Understanding Digital Marketing

Also available by Damian Ryan:

The Best Digital Marketing Campaigns in the World II

In the second collection of *The Best Digital Marketing Campaigns in the World*, Damian Ryan presents an international showcase of the most successful digital marketing campaigns in recent history.

Full of behind-the-scenes insights into campaign strategy, implementation and results, it explores how businesses and agencies, large and small, have harnessed social media, blogs, video, e-mail, mobile and search to boost their brand and engage with consumers. Covering a wide range of world-class, award-winning campaigns including Red Bull and Stratos, Peugeot: Let Your Body Drive, and Students Beans' Freshersfields.com, *The Best Digital Marketing Campaigns in the World II* is an inspirational showcase of digital creativity. Providing a fascinating snapshot of the digital landscape and a privileged insight into some of the freshest, most creative thinking in the industry, this is a must-read for everyone studying or working in marketing and advertising.

ISBN: 978 0 7494 6968 9
Published by Kogan Page

THIRD EDITION

Understanding Digital Marketing

Marketing strategies for engaging the digital generation

Damian Ryan

KoganPage

LONDON PHILADELPHIA NEW DELHI

First published in Great Britain and the United States in 2009 by Kogan Page Limited
Second edition 2012
Third edition 2014

2nd Floor, 45 Gee Street
London EC1V 3RS
United Kingdom
www.koganpage.com

1518 Walnut Street, Suite 1100
Philadelphia PA 19102
USA

4737/23 Ansari Road
Daryaganj
New Delhi 110002
India

© Damian Ryan, 2014

ISBN   978 0 7494 7102 6
E-ISBN   978 0 7494 7103 3

British Library Cataloguing-in-Publication Data

A CIP record for this book is available from the British Library.

Library of Congress Cataloging-in-Publication Data

Ryan, Damian.
   Understanding digital marketing / Damian Ryan. – Third edition.
      pages cm
      ISBN 978-0-7494-7102-6 (paperback) – ISBN 978-0-7494-7103-3 (ebook)   1. Internet marketing.
2. Social media.   3. Strategic planning.   4. Marketing–Management.   I. Title.
   HF5415.1265.R93 2014
   658.8'72–dc23
                                                                                2014013409

Typeset by Graphicraft Limited, Hong Kong
Print production managed by Jellyfish
Printed and bound by CPI Group (UK) Ltd, Croydon, CR0 4YY

CONTENTS

11   Understanding content marketing 298

12   Convincing your boss to invest in digital marketing 327

13   What's next? 367

PREFACE

If you are reading this...

You already know the world of digital media is changing at a phenomenal pace. Its constantly evolving technologies, and the way people are using them, is transforming not just how you access your information, but how you interact and communicate with your friends and colleagues on a global scale.

It has also changed the way you choose and buy products and services.

People are embracing digital technology to communicate in ways that would have been inconceivable just a few short years ago. No longer the preserve of tech-savvy early adopters, today ordinary people are integrating digital technologies seamlessly into their everyday lives.

From SMS updates on their favourite sports teams, to a free video call with relatives on the other side of the globe, to collaborative online gaming and much, much more: ordinary people – your customers – are starting to use digital media without giving it a second thought.

The global online population was around 2.1 billion at the end of March 2011 (Internet World Stats). By mid 2012 the figure had already climbed to almost 2.5 billion people online or just over one-third of the 7 billion people on the planet being connected to the net. There is no doubt this figure is set to double in the years ahead – this means 5 billion of the 7 billion people in the world will be online in one manner or another: the question is no longer 'if' – it's about 'when'. The answer to 'when' is hotly debated by a lot of researchers, but if I take an average view it looks like 2018.

However, it's how we consume data, and the sheer volume of this data created by the soaring online population and the move towards more portable access, that change the game out of all recognition. More video, more rich media, faster and faster access by more people in more parts of the world change the fabric of business and mean that digital marketing – and mastering the art thereof – is now a prequisite of any enterprise or individual planning to compete in the years ahead.

Zettabytes? Because of this massive volume of data we need to invent new words and definitions to describe and rationalize the type of world ahead. A zettabyte is a number with 21 zeroes – equivalent to a trillion gigabytes and the similar level of data to 1 billion DVDs downloaded every day for a year!

According to Cisco, the global consumption of data by 2017 will be three times the level (measured in zettabytes) of December 2013, as I am writing this. So hang on!

What makes this digital revolution so exciting is that it's happening right now. We're living through it, and you have a unique opportunity to jump in and be part of this historical transition.

In the pages that follow I'll take you on a journey into the world of digital marketing. I'll show you how it all started, how it got to where it is today, and where thought leaders in the industry believe it's heading in the future. Most importantly of all, I'll show you – in a practical, no-nonsense way – how you can harness the burgeoning power of digital media to drive your business to the crest of this digital marketing wave, and how to keep it there.

This book will:

- help you and your business to choose online advertising and marketing channels that will get your ideas, products and services to a massive and ever-expanding market;

- give you that elusive competitive edge that will keep you ahead of the pack;

- future-proof your business by helping you to understand the origins of digital marketing and the trends that are shaping its future;

- give you a concept of the scale of the online marketplace, the unfolding opportunities and the digital service providers who will help your business to capitalize on them;

- provide practical, real-world examples of digital marketing successes – including leading brands that have become household names in a relatively short space of time;

- offer insight through interviews, analysis and contributions from digital marketing experts;

- ... ultimately, give you the tools you need to harness the power of the internet in order to take your business wherever you want it to go.

I'll also help you to convince your colleagues and shareholders why they should invest in digital marketing too.

Understanding Digital Marketing sets out to unravel the mysteries of digital marketing by taking you on a journey. As you travel into this digital world the book will reveal how leading marketers in sectors as diverse as travel, retail, gambling and adult entertainment have stumbled on incredibly effective techniques to turn people on to doing business online, reaping literally millions as a result. The book will show you how to apply their experience to transform your own digital enterprise.

Whether you're looking to start up your own home-based internet business, work for a large multinational or are anywhere in between, if you want to connect with your customers today and into the future, you need digital channels as part of your marketing mix.

The internet has become the medium of choice for a generation of consumers: the first generation to have grown up taking for granted instant access to digital information. This generation integrates digital media into every facet of its daily life, in ways we could never have conceived in even the recent past. Today this generation of digital natives is entering the workplace and is spending like never before. This is the mass market of tomorrow, and for business people and marketers the challenge is to become fluent in this new digital language so that we can talk effectively to our target audience.

Television froze a generation of consumers to the couch for years, now digital media is engaging consumers and customers in ways that the early architects of the technology could never have dreamed. The advent of 'two-screen' or even 'three-screen' marketing is now becoming a real consideration – just look at how our own lives are changing and how we soak up data... How many of us regularly sit in front of the television with our laptops, tablets and mobile phones all on the go at the same time?!

When the Apple Mac came along it opened up the art of publishing and, as a result, print media boomed. Today the same thing is happening online, through the phenomenon of user-generated content (UGC) and social networking: ordinary people are becoming the directors, producers, editors and distributors of their own media-rich content – the content that they, their friends and the world want to see. But that's only the start.

Prime-time television audiences are falling, print media is coming under increasing pressure to address dropping circulation figures – and while the old school sits on the sidelines, bloated and slowly atrophying, digital media has transformed itself into a finely tuned engine delivering more power, opportunity and control than any other form of media could dream of.

In other words – it's time to follow the smart money!

Over the last 20 years I've had the absolute pleasure of working at the coalface of this burgeoning and insistent new media. I've met lots of smart people and spoken to literally hundreds of organizations with massively diverse and challenging agendas. The one common factor was a hunger for data and knowledge: anything that would give their particular brand that elusive competitive edge.

When putting this book together I wanted to make it as informative and practical as possible. Each chapter begins with a summary of its content, so you can easily browse through the chapters and select the one that addresses the topic you're interested in. I've purposely left out the jargon – and where technical terms have been absolutely necessary I've supplied a clear definition in the text, backed up by a complete glossary at the back of the book that explains all of the terms that digital marketers use in plain English. The result, I hope, is a book that is clear, informative and entertaining, even for the complete digital novice.

In your hands you hold what independent marketers around the world have been crying out for: a book that shows you how to successfully use the internet to sell your products or services. It begins with the origins of the medium and takes you through the various disciplines of digital marketing campaigns. The book travels around the world collecting facts, figures, comment and opinion from acknowledged experts, brands and organizations in different fields, getting them to spill the beans on how the net delivered the goods for them.

This edition (the third) marks a fundamental change in the way the book has been constructed. I started writing these books with Calvin Jones in 2007 but over the last year Calvin has moved on to other projects, although his influence and contribution are still obvious and present in this edition. It's fun looking back on the original creation of some of the chapters and remembering the journey. Calvin has been, and is, a terrific collaborator and a good buddy too! The key change, however, is my realization of just how fast the digital marketing world is evolving, and my fundamental belief that no one person can claim to be an expert across all disciplines. Because of this I have increased the number of collaborators in this edition and sought out experts in their own particular fields of influence to work closely with me on the creation of the book. The end result is, I hope, a better product with more chapters and a deeper, more advanced level of expertise in core areas such as search, analytics, online PR and content marketing.

Aside from these disciplines I have also revisited every other chapter from the first two editions and ensured they are up to date and include valid, practical examples of digital marketing in action. Due to several requests I have also included a chapter to help you convince your colleagues to invest in digital marketing.

Digital marketing has its sinister side too – while many marketers play above board, some have been tempted by the dark side of the force and find more return on investment (ROI) by using unscrupulous tactics to undermine their rivals and gain competitive advantage. The book will examine the world of 'black hat marketing'.

It took television 22 years to reach 50 million households – it took the internet just five to achieve the same level of penetration. Things are progressing at an unbelievable rate, and we're approaching a pivotal point in marketing history – a time when digital marketing will overtake traditional mass media as the medium of choice for reaching the consumer of tomorrow.

In the summer of 1993 I interviewed Jerry Reitman, head of direct marketing for Leo Burnetts in Chicago, for my magazine *GO Direct*. During our conversation Jerry pointed at the computer on his desk and said: 'And that... that's where it's going'. I wondered what he was talking about.

Twenty years on and practically one-third of the world is online. And it's not just about North America and Europe either... these markets only count for one-third of the world's online population. The growth will come from Africa, Asia and the Middle East.

Consumers have grown tired of mass media marketing, and are turning instead to the internet. They want more engagement, more interaction. They're starting to spend most of their leisure time in a digital world, and creative digital marketing is the way your business will reach them.

Writing a book about this subject has always been too great a challenge without adopting a collaborative approach. The book set out to democratize the digital marketing knowledge that exists in the world. While I believe I have gone some way to achieving this objective, I now believe the best path from here is to open up this challenge to digital marketers everywhere, to create a place where they can connect with one another, collaborate on all digital marketing-related subject matter and ultimately build knowledge and prosper as a result. Over the last year I have, together with colleagues from all over the world, been putting a platform together to achieve this objective and now invite you to get on board. Please visit **www.gogadm.com** and join the movement.

CONTRIBUTORS' BIOGRAPHIES

Simon Kingsnorth

A global digital-marketing expert, Simon has worked client-side for a wide range of businesses, including start-ups and marketing leading corporations across a range of industries. He has built a large number of successful digital marketing strategies, both nationally and globally, and consulted for companies across the world. As a marketing leader he has contributed to the significant growth of several businesses in areas including digital marketing, offline marketing, branding, relationship management, contract negotiation and product development.

Nick Massey

A serial CEO, Nick was a strategy consultant with PA Consulting Group, then joined Coca-Cola in commercial and strategy roles in the UK and United States. As CEO of Octagon he won the 'Agency of the Year' award. He worked with Goldman Sachs as CEO of Box-clever, and was CEO of digital music service rara.com.

Ben Knight

Operations Director for Croud, before which he was at Harvest as Head of Performance Digital; his remit included ultimate responsibility for paid and natural search, social media and the analytics channels. Ben has nearly 10 years' experience in search, and a wealth of full-service digital experience, managing the largest blue-chip clients in the UK.

Throughout Ben's career he has worked and managed brands from a variety of verticals, developing intimate search knowledge and strategy for clients as diverse as Gocompare, Experian, Virgin Holidays, Betfair, Date the UK, Friends Reunited and Carphone Warehouse. Ben sits on the IAB's Search Council.

Prior to Harvest Ben worked from 2002 to 2008 at The Search Works. He joined a small company of 12 people and helped it grow to over 100, becoming at that time the UK's largest search specialist agency. His last two years at the agency involved him heading up the financial vertical, working as the Account Director and overseeing monthly spend in excess of £5 million.

Adrian Brady

Adrian's early career was in the rapidly growing Irish tourism industry before coming to London in 1993. Adrian then moved into the PR agency world, working across a range of business and consumer brands such as Royal Mail and Whitbread. In 1996 Adrian launched Eulogy! The agency was noted by *Marketing* magazine as one of the country's fastest-growing PR agencies in the late 1990s. Eulogy!'s industry awards success includes the prestigious *PR Week*, the

B2B 'Campaign of the Year', and the International Public Relations Association 'Golden World' accolade, as well as being voted by *PR Week* as one of the Top 40 independent PR agencies.

Dale Lovell

Publishing Director and co-founder of Content Amp, a global leader in content-marketing services to leading brands and agencies, Dale has worked in online publishing, content strategy and creative marketing for over 14 years. From 2000 to 2008 he worked for several successful online publishing ventures in both the UK and the United States, the last of which was sold to Fox International Channels, a NewsCorp company. From 2008 to 2010 Dale worked with brands such as the National Geographic Channel, offering online content-marketing direction and publishing development. In 2010, recognizing the growing requirement for branded content and creative marketing services by brands online, Dale co-founded Content Amp. Today Content Amp works with leading brands and agencies on content strategy and digital content-amplification campaigns.

Dale has a history degree from the University of Reading and has contributed as a journalist to over 50 leading publications globally. He is a regular commentator on the digital marketing industry.

Andrew Copeland

Head of Publisher Development, EMEA at Undertone, Andrew has over seven years' experience in affiliate marketing and has worked with a number of brands such as Lloyds, Barclaycard, Toshiba and Mazuma Mobile, developing successful performance-marketing strategies to deliver against each clients' objectives. This is not the first time Andrew has contributed to this book (or, in fact, its sister publication, *Understanding Digital Marketing*). An expert in every sense of the word.

Richard Foan

Group Executive Director of Communication & Innovation at ABC, Richard is a very well-known personality in the digital media industry who is respected for his experience and informed opinion. He facilitates innovation and communication at ABC in line with industry needs. Richard is Chairman of the global IFABC Web Standards Group and Chairman of JICWEBS (Joint Industry Committee for Web Standards in the UK and Ireland). He regularly presents to the global media industry on issues associated with the accountability of digital media.

Hannah Squirrell

Director of Marketing and eCommerce for Bennetts, the UK's No 1 for motorbike insurance, Hannah is responsible for the delivery of Bennetts' business plan across marketing, e-commerce and aggregation to enhance its market leadership position and continue to deliver exceptional growth.

Hannah has extensive experience of developing and implementing multichannel brand-marketing strategies across a number of businesses. She was a founding member of the Capital One marketing team, where she was instrumental in managing its media strategy and marketing channels. Hannah then joined a 'Top 5' London independent advertising agency, where she set up and managed the digital function working across brands such as Tesco, 3M, Haven Holidays, Thorntons and Avon Cosmetics.

Brook Zimmatore

The co-founder of Massive PR International and Sterling Kreative in London, Brook oversees all aspects of technical production, including implementing the rock solid creative and defensive strategies to effectively control the online image of brands and private clients.

ACKNOWLEDGEMENTS

Whenever I write this page I know I am going to forget to thank someone and then remember it about a week later. *This has actually just happened – am on train from Preston back to London and suddenly remembered I forgot to thank my parents and family ... luckily, Philippa is going to manage to squeeze this in right???*

This edition is especially challenging as I had more people involved in this version than any of the five books in the series to date. It is also the first edition of *Understanding Digital Marketing* where I didn't have my colleague and friend, Calvin Jones, as co-writer, and believe me he was sorely missed, but you can still see his influence in some of the chapters that follow. Happily, Calvin and I are now working on another project (**www.gogadm.com**) so there's still plenty of banter and collaboration going on regardless.

Thank you to all the contributors and collaborators. At the last count there were in excess of 50 people involved in either research, writing, or case studies and so on, and believe me this was the minimum number required to achieve this edition – for starters it's about 50 per cent larger than the 2nd edition and I sincerely hope that size does matter!

Thanks to the team at Kogan Page – Helen, Maddie, Mark, Sonya, Philippa and everyone else who supports me in this pursuit.

To my colleagues at Mediaventura and GADM – (particularly Chris, Ed, Dennis, Jan, Martin, Jools, Beckie and Sukhi) thanks for all the collaboration. It's been a bit tough juggling all these balls over the last year but there's never been a time where I instinctively felt I was doing the wrong thing and believe me I would know!!

It's been a great year for catching up with old friends and making loads of new ones. Some highlights include the arrival of Lola, Christmas with Richard and friends in Australia, turning 50 in a blaze of glory with the Marlow Entrepreneurs in tow, meeting the Toorak Two: the beautiful Tamara Williams and fabulous Jodie O'Brien – not a bad year all in all!

Finally a big thanks to all the academics who read and recommend this book. One of the greatest challenges for the digital marketing sector is the widening skills shortage gap. While this book may enlighten some, it's the instructors and providers of hands-on course material and education who should be singled out too – keeping up to speed with digital marketing is not easy, it moves so quickly! We hope that our work with **www.gogadm.com**

will help facilitate the discussion and empower academics and educators like never before.

The last word as always goes to my twin daughters – when I started on the first edition they were three years old. Now they're turning eleven and showing me how to navigate my way around iMovie!! I recently had to explain what a typewriter was – am getting old.

This book is dedicated to the fond
memory of Paul G Oughton, a great friend,
legal genius and connoisseur of fine wine and guitars!

'... it isn't going to be a late one'!

So... you want to go digital???

OUR CHAPTER PLEDGE TO YOU

When you reach the end of this chapter you'll have answers to the following questions:

- How did we reach the dawn of a digital age in marketing?
- What are the similarities between the internet and historical global communications revolutions?
- How many people are on the internet and how quickly is it growing?
- How is digital technology influencing consumer behaviour?

In the beginning...

Etched on a dusty curbstone amidst the ruins of the ancient Roman city of Pompeii, you'll find an engraved penis, strategically carved to point the way to what, at the time, was one of the most popular brothels in the area. Guides will tell you it's the 'oldest advertisement in the world, for the oldest business in the world...'. While the truth of that claim is debatable, the phallic ad is certainly very old.

The Pompeii penis was buried by the eruption of Mount Vesuvius, which destroyed the city on 24 August AD 79, but the true origins of marketing go back much further than that. Although, according to business historians, marketing as a discreet business discipline wasn't born until the 1950s, marketing activities have played a fundamental role in the success of businesses from, well, the very first business. There are few certainties in the world of business, but one thing is for sure: if you don't let customers know about your business, you won't stay in business for very long.

But this is a book about marketing in the digital age – the present, and the future

That is true. We're here to talk about the exciting new world of digital marketing as it has emerged from relative obscurity in the late 1990s into the mainstream of business in 2014. We're going to look at how businesses just like yours can harness the power of this online revolution to connect with a new wave of consumers: consumers who take this pervasive technology and integrate it seamlessly into their everyday lives in ways we could never have conceived of as recently as a decade ago.

This book is about the future of marketing. So why are we starting by looking backwards? In his 1960s classic *Understanding Media: The Extensions of Man*, Canadian communications theorist and philosopher Marshall McLuhan noted 'It is instructive to follow the embryonic stages of any new growth, for during this period of development it is much mis-understood, whether it be printing or the motor car or TV.' As is so often the case, having a basic grasp of the past can help our understanding of the present, and ultimately illuminate our view of the future.

So buckle your seatbelt as we take a whistle-stop tour of how marketing has evolved over the years, and how advertising and technology have converged to define a new marketing landscape that is just beginning to mature, and is still gravid with opportunity.

The changing face of advertising

Advertising can be intoxicating. The spin, the story, the message, the call to action, the image, the placement, the measurement, the refinement. It all adds up to a powerful cocktail that can ultimately change the world. At its core, advertising is all about influencing people – persuading them to take the actions we want, whether that is choosing a particular brand of tooth-paste, picking up the phone, filling in a mailing coupon or visiting a website. Done well, the power of advertising can achieve amazing things, and if you're in business you're already doing it, and will continue to do so.

Advertising through the ages

Advertising, an essential component in the marketing of any business, has been around for a long time. The Pompeii penis is positively modern compared to some of the advertising relics that archaeologists have unearthed in ancient Arabia, China, Egypt, Greece and Rome. The Egyptians used papyrus to create posters and flyers, while lost-and-found advertising (also on papyrus, and often relating to 'missing' slaves) was common in both ancient Greece and Rome. Posters, signs and flyers were widely employed in the ancient cities of Rome, Pompeii and Carthage to publicize events such as circuses, games and gladiatorial contests.

People have been trying to influence other people since the dawn of human existence, utilizing whatever means and media they had at their disposal at the time. The human voice and word of mouth, of course, came first. Then someone picked up a piece of stone and started etching images on a cave wall: enduring images that told stories, communicated ideas and promoted certain ways of doing things.

The first advertising? That is debatable, but these images, some of which are around to this day, certainly demonstrate an early recognition of the power of images and messages to influence the perception and behaviour of others.

The development of printing during the 15th and 16th centuries heralded a significant milestone in advertising, making it more cost-effective for marketers to reach a much wider audience. In the 17th century, adverts began to appear in early newspapers in England, and then spread across the globe. The first form of mass-media advertising was born.

The 18th and 19th centuries saw a further expansion in newspaper advertising, and alongside it the birth of mail-order advertising – which would evolve into the massive direct mail/direct response industry we know and love today. It also saw the establishment of the first advertising agency, set up in Philadelphia in 1843 by the pioneering Volney Palmer. Initially ad agencies acted as simple brokers for newspaper space, but before long they developed into full-service operations, offering their clients a suite of creative and ad-placement services.

The 20th century saw the dawn of another new advertising age, with the advent of radio offering a completely new medium through which advertisers could reach out to prospective clients. Then came television, which shifted the advertising landscape yet again, and towards the end of the century a new force – the internet – began moving out of the realm of 'techies' and early adopters to become a valuable business and communication tool for the masses. The era of digital marketing was born.

Technological advances have punctuated the evolution of advertising throughout history, each fundamentally altering the way that businesses could communicate with their customers. Interestingly, however, none of these groundbreaking developments superseded those that came before. Rather they served to augment them, offering marketers more diversity, allowing them to connect with a broader cross section of consumers. In today's sophisticated age of paid search placement, keyword-targeted pay-per-click advertising and social networking, you'll still find the earliest forms of advertising alive and well.

Stroll through any market, practically anywhere in the world – from the food markets of central London to the bazaars of North Africa, to the street markets of India – and you'll be greeted by a cacophony of noise as vendors use their voices to vie for the attention of passing customers. The human voice, the first marketing medium in history, still going strong in the digital age.

The technology behind digital marketing

As we have already mentioned, developments in technology and the evolution of marketing are inextricably intertwined. Technology has underpinned major milestones in the history of marketing since its inception. The process tends to go something like this:

1 New technology emerges and is initially the preserve of technologists and early adopters.

2 The technology gains a firmer foothold in the market and starts to become more popular, putting it on the marketing radar.

3 Innovative marketers jump in to explore ways that they can harness the power of this emerging technology to connect with their target audience.

4 The technology migrates to the mainstream and is adopted into standard marketing practice.

The printing press, radio, television and now the internet are all examples of major breakthroughs in technology that ultimately altered forever the relationships between marketers and consumers, and did so on a global scale. But of course marketing isn't about technology, it's about people: technology is only interesting, from a marketing perspective, when it connects people with other people more effectively.

There are plenty of examples of technology through the ages having a significant impact on various markets – technology that may seem obscure, even irrelevant today. Remember Muzak – the company that brought elevator music to the masses back in the 1930s? The technology for piping audio over power lines was patented in 1922 by retired Major General George O Squier, and exclusive rights to the patent were bought by the North American Company. In 1934, under the corporate umbrella of 'Muzak', they started piping music into Cleveland homes.

Muzak seemed to have hit on a winning formula, but the advent of free commercial radio sounded the death knell for the company's chosen route to market. With free music available on shiny new wirelesses, households were no longer prepared to pay for the Muzak service. Undeterred, the company focused its efforts on New York City businesses. As buildings in New York soared skywards, the lift/elevator became practically ubiquitous. Muzak had found its niche, and 'elevator music' was born.

So what, you might think.

It's true that, compared to behemoths of contemporary media such as radio, television and now the internet, elevator music is small potatoes. But back in its heyday this was cutting-edge stuff, and it reached a lot of people. Muzak had the power to sway opinions and influence markets, so much so that for music artists of that era, having your track played on the Muzak network practically guaranteed a hit.

The point is that technology has the ability to open up completely new markets, and to radically shake up existing ones. The mainstream adoption of digital technology – the internet, the software applications that run on it, and the devices that allow people to connect to both the network and each other whenever, wherever and however they want to – promises to dwarf all that has come before it. It heralds the single most disruptive development in the history of marketing.

Whether that disruption represents an opportunity or a threat to you as a marketer depends largely on your perspective. We hope the fact that you're reading this book means that you see it as an opportunity.

The first global communications network: 'the highway of thought'

To understand the explosive growth of the internet we need to look back at how early communications technology evolved into the global network of interconnected computers that today we call the internet. The story of electronic communication begins with the wired telegraph – a network that grew rapidly to cover the globe, connected people across vast distances in a way that seemed almost magical, and changed the world forever.

Tom Standage, in his book *The Victorian Internet*, looks at the wired telegraph and draws some astonishing parallels between the growth of the world's first electronic communications network and the growth of the modern-day internet. Standage describes the origins of the telegraph, and the quest to deliver information from point to point more rapidly in the days when speedy communication relied on a fast horse and a skilled rider:

> On an April day in 1746 at the grand convent of the Carthusians in Paris about 200 monks arranged themselves in a long, snaking line. Each monk held one end of a 25 foot iron wire in each hand connecting him to his neighbour on either side. Together the monks and their connecting wires formed a line over a mile long. Once the line was complete the Abbot, Jean-Antoine Nollet, a noted French scientist, took a primitive battery and, without warning, connected it to the line of monks – giving all of them a powerful electric shock.

These 'electric monks' demonstrated conclusively that electricity could transmit a message (albeit a painful one) from one location to another in an instant, and laid the foundation for a communications revolution.

In 1830 Joseph Henry (1797–1878), an eminent US scientist who went on to become the first Director of the Smithsonian Institute, took the concept a step further. He demonstrated the potential of the electromagnet for long-distance communications when he passed an electric current through a mile-long cable to ring an electromagnetic bell connected to the other end. Samuel Morse (1791–1872), the inventor of Morse code, took Henry's concept a step further and made a commercial success of it: the electronic telegraph was born.

In 1842 Morse demonstrated a working telegraph between two committee rooms in Washington, and congress voted slimly in favour of investing US $30,000 for an experimental telegraph line between Washington and Baltimore. It was a very close call: 89 votes for the prototype, 83 against and 70 abstentions by congressmen looking 'to avoid the responsibility of spending the public money for a machine they could not understand'.

Despite the reservations of the congressmen, the new network was a huge success. It grew at a phenomenal rate: by 1850 there were more than 12,000 miles of telegraph line criss-crossing the United States, two years later there was more than twice that, and the network of connected wires was spreading rapidly around the globe.

This spellbinding new network delivered news in moments rather than the weeks and months people were used to. It connected people over vast distances in ways previously inconceivable, and to many remained completely incomprehensible.

Governments tried and failed to control this raw new communications medium. Its advocates hailed it as revolutionary, and its popularity grew at an unprecedented rate. Newspapers began publishing news just hours rather than weeks after the event, romance blossomed over the wires, couples were married 'online', gamblers used the new network to 'cheat' on the horses, and it transformed the way that business was conducted around the world. In the space of a generation, the telegraph literally altered the fabric of society.

Does any of this sound familiar...?

A *New York Times* article published on Wednesday 14 September 1852 describes the telegraph network as '... the highway of thought'; not much of a stretch from the 'information superhighway' label we apply to our modern-day revolutionary network. If anything, the communications revolution instigated by the telegraph must have represented more of a cultural upheaval than the explosive growth of the internet today.

For the first time, people grasped that they could communicate almost instantly across continents and even oceans. They felt a sense of closeness, a togetherness that simply hadn't been possible before. The telegraph system was hailed by some as a harbinger of peace and solidarity: a network of wires that would ultimately bind countries, creeds and cultures in a way hitherto unimaginable. Others, of course, used the network to wage war more efficiently. The sheer expansion of ideas and dreams that ensued must have been truly staggering, the opportunities and potential for change bewildering.

For rapid, long-distance communications the telegraph remained the only game in town until 1877, when two rival inventors battled to be the first to patent another new technology set to turn the world of electronic communications on its head. Its name, the telephone; the inventors, Elisha Gray and Alexander Graham Bell. They submitted their patent applications within hours of one another – but Bell pipped Gray to the post, and a now famous legal battle ensued.

The first words ever transmitted into a telephone were uttered by Bell, speaking to his research assistant, Thomas Watson, in the next room. He simply said: 'Mr Watson – come here – I want to see you.'

Early networks

The internet story really starts in 1957, with the USSR's launch of the sputnik satellite. It signalled that the United States was falling behind the Russians in the technology stakes, prompting the US government to invest heavily in science and technology. In 1958, the US Department of Defense set up the Advanced Research Projects Agency (ARPA) – a specialist agency established with a specific remit: making sure the United States stayed ahead of its cold war nemesis in the accelerating technology race.

In August 1962 a computer scientist, Joseph Carl Robnett Licklider (1915–1990), Vice President at technology company Bolt Beranek and Newman, wrote a series of memos discussing the concept of an 'Intergalactic Computer Network'. Licklider's revolutionary ideas, amazingly, encompassed practically everything that the internet has today become.

In October 1963, Licklider was appointed head of the Behavioral Sciences and Command and Control programmes at ARPA. During his two-year tenure he convinced the agency of the importance of developing computer networks, and although he left ARPA before work on his theories began, the seed for the Advanced Research Projects Agency Network (ARPANET) – the precursor to the internet – had been sown.

In 1965 researchers hooked up a computer at Massachusetts Institute of Technology's (MIT) Lincoln Lab with a US Air Force computer in California. For the first time, two computers communicated with each other using 'packet'-based information transmitted over a network.

ARPA (since renamed Defense Advanced Research Projects Agency (DARPA) – **www.darpa.mil**) started the ARPANET project in 1966, claiming that it would allow the powerful computers owned by the government, universities and research institutions around the United States to communicate with one another and to share valuable computing resources. IBM and other large computer companies at the time were sceptical, reportedly claiming that the network ARPA proposed couldn't be built.

ARPA ploughed on, and on 21 November 1969 the first two computers were connected to the fledgling ARPANET, one at University of California Los Angeles, the other at Stanford Research Institute. By 5 December the same year, the network doubled in size as they were joined by two other computers: one at University of California Santa Barbara, the other at University of Utah's graphics department. The new network grew quickly. By 1971, 15 US institutions were connected to ARPANET, and by 1974 the number had grown to 46, and had spread to include overseas nodes in Hawaii, Norway and London.

You've got mail

E-mail, which is still often described as the internet's 'killer application', began life in the early 1960s as a facility that allowed users of mainframe computers to send simple text-based messages to another user's mailbox on the same computer. But it wasn't until the advent of ARPANET that anyone considered sending electronic mail from one user to another across a network.

In 1971 Ray Tomlinson, an engineer working on ARPANET, wrote the first program capable of sending mail from a user on one host computer to another user's mailbox on another host computer. As an identifier to distinguish network mail from local mail Tomlinson decided to append the host name of the user's computer to their user login name. To separate the two names he chose the @ symbol.

'I am frequently asked why I chose the at sign, but the at sign just makes sense,' writes Tomlinson on his website. 'The purpose of the at sign (in English) was to indicate a unit price (for example, 10 items @ US $1.95). I used the at sign to indicate that the user was 'at' some other host rather than being local.'

E-mail, one of the internet's most widely used applications – and one of the most critical for internet marketers – began life as a programmer's afterthought. Tomlinson created e-mail because he thought it 'seemed like a neat idea' at the time. 'There was no directive to 'go forth and invent e-mail'. The ARPANET was a solution looking for a problem. A colleague suggested that I not tell my boss what I had done because e-mail wasn't in our statement of work,' he said.

From ARPANET to internet

The term 'internet' was first used in 1974 by US computer scientist Vint Cerf (commonly referred to as one of the 'fathers of the internet', and now a senior executive and internet evangelist with Google). Cerf was working with Robert Khan at DARPA on a way to standardize the way that different host computers communicated across both the growing ARPANET and between the ARPANET and other emerging computer networks. The TCP (Transmission Control Program) network protocol they defined evolved to become the TCP/IP (Transmission Control Program/Internet Protocol) protocol suit that is still used to this day to pass packets of information backwards and forwards across the internet.

In 1983 the ARPANET started using the TCP/IP protocol – a move that many consider to signal the true 'birth' of the internet as we know it. That year, too, the system of domain names (.com, .net, etc) was invented. By 1984 the number of 'nodes' on the still fledgling network passed 1,000 and began climbing rapidly. By 1989 there were more than 100,000 hosts connected to the internet, and the growth continued.

Making connections – birth of the web

It was in 1989 that Tim Berners-Lee, a British developer working at CERN (the European Organization for Nuclear Research) in Geneva, proposed a system of information cross-referencing, access and retrieval across the rapidly growing internet, based on 'hypertext' links. The concept of a hypertext information architecture was nothing new, and was already being used in individual programs running on individual computers around the world. The idea of linking documents stored on different computers across the rapidly growing internet, though, was nothing short of revolutionary.

The building blocks for the world wide web were already in place – but it was Tim Berners-Lee's vision that brought them together. 'I just had to take the hypertext idea and connect it to the TCP and DNS ideas and – ta-da! – the World Wide Web,' Berners-Lee comments on the W3C (World Wide Web Consortium) website.

The first web page on the internet was built at CERN, and went online on 6 August 1991. It contained information about the new world wide web, how to get a web browser and how to set up a web server. Over time it also became the first ever web directory, as Berners-Lee maintained a list of links to other websites on the page as they appeared.

The wild wide web – a new frontier

Up to this point, the internet had been the realm of technologists and scientists at research institutions. But the advent of the web changed the landscape, making online information accessible to a much broader audience. What happened next was explosive. Between 1991 and 1997 the web grew at an astonishing 850 per cent per annum, eclipsing all expectations. With more websites and more people joining the online party every day, it was only a matter of time before innovative tech-savvy marketers started to notice the web's potential as an avenue for the marketing message.

The mid 1990s saw an explosion in new online ventures as pioneering entrepreneurs, grasping the burgeoning potential of this exciting new medium, scrambled to stake their claim on this virtual new frontier. In August 1995 there were 18,957 websites online; by August 1996 there were 342,081 ('15 Years of the Web, Internet Timeline', **www.bbc.co.uk**). Note there are now *approximately 635 million* websites online.

Silicon Valley was awash with venture capital as investors bet big bucks on the internet's next big thing – some with viable business plans, others with charismatic founders riding on the coat tails of the prevailing net mania. New ventures sprung up almost daily, selling everything imaginable – or selling nothing at all. Fledgling companies spent vast amounts of money, growing quickly with scant regard for turning a profit, betting their future on building strong online brands that could win the hearts and minds of net consumers. The profits would come later... at least, that was the theory. Some of these companies were destined to become household names in a few short years; others would vanish into obscurity just as quickly.

These were heady, almost euphoric times. The internet had acquired the mythical Midas touch: a business with .com in its name, it seemed, was destined for great things. Initial Public Offerings (IPOs) of dot.com companies made millionaires of founders, and made the headlines, fuelling further mania. It was an era that saw the birth of some of today's most well-known online brands: sites such as Amazon.com, Yahoo!, eBay... and, in September 1998, Google Inc.

Boom, boom... bang!

For a time it seemed like the halcyon days of the late 1990s would continue forever, that the dot.com bubble was impervious to bursting. Fuelled by speculative investment and high-profile high-tech IPOs, the Nasdaq Composite stock index continued to rocket upwards. Each new dot.com success fuelled the fervour for technology stocks, blowing the bubble up a little more. On 10 March 2000 the Nasdaq index hit an intra-day high of 5,132.52 before settling to an all-time closing high of 5,046 points.

And then it went into free fall.

What happened to the railways in the 1840s, radio in the 1920s and transistor electronics in the 1950s had finally hit the dot.com boom. Between March 2000 and October 2002 some US $5 trillion in all was wiped off the market value of technology stocks. Speculative investment suddenly stopped, venture capitalists were less cavalier with their cash, and high-risk start-ups with dubious business plans ran out of places to source funding. With profits still a distant dream, even for high-profile internet start-ups, the coffers soon began to run dry. It signalled the end of the road for many.

Despite the occasional 'blip', both the stock market index and the fortunes of internet businesses continued to wane until 2003 when, slowly but surely, the tide turned and things started to look up. Although there had been some high-profile closures, mergers and acquisitions in the wake of the crash, the reality is that, for the internet industry as a whole, the inevitable 'readjustment' had a positive impact. It essentially cleared the decks – sweeping away a plethora of unviable, poorly conceived and poorly managed businesses – and served as a poignant reality check to those who remained. Yes, there were casualties, but overall the industry emerged stronger, more focused and both optimistic and, crucially, realistic about the future.

Two other critical elements helped fuel the recovery, and to some extent the public fascination with the internet: one was the meteoric rise of Google from relative obscurity to dominate the world of internet search, the other was the accelerated roll-out of high-speed, always-on broadband access for residential users.

People could suddenly find what they were looking for online – could get access to what they wanted, when they wanted it – without having to go through the frustrating rigmarole of a dial-up connection. It transformed the online experience, turning it from a passing curiosity into a useful every-day tool for a much wider demographic of users. And the more people who used the internet, the more indispensable it became.

Enough technology... let's talk about people

If you're non-technical the world of digital marketing may seem a bit daunting at first. All that technology must be really complicated... right? Not necessarily.

One of the key things to remember if you're new to digital marketing is this: digital marketing isn't actually about technology at all, it's all about people. In that sense it's similar to traditional marketing: it's about people (marketers) connecting with other people (consumers) to build relationships and ultimately drive sales.

Technology merely affords you, the marketer, new and exciting platforms that allow you to connect with people in increasingly diverse and relevant ways. Digital marketing is not about understanding the underlying technology, but rather about understanding people, how they are using that technology, and how you can leverage that to engage with them more effectively. Yes, you have to learn to use the tools at your disposal – but understanding people is the real key to unlocking the potential of digital marketing.

A huge and growing market

Although internet companies suffered bruised finances and a tarnished public image in the wake of the dot.com crash, the internet itself never stopped growing, both in terms of the number of websites online, and, crucially from a marketing perspective, the number of people with internet access. In March 2000, when the dot.com bubble burst, there were an estimated 304 million people in the world with internet access. By March 2003 that figure

FIGURE 1.1   The global distribution of the world's 2.1 billion internet users by region (according to Internet World Stats, March 2011)

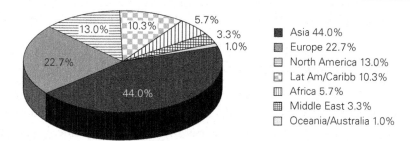

SOURCE: Internet World Stats – **www.internetworldstats.com/stats.htm**
BASIS: 2,095,006,005 Internet users on March 31, 2011
Copyright © 2011, Miniwatts Marketing Group

had doubled to 608 million, and in December 2005 the global online population passed 1 billion. As of June 2012 the figure sits at 2.4 billion people. That is about one-third of the global population... and it's still climbing (see Figure 1.1; Internet World Stats, **www.internetworldstats.com**).

As global and local online populations have spiralled upwards, so too have the levels of broadband penetration, which means that not only are there more people online, but they are also online more often, for much longer periods of time and can do much more with that time. All of which means that the market penetration of digital channels is growing rapidly. As the potential audience grows, so too does the allure of digital marketing. Marketers around the world are sitting up and taking notice, and big-name brands are taking the internet and other digital marketing channels seriously: loosening the purse strings and redistributing their advertising spend.

Recent figures released from the joint survey of IAB (Internet Advertising Bureau UK) and PricewaterhouseCoopers (PWC) show that online ad spend continues to impress with figures from the first half of 2013 revealing an increase of 17.5 per cent as the UK online market looks set to crack the £6 billion mark – a record high. This equates to approximately £10 marketing spend per month per online UK consumer.

Mobile advertising is now unsurprisingly experiencing rapid growth, up 127 per cent in the first half of 2013 to a market value of £429 million, and video ads continued to impress with growth of 86 per cent to a market value of £135 million. The fastest growth of all in this survey was mobile video advertising, showing growth of 1,260 per cent albeit from a small base to a current market size of £23 million but fuelled by the roll-out of new 4G networks, surely a bet for future marketers right here.

Meanwhile, stateside... according to Zenith Optimedia 2013 survey, digital now represents 22 per cent of all ad spend globally, which has increased from 19 per cent in 2012. Mobile is growing at 81 per cent and search still remains the most popular form of online advertising.

Introducing Consumer 2.0

Unless you have been hiding under a rock in the Outer Hebrides since about 2004 you will be familiar with the Web 2.0 (pronounced two-point-oh) moniker. It is bandied about with alacrity by the web-savvy elite, but what exactly does it mean?

Let's start off with what Web 2.0 is not: it's not a new version of Web 1.0. Web 2.0 is not a revolution in technology, it's an evolution in the way people are using technology. It's about harnessing the distributed collaborative potential of the internet to connect and communicate with other like-minded people wherever they are: creating communities and sharing knowledge, thoughts, ideas and dreams.

If you've ever shared photos on Flickr, read and commented on a blog, looked for friends on Facebook, watched a video clip on YouTube, tried to find your house on Google Maps, video-called friends or family abroad using Skype or looked up an article on Wikipedia, then you have used Web 2.0 technologies.

Suddenly it seems we have been inundated with version 2.0 of anything and everything as different sectors of society seek to demonstrate that they are current and progressive. We have Business 2.0, Government 2.0, Education 2.0, Careers 2.0... and, of course, Marketing 2.0. Well, not to be outdone, we would like to introduce you to the new, improved, Consumer 2.0.

One upon a time, consumers were quite happy to sit in front of passive broadcast media, accepting whatever was being peddled their way by editors and programme schedulers. Yes, there was an element of choice – you could buy a different newspaper, listen to a different station or choose a different channel – but the ultimate decision in terms of the content available to you rested with somebody else.

Then along came the web, and changed all the rules. Now, with Web 2.0, broadband and rich media content, today's consumers are in control like never before. They can choose the content they want, when they want it, in the way that they want it... they can even create their own and share it with their friends, their peers and the world for free.

'Consumers are becoming better informed, better connected, more communicative, and more in control than ever,' highlights Julian Smith, an analyst with Jupiter Research writing for the ClickZ network. 'They're better informed through the increased ability to access and sift an abundance of information any time, anywhere. They're better connected through the ability to instantaneously communicate with others across time zones and social strata. They're more communicative through the ability to publish and share their ideas and opinions. They're more in control through the ability not only to personalize their information and entertainment consumption, marketing messages, and the products and services they buy, but also to gain satisfaction on demand.'

Analysts at Jupiter Research identified seven key ways in which the increasingly widespread adoption of technology is influencing consumer behaviour:

- **Interconnectivity:** networked digital technology is enabling consumers to connect with each other more readily, be it through e-mail, instant messaging (IM), mobile messaging, or web-based social networking platforms such as Facebook, Twitter and LinkedIn – or more likely a combination of all of these platforms. Consumers are interacting with like-minded people around the world, paying scant regard for trifling concerns such as time zones or geography. Peer-to-peer interaction is reinforcing social networks, and building new virtual communities.

- **Technology is levelling the information playing field:** with digital technology, content can be created, published, accessed and consumed quickly and easily. As a result, the scope of news, opinion and information available to consumers is broader and deeper than ever. Consumers can conduct their own unbiased research, comparing and contrasting products and services before they buy. Knowledge is power... and digital technology is shifting the balance of power in favour of the consumer.

- **Relevance filtering is increasing:** with such a glut of information available to digital consumers, they are through necessity learning to filter out items relevant to them and to ignore anything they perceive as irrelevant. Increasingly digital consumers look to have their information aggregated, categorized and delivered (whether through e-mail or really simple syndication (RSS) feeds – a way to automatically retrieve updated posts/articles from a website). They use personalization features to block out irrelevant content and increasingly employ software solutions to exclude unsolicited commercial messages.

- **Niche aggregation is growing:** the abundance and diversity of online content allows consumers to participate and indulge their specialist interests and hobbies. Aggregations of like-minded individuals congregate online; the homogeneous mass consumer population is fragmenting into ever smaller niche groups, with increasingly individual requirements.

- **Micropublishing of personal content is blossoming:** digital media's interactive and interconnected nature allows consumers to express themselves online. Publishing your own content costs little more than a bit of time and imagination, whether through discussion forums, message boards, feedback forms, voting platforms, personal photo galleries, or blogs. Users are posting their opinions online for all to see, and are consulting the opinion of their online peers before making purchasing decisions. How often do you check an online review before booking a table at an unknown restaurant, a weekend break at a hotel, or even buying a new car?

- **Rise of the 'prosumer':** online consumers are getting increasingly involved in the creation of the products and services they purchase, shifting the balance of power from producer to consumer. They are letting producers know what they want in no uncertain terms: the level of interaction between producer and consumer is unprecedented. Individuals are more involved in specifying, creating and customizing products to suit their requirements, and are able to shape and mould the experiences and communications they receive from producers. Traditional mass-production and mass-marketing concepts are rapidly becoming a thing of the past.

- **On-demand; any time, any place, anywhere:** as digital technology becomes more ubiquitous in people's lives, the corresponding acceleration of business processes means that consumers can satisfy their needs more quickly, more easily and with fewer barriers. In the digital economy, trifling concerns such as time, geography, location and physical storage space are becoming irrelevant. It is a world of almost instant gratification – and the more consumers get of it, the more they want it... now, now, now!

For marketers this evolution of the marketplace, and the shift in consumer mindset that it heralds, presents a plethora of new challenges. As consumers increasingly embrace new ways of communicating, take greater ownership of the information and entertainment they consume, and aggregate in increasingly specialized niche online communities, marketers must shift their approach if they want to connect with them.

And that is what the rest of this book is all about.

CASE STUDY   Harley-Davidson

(As showcased in *The Best Digital Marketing Campaigns in the World II*.)

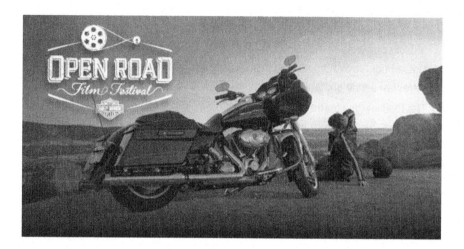

Comment

How smart digital increased sales by 43 per cent. More than just a motorbike, a Harley-Davidson comes with a lifestyle, but how do you sell a lifestyle on a 30-minute test ride? And so 24-hour test rides were born.

Location

Australia.

The challenge

Harley-Davidson wanted to lift sales for its touring range of motorbikes and create audience-engaging content.

Campaign budget

US $250,000 to $300,000.

Target audience

Customers and potential customers of Harley-Davidson motorbikes.

Action

- To launch 24-hour test rides, the agency created the end sequence to a short film where a man wakes up with a Harley. They then invited young film-makers to view the film online, and challenged them to show how the film begins.
- This resulted in multiple films being made, all with different beginnings, but all leading to one common ending.
- The agency then staged 'The Open Road Film Festival' event. This was a public screening of the top eight films. The event took place at The Bucket List, a popular nightspot in Australia's legendary Bondi Beach area, and attracted a vast audience including many of Australia's own film celebrities.
- The festival was featured online where thousands of viewers across Australia and New Zealand watched and voted for their favourite films. Prizes were awarded to film-makers and voters, including a Harley-Davidson Iron 883 and much-desired Canon cameras and equipment.
- Inspired by the Harley adventures in these films, many film viewers went on to join a waiting list for 24-hour test rides.
- The campaign generated far more interaction than anyone had anticipated or hoped for and, importantly, met the brief of: 1) getting branded content created by film-makers that brought to life the excitement of owning a Harley through dramatizing what could happen with a Harley in 24 hours; 2) lifting the sales of the touring bike range.

Results

- 59,383: number of site visits over the festival and campaign period.
- 41,340: number of unique site visits.
- 33,072: total number of collective minutes spent on the site.
- 10,599: total number of views of the top eight films.
- 171: number of film-makers who signed up for film tips from Gregor Jordan and Bryan Brown.
- 65: number of film-script submissions and grant applications.
- 25: number of finished films uploaded.
- 43 per cent sales uplift: the campaign contributed to a 43 per cent sales uplift for touring models during the campaign period versus the exact same period of the previous year. A resounding success.

Links to campaign

http://openroadfilmfestival.com/

About the creator

303Lowe is a boutique full-service agency with offices in both Sydney and Perth, Australia. Together, we are small enough to be nimble and responsive, yet big enough to take on the greatest challenges. We've built our agency on the belief that for too long, advertising has simply interrupted people. We see engagement and interaction as a more effective way of communicating with customers, which is why we've put digital skill sets at the heart of our agency.

We believe a big idea can beat the weight of a media schedule; that ingenuity and creativity are more critical to effectiveness than the size of the campaign budget. Bigger thinking can and does win hearts and minds. It's how in 2012, we won more Effie awards for more clients than any other agency in Australia, including The Grand Effie. A tally we've since proudly added further to in 2013.

Credits

The 'Wake up with a Harley' campaign received Digital Campaign of the Year at Australia's WA Campaign Brief Awards in 2012. Its credits:

- Executive Creative Director: Simon Langley.
- Creative Director/s: Richard Berney, Steve Straw.
- Art Director: Helen King.
- Head of Business Management: Matt Clarke.
- Business Manager: Katie Wong-Hee, Brodie Neader.
- Head of Digital: Nic Chamberlain.
- Digital Producer: Matt Pratley.
- Web Designer: Pete Herekiuha, Fed Barera, Baptiste David.
- Director: Gregor Jordan.
- Production: Finch Company.

Additional comments

Producer Bryan Brown said: 'The more opportunities for young Australian film-makers, the more creative the Oz film industry can be. The Open Road Film Festival is fantastic because it has the potential to help new directors get noticed. The prizes are pretty good too.'

Matt Clarke, Head of Business Management at 303Lowe, said: 'After presenting the idea to Harley just over a year ago, to see it conclude with eight diverse and interesting films is extremely rewarding and has created some excellent content. It builds on Harley's association with film going back to the likes of *Easy Rider*.'

Richard Berney, Creative Director, said: 'Great to see this work so well. This was a new way to generate content, and use the burning creativity that is in the Australian film industry for the benefit of both Harley and young Aussie film-makers.'

Adam Wright, Director of Marketing for Harley-Davidson Australia and New Zealand, said: 'Harley-Davidson has a great heritage in the international film scene. We're proud to be a part of this brave new festival, and seeing our bikes in these great stories is just amazing.'

@first... think!

02

OUR CHAPTER PLEDGE TO YOU

When you reach the end of this chapter you'll have answers to the following questions:

- What is a digital marketing strategy and why do I need one?
- How do I know if digital marketing is right for my business?
- How do I formulate a digital marketing strategy?
- Are my customers ready for digital marketing?

Why you need a digital marketing strategy

Why do you need a digital marketing strategy? The simple answer: because without one you will miss opportunities and lose business. Formulating a digital marketing strategy will help you to make informed decisions about your foray into the digital marketing arena, and ensure that your efforts are focused on the elements of digital marketing that are most relevant to your business. It is a crucial first step towards understanding how the constantly evolving digital marketplace relates to you, and how it affects the relationship between your business or brand, and your customers and prospects.

It doesn't matter what business you're in, it's a fairly safe bet that an increasing number of your target market rely on digital technology every day to research, evaluate and purchase the products and services they consume. Without a coherent strategy of engagement and retention through digital channels your business is at best missing a golden opportunity, and at worst could be left behind, watching your competitors pull away across an ever-widening digital divide.

Unlike conventional forms of mass-media marketing, the internet is unique in its capacity to both broaden the scope of your marketing reach and narrow its focus *at the same time*. Using digital channels you can transcend traditional constraints such as geography and time zones to connect with a much wider audience. At the same time, digital technology allows you to hone your marketing message with laser-like precision to target very specific niche segments within that wider market. Implemented effectively it can be an incredibly powerful combination.

It is often stated that the internet puts consumers in control like never before. But it is important to remember that the internet also delivers an unprecedented suite of tools, techniques and tactics that allow marketers to reach out and engage with those same consumers. The marketing landscape has never been more challenging, dynamic and diverse.

And therein lies the crux of our need for a cohesive digital marketing strategy. If you're going to harness the power of digital marketing to drive your online business to dizzying new heights, you need a thorough understanding of your market, how your customers are using digital technology, and how your business can best utilize that same technology to build enduring and mutually rewarding relationships with them.

As digital channels continue to broaden the scope available to us as marketers, so they add to the potential complexity of any digital marketing campaign. Having a clearly defined strategy will help to keep you focused, ensure that your marketing activities are always aligned with your business goals and, crucially, that you're targeting the right people.

Your business and digital marketing

Whether or not your business is suited to digital marketing depends very much on the nature of that business, where it is now, and where you want it to go in the future. If, for example, you're a dairy farmer in rural Ireland, have a fixed contract to supply milk to the local co-operative, and have little, if any, scope or ambition to diversify and grow your business year-on-year, then digital marketing probably isn't for you. Likewise, if you're a local butcher with an established client base in a thriving market town in the English Peak District, and simply want to maintain the status quo, then again you'll probably do just fine without digital marketing.

If, however, you're a Peak District butcher looking to diversify your product offering, broaden the scope of your business and want to start selling your quality organic produce to restaurants and hotels around the country... well then, welcome to the world of digital marketing.

In truth, there are very few businesses today that can't benefit from at least some degree of digital marketing – even if it is just providing a basic online brochure telling people what you do, and sending out the occasional update to existing customers via an e-mail newsletter or RSS feed.

Whether you are running a home-based 'lifestyle' business selling hand-embroidered cushion covers, are a small-scale artisan food producer, an up-and-coming restaurateur or managing a large multinational corporation, a growing proportion of your customer base is already online, with more joining them every day (see Figure 2.1). Obviously, the more your target market comes to rely on these online channels for its information, research and purchasing needs, the more critical digital marketing will become to the ongoing success of your business.

Digital marketing – yes or no

There are really only two key questions you need to answer when it comes to deciding whether or not your business needs a digital marketing strategy. They are:

1 **Is my audience online/is it going to be online?** If your customers use digital technology to research and/or purchase the products and services you provide, then you absolutely need to embrace digital marketing now in order to engage with them and retain them. If they don't, then you don't. It really is that simple. Just bear in mind that as the next generation of consumers start to become your new customers, they are likely to demand more digital interaction from your business. If you're not in a position to deliver that, they could well choose to spend their money elsewhere.

2 **Are my products/services/brands suited to digital marketing?** This can be a tricky one – but the answer is usually yes. Typically it doesn't matter what your product, service or brand is: as long as you have established that there is a viable online audience for it (see question 1), then you should be promoting it online. While some products and services are obviously more suited to online purchase and fulfilment than others (digital files, such as e-books or music, spring to mind), you will also find being marketed effectively through digital channels plenty of items that few people would ever dream of actually purchasing over the internet. Consumers go online to research, evaluate and compare their choices. They make purchasing decisions based on the quality of their online experience, then head to a bricks-and-mortar store to hand over their cash. Boats, cars, houses, apartments, horses, tractors – you name it – they are all being actively and successfully marketed online.

FIGURE 2.1 Are your customers online? Figures from the Pew Internet & American Life Project April–May 2013 showing the proportion of US adults now online, and a breakdown of their demographic make-up

Demographics of internet users

% of adults in each group who use the internet (the number of respondents in each group listed as 'n' for the group)

		Use the Internet
All adults (n = 2,252)		**85%**
a	Men (n = 1,029)	85
b	Women (n = 1,223)	84
Race/ethnicity		
a	White, Non-Hispanic (n = 1,571)	86^c
b	Black, Non-Hispanic (n = 252)	85^c
c	Hispanic (n = 249)	76
Age		
a	18–29 (n = 404)	98^{bcd}
b	30–49 (n = 577)	92^{cd}
c	50–64 (n = 641)	83^d
d	65+ (n = 570)	56
Education attainment		
a	Less than high school (n = 168)	59
b	High school grad (n = 630)	78^a
c	Some College (n = 588)	92^{ab}
d	College + (n = 834)	96^{abc}
Household income		
a	Less than $30,000/yr (n = 580)	76
b	$30,000–$49,999 (n = 374)	88^a
c	$50,000–$74,999 (n = 298)	94^{ab}
d	$75,000+ (n = 582)	96^{ab}
Urbanity		
a	Urban (n = 763)	86^c
b	Suburban (n = 1,037)	86^c
c	Rural (n = 450)	80

SOURCE: Pew Research Center's Internet & American Life Project Spring Tracking Survey, April 17 – May 19, 2013. N = 2,252 adults. Interviews were conducted in English and Spanish and on landline and cell phones. Margin of error is +/– 2.3 percentage points for results based on internet users.

NOTE: Percentages marked with a superscript letter (eg, ^{a}) indicate a statistically significant difference between that row and the row designated by that superscript letter, among categories of each demographic characteristic (eg age).

Defining your digital marketing strategy

Once you've decided that you do, in fact, need to pursue some form of digital marketing, the next step is to actually sit down and define your strategy. Unfortunately, there is no 'one size fits all' strategic panacea here. We don't have a magic recipe to ensure your digital marketing success, and neither does anybody else (despite some of the online hyperbola you may read on the subject).

Basically, every business needs to 'bake' its own unique strategy based on its own particular set of circumstances. While the available ingredients are the same (and we'll cover the major ones later in the book), the resulting strategies can be radically different.

It's common sense really. If you sell apples to local grocers by the truck-load your strategy will bear little resemblance to that of a company selling downloadable e-books and reports on financial trading, which will in turn be very different to the strategy adopted by a sports clothing manufacturer who wants to cut out the middle man and sell directly to consumers over the web.

Different products, different markets, different needs... different solutions. What it ultimately boils down to is this: the best people to define your digital marketing strategy, curiously enough, are the people who best know your business.

Laying strong digital foundations

The good news is that you've almost certainly already started the process of defining your digital marketing strategy. Before even picking up this book you've probably been thinking about digital marketing in the context of your business, about what your competitors are doing online and why, about how your customers and prospects are integrating digital technology into their lives, and about how you can best exploit these new and exciting digital channels to foster longer, more productive relationships with them. These are the components that will form the foundation of your digital marketing strategy:

- **Know your business:** is your business ready to embrace digital marketing? Are your products/services suited to online promotion? Do you have the right technology/skills/infrastructure in place? How will digital marketing fit into your existing business processes? Do those processes need to change, and are you and your staff ready to accommodate those changes?

- **Know the competition:** who are your main competitors in the digital marketplace? Are they the same as your offline competitors? What are they doing right (emulate them)? What are they doing wrong (learn from them)? What aren't they doing at all (is there an opportunity there for you?)? How can you differentiate your online offering from theirs? Remember, competition in the digital world can come from just around the corner, or from right around the globe. The same technologies that allow you to reach out to a broader geographical market also allow others to reach in to your local market. When you venture online you are entering a global game, so don't limit your analysis to local competition.

- **Know your customers:** who are your customers and what do they want from you? Are you going to be servicing the same customer base online, or are you fishing for business from a completely new demographic? How do the customers you're targeting use digital technology, and how can you harness that knowledge to engage in a productive and ongoing relationship with them?

- **Know what you want to achieve:** if you don't know where you're going, there's a pretty fair chance you'll never get there. What do you want to get out of digital marketing? Setting clear, measurable and achievable goals is a key part of your digital marketing strategy. Are you looking to generate online sales, create a source of targeted sales leads, improve your brand awareness among online communities, all of the above or perhaps something completely different? Your goals are the yardsticks against which you can measure the progress of your digital marketing campaigns.

- **Know how you're doing:** the beauty of digital marketing is that, compared to many forms of advertising, results are so much more measurable. Check out our chapter on analytics later in the book (Chapter 4)! You can track everything that happens online and compare your progress against predefined goals and key performance indicators (KPIs). How is your digital campaign progressing? Are certain digital channels delivering more traffic than others? Why is that? What about conversion rates – how much of that increased traffic results in tangible value to your business? Measure, tweak, refine, re-measure. Digital marketing is an ongoing iterative process.

The process of formally defining your digital marketing strategy forces you to sit down and analyse with a critical eye the market in which you're operating, and to really think about the different components of your business and how digital marketing can help you to achieve your business goals.

Don't get too bogged down in the technical details – remember, digital marketing is about people communicating with other people, the technology is just the bit in the middle that helps it to happen. Your strategy should provide you with a high-level framework – a bird's-eye view of the digital marketing landscape with your business centre stage – the details will come later.

Understanding the digital consumer

There is a notion that pervades marketing circles today, a notion of mysterious ethereal creatures who exist in a hyper-connected, multifaceted cyber world of their own. They are an enigma: they speak a different language, communicate in ways we don't understand, and they are turning the world of marketing on its head. These are the ephemeral, wraith-like 'digital consumers', who slip effortlessly through the marketer's grasp. Digital consumers are different, we're told... but are they really?

The digital consumer revealed

The first thing to realize about digital consumers is that there is basically no such thing. The customers and prospects you encounter online are the very same people who walk into your store every day, call you on the telephone, or order something from your mail-order catalogue. There's nothing dark, sinister or mysterious about them. They are people – like everybody else.

'There is no great mystery about how [digital consumers] think and what they want', maintains interactive marketing expert Giles Rhys Jones of Interactive Marketing Trends (**http://interactivemarketingtrends.blogspot.com**):

> These consumers are doing exactly what people have been doing for thousands of years – communicating with each other.
>
> The fact that technology is enabling them to communicate with each other faster, over distance, over mobiles and in 3D worlds is being perceived as something dangerous, unique and extraordinary, something that needs to be controlled and pinned down. People talk to each other – they always have. They are talking the same language and saying the same things, they are just not necessarily sitting in the pub talking to 1 or 5 people, but doing it online to 15 or 5,000.

Making the web their own

Consumers, whatever their 'flavour', don't care about the way that marketers define what they do. Concepts like above the line, through the line, below the line, digital, traditional, experiential, linear, analogue, mobile, direct, indirect – or any other 'box' we care to slip our marketing endeavours into – are

FIGURE 2.2   Digital consumption survey

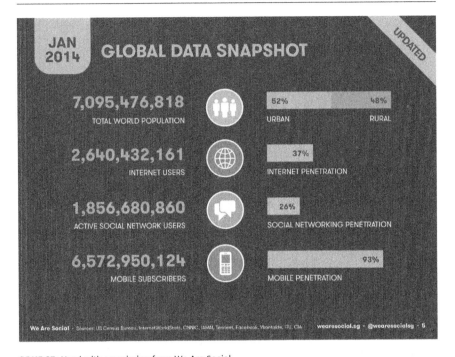

SOURCE: Used with permission from We Are Social.

completely meaningless to them. All consumers care about is the experience – how the marketing available to them can enhance the experience and help them to make more informed decisions.

People are the single most important element in any form of marketing. That is just as true in the digital space as it is in any other sphere of the discipline. As a marketer you need to understand people and their behaviour – and here's where the notion of the digital consumer does carry some weight, because consumer behaviour is changing, and it's changing because of the pervasive, evocative and enabling nature of digital technology (see Figure 2.2).

'The majority of today's consumers are actively personalizing their digital experiences and sampling niche content and video with increasing frequency,' said Dave Friedman, president of the central region for Avenue A | Razorfish, writing in an article for Chief Marketer (**www.chiefmarketer.com**).

'We've reached a collective digital tipping point as a majority of consumers are tapping into a variety of emerging technologies and social media to increasingly personalize their digital experiences,' said Friedman. 'From recommendation engines, to blogs, to customized start pages, today's "connected consumer" navigates a landscape that is much more niche and personalized than we ever expected.'

The practice of broadcasting generic advertising messages to the mass market is rapidly being usurped by specifically targeted, narrow-cast marketing, through digital channels, to an increasingly diverse and segmented marketplace. Even, ultimately, to a target market of one. Digital marketing allows us to build uniquely tailored ongoing relationships with individual customers. This is a conversation, not a lecture. Marketing in the digital age has been transformed into a process of dialogue, as much about listening as it is about telling.

I don't know you and you don't know me

On the internet, no one knows you're a dog... right? Perceived anonymity is another online trait that can have a profound effect on consumer behaviour. It liberates consumers from the social shackles that bind them in the real world; online they are free to do and say as they please with scant regard for the social propriety that holds sway in 'real life'. In a bricks-and-mortar store, shoppers will wait patiently for service, and will often endure a less than flawless shopping experience to get what they want. Online they won't; they demand instant gratification and a flawless customer experience. You have to deliver, first time, every time. If you fail to engage, retain and fulfil their expectations on demand, they're gone, vanishing into the ether of cyberspace as quickly as they came; the only trace a fleeting, solitary record on your web server's log file...

And then they will tell all their online friends about their less than stellar experience.

Key traits of the online consumer

We are all familiar with the old road-rage analogy of the congenial, neighbourly man or woman who suddenly becomes a raving speed demon when they get behind the wheel of a car. Well, there is something about the immediacy and anonymity of the digital experience that has a similar effect on people.

It's always risky to generalize and make assumptions about people – especially in a field as dynamic and fast-moving as this one. The only real way to know your market intimately is to conduct original research within your particular target group. That said, a lot of research work has been done (and continues to be done) on the behavioural traits of online consumers, and a broad consensus has emerged around the key characteristics that epitomize the digital consumer:

1 **Digital consumers are increasingly comfortable with the medium:**
   many online consumers have been using the internet for many years
   at this stage – and while the user demographic is still skewed in
   favour of younger people, older users are becoming increasingly
   internet savvy. 'It's almost like a piano player who plays faster once
   they know the instrument. In the beginning people "pling, pling,
   pling" very carefully, and then they move on to playing symphonies,'
   said web usability guru Jacob Nielsen in an interview with the BBC.
   As people become more comfortable with the medium they use it
   more efficiently and effectively, which means they don't hang around
   for long: your content needs to deliver what they want, and it needs
   to deliver quickly.

2 **They want it all, and they want it now:** in the digital world, where
   everything happens at a million miles per hour, consumers have
   grown accustomed to getting their information on demand from
   multiple sources simultaneously. Their time is a precious commodity,
   so they want information in a format that they can scan for relevance
   before investing time in examining the detail. Designers and
   marketers need to accommodate this desire for 'scanability' and
   instant gratification when constructing their online offering.
   Think about 'value for time' as well as 'value for money'.

3 **They're in control:** the web is no passive medium. Users are in control
   – in the Web 2.0 world more than ever before. Fail to grasp that
   simple fact and your target audience won't just fail to engage with
   you, they will actively disengage. We need to tailor our marketing to
   be user centric, elective or permission based, and offer a real value
   proposition to the consumer in order to garner positive results.

4 **They're fickle:** the transparency and immediacy of the internet doesn't
   eradicate the concept of brand or vendor loyalty, but it does erode it.
   Building trust in a brand is still a crucial element of digital marketing,
   but today's consumer has literally at their fingertips the power to
   compare and contrast competing brands. How does your value
   proposition stack up against the competition around the country and
   across the globe? Your brand identity may be valuable, but if your
   overall value proposition doesn't stack up then you will lose out.

5 **They're vocal:** online consumers talk to each other... a lot. Through
   peer reviews, blogs, social networks, online forums and communities
   they're telling each other about their positive online experiences...
   and the negative ones. From a marketing perspective this is

something of a double-edged sword – harness the positive aspects and you have incredible viral potential to propagate your message; get it wrong and you could just as easily be on the receiving end of an uncomfortable online backlash.

21 minutes in my digital life, 13 December 2013

It is 7 am. I wake to the sound of my iPhone cranking out a Paul Weller number. After several stabs in the dark I manage to turn it off before checking a number of texts that arrived during the night from Australia and the United States. While my right arm remains trapped by the duvet, my left thumb whacks off a reply to Richard in Melbourne and Senay in San Francisco. I then drift over to check both my personal and business Twitter accounts. Not much to retweet there so have a quick look at Facebook to see if anyone liked the picture of my father's 80th birthday party. Excellent. There were loads of likes and a few nice comments too.

Because I live in an upside-down house (bedrooms downstairs) I head upstairs to my desk – the laptop already open I check e-mails into my Mediaventura account, gaze blearily at the online itinerary on iCal from Beckie and look at the various discussions among the team on current projects – I note that dropbox has been updated with more data on our latest deal.

A text pings in from Christophe (he's up early) to say that the new designs for **www.gogadm.com** are expected from the team in Serbia any second and I reply back to confirm our get-together in London later on in the day.

In all, I have received 24 messages since 8 pm the previous day – half of these are newsletters and LinkedIn groups – some I delete straightaway and the rest I will leave for later or never. The other 12 messages sort of prioritize themselves in front of me – of course I immediately open the e-mail from Amazon confirming the order for Christmas presents for my kids and then take a quick look at **www.ticketmaster.co.uk** to see if there is any hope of getting them tickets for One Direction. I hear the familiar sound of Skype popping away in the background as more of my contacts wake up and hit their respective desks too – then another bleep goes off and there's Barry on IM wanting to chat about our meeting planned for 11 am. We chat for a bit and then I sign off in need of a cup of rosie.

... it's 7:21 am, time for a shower, then breakfast.

Welcome to the world of me, the digital immigrant – unlike the droves of digital natives I didn't start to use the net until I was 30. While it feels completely natural now, I recognize this is nothing compared to the manner in which digital natives see things. For me I am still full of wonder about the miracles of Skype and the instantaneousness of the net, but that's me and I reckon I am just about typical of people around me. However, for anyone under the age of 25 it's a completely different experience – a hyper-connected, high-octane world of instant access and gratification with digital technology at its core. To young people today, these aren't merely digital tools, they are essential, seamlessly integrated elements of their daily lives. These are digital consumers, the net-generation, generation Y... call them what you will. They are insistent, impatient, demanding, multitasking information junkies. They are the mass market of tomorrow – and, as marketers, it's absolutely imperative that we learn to speak their language today.

Using influencers to help spread the word

There is one particular category of users online that warrants a special mention when it comes to defining your digital marketing strategy. Dubbed 'influencers' these early adopters are the online opinion leaders. Through blogs, podcasts, forums and social networks they harness the power of the web to extol the virtues of products and brands that they like, and equally to denigrate those they find unsatisfactory.

Why are influencers important to you as a marketer? Because they have the virtual-ear of the online masses. People read and listen to what they have to say; they value their opinion and trust their judgement. These online influencers have already won the pivotal battle for the hearts and minds of online consumers. Engage positively with them, and you essentially recruit a team of powerful online advocates who can have a potentially massive impact on a much wider group of consumers. This is the online equivalent of 'word-of-mouth' marketing on steroids. Of course, give them a negative experience and... well, you can guess the rest.

But how exactly will you recognize these online influencers?

A December 2006 report by DoubleClick ('Influencing the Influencers: How Online Advertising and Media Impact Word of Mouth') defined an influencer as a person who 'strongly agreed' to three or more of the following statements:

- They consider themselves expert in certain areas (such as their work, hobbies or interests).

- People often ask their advice about purchases in areas where they are knowledgeable.
- When they encounter a new product they like, they tend to recommend it to friends.
- They have a large social circle and often refer people to one another based on their interests.
- They are active online, using blogs, social networking sites, e-mail, discussion groups, online community boards, etc, to connect with their peers.

Identifying the influencers within your market sector, analysing their behaviour and tailoring part of your digital campaign to target this small but influential group can result in disproportionate knock-on benefits. Don't neglect your core market, of course – but certainly consider targeting influencers as part of your overall digital marketing strategy.

Mind your Ps

You might be asking yourself how all this newfangled digital 'stuff' fits in to the traditional marketing mix: the venerable four Ps of Product, Price, Promotion and Place. Well, it breaks down something like this.

Place

Let's start with the obvious one: it's the internet. It's the 2.4 billion plus people around the world who have decided it is better to be connected... whether it is accessed through a computer, a mobile device, internet protocol television (IPTV) or whatever else might come along. That's really it.

Price

Pricing is critical online. You have to be competitive: this is the internet, and pricing is transparent. You don't necessarily have to be the cheapest – but to compete you need to make sure your overall value proposition to the customer is compelling. Overprice your product and a host of price comparison sites will soon highlight the fact, as will the countless peer review communities where consumers actively debate the relative merits (or otherwise) of everything from financial products to wedding stationery (see Figure 2.3).

FIGURE 2.3 Moneysupermarket.com, billed as 'the UK's leading finance price-comparison website and a leading UK travel price comparison website'

Product

This is what you have to offer – your unique value proposition to your customers. A good product, of course, is the cornerstone of all successful marketing, but it is particularly crucial in the digital arena. A product that delivers tangible benefits and fills a real need in the marketplace – something that leaves the customer with a genuine perception of value – gives marketers the scope they need to do their job effectively. When you're promoting something viable, it's much easier to engage with consumers and to convince them to buy.

Conversely, the best marketing minds in the world will struggle to promote a product that doesn't deliver the goods. And this is where the all-pervading, viral nature of the internet can really come back to bite you. If you promote a product online and that product doesn't deliver, you had better be prepared for the backlash.

Digital consumers are no wallflowers – they are vociferous and well-connected. They won't keep the shortcomings of your product or business to themselves – they'll shout about it from the tallest building in cyberspace, and others will quickly pick up the cry. Once that happens you can pretty much shelve your marketing ambitions and go back to the drawing board.

So, it is important to make sure your product and the entire customer value chain associated with it is right from the start. You need a solid foundation if you're going to build a sustainable online business, and that all starts with a sound product.

Promotion

Promotion is everything you do, online and offline, to get your product in front of your prospects, acquire new customers and retain existing ones. Examining those options will form the bulk of the rest of this book: in the following chapters we'll discuss the major forms of online promotion available now, and will go on to look at emerging and future trends. Here we summarize the main elements in order to whet your appetite:

- **Your website**: your website is the hub of your digital world – and perhaps the most important element in your whole digital marketing strategy. It's a vital piece of online real estate to which all of your other online activity will direct your prospects. A lot of the digital marketing techniques discussed in this book are about generating traffic to your website – but traffic in itself is worthless. To become valuable, traffic must be converted – and that is essentially what your website should be: a conversion engine for the traffic being directed to it.

- **Search engine optimization (SEO)**: part and parcel of the website is SEO, or the process of aligning content on your website to what your prospects are actively searching for, and presenting it in a manner that makes it accessible to both people and search engines. The organic or natural search results (the results in the middle of the search engine results page) is **the** place to be if you want to increase targeted traffic to your website.

- **Pay per click search advertising (PPC)**: pay per click advertising offers you a way to buy your way onto the search results pages for chosen keywords or key phrases. Depending on your business and what keywords you want to rank for, this can be an extremely effective way of generating search engine traffic quickly, although as the medium continues to gain in popularity more competitive keywords are becoming prohibitively expensive for smaller businesses.

- **Affiliate/performance marketing and strategic partnerships:** how to partner with other organizations and websites in mutually beneficial relationships to promote your products or services.

- **Online public relations:** using online channels such as press releases, article syndication and blogs to create a positive perception of your brand and/or position you as an authority in your particular field.

- **Social media:** the focus of Web 2.0 and a massive growth area for marketers online and one that can potentially offer highly targeted advertising to niche social groups based on profile information they volunteer through sites such as Facebook, Twitter, Pinterest, Tumblr and so on. Social media and social networking is an entire branch of digital marketing that is producing incredibly exciting results.

- **E-mail marketing:** the granddaddy of internet marketing, suffering something of a crisis in the wake of perpetual spam bombardment, but still an important tool in the digital marketer's arsenal, particularly when it comes to maintaining ongoing relationships with existing customers and prospects who have 'opted in' to receive information.

- **Mobile marketing:** the up-and-coming star of digital... mobile is finally poised to deliver on the latent potential that has been promising to erupt for years. With smartphone penetration growing and fast mobile internet becoming almost ubiquitous, at least in urban centres, mobile means your customers now have access to your content any time, any place, anywhere!

- **Customer relationship management:** retaining existing customers, and building mutually rewarding relationships with them, is another important element of digital marketing. Digital technology makes developing an enduring connection with your customers more straightforward and effective than ever before.

- **Content marketing...** I feel people have always understood the importance of good content but now that Google and other search engines will rank your pages based upon its content offering – and the fact that content is pulling better response (at times) than display media – it cannot be ignored (please refer to Chapter 11).

- **Display media:** what used to be just plain old online advertising has developed into its own science, with incredible results and new technologies every day. Retargeting, in particular, is an area worthy of examination. Online video, online audio, real-time bidding – lots to consider here.

Eyes on the prize

Another crucially important area of your digital marketing strategy is setting realistic goals. Your strategy should explicitly define the business goals you want your digital marketing efforts to help you achieve. As with any other journey, you can only plan an effective route if you have a clear, unambiguous destination in mind from the start. Or to put it another way, you might be the world's best archer – but if no one gives you a target to aim at, what good will it do you?

To measure your progress towards those goals, you also need to set milestones along the way, consistently measuring your achievements and steering your digital campaign towards your ultimate destination. Here, again, the digital realm offers a raft of tools and techniques to help marketers reap a better return from their investment.

We'll be examining the topic of web metrics and website intelligence in Chapter 4, but the crucial thing to remember here is that digital marketing is an iterative process of continuous improvement and refinement. You can monitor and analyse the effectiveness of your digital marketing campaigns in practically real time. You can measure everything, and even run alternative ads and strategies side-by-side to see what works best before committing to a given course: test, refine, re-test and then decide where to make your investment, based on real data from real customers.

Tracking accountability

When a computer or mobile phone – in fact let's call it a digital media device – hits a site, a record is created in the web server's log file based on the unique IP address of that user, and tracks their navigation through the site. Software on the web server also sends a small, unobtrusive file to the user's browser known as a 'cookie', which essentially allows the web server to recognize the same user when they come back to the site again.

Based on information in the log file, marketers can tell a surprising amount about the user's activity on the site:

- We know the broad geographical location based on the digits in the IP address.

- We know when they arrived and from where.

- We know what type of browser and operating system they're using.

So far we know very little but we can already start to be more accountable. For example, we can now order our advertising and marketing messages to be delivered only to people with a Mac who live in Ireland and don't like working before lunchtime but are seriously interested in sports.

Now let's make things a little more interesting.

By adding specific 'page tags' to our website (with the help of a website developer, webmaster and analytics partner) we can start to do some very clever things – following website visitors to the purchase point and beyond.

For example, say we choose to run a banner ad campaign. We can detect not only the people who click on the banner and go through the site to become purchasers, we can also detect those people who do NOT click on the banner, but then go ahead and buy the product anyway a few weeks later. This is really exciting stuff for marketers because ultimately it dispenses with our whole fascination with the value of the click-through.

Not long ago, digital marketing metrics were all about clicks, clicks, clicks. Today, while clicks remain an important guideline, ultimately they are about as useful as saying 230 people noticed my ad today, isn't that great. Well, in a word, no.

Today's online marketing investment is about tangible returns, it is about conversion and return on investment (ROI); ultimately it is about the accountability of the brand, the price, the ad campaign and the job of the marketer.

Which scenario would you rather: a warm post-campaign glow when the research company pats you on the back and says well done for achieving a 10 per cent increase in brand recall among 18–24 year olds, or 1,293 enquiries about your product and the names and addresses (e-mail, of course) of the 233 new customers who now own your product?

Online marketing is very like direct marketing in that regard. You invest, you sell, you weigh up your ROI, you learn, you adapt, you move on. Except that, online, the process is much accelerated. Yes, of course there is still value in brand-based advertising. The drum-playing gorilla who makes you want to eat Dairy Milk, or the girl on the bench who makes you want to whistle the 'Nokia' tune and give her your Coca-Cola... it's all good brand-building stuff, and the kind of advertising that is sure to remain with us. The big problem with it is its lack of accountability.

The truth is that digital is simply more accountable. You have far more control and can make far more informed decisions based on the feedback and information that the technology provides. It is easy to control the pace and flow of your marketing budget, to turn it up or down and to channel it in different directions.

If you are selling holidays, for example, you already know enough about your customers to realize that certain times of the year (holiday season) are less effective for advertising than others (freezing winter days). But how cool would it be if you could target your holiday advertising so that your ads start to run when the temperature drops below 10°C in a particular region? What about being able to advertise your currency-exchange services based on the performance of the markets? Well, in the digital world, you can do that. The potential is boundless.

Bringing it all together

There is a lot to think about when defining your digital marketing strategy but, in the end, the process is about researching, analysing and understanding three things that are crucial to your success: your business, your competition and your customers. Your strategy lays the foundation for everything you do as a digital marketer, and will guide the decisions you make as you implement some of the techniques outlined in the coming chapters – and choose not to implement others, precisely because they don't fit with your chosen strategy.

Effective digital marketing is about boxing clever. You pick and choose the elements that are specifically relevant to your business. Going through the process of defining a clear strategy, based on a thorough analysis of where your business is now, and where you want digital marketing to take it, puts you in the ideal position to know what is likely to work for you, and just as importantly, what probably won't.

CASE STUDY MercadoLibre

Comment

e-commerce giant gets personal on a massive scale with dynamic ads.

Founded in Buenos Aires, Argentina, in 1999 and now eBay's official Latin America partner, MercadoLibre is an online platform dedicated to e-commerce and online auctions. As Latin America's top e-commerce advertiser, MercadoLibre offers thousands of products in hundreds of product categories for all types of audiences.

Location

Argentina.

The challenge

To engage MercadoLibre customers and increase conversion through targeted ads.

Target audience

Consumers in Latin America.

Action

- The initial user pool identified by first-party data was retargeted with dynamic banners based on their previous behaviour on the advertiser's site.

- Messages and image versions were tailored to each user based on their previous activities, products they browsed or the date of their last purchase.

- Headway Digital set up XML (Extensible Markup Language) feeds and application programming interfaces (APIs) to serve the most relevant ad version for each user – automatically and with no manual versioning, using Headway DSP.

The retargeting strategy fell into two categories:

Scenario 1:

1 A user visits the advertising site, looks at mobile phones, but does not complete a transaction.

2 The user is retargeted across real-time bidding (RTB) sites, including Google network and Facebook, and is served an ad featuring the mobile phone along with suggested options.

Scenario 2:

1 A user completes a mobile phone purchase at the advertiser's site.

2 The user is retargeted across RTB sites and is served an ad displaying accessories compatible with the model purchased.

By serving highly relevant ads to each user, this advertiser was able to generate higher conversions and higher average spend than static ads, with extremely low production costs and cost per acquisition (CPA).

Results

- Return on ad spend + 300 per cent.

- Conversion rate + 212 per cent.

- Clicks per conversion –68 per cent.

- Conversions + 1,167 per cent.

Links to campaign

- http://www.headwaydigital.com/

- http://www.mercadolibre.com/

About the creator

Headway Digital, is a digital media trading desk, connecting media buyers directly with multiple real-time display advertising marketplaces around the world.

Headway Digital technology integrates and provides access to third party data providers, ad networks, ad exchanges, and other top third-party providers in order to achieve data-driven media-buying power.

Quote

Guillermina Coto, MercadoLibre marketing manager, said: 'This dynamic campaign enabled us to deliver personalized ads based on each consumer's interest and status in the purchase cycle – with excellent results. Headway Digital's DCO capabilities with API and XML meant the retargeting strategy was efficiently executed.'

Then build your channel

03

Your website – the hub of your digital marketing world

Before we get going on this chapter we need to agree something together – whether your website appears as a shop window on a person's 'connected' television set or it materializes as a mobile site enabled for a smartphone, or is just a simple old-fashioned homepage on a computer screen – it is still a shop window to your digital world and it is still a website. Later in the chapter you will read about developments in the world of 'responsive web design' and that is impacting the creation and evolution of sites, but now this is all we need to agree on: a website is increasingly EVERYWHERE and as long as you can access and acquire your products and services do we really need to get into semantics?

As a digital marketer, your website is your place of business. You may have all sorts of campaigns out there, tapping the far-flung reaches of cyberspace for a rich vein of new customers, but ultimately everything will be channelled back through a single point: your website. That makes your website incredibly valuable. In fact, it is the single most valuable piece of digital real-estate you will ever own. Get your digital marketing strategy right, and who knows, it could well end up being the most valuable piece of real estate you own: period.

We can't stress this point enough. In an uncertain and constantly evolving digital world, your website is the one thing over which you have complete and explicit control. You can change anything and everything on your website; you can tweak it, tune it and manipulate it in any way you want; you can build in ways to track and measure *all* of the activity on your website. You own it, it's yours, and it's the yardstick by which your entire online business will be measured.

A conversion engine for traffic

All of the digital marketing techniques we discuss in the coming chapters have one thing in common: they are designed to drive targeted, pre-qualified traffic to your website. But *traffic on its own does nothing but consume internet bandwidth*: it is your website that converts that traffic into prospects and customers – taking the numbers and transforming them into something of tangible value to your business.

As a digital marketer your website IS NOT just an online brochure to let people know who you are and what you do. Granted, some of the information you provide on your site will serve that purpose – but only in a periphery capacity. Nor is it simply there to garner search engine 'mojo' and generate huge volumes of traffic. Think of your website primarily as a *conversion engine* for the traffic you garner through all of your other digital marketing endeavours.

Yes, you need to provide information about your business, products and services – but always with your conversion goals in mind. Everything on your website should be geared towards achieving those conversion goals, either directly (products and service information, online ordering/ sales functionality, sales-focused copy and calls to action, enquiry forms, newsletter sign-up, etc) or indirectly (business and brand information that builds trust, content that encourages repeat visits and/or establishes your authority/reputation in your field).

Your conversion goals could be anything from an actual online purchase (a sales transaction) to an online query (lead generation), to subscribing for your online newsletter (opt-in for future marketing)... or whatever else you decide is important for your business and appropriate for your customers. You can, of course, have multiple, tiered conversion goals. Your primary goal might be an online sale or booking, your secondary goal could be online lead generation and your tertiary goal could be to harvest opt-in e-mail addresses for your mailing list.

It doesn't matter what your goals are, or whether your website is a small information/brochure-type site or a huge online store, the important thing is that you keep your goals in mind when you design (or redesign) your website. Remember, conversion is the key to digital marketing success; your website, and the user experience you deliver through it, is what will ultimately drive that conversion.

Building an effective website

An effective website is essentially about the convergence of two things: your business goals and the needs of your target market. Build something that aligns the two and you will end up with an effective website. Broken down like that it sounds simple, but achieving that convergence can be a tricky process – and a quick surf around the web will soon demonstrate that it is easier to get it wrong than to get it right.

You'll note we used the word effective, rather than successful. For a website to be successful people need to be able to find it (which we cover in the next chapter), but if you build your site to cater for the right people's needs you significantly increase the chance that, once they arrive, they will become more than just a passing statistic.

First, let's state here and now that this is not a definitive guide to website development. This is a book about digital marketing. In this chapter we explore how to approach your website with digital marketing in mind. Our focus is to maximize the effectiveness of your website with a view to your digital marketing endeavours.

What follows is a high-level overview of the important elements to consider when designing your website from a digital marketing perspective. It is not meant to be an exhaustive guide. Most of the topics we touch on here would warrant an entire book to themselves. In fact, if you surf on Amazon you will find a swathe of titles available in each category. You'll also find an avalanche of relevant (and, of course, irrelevant) information on the web.

Here, our aim is to arm you with the high-level knowledge you need to make informed decisions about your website design in a digital marketing context, and to communicate exactly what you need in order to engage with your web design partners when it is time to construct your digital hub.

The main steps of building your website

Different businesses will follow different processes involving different groups of people when designing, developing and implementing a website, but regardless of the approach you choose to take, how formal or informal the process, there are a number of key stages that generally form part of any web development project:

- **Planning:** establish your goals for the site; analyse the competition; define who your target market is, how they will find you online and what they will be looking for when they arrive; map out a schedule and decide who will do what and when.

- **Design:** decide on the 'look and feel' of the site: colours, graphics, information architecture (the arrangement or structure of the information), navigation, etc. The way that information is arranged can have a big impact on a site's usability and its perceived relevance and authority both for users and search engines.

- **Development:** putting it all together, taking the agreed design and constructing the actual pages of the site, crafting the content, links and navigation hierarchy.

- **Testing:** making sure everything works the way it should before you let it out onto the big bad internet.

- **Responsive web design (RWD)** – if your customers are mobile then you would probably be wise to design your site with mobile screen sizes and functionality in mind (more on this later in this chapter).

- **Deployment:** your new site becomes live on the internet for the whole world to find... or not, as the case may be.

Before you start

Know why you are building a website

'What is my website for?' It's a simple enough question, yet you might be amazed at how many businesses have never asked it. They have a website because everyone else has one and it seemed like a good idea at the time. The result is a site – invariably an isolated little island in the backwaters of cyber-space – that brings nothing to the business but the expense of annual hosting and maintenance. Ideally you should have a clear idea of exactly what your organization wants to achieve from a website *before* you start to build it.

Know who your website is for

Knowing who exactly you are creating your website for is also crucial to its success. Yet, surprisingly, it is another thing that is often overlooked in the process. Far too many websites end up being designed to appeal to the committee of executives who ultimately sign off on the project, instead of the people who will actually be using them. Don't fall into that trap. For your website to succeed it needs to appeal to one group of people, and one group of people only: your target market.

Think about how your users will access your website, what will they want to find when they get there, and how your site can fulfil those needs. Put yourself in their shoes, or better still, ask them directly what they want to see/do on your website. Try conducting some informal market research with people who would potentially use your website (online and/or offline). The results may be illuminating, and could be the difference between a successful website and an expensive online experiment.

Build usability and accessibility into your website design

Usability and accessibility are central to good web design... and yet both are frequently ignored, or at least are not given the weighting they warrant when it comes to making design decisions. They are about making sure that your site content can be accessed by the widest possible audience, and delivering the information and functionality users want in a way they're comfortable and familiar with.

Usability

The theory behind web usability is straightforward enough: simple, elegant and functional design helps users to achieve what they want to achieve online more effectively. It's about taking the frustration out of the user experience, making sure things work intuitively, eliminating barriers so that users accomplish their goals almost effortlessly. Your goal is to help the user to do what they want to do in the most efficient and effective way possible. Everything else is just web clutter. Achieving a simple, elegant design that delivers what the user wants with a minimum of fuss isn't easy, but putting in the effort can pay huge dividends.

Optimizing your mobile presence

By Matt Brocklehurst, Product Marketing at Google

Many brands ask, 'Should we create a mobile site or an app?' If you have to choose, your first priority should be a mobile-optimized site. Once it's live, then consider launching an app to cater to loyal users.

Designing a site for mobile demands more than taking content from your desktop website and fitting it into a small screen. First, understand how customers interact with your existing site, paying particular attention to mobile visitor habits. From here, adapt your value proposition to mobile by tailoring content to specific audiences. Get input from your agency about implementation options: building using responsive web design, dynamically serving different HTML on the same URL, or creating a separate URL for mobile. Tag your mobile site to track and analyse user behaviour. And be aware that the work is never finished – evaluate site performance and iterate based on insights about user interactions.

To enrich relationships with users, you can next think about building a branded app – but be clear about its purpose. Will it offer entertainment, utility or both? Don't be tempted to just port your mobile site into the app. Instead, design a made-for-app experience using those special features a site can't deliver, like notifications, camera integration or one-click purchasing. If resources require prioritization, design for mobile platforms that represent the majority of the smartphone-installed base. You could also consider developing a single hybrid app that automatically adapts its layout to tablets and smartphones. Once your app has launched, encourage downloads through site links, in-app ads, mobile search ads and PR activity.

Of course, you're still not done; think past the install and contemplate how to actively engage the user base to drive incremental transactions. For example, new remarketing technologies make it possible to reach app users by serving targeted ads only to those individuals who have downloaded your app. Meanwhile, many analytics packages can now measure app engagement and model lifetime value for app users. By tapping into these insights and optimizing accordingly, you can deliver a consistently great mobile experience for your users.

CASE STUDY Alpharooms

Alpharooms, the online travel company, noted steady traffic growth from smartphones and tablets to its desktop site, but conversion rates on these devices were poor. The company decided to launch a multi-screen strategy and built a new site using responsive web design. The launch saw the bounce rate from mobile traffic drop by 35 per cent, while overall conversion rate doubled and mobile conversions increased fourfold.

For a step-by-step guide to usability, and a comprehensive downloadable e-book of research-based web design and usability guidelines, check out the US Government's usability website at **www.usability.gov**.

Accessibility

The term accessibility, in relation to the web, refers to the process of designing your website to be equally accessible to everyone. A well-designed website should allow all users equal access to the information and functionality they deliver. By adhering to accessibility guidelines when designing your site you are basically making sure that it is useful to as broad a cross-section of your target audience as possible.

If your site complies with accessibility guidelines it will also work seamlessly with hardware and software designed to make the internet more accessible to people with disabilities. For example, by making sure you include descriptive text alternatives to images and multimedia content on your website you can help visually impaired or even completely sightless visitors to access your site through special text-to-speech software and/or text-to-Braille hardware. How stringently you choose to adhere to these accessibility guidelines will depend on several factors, including the nature of your site, your target audience and, in some circumstances, the requirements of local accessibility legislation.

With both accessibility and usability, very small and simple steps can make a big difference; even something as small as ensuring that the text on your website resizes according to the user's browser preferences can have a huge impact on some people's ability to use your site effectively.

A more detailed look at website accessibility, including all of the most current accessibility standards and guidelines, can be found on the W3C website at **www.w3.org/WAI/**.

A word about the W3C and web standards

The World Wide Web Consortium (W3C, **www.w3.org**) is the gatekeeper of web standards. Its mission: 'to lead the World Wide Web to its full potential by developing protocols and guidelines that ensure long-term growth for the Web.'

Since its inception in 1994 the consortium has published more than 110 of these standards, which it calls W3C Recommendations. These open standards are primarily designed to ensure what the W3C calls the 'interoperability of the web' – or basically to make sure that all of the different computers, platforms and technologies that make up and access the web can work together seamlessly.

In practice it is a good idea to make sure that your website is designed and implemented to be web-standards compliant. A standards-compliant website is much more likely to work consistently across the different browsers and operating systems used by your target market. It also future proofs your site to some extent, reducing the need for maintenance. Standards-compliant sites should (in theory at least) continue to work consistently with new browser versions (which *should* be backward compatible with the standards), while a non-compliant site may not.

Maintaining a standards-compliant site is also more straightforward, because the code that makes up the pages is, you guessed it, *standard*. It makes it easier for a web developer to pick up and maintain somebody else's code – which could be important if you decide to change your web designer, or to bring the entire process in-house in the future.

In general, you should aim to make sure your site is as standards compliant as possible while still achieving what you need. Make sure your web designer knows you are aware of web standards, and that you want your site to adhere to them. All of the standards are available on the W3C site, and there are online validators that will screen your pages for compliance. You can even download a little 'badge' to display in the footer of your standards-compliant website to prove to the world that your pages validate.

Words make your website tick

The world of the web is dominated by words. Audio, video, flash and animation may seem to be everywhere online, but even in an era where multimedia content seems to be taking over, at its core the web is still all about text, and the connections between different words and phrases on and between websites. As a digital marketer, some of those words and phrases are more important to you than others, and knowing which words are relevant to your business is essential to building an effective website.

These are your keywords or key phrases, and in the search-dominated world of the digital marketer they are... in a word, key. Exactly what they are will depend on your business, the digital marketing goals you defined as part of your overall strategy, and on the online behaviour of your target market. But you need to know what they are.

Keywords are practically synonymous with search, so we cover the basics of keyword research and selection in the Search chapter (Chapter 5). But it is a very good idea to have your list of target keywords in mind from the very beginning. It's much easier to optimize a site for search engines as you build it, than it is to retro-fit search engine optimization after the fact. Your keywords will help to guide everything, from your site design to your information architecture and navigation, right down to the content on the individual pages of your website.

Know your competition

Identifying your competition, analysing what they are trying to achieve with their websites, where they are succeeding and where they are failing, can be a great way of getting ideas and looking at different ways to compete online. Take the keyword phrases you have identified for your website and type them into leading search engines – the sites that rank highly for your keywords are your online competition.

What are they doing well, and how easy would it be for you to emulate and improve on those things? Put yourself in the user's shoes. What sort of user experience are they offering? How could it be improved upon? What about the content?

A thorough analysis of your online competition can reveal a lot, not just about them and what they offer online, but about the direction you choose to take with your website in order to compete effectively.

Choosing your domain name

Every website on the internet has a unique address (a slight simplification, but we don't need to get into the complexities here). It is called an IP address, and is not very interesting, informative or memorable to most humans. It consists of a series of numbers something like 209.85.143.99 (type that address into your browser and see where it takes you).

While this is fine for computers and the occasional numerically inclined tech-head, it's not much use to the rest of us. So, back in the early days of the internet, the domain name system was developed to assign human-readable names to these numeric addresses. These domain names – things like digitalmarketingsuccess.com, google.com, wikipedia.org or harvard.edu – are naturally much more useful and memorable to your average human than the IP addresses they relate to.

You need your own domain name

If you don't have your own domain name, you need to register one. As a business, if you want to be taken seriously online, piggybacking on someone else's domain is completely unacceptable. An address like www.mysite. someothersite.com or www.someothersite.com/mysite/ looks unprofessional, makes your web address difficult to remember, won't do you any favours with search engines and generally tarnishes your business image wherever you publicize it, online and off.

The good news is that registering a domain is cheap (less than US $10 per year, depending on the domain registrar you choose) and easy. It may be included as part of the package offered by your website developer, or you can easily register a domain yourself. You can check availability, select your domain and register it in minutes online (**www.mydomain.com** is the registrar we used to register the domain associated with this book; there are plenty more to choose from, just type 'domain registration' into your favourite search engine and you'll be presented with plenty of options).

It is worth noting that while most domains operate on a first-come-first served basis, some country specific domains (such as Ireland's .ie domains) have special eligibility conditions that need to be satisfied before the registration is confirmed. Check with the relevant country's domain name authority to see if any country-specific conditions apply to the domain(s) you're interested in.

Some things to bear in mind when choosing your domain name are:

- **Make it catchy, memorable and relevant:** choose an easily identifiable domain name that is relevant to your business and *easy for people to remember*.

- **Use a country-specific top level domain (TLD) to appeal to a local audience:** the TLD is the element of an internet domain name that comes after the 'dot'. For instance in the domain name understandingdigital.com the top-level domain is com or COM.

If your market is local, it often pays to register the local version
of the domain (.co.uk or .ie, for example) instead (or as well as)
the more generic .com, .net or .org. If you're appealing to an
international audience, a generic TLD may serve you better. Of the
generic TLDs .com is by far the most universally accepted and
popular – making it the most valuable one to secure.

- **You can buy multiple domain names:** there is nothing to stop you
  buying more than one domain to prevent others from registering
  them. You can then *redirect* the secondary domains to point to your
  main website. Another option is registering country-specific domains
  to give yourself an online 'presence' in each country you do business
  in. You can then deploy a regionally tailored version of your website
  to each of those domains (the preferable option), or redirect them to
  a localized section on your main website.

- **Consider different suffixes:** there are so many available these days
  .mobi . insurance .sport and so on. Maybe one of these suffixes is
  a cool idea for your particular brand?

- **Keywords in a domain name can be beneficial:** you may decide to
  incorporate one of your keyword phrases into your domain name.
  Opinion varies on the significance of this in terms of its impact on
  your search engine ranking, but it may help both search engines and
  users to establish what your site is about right from the start.

Hosting – your website's home on the internet

The other bit of housekeeping you need to take care of before your site goes
live is hosting. Your finished site will consist of files, applications and possibly a database, all of which sit on a computer that is permanently connected to the internet. This computer is your web server, and will be running
special software that will accept requests from users' web browsers and
deliver your web pages by return. It's a bit more complicated, but basically
that is what it boils down to.

Unless you belong to a large organization with its own data centre that
has a permanent connection to the internet backbone, it is highly unlikely
that you will host your site in-house. A much more likely scenario is to
arrange a hosting solution through a specialist hosting provider.

Different types of hosting

There are basically three different types of hosting offered by web hosting companies – all of which are perfectly acceptable for your business website. Which option you choose will depend largely on your budget, how busy you anticipate your website will be (in terms of visitor traffic), and the amount of control you want over the configuration of the server (whether you need to install your own custom software, change security settings, configure web server options, etc).

A word of warning here: avoid 'free' hosting accounts. While they may be tempting for a small business site to begin with, they tend to be unreliable, often serve up annoying ads at the top of your site, don't offer the flexibility or functionality of a paid hosting account, may not support the use of your own domain name, offer limited (if any) support, and present a greater risk that you will be sharing your server with some less than desirable neighbours – which can hurt your search engine rankings.

Shared hosting accounts

With shared hosting you are essentially renting space on a powerful server where your website(s) will sit alongside a number of other websites (typically hundreds, sometimes thousands on a single server). Each hosting account has its own, secure virtual space on the server where you can upload your site's files. A dedicated control panel for account administration offers some degree of control over server configuration and usually provides access to a suite of additional software and tools to help you (or your webmaster) manage your website(s). All of the websites on a server typically share system resources such as CPU, RAM, etc.

Shared hosting is the most common and cheapest form of hosting, and it is how the majority of websites – particularly for small to medium businesses – start out. Most shared hosting accounts have space restrictions and a monthly bandwidth cap. They are ideal for small-to-medium businesses and websites with average levels of traffic. In most instances this is the most cost-effective form of hosting.

Virtual dedicated hosting

With virtual dedicated hosting a single server is 'split' into a number of virtual servers. Each user feels like they're on their own dedicated computer, when in fact they're sharing the resources of the same physical machine. The users will typically have complete administrative control over their own virtual space. This is also known as a virtual private server (VPS). While virtual dedicated hosting offers complete flexibility in terms of the administration, software and configuration options available, you're still sharing server resources with other users/ websites.

Dedicated hosting

Dedicated hosting solutions provide a dedicated, high-powered server for your website(s), and your website(s) alone. You don't share space or system resources with anybody else – which means you don't share the cost either... making dedicated hosting comparatively expensive.

Dedicated servers offer much more power and flexibility, because changes made to the server affect only your website(s). That means that you (or your webmaster/technical team) have complete control over server configuration, security, software and settings. They also typically offer much more capacity in terms of space and bandwidth than shared hosting – making them suitable for high-traffic sites.

Because of the flexibility and control offered by dedicated hosting solutions (complete control over the host computer), they tend to require more technical ability to administer than shared hosting environments.

Server co-location

Co-location is essentially the same as dedicated hosting, except that instead of the hosting company providing a preconfigured dedicated server for your website, you buy and configure your own server, which is then hosted at their dedicated hosting facility. This offers perhaps the ultimate in flexibility, because you have complete control not only over the software and setting on the server, but also over the hardware specification, operating system, software, security... everything. Co-location is essentially the same as hosting your own server in your own office – except that your server is plugged in to a rack in a dedicated hosting facility with all of the bells and whistles you'd expect.

Cloud-based hosting

Cloud-based hosting is different to traditional hosting models in that you pay for your hosting based on the resources you use, rather than paying for a fixed hardware resource and monthly allowance of space and bandwidth. Essentially, when you're hosting in the 'cloud' your web server is a virtual entity, it doesn't exist on a single physical server, it is distributed across multiple clustered servers, sharing resources between them. In theory, cloud-based hosting can be cost-effective, because you only pay for the resources you use; instantly scalable, because you can tap into practically limitless computing resources on-the-fly; and inherently reliable, as there is no single point of failure. If one physical machine keels over, the others share the load until another comes on stream to replace it. That is a very simplistic explanation of how cloud computing works... but you get the idea.

Cloud computing, which encompasses cloud-based hosting, is not without its issues. These largely revolve around data ownership, privacy and security; the debate, as always, is ongoing. That said, cloud-based hosting is really gaining traction in the marketplace, and increasing numbers of hosting providers are now offering a cloud-based 'pay for what you use' option as part of their portfolio. As always, you need to weigh the merits of what is on offer and decide what works best for your business.

Choosing your hosting company

Your website developer will be able to help you decide which web hosting option is right for you, based on the size, design, functionality and configuration of your website, and your anticipated levels of traffic based on your business goals. They should also be able to recommend a reliable web hosting company that will serve your needs.

When choosing your web host, bear the following in mind:

- **Choose a host in the country where your primary target market lives:** this is important, because search engines deliver local search results to users based in part on the geographical location of the server on which the web pages reside (which they can infer from the server IP address).

- **Make sure the host is reliable:** do they offer guaranteed uptime/levels of service? Many hosts publish live server statistics that demonstrate the reliability of their services. You should expect a service level approaching 100 per cent from a high-quality hosting service.

- **What sort of support do they offer:** make sure the hosting you choose includes efficient and effective support 24/7. If your website goes down you need to be confident you can call on your host for assistance whatever time of the day or night.

- **Backup and disaster recovery:** if the worst happens and the server goes belly up, what sort of disaster recovery options does the host have in place? Ideally your host should take several daily snapshots of your entire account/server, allowing them to restore it and get your site back up and running as quickly as possible, should the worst happen.

- **What do others think:** find out what other customers think. Read testimonials, and search for discussions on webmaster forums and social media sites relating to the hosts you are considering. Are other people's experiences good or bad? Post a few questions.

- **Shop around:** hosting is an incredibly competitive industry, so shop around for the best deal – but bear in mind that the cheapest option *isn't always the best choice.*

How to choose a web designer/developer

Unless you are a web designer yourself, or have access to a dedicated in-house web development team, you need to bring in a professional web design firm to help with your website project. You'll find a host of options out there, offering a range of services that will literally boggle your mind. The good news is, if you've done your preliminary work, you should already have a fair idea of what you want out of your website, who it is aimed at and the sort of features you want to include. Armed with that knowledge, you can start to whittle down the list of potential designers to something more manageable.

Look at their own website: in trying to assess the relative merits of a web design company, the best place to start is with their own website. What is their site like? Examine it with a critical eye. Does it look professional? Is it functional? Think about what they are trying to achieve, and how well the site addresses the needs of its target audience (you, in this case). Is it easy to find what you want? Does it meet or exceed your expectations? If not, do you really want the same people working on your website?

Examine their portfolio: practically every web design firms offer an online portfolio showing recent website projects they have worked on. Look at these – but go beyond the portfolio pages and click through to the actual websites themselves. Again, put your analytical hat on and ask what the sites are trying to achieve, who they are aimed at and how well the designers have achieved those goals.

That should give you enough of a steer to produce a reasonable shortlist of potential candidates. Now you can dig a little deeper:

- **Ask their customers for recommendations:** go back to the best of the portfolio sites for your shortlisted designers. Go to the 'contact us' page and drop them a line by e-mail or pick up the phone to ask for some honest feedback on their web design experience. Would they recommend the firm?

- **What is their online reputation like**: web forums, online communities and peer review sites are another good place to look for information about your shortlisted web design firms. Is the online vibe positive or negative? What are people saying about them?

- **Are they designing sites to be found**: your website is only as good as the quality traffic it gets. Are your shortlisted designers search engine savvy? Go back to the portfolio sites you looked at, and pick out some of the keyword phrases you would expect them to rank for in a search engine. Now go to the search engines and type in those keyword phrases. Have those sites been indexed? Where do they rank on the search results page? Low ranking doesn't necessarily indicate a problem with their web design – there are many components that contribute to search engine ranking (see the next chapter), but it may be something you should ask them to clarify before making your decision.

- **Do they adhere to web standards**: go to the W3Cs website validation page (**www.w3.org/QA/Tools/**) and run the web addresses of your shortlisted web designers through the MarkUp Validator, Link Checker and CSS Validator. Do the sites validate as web-standards compliant? You shouldn't necessarily discount your favourite designers because of this – but it is something else you should ask them about before making your final decision.

By now you should have whittled your shortlist down to a few competent and professional companies that you want to quote/tender on your website project. The final decision is, of course, up to you.

Arranging your information

Your site structure – the way you arrange and group your information and how users navigate their way around it – can have a massive impact on its usability, its visibility to search engine spiders, its rank in search engine results pages (SERPS – a term in search engine marketing that refers to the results pages returned when a user submits a query to the search engine) and its potential to convert traffic once it arrives. Getting your information architecture right is absolutely critical to the success of your website.

It can be difficult to know where to start. You know what information you want on your site, but what is the best way of arranging it so that users can access it intuitively, at the level of granularity they desire, while also providing you with maximum exposure in the search engines for specific keywords? The answer, as is so often the case in digital marketing, is that it depends.

It depends on the sort of business you're in, the type of site you're building, your target audience, your business goals and a whole host of other variables.

Start with your keywords

The keywords your potential users are searching on should give you a good indication of both the content they are looking for and the search terms you want your site to rank for in the SERPs. Take those keywords and arrange them into logical categories or themes. These themes, along with the staple 'homepage', 'about us' and 'contact us' links, give you the primary navigation structure for your site.

Define your content structure

Look at your main themes, the keywords you have associated with each of them and the corresponding information or content you want to include beneath each. Now define a tiered hierarchy of subcategories (your secondary, tertiary navigation levels, etc) within each theme as necessary until you have all of your targeted keywords covered. Arrange your content so that the most important information is summarized at the highest levels, allowing the user to drill down to more detailed but less important information on the specific topic as required. Try not to go too deep in terms of navigation subcategories – it is rarely necessary to go beyond three, in exceptional cases four, levels deep from the homepage (see Figure 3.1).

FIGURE 3.1   A simple website information hierarchy

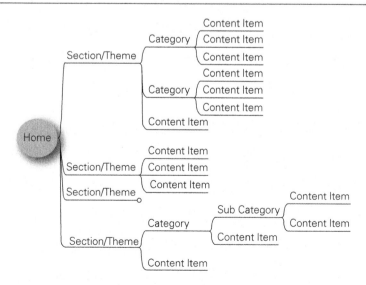

Your homepage

The homepage is often perceived as one of the most important pages on your site, but is potentially one of the least useful, both to your business and to your site visitors. For a start, homepages tend, by necessity, to be relatively generic. Too generic to answer a user's specific query or to instantly entice the conversion you crave. Indeed, many of your visitors – especially those arriving from a search engine, or by clicking on a link from another website or an online advertisement – will tend to land on a much more focused internal page, one that deals with the specific topic that they have searched for or clicked on. This deeper page should be much better at satisfying their immediate requirements.

Where a homepage comes into its own is as a central reference point for navigating your content. A breadcrumb trail or navigation path along the top of your site can tell a user at a glance exactly where they are on your site in relation to a fixed point: your homepage. It is also a convenient central location that users can easily return to. No matter where they wander on your site, users are always only one click from home... which reassures them that they cannot get lost.

Your homepage should be a 'jumping off point' for the rest of your site, offering intuitive one-click navigation to all of your main sections or themes, and telling people immediately what your site is about, and how it can help them. It is also a good place to highlight new products and services, special offers, incentives, news or anything else you want to promote on your site.

Avoid splash screens that simply show your company logo and a 'click here to enter' button – they offer no benefit at all to your users or to your business – they are web clutter at its worst. Likewise flash intros – the 'skip intro' button is one of the most widely clicked buttons on the web. Remember: you want to make it as easy as possible for your visitors to achieve their goals, so avoid putting obstacles between them and your real content.

Writing effective web content

Now you have defined a structure for your information you're ready to put together your content.

Stop! Don't make the mistake that often happens with new websites. You can't simply take your offline marketing collateral and paste the same copy into your web pages and expect it to work.

The golden rule of writing effectively in any medium is to know your audience – the more your writing is tailored to your audience, the more effective it is. It is exactly the same on the web. The difference between effective web writing and effective print writing reflects the core difference in the nature of the audience. Print is a linear medium, the web is random access; people read through printed material from beginning to end, on the web they scan and skip; offline readers are patient, online readers want the information they are looking for now, now, now.

We already know a bit about the characteristics of online users from our look at online consumer behaviour in the last chapter – writing effective web content is about taking what we know about web users in general, and the target audience of our website in particular, and applying that knowledge to deliver our information in a format that meets those readers' needs:

- **Grab attention:** web users are impatient – forget flowery introductions and verbose descriptions, make your writing clear, concise and to the point from the start.

- **Make it scannable:** avoid large blocks of uninterrupted text. Use headings, subheadings and bullet points to break up the text into manageable, scannable stand-alone chunks.

- **Make it original:** unique, original content is a great way to engage your users, establish your relevance and authority, and search engines love it.

- **Use the inverted pyramid:** the inverted pyramid writing style often used for newspaper stories tends to work well on the web. Aim to deliver the most important points of your story first, going on to deliver supporting details in order of decreasing importance down the page. Ideally, the user should be able to stop reading at any point and still get the gist of the content.

- **Be consistent:** use a simple, easy-to-read writing style, and keep things consistent across the site. If you have a number of people creating your content, consider developing a style guide or house style to help maintain consistency.

- **Engage with your reader:** use a conversational style, and write as if you were talking to an *individual* rather than an audience. It will help your writing to engage with the reader on a much more personal level.

- See our chapter on content marketing in this edition of UDM – this is certainly going to be one of the hottest growth areas online in the years ahead.

Top 12 web design mistakes to avoid, by Pauline Cabrera

(http://www.twelveskip.com/guide/website/966/12-top-web-design-mistakes-to-avoid)

1. The design does not speak for itself

If you are a policeman and you want yourself to be identified as one, then you must always wear the right uniform and the right badge. The same principle goes with web design: you have to wear the right 'tie' for your users to know who you are and what you do. If you are selling e-books and tutorials, then you don't want to let people think that your site is that of a local restaurant they are familiar with.

Start asking if you have solid branding. Do the colours, the font styles, and the objectives of your company reflect your website design, and vice versa? Do you use only the necessary and the right elements for your company to be clearly identified? Do you use trigger keywords to make people understand at once what you offer? People don't take more than a minute to guess what your website is about, so you had better show the right face at once.

2. Noisy, unorganized visuals

Since design is about visuals, you must show how user-friendly your website is. User-friendliness is just another technical way of understanding user-centeredness, and if your design is poor in this respect, then it is another way of saying that you don't deserve a user.

Noisy and unorganized visuals here mean that your content is not properly laid on the surface. Do you have clear navigation? Do the elements of your website fall on the right sections or areas of the page as a whole? Do your posts have a clear readability, ie are they well-spaced, scannable and friendly to the eyes? Do your ads and banners fall on the right areas, so as not to be mistaken for something else? Are there too many distracting elements, like flashy banners and animated texts?

3. Your design manipulates or prohibits users from spontaneity

This may sound very harsh, but you may not be aware of it yet. You know these terms for sure, but for web design, this means that a part or the whole of your design forces users to do something or not to do something. If people don't want to enter into your survey, don't force them to do so in exchange for access to something they're asking for.

How about a pop-up window? Any sudden music playback? Do any links of yours require a new window? We all know that these things are annoying. How about access to some materials or pages? Do you require your users to sign up first? If you are really strict with your content, at least you make yourself clear about why things should be kept that way.

4. Unclear or broken navigation and structure

People hate it when they click a broken link, or worse, a link that leads them to somewhere else. More so, despite the fact that you have a navigation bar, sometimes people want to look for something immediately and specifically without scrolling on your hover buttons one by one. The question now is, do you have an internal search engine and a link to your sitemap?

It is always a failure for websites if their goals are naturally and usually not met. People are being led to your site for a reason, and you only want to satisfy their need. If they cannot find what they are looking for in the first few minutes, then all your efforts and planning fail.

5. Confusing and misleading links

Links are but the circulatory system of the internet. These are the necessary elements wherein all (relevant) pages meet and are anchored upon. Knowing how important links are, you should treat links with respect, and so your users as well. Let the links say what they are about to see and nothing else.

Make a clear distinction also of the differences between your underlined or coloured words or phrases with your links. Make sure also that your links at different states (hover, on, off, etc) portray a different visual cue so as to aid people in knowing which links they have already clicked or not. Lastly, buttons should appear as buttons, and those which are not should not appear as such.

6. 'Long' pages

The word 'long' here equates to two aspects of a web design: length and time. In length, your website should not be so long (vertically or horizontally) that people get sick going back to some key areas they find important. If you are providing a single-page website, make sure that you give assistance to your users by anchor links which will help them jump from one section to another, or even back to the top of the page.

Long texts and content should also be broken down into pieces or 'chapters.' You can lay these chapters out in separate pages which is done in a lot of designs. If you are about to integrate a presentation or a PDF, be sure that at least you provide the first few pages or slides first – those that don't take the most amount of time to load or download. Afterwards, always give users the link to the whole file.

Additionally, you must realize that people hate it when their data connection is slow, and worse, when the website they are in need of connecting to is darn slow and even non-responsive. That's where optimization comes in, and that's where you really need to learn to trim your content to a loadable limit. If you are really a good resource, then be a good resource.

7. User filtration

I have discussed manipulative web designs, but I would like to give more space to user experience as a whole. Remember that readers are impatient, and you cannot blame them if they are seeking only convenience. Do any of your pages or resources need a 'higher clearance level' for them to get access to, such as a required membership? If you are really serious about membership and if you want to take control of and grant access to specific content, at least you must make it easy and clear.

Users won't be happy if it requires them to fill in personal information over and over again; they are lucky if their browsers have an auto-fill feature. How about you allow other registration methods, such as linking a Facebook or Google account which is quicker? The same also goes for purchases and payments. Do you provide prices at once? Do you make them feel safe when they enter credit card details, or at least provide a PayPal assurance? Does your CAPTCHA look too blurry or is it illegible, meaning that people will just get frustrated making too many attempts?

Remember that making that utmost appeal to your potential clients or customers is not enough; you must actually guide them along up to the last step and not leave them coughing in the middle. User filtration comes in when they are about to bite what you offer, but turn away frustrated in the middle of the process.

8. Unreachable contact details

Don't ever forget to include contact details that are visible, comprehensive, and offer a lot of options. Make sure also that the options you offer on your contact area are all working fine and someone is ready to respond. Remember that your contact information is what makes your users feel assured that they are understood by humans, so you don't want to compromise it by letting users call an offline channel.

9. Designs that will only work when...

If someone is knocking on your door, you don't want to send them back to their homes just to put on the right pair of sandals. The same goes with a healthy design. You don't want to use any programming languages that will require every user of yours to get a specific plug-in or software first. Aside from the fact that many of these plug-ins are suspicious nowadays, it is really annoying and inconvenient.

The same also goes for browser compatibility. Did you make sure that your design works and displays well when viewed in a different browser? How about making your website flow and respond to different screen sizes, which is already an ongoing norm? Is your domain good for all countries, and won't blacklist an IP address, preventing access to your site? Checking all these factors will make your website a lot friendlier for ordinary people.

10. Using splash pages

No, this is not really a sacrilege to web design, but you must understand that using splash pages will create a very rigid barrier between search engines and your site. If you are really worried about SEO stats and reports, then removing the barrier will lead to better results.

Using splash pages can often be seen as an amateur way of advertising as well; it is the equivalent to a shout-out. Do your marketing the natural way, and people will visit you naturally as well.

11. Old design and content

Carefully look at how your website is designed. Is it already out of date? Is the content updated at least regularly? Will there still be somebody looking for your old product?

Always consult a professional if you are not sure if your site needs a redesign. If you have trouble loading your site with content, you can always outsource for talented individuals. If you are really serious about your site's goals, then you need to do something.

12. No further analytics

That's why analytics are there: to let you know what's going on with your website and its content. If you are serious about what you have planted, you should be more than excited with how it is growing (or shrinking), and of course, take necessary action. You don't want to throw corn pellets on the ground, without checking if the birds have come or not.

Your website is your investment, and you should consider it as such at all times. Avoid the above listed mistakes, and you will gain a better-functioning website that people will love to use.

That's it: your new site is ready, it is live online… it's there for all the world to see, and it looks great. Now all you need is traffic, and in the chapters that follow we'll show you exactly how to get it!

CASE STUDY   Hg2

Hg2 – a hedonist's guide to… publishes sophisticated independent travel guides from around the world.

Location

Global.

The challenge

Target iPhone users, using Hg2 content to raise awareness of and increase downloads of the Hg2 app. While creating content is not a problem for Hg2, when it launched its iPhone app it wanted to target digitally savvy iPhone uses and so turned to Outbrain to help find and target this audience via Outbrain Mobile.

Target audience

iPhone users around the world.

Action

- Hg2 worked with Outbrain to amplify some of its own high-quality editorial content that highlighted how the app could help travellers when abroad.

- The content had strong calls-to-action to prompt users to download the app should they want to.

- Hg2 content was amplified over Outbrain's network on a PPC basis, with Outbrain recommending the content to users who were most likely to be interested in it.

- Only users accessing content on their iPhones, rather than a desktop or other mobile device, were shown Hg2 content.

- All content was mobile-optimized and headlines were targeted towards an iPhone audience, eg 'From Almaty to Zurich in one beautiful app'.

- Users clicking on this content were already interested in understanding more about the iPhone app and therefore even more highly targeted.

Results

- Over a two-week period Outbrain drove high volumes of users to the content and saw that over 17 per cent of users went on to download the app.

- Outbrain delivered 16,239 clicks to Hg2 content.

Links to campaign

- http://www.outbrain.com/
- http://www.hg2.com/
- https://itunes.apple.com/gb/app/hg2-a-hedonists-guide/id431859092?mt=8

About the creator

- Outbrain is a global agency that prides itself on recommending articles, mobile and video content on client's websites and on premium publisher sites to expose it to highly engaged audiences.
- They work to increase engagement for all of your content while earning revenue with links to high-quality third-party content.
- Their strategy aims to drive traffic to your content by recommending it alongside the editorial on top publisher sites.
- One of their strengths is offering a more personalized reader experience and power cross-platform content discovery with one solution.
- Using a cost-efficient, pay-per-click model, they gain insights to refine your content and media strategies.
- Current clients include CNN, Rolling Stone and TIME.

Quote

Tremayne Carew Pole, publisher and founder of Hg2, said:

We had a specific remit – which was to target iPhone users to drive downloads of the app. Outbrain's solution for mobile made perfect sense to achieve this and the hugely impressive results speak for themselves.

Is it working?

04

OUR CHAPTER PLEDGE TO YOU

By the end of this chapter you will understand:

- The importance of measurement
- The differences between owned, paid for and earned media
- Why testing is vital
- What attribution modelling is all about
- The return of GRP (sounds like Tolkien? It isn't!)
- How to choose effective KPIs

The internet has always been trumpeted as the most measurable medium for marketing – and it is. It offers unprecedented levels of information about who your customers are and what they are doing, and allows a deeper understanding than any other medium of how your marketing efforts are performing.

For businesses that sell online in particular, it's possible to link an initial enquiry to a completed sale – and beyond. The spread of interactive technology also means that this degree of detail is starting to become available in more traditional channels – smart TV and digital outdoor are the obvious examples – with the promise of more to come.

But saying that the internet is the most measurable medium yet invented is not the same as saying it is without flaws, that it allows everything to be measured. This myth arose in the dot.com boom of the early 2000s, and the internet industry has not done enough to dispel it. The result has not only been fertile ground for misunderstanding and confusion. It has also left online marketing vulnerable to criticism and suspicion, which has in turn discouraged investment in online marketing as marketers have shied away from a medium whose metrics many feel are untrustworthy – perhaps one explanation for the continuing gap between the amount of time people spend online and the amount of money that marketers spend trying to reach them there.

The truth is that despite online ubiquity, it is still a young medium, and one that is changing all the time. The commercial internet itself is less than 20 years old, and the pillars of our current online experience are younger still. Google was founded in 1998, Facebook in 2004 and YouTube in 2005. Similarly, the best ways to approach online marketing – and how to measure it – continue to evolve. New techniques are being developed, new technologies and channels integrated, and discrepancies resolved. The picture becomes clearer every year, as do the limitations of the medium.

Because all media have their limitations. The irony of online marketing is that many of those who criticize the measurement failings of interactive media understand and are happy to work with the shortcomings of other channels – the panel-based approach of traditional TV and radio, or the proximity and footfall used for out-of-home media, for example. The one key difference with digital is the availability of census (action-based) data.

So by the end of this chapter we aim to have shown you just how powerful the measurement techniques available online are, and how to apply them. Equally importantly, we aim to show you what their shortcomings are, what pitfalls those shortcomings create, and how to understand and manage them.

Owned, paid and earned

The most common way of thinking about online marketing at present is to think in terms of the three types of media available to marketers: owned, paid and earned. In other words, properties that the business has total control over, such as its own websites; properties that it pays for its messages to appear on, ie advertising; and properties where other people talk about its products and services, ie social media. Each of these has its own ways of measuring results, and its own associated questions of which marketers should be aware.

The simplest place to start is with owned media; your own website. Web analytics technology allows you to measure how many browsers (which may be approximated to the number of people when the right measurement techniques are applied) engaged with your website; where they came from (both on the internet and geographically); what browser and operating system they used; what keywords they used to find your site and on which search engine; the page they arrived at; how long they stayed; which pages they visited while they were there; which page they left from and whether or not they came back again. That in turn gives you information about how your users find your site; whether you are giving them what they want; whether your site is optimized for the right search keywords; how effective your different forms of advertising are at driving traffic to your site; and what proportion of that traffic is taking a desired action (buying something or requesting further information, for example). And this is all information that is readily volunteered by the user or the user's browser.

There are two main ways of collecting information about your website visitors. You can analyse the web access logs created by your own web server, or you can embed some code, called a page tag, in every page on your website, which will then send similar information to your chosen analytics service provider.

In the case of web server logs, every time your web server receives a request for a resource (a file) on your website, it stores details of that request in its server access logs. What exactly is recorded depends on a variety of factors, including the way the server is set up, the format of the log files it produces and the settings of the user's browser. That said, a server log file will typically contain the following pieces of information for every browser request it receives:

- the unique IP address of the network or computer making the request;
- a time stamp showing the date and time the request was made;
- the URL of the requested resource;
- a status code confirming the result of the request;
- the file size of the returned resource;
- the URL of the page the request came from;
- other information supplied by the 'user agent' (typically browser type/version, language and operating system).

Most web hosts provide some form of basic log file analysis software as part of their hosting package, so it's worth looking at these first to get a basic idea of the kind of information that is available in your log files. There are a wide range of software options available, ranging from free open source offerings (such as Webalizer, AWStats and Analog) to costly enterprise-level solutions from leading industry players like Webtrends and Adobe.

The second method, page tagging, has grown with the rising popularity of the software-as-a-service (SaaS) concept, and has been fuelled by the introduction of free, powerful and highly configurable analytics services such as StatCounter and Google Analytics. You just have to make sure that the tracking code is included on every page on your site that you want to track (including new pages you may add over time) and your service provider will look after the rest. For most sites, the code will simply need to be inserted once into the main template file. To track human activity requires assurance that robot and spider traffic is effectively filtered out.

Log files versus page tagging

Advantages of log file analysis:

- Your server will generally already be producing log files, so the raw data is already available for analysis. Collecting data using page tags requires changes to the website, and tracking can only begin once the changes have been made.

- Every transaction your web server makes is recorded in the log file. Page tagging relies on settings in the visitors' browser (such as JavaScript being enabled), so a certain (small) proportion of visitors may go undetected.

- The data collected in your log files is *your data,* and is in a standard format that makes it easy for you to migrate to analytics software from different vendors, use more than one package to give you a broader view of your data, and analyse historical data using any log file analysis program you choose. Page tagging solutions usually mean you're locked in to the relationship with your chosen provider – if you change providers you typically have to start collecting data again from scratch.

- Your log files capture visits by search engine spiders and other automated bots as well as human users. Although it is important that your analytics software can differentiate these from your human visitors, knowing which spiders have crawled your site and when can be important for search engine optimization. Page tagging solutions typically overlook non-human visitors.

- Server logs record information on failed requests, giving you insight into potential problems with your website. Page tagging, on the other hand, only records an event when a page is successfully viewed.

Advantages of page tagging:

- The tagging code (typically JavaScript) is automatically run every time the page is loaded, so even viewing a cached page will generate a visit. Because viewing a page from a cache doesn't require communication with the server, log files contain no records of cached page views.

- It is easier for developers to add custom information to page tagging code to be collected by the remote server (for example information about a visitors' screen resolution, or about the goods they purchased). With log file analysis, custom information that is not routinely collected by the web server can only be recorded by appending information to the URL.

- Page tagging can collect data based on events that don't involve sending a request to the web server, such as interactions with Flash, Ajax and other rich media content.

- Cookies are assigned and handled by the page tagging service; with log file analysis your server has to be specially configured to use cookies.

- Page tagging will work even if you can't access to your web server logs.

However, you are not restricted to using one type of analytics solution or the other – you're free to use both as necessary, extracting the best information from each to suit your particular needs. There are also what are known as hybrid analytics solutions. A number of analytics solutions on the market, particularly at the enterprise level, have the ability to combine log file analysis and page tagging methods within the same analytics suite. These hybrid systems analyse all of the data, and consolidate the information to present seamless reporting to the analyst. While these may offer the most comprehensive analytics solutions, with each data collection method compensating in part for the inadequacies of the other, it is important to remember that no analytics solution is 100 per cent accurate. Most, however, are near enough to the mark to allow you to spot trends and make informed decisions.

Augmenting information using cookies

While the IP address you collect by either method *may* also help track a user's path through your site, using IP addresses to uniquely identify visitors is inconsistent and inaccurate for a variety of reasons, no matter which of the tracking methods above you choose to use. For instance, a large number of internet users may share a single IP address assigned by their internet service provider (ISP). That means that if your analytics solution relies solely on IP addresses to identify unique visitors, it will count these multiple users as the same visitor, skewing your data. On the flip side, users with mobile devices will be assigned a different IP address whenever they connect to a new Wi-Fi network, so a person returning to your site would be identified as a new visitor rather than a returning one, unless the analytics in place have an effective device-specific identifier applied for situations where cookies do not work. At home, rebooting the household broadband router will often have a similar effect.

To get around these limitations, and to remember site settings that help to improve the user experience, many websites and third-party tracking services employ hypertext transfer protocol (HTTP) cookies to identify individual users. Cookies are small files that are sent to the user's browser and stored on their local hard drive. Typically they store a unique ID that allows the site (or tracking service) to identify a returning visitor, store site preference and personalization settings, and help to track that visitor's navigation around a website.

Cookies get a bad press because of the potential privacy issues associated with what are called *persistent third-party cookies*, or cookies that are set by a domain other than the one you're visiting (by content on the page pulled from another domain, such as ads, widgets or embedded video, for example), and that persist beyond the scope of your existing browser session. In theory, these cookies could be used to track visitor behaviour across multiple websites, building up a picture of user browsing behaviour as they surf the web. That is perceived as a bad thing, because large ad-serving and tracking companies can potentially use cookies to build up profiles of user behaviour across all the websites they serve, without explicit consent from the user.

In practice, while cookies *can* be used to glean user data without explicit consent, they tend to be largely harmless. The plus side is that they allow websites to deliver a better user experience to their customers and allow more accurate tracking of website statistics, which in turn allow website owners to optimize content and improve the visitor experience still further.

The vast majority of internet users' browsers are set to accept cookies by default, but it is important to note that some people choose to reject cookies out of hand. Others accept them only for the duration of their current browser session and then delete them, while still others choose to accept first-party cookies but reject third-party cookies. All of these factors can affect the accuracy of cookie-based information.

As a rule of thumb, if you use cookies, it is best practice to include an entry in your site's privacy policy explicitly stating what you use cookies for, what information they contain, and with whom (if anyone) that information is shared.

Test and test again

While collecting and analysing statistics through web analytics is incredibly powerful, it is also inherently limited. It can only tell you *what* happened on your site; it can never tell you *why*. That's where the human element comes into play: the ability to analyse the what, and infer the why. There is almost always more than one explanation for why your users are behaving in a certain way on your site.

Suppose, for example, you notice that the bounce rate for visitors from a particular PPC campaign seems unusually high. That could mean there is a problem with the ad itself (copy appealing to an audience that is too generic), the choice of keyword you're bidding on (keyword choice too generic to drive targeted traffic), or that the value proposition on your landing page is not compelling enough.

The beauty of the web is that we can try fixing these things one by one, and measure the results to pinpoint exactly where the problem lies. Because we can measure everything, we can test each possible variation, and use real data from actual visitors to our site to identify which change delivers optimum results.

The role of testing in online marketing really cannot be overstated. When you can measure, you can test, and when you can test you can make changes based on actual visitor behaviour. You eliminate the guesswork, which in turn eliminates much of the risk.

The A/B split test is a familiar tool in the marketer's arsenal. It basically means running two different versions of an ad or a page and measuring which version produces the best results.

The main problem with A/B split testing is that you can only use it effectively to test variances in the impact of a single page element at a time. Change more than one element, and you can't be sure which change was responsible for the change you see in the results. It is very difficult to conduct accurate tests that measure the impact of varying different components on the same landing page, and how the changes combine to impact your visitor behaviour. Or at least, it was until relatively recently.

Enter multivariate testing, a process that enables website owners to test multiple components on a web page simultaneously in a live environment. Think of it as conducting tens, hundreds or even thousands of A/B split tests simultaneously, and being able to ascertain, based on real data from real visitors to your site, which combination of the variables produce the best results.

Multivariate testing is rapidly becoming the conversion optimization method of choice among digital marketers, largely because it allows for far more complex testing options than simple A/B split tests, delivers results in a short space of time and can have a dramatic impact on conversion rates.

For example, let's say you had a landing page that was underperforming, and you wanted to optimize it. To keep things simple, let's say you wanted to try out two different headlines, two different images, and whether to use a text link or a 'buy-now' button as a call to action.

That's $2 \times 2 \times 2$ variations – or eight possible combinations to test. With multivariate testing tools you simply set up a straightforward experiment that will dynamically serve variations of your page to your visitors and record the corresponding conversions. At the end of the experiment you are presented with data showing how each of the different combinations performed, allowing you to choose the most effective of them and implement it permanently on your site.

There are numerous commercial tools available for conducting multi-variate testing, including a tool called Website Optimizer from Google, which, like Google's other products, is absolutely free, making it an ideal place to start.

Measuring paid media

So far we've looked at the information you can collect from your own website. Clearly, much of this information can be used to inform your online advertising. Knowing where traffic comes from, for example, helps you make decisions about where to advertise. But online advertising comes with its own complexities that need to be understood in order to take advantage of it fully.

The first complication is the distinction between brand and direct response advertising. It may seem hard to believe, but in the early 2000s there was a belief that internet advertising couldn't build brands. Indeed, when the dot.com bubble burst and advertising agencies looked to put their digital subsidiaries on to the back-burner, they most often folded them into their direct response (DR) arms.

Part of the problem was the click. The big selling point of online advertising in the early years was its measurability, and the most significant aspect of that was the click. For the first time, advertisers knew for certain if an ad had worked, because they knew if someone had clicked on it. With the rise of search, online quickly became the most efficient and often the most scalable direct response medium ever seen. But as the click got more and more attention, it came to dominate the discussion, and the notion that advertising didn't always have to elicit a direct response to be successful got lost. The fact that traditional brand metrics – such as propensity to purchase, and prompted and unprompted recall – were no easier to measure online than they were offline saw them being further ignored as the online marketing industry chased direct response budgets.

Direct response – and search in particular – still dominates online advertising spend in mature markets, but the significance of the click is diminishing for two reasons. The first is the growing importance of social media, which many marketers think has little role in direct response. The second is the increasing realization that click-based approaches give a distorted view of how different channels perform in a customer's journey from prospect to purchaser.

In fact, while concentrating on the click can look as if it is helping to optimize spend, it can actually be doing the opposite. This is because different media are more efficient in cost per acquisition (CPA) terms as you move down the sales funnel. But concentrating on optimizing CPA at the bottom of the funnel can lead to marketers ignoring the need to prospect for new leads at the top, ultimately pushing up the overall cost of a sale. Broadly speaking, search and other channels close to the bottom of the funnel harvest demand. And while display can also do this, its more important role is to grow demand by allowing you to prospect for new potential customers within your target groups. If your CPA for display is £10 and it is £2 for e-mail, your finance department may well say 'stop doing display'. But you may find that you end up having to spend more on e-mails to sell to a group of customers that isn't growing any more.

It is also important to remember that for online, increasing the amount you spend in CPA terms can result in a significant increase in profit because, especially in search, it is an auction model. Being in first, second or third place on Google can result in a big rise in profitability, because those positions attract the vast majority of clicks. If you can make the bid required to be in one of those slots and retain profitability, you can scale your sales significantly.

Attribution modelling

The emphasis on direct response led to a situation known as 'last click wins', where the entire value of a conversion is attributed to the site that delivered the customer to the transaction site ready to convert. One of the most significant trends in the last few years has been advertisers looking to move away from this model, and to find ways of attributing value more accurately across all the channels they use, in order to then maximize the effectiveness of their overall spend.

This process is known as attribution modelling. 'Last click wins' is itself an attribution model, flawed though it is. The problem is that finding better models is difficult, since tracking an entire consumer journey, even one that solely takes place online, remains challenging. It is all but impossible to tie a visit to a brand site, reading reviews, seeing an online display ad and research on a price comparison site together as a single customer journey. Add offline media and mobile into that list and impossible barely covers it. So most companies take an iterative approach. They adopt a slightly more advanced model than last-click-wins, perhaps attributing a conversion equally to both the last click and the first, and test that against the data, then repeat the process until a robust model emerges.

A simple first step is to add post-impression sales in with those attributed to the last click. Post-impression simply means dropping a cookie on a person's browser when they see an ad, then recognizing it when that person comes to the advertiser's site to convert. It is a way of including the 'halo' effect of display media on sales. The critical issue is to make sure that the correct time limit is set for sales to be attributed to a display impression. This is called the cookie window, and it will vary from sector to sector and company to company. Setting the right window, based on analysis of impression and click data, will help prevent sales being attributed to media that played no part in the conversion to sales.

In simple terms, there are two types of attribution: whole attribution, where sales are attributed one by one to each channel in use by the advertiser; and advanced (or fractal) attribution, where sales are weighted by the combination of media used. In each case, as we saw with A/B split testing and multivariate testing, the mantra is test, optimize, test again.

The other big impact that attribution modelling is having is that the barriers between measurement of different channels are starting to break down. Until recently, data about the effects of activity in one channel would not be shared regularly with those responsible for other channels, but the post-crash pressure on marketers to show that their budgets are being spent as effectively as possible has meant a significant impetus for this to change. Brand and direct response teams need to understand how their media activity in the digital environment affects the consumer's path to purchase, and therefore the effectiveness and efficiency of the overall marketing plan.

And not just at the level of digital marketing. The convergence of online and offline channels, and the recognition that consumers move seamlessly between them, regardless of any functional separations within the business, is forcing marketers to look for a single view of the customer. This of course adds a further layer of complication. All the channels are interdependent, and changing your activity in one will impact on all the others. It has been known for some years, for example, that search costs go down when a company is running a TV campaign, because people are more aware of the brand, and brand keywords are cheaper to bid on than generic search terms.

So another thing to remember is that as well as measuring against the planning and targeting of campaigns, it is really important to measure all your channel activity against return on investment or profit. This allows you to look at all your activity holistically. You might find, for example, that you are making a loss on your display spending, but in doing so you actually generate more profit overall. It also makes it easier to scale your marketing activities.

Of course, linking online and offline activity is easier for some businesses than others. E-commerce companies can link a sale to an online ad being viewed much more easily than traditional retailers can, for example. In fact one of the growing areas of activity is finding ways of closing the loop between online and offline in terms of conversions. Analyst Greg Sterling estimates that, in the United States, the value of cross-channel commerce is ten times greater than that of e-commerce, so the impetus is considerable.

Another drier is the increasing use of smartphones, which are used for consuming media, including marketing messages, but much less for transactions than either PCs/laptops or tablets. Strategies being tried to close the loop include such proxy metrics as clicks-to-call or map look-ups from the retailer's site; coupons; check-ins or scanning quick response (QR) codes at the point of sale; mobile wallets; partnerships between media owners and offline loyalty card providers; and, of course, 'click & collect'.

Even above the level of general marketing, convergence means that media cannot be treated separately any more. Online listening, for example, means that traditional metrics for radio are having to take the internet into account. And all of this is fuelling a move towards the introduction of the long-established offline metric of gross rating points (GRP) as an online measurement, as we'll see shortly.

Who am I talking to?

The second reason for the complexity of measuring online display advertising is related to the online dominance of performance advertising over brand. It also lies in history, and in the development of two parallel, incompatible advertising currencies. The first is panel-based, as developed by companies such as comScore and Nielsen, and is used for planning. The second is ad server-based, as we saw with site metrics, and is used for buying.

Part of the problem is that just because an ad is served doesn't mean it is served to a member of the audience for which it is intended. According to comScore, the main reasons are that more than 60 per cent of computers are shared, so ads can be shown to the wrong person; demographic data is used for targeting ages and becomes outdated; not all registration data is accurate; and some targeting infers demography based on content consumption.

Equally, just because an ad is served doesn't mean someone actually saw it. Users may leave the page in less than a second (the minimum amount of time an ad must be in view to count as being viewable according to the IAB definition); the ad may appear 'below the fold' – in a part of the page that the user doesn't actually see; or the ad may be served to a non-human visitor – a bot or a spider. comScore estimates that overall only 46 per cent of ads are actually viewable by people.

These discrepancies have led to a drive to reconcile the two forms of data, but as Paul Goode, SVP Marketing, EMEA/APAC/LATAM at comScore points out, this is not the responsibility of marketers. However, marketers should make sure that their agencies are doing due diligence on the data they use in order to make sure it is not panel – or census – only.

At the same time we have seen a switch – driven by advertisers' desire for better targeting and media owners' need to increase the value of their inventory – from buying media as a proxy for audiences to buying audiences themselves. This really started with behavioural targeting and retargeting, and its latest iteration is programmatic trading, or real-time bidding (RTB).

RTB can be thought of as applying the techniques of PPC to display advertising. Instead of the ads being sold beforehand in the traditional way, the inventory is auctioned to the highest bidder as the page is being assembled, based on attributes – either explicit or inferred – of the user as reflected in the cookies stored on their browser.

There are two main benefits to RTB: improved targeting of advertising and improved efficiency in the process of delivering it. At present most of the benefits are being seen in the latter, with the effect that agencies are very excited and most advertisers are wondering what all the fuss is about, although the most advanced advertiser, such as Sky in the UK, have been auditing their agencies to make sure they can respond to the challenges of the new environment. The obvious problem, at least as far as measurement is concerned, is that RTB relies on cookies, with all the attendant issues of accuracy that we have already discussed.

In fact those accuracy questions are the latest point of discussion in online advertising measurement. Expectations of the accuracy achievable by online targeting and the viewability of online display ads have become inflated, and discussions are under way on the need for standards of viewability.

In the meantime, as Goode says, the key question is whether, as an advertiser, your advertising is reaching real people: 'Cookies aren't people, and the problems with them will only get worse as the number of devices proliferates. And if you don't get the people part right, all your other metrics will be flawed.'

In fact, difficulties surrounding cookies – privacy legislation, consumers increasingly taking action to block or delete cookies, the growing importance of mobile ecosystems that don't allow third-party cookies – mean media owners are looking for alternatives. Google, for example, is looking at an ad ID that could allow it to track a user not only across different media but also channels (such as mobile and desktop).

Making Measurement Make Sense (3MS)

One of the most important initiatives to result from these difficulties is Making Measurement Make Sense (3MS), which was launched in the United States by the American Association of Advertising Agencies, the Association of National Advertisers and the Interactive Advertising Bureau in February 2011. Its aim is to make 'digital media more hospitable to brands by evolving the way the value of interactive advertising is measured', and it intends 'to make digital media measurements directly comparable to those of traditional media, while maintaining the ability to evaluate the unique value that interactivity brings to brand campaigns'.

The five guiding principles of digital measurement as defined by Making Measurement Make Sense (3MS)

Principle 1 – move to a 'viewable impressions' standard and count real exposures online

Today we count 'served impressions' as recorded by ad servers. Often, ad units are not in a viewable space to the end user or fail to fully load on the screen – potentially resulting in substantial overcounting of impressions. Viewable exposures are increasingly the norm across other media and better address the needs of brand marketers.

Principle 2 – online advertising must migrate to a currency based on audience impressions, not gross ad impressions

Brand marketers target specific audiences. Marketers need to understand the quality and number of exposures against their targets – and the respective reach and frequency of such exposures. The existing digital currency makes this extremely difficult. Moreover, the practice of selling ad impressions makes cross-media comparisons extremely difficult, if not impossible.

Principle 3 – because all ad units are not created equal, we must create a transparent classification system

Unlike traditional media, which have a limited number of inventory types (eg 30-sec spot, full-page back cover), digital has a myriad of units. Making Measurement Make Sense advocates a transparent classification system, adhered to by all publishers. Such a system will enable marketers to identify and spotlight the best offerings for brand building, and for other marketing objectives.

Principle 4 – determine interactivity 'metrics that matter' for brand marketers, so that marketers can better evaluate online's contribution to brand building

Currently, the industry is awash in digital interaction metrics. However, these metrics are not necessarily relevant for brand marketers. Aside from click-throughs, there are few standards for enabling reliable comparison across sites. The industry must identify and define the specific metrics most valuable to brand marketers and define and implement reliable standards for existing metrics.

Principle 5 – digital media measurement must become increasingly comparable and integrated with other media

Measurement solutions must facilitate cross-media platform planning, buying and evaluating of marketing and media. This is a substantial issue that hampers analysis and decision making throughout the ecosystem.

(Source: Making Measurement Make Sense. For more information, go to **http://www.measurementnow.net**)

The return of GRP

The participants in the 3MS initiative turned the five principles into the Five-Part Digital Marketing Measurement Solution (see box below), one of which was to establish an audience currency: 'an online Gross Ratings Point metric, providing reach and frequency reporting of viewable impressions'. GRP is an established offline metric and is defined as the cumulative number of impressions generated by an ad campaign. It is calculated by multiplying the audience reached (as a percentage of the total audience) by the frequency the ad was shown. The important distinction in the case of online advertising, and 3MS in particular, is that the impressions reported should be viewable under the IAB definition.

The Five-Part Digital Marketing Measurement Solution

- Define impression: shift from a 'served' to a viewable impression standard.

- Establish audience currency: introduce an online GRP metric, providing reach and frequency reporting of viewable impressions.

- Standard classification of ad units: implement a classification system and taxonomy for banner, rich media and streaming video ads.

- Brand ad performance metrics: define standard and transparent metrics for view-through reporting and cumulative social activity.

- Brand attitudinal measures: establish standards and vendor validation to improve the methodology for online brand attitudinal studies.

(Source: Making Measurement Make Sense. For more information, go to **http://www.measurementnow.net**)

The problem of earned media

The final part of our media triumvirate – earned media – is exactly what the name suggests; media where a marketers' presence is not determined by what they spend, but by how interesting people think their company and its products and services are. It is social media in the broad sense.

Social media metrics are evolving just as quickly as those in any other part of digital marketing, but as yet few companies have really established ways of measuring return on investment from social. For most, their social activity exists aside from conventional metrics, measurable only on its own terms. In this, social is analogous to such marketing activities as online games – easy to measure in terms of number of plays, but much harder to link to business results such as sales.

Just as in the early days of online, the first measurements of social media were simple numbers of participants – how many friends, fans or followers you had. Thinking has moved on to look more at the interactions of these fans with the brand, with sharing being a popular metric for the success of a social communication.

However, recent research from Germany argues that return on investment from social can be measured. A St Gallen University study – in co-operation with Adobe, Publicis and Akamai – last year found that most companies struggle to measure social ROI because their use of social media is not sufficiently integrated with their business objectives. The study looked at 186 large and medium-sized companies across multiple industries in Germany, and found that the majority have social media strategies that merely focus on communication tactics and are not integrated into the actual business model. The result is severe measurement problems, because the impact of communications targets on financial results is not clear. But the flipside is that if social media objectives can be mapped across to business objectives, the ROI of social media can be measured more accurately.

What are you trying to achieve?

This leads on to another key issue for digital marketers – the need to set key performance indicators (KPIs) for the business. As discussed earlier, measuring marketing activity across all channels against ROI or profitability allows you to take a holistic view of what is going on. Setting the right KPIs enables you to do a similar thing.

The concept of KPIs is nothing new, and has been common in the world of business analysis for many years. KPIs are used to distill key trends from complex, often disparate pools of data, and to present them as a series of clear, unequivocal indices – a snapshot of how your organization (or website, in our case) is performing at any given time. KPIs do 'exactly what it says on the tin'. They *indicate* progress (or lack of it) in areas that are *key* to your website's *performance*.

Why KPIs are important

The real value of KPIs is that they let you extract meaning from your data at a glance. Without them, it is all too easy to drown in the proliferation of data that your web analytics solution churns out. It is a classic case of not seeing the wood for the trees.

By defining and measuring your KPIs you are creating a regular snapshot that allows you to monitor the performance of your marketing over time. You know that if this KPI is going up it means one thing, if that one's going down it means another, and so on. Your KPIs not only give you an immediate sense of the overall health of your marketing, but also help to highlight potential problems, and point you in the right direction before you delve deeper into your data looking for solutions.

Choosing effective KPIs

In the document 'Web Analytics Key Metrics and KPIs' (Creese & Burby, 2005) the Web Analytics Association (WAA) defines a KPI in the context of web analytics as:

> KPI (Key Performance Indicator): while a KPI can be either a count or a ratio, it is frequently a ratio. While basic counts and ratios can be used by all Web site types, a KPI is infused with business strategy – hence the term 'Key' – and therefore the set of appropriate KPIs typically differs between site and process types.

Another thing to note is that the term *KPI* and *metric* are often used interchangeably. This is misleading, because although a KPI is *always* a metric, a metric is not necessarily a KPI. So how do you tell the difference?

- KPIs are always clearly aligned to strategic business goals.
- KPIs are defined by management: decision makers have to identify, define and take ownership of the key drivers of their organization's success.
- KPIs are tied to value drivers critical to achieving key business goals: they should represent the 'deal breakers' in the pursuit of your organizational goals.
- KPIs need to be based on valid data: you only get out what you put in.
- KPIs need to be quantifiable: you have to be able to measure your KPIs in a consistent and meaningful way over time.
- KPIs need to be easy to understand: they should be a barometer of your sites of performance – a quick glance at your KPIs should tell anyone in your organization, from management to intern, how well your marketing is performing.
- KPIs can be influenced by, and used as triggers for, positive action: one of the main values of KPIs is that they immediately highlight where your organization 'could do better', and highlight areas where action is required to get things back on track.

From a digital marketing perspective, choosing the right KPIs is crucial to monitoring your marketing's performance effectively, and allowing you to make informed decisions for continuous improvement. But with a bewildering array of different metrics to choose from, it is also notoriously difficult to pin down exactly what represents a KPI for your site.

If you find yourself struggling with this, it is an area where a session or two with a professional web analytics consultant could be money well spent. Don't let the consultant take over – you know your own business better than they ever will; rather, leverage their expertise with web metrics to help you define your own KPIs. The important thing is that you end up with a manageable suite of KPIs (usually numbering in the single figures) that together encapsulate the performance of your website.

Some generic web-based KPIs you may find useful:

- **Conversion rate:** this is the proportion of visitors to your site who go on to perform a predefined action – such as complete a purchase, subscribe to your online newsletter, register on the forum, fill in an enquiry form or any other conversion factor you have defined. Naturally, the higher your conversion rate, the more of your visitors are carrying out the actions you want them to perform on the site, and the better your site's performance (to get an idea of some average conversion rates across a variety of online business categories see **http://index.fireclick.com**).

- **Page views:** simple and straightforward, this is the number of pages viewed by your visitors over a given period, providing you filter out robot and spider traffic and manage measurement of viewability of course!

- **Absolute unique visitors:** the number of individuals who visited your site over a given period (as opposed to visits, where each returning visitor is counted again).

- **New v returning visitors:** the proportion of your visitors who have been to your site before, assuming the analytics package can recognize them through reconciliation with other data (for example they accept and haven't deleted cookies).

- **Bounce rate:** the bounce rate is the number of people who arrive on your site, and then leave again having only looked at that single landing page. This can be an important metric, potentially highlighting that your traffic perhaps isn't targeted enough (your keyword choices might be too generic) or your landing page isn't delivering what visitors expect when they arrive. Bear in mind, though, that some sites will have a naturally high bounce rate (think of a dictionary site, for example: a visitor arrives at the definition page for the word they were searching for, reads the definition and leaves).

- **Abandonment rate:** abandonment rate comes in a variety of flavours – it basically highlights the proportion of your visitors who start down a predefined conversion funnel (a series of pages leading to a target action or conversion), but bail out before committing to the desired action. The classic example is visitors dumping an e-commerce shopping cart before checking out, or abandoning the checkout process.

- **Cost per conversion (CPC):** this is basically a calculation of the total cost of advertising (or of a particular advertising campaign where you have tagged the ads so that your analytics software can differentiate resulting traffic) divided by the total number of conversions generated as a result.

There are plenty more. A look at the dashboard or overview page of your web analytics package of choice will offer plenty more, and you'll find literally hundreds of suggested KPIs online. In the end, picking the metrics that are relevant as KPIs for your website is down to you.

Unique visitors may be unique, but are they enough? – Rob Norman, chief digital officer global, GroupM

Consider the following. In September 2013 comScore, for the United States, reported that six web properties had more than 100 million unique users, 15 more had at least 50 million uniques, and that a further 29 had 25 million or more. Of these 50 sites, over 40 of them are funded by advertising. In addition, comScore also publishes the number of unique visitors to inventory represented by ad networks and exchanges, and lists 20 with more than 120 million unique visitors. In this case, unique is defined as 'un-duplicated single user visits to a given property'. These users are not unique or exclusive to that property.

Other than confirming that there are many very large sources of internet audiences, this information is uniquely useless because it tells us ridiculously little about real user engagement with the properties in question other than the raw reach of any one site; if we buy a page in *Vogue* we buy the whole reach, when we buy Yahoo, for the most part we don't. Of course we can de-duplicate audiences in the pursuit of optimizing reach and frequency, and apply behavioural and other data but it would be helpful to know more.

More pertinent data, in addition to monthly unique visitors, would be:

- **Daily unique visitors:** an indicator of the frequency of visits and by extension the value placed on that property by the user; three quarters of Facebook users visit daily, one half of LinkedIn users visit monthly – do the maths.

- **Average time spent per daily unique within five user quintiles from most to least time spent:** an indicator of the depth of the relationship between property and user.

- **A frequency distribution with accompanying geodemographic and device data by user quintile from the heaviest users to the lightest users:** indicating the characteristics of the most and least committed users, such as the relationship between the relatively small cohort of active Tweeters as opposed to the larger cohort of passive followers and the relationship between YouTube devotees and those who view occasionally.

- **Volume of content shared to Facebook, Twitter, LinkedIn and YouTube per unique visitor:** showing the likelihood of that property being a source of influence. The majority of the 10 most shared sources on Facebook and Twitter are news organizations with their roots in television or newspapers. Two of the other three are Buzzfeed and the Huffington Post. What might this imply? At another level, two recipe sites with a vastly different sharing profile may indicate a difference in value to advertisers.

- **The application of unified IDs:** showing consumption of content by device type and the nature of cross-device contiguous consumption.

These five data points, if made available as standard measures, will paint a far more textured view of the web's leading properties than exists today, and infuse audience data with real meaning.

Even in this data-driven age, buyers of media, creators of advertising and owners of brands have an interest in the composition and characteristics of the environments in which their advertising and brands appear. Knowing why someone does something, and how often, is every bit as interesting as knowing *how many* do it. This is particularly relevant when the pursuit of long-term marketing effect and brand health are priorities supported by the need to tell stories rather than a simple focus on immediate actions.

The most likely beneficiaries of these data sets are publishers, platforms and aggregators that have deep and frequent purpose-driven interactions with their audiences. That might imply that the data could hold significant advantages for the creators of original content who often don't top the unique user charts, as well as high-utility destinations such as Google. Frequently a perceived lack of scale disguises the value inherent in strong relationships and the influence of those relationships on both the formation of opinions, decision making and the creation and transmission of influence.

Ultimately, efficiency and effectiveness in advertising lies in the content of the message, its context, its relevance to the recipient and the price and timing of its delivery. If it is true that context and relevance are elevated by user engagement with adjacent content, the data sets proposed above are likely to be contributors to success, or at least a valuable price modifier to available inventory. If this is not true, the data will tell us soon enough.

The need for trust

What is clear from these thoughts from across the world is that the future of media measurement in the context of digital depends on trust. In this increasingly fragmented, detailed, flexible, agile and accelerating world, key decision makers will benefit from knowing who to trust. Of course this need has always been there; the complexity and pace that we face just makes it more important going forward. Which data is trusted? Why? From whom? Knowing the basis on which the data your business is using is built (whether internally or externally sourced) is important when you are convincing others about your business case.

Key to trust is transparency and, in the case of digital analytics, this transparency comes from standard metrics and knowing that these have actually been applied professionally. Hybrid data that enables cross-content/ environment comparison is crucial to understanding contextual advertising, but advertisers will have to be able to trust the suppliers of that data and the processes they use to pull it together if digital is going to reach the balance we mentioned in the opening few paragraphs of this chapter.

As digital continues to enable trading at pace, regional differences in data metrics will become more visible and the role of global standards for local markets will become even more important.

A good source of knowledge in this area includes **www.ifabc.org** – an alliance of 40 independent organizations set up by and for the industry. This group has built digital media measurement metrics since founding its own www standards group in 1996. In addition, many of its members deliver independent verification of the application of digital media measurement.

While the numbers we use are important, the scale and pace referred to throughout this chapter underlines the next level of accountability that will be taken for granted in a few years' time. We will rely more and more on criteria based on proof-of-context – examples of this will be standards for checking the viewability of advertising in digital and the processes by which the parties involved reduce the risk of ad misplacement. The latter extends the subject of analytics, as we tie the topic of data and data ethics in general to the ongoing debate around KPIs – but that is another chapter for the next book.

Realism rather than idealism helps balance the time available to understand measurement, with the volume, fragmentation and speed of available data. Using data sourced with the independent stamp of trust removes a large part of the uncertainty involved.

Setting up simple measurement step-by-step – a brand perspective, Alex Tait

- Set KPIs relevant for your customer journey. These will vary by sector and business model.

- Implement tracking used for all campaign activity and at least the key points of your onsite journey. Analytics for the onsite journey such as the homepage, landing and thank you pages – Google Analytics and Omniture are two examples of packages you could use. For offsite media such as PPC and display, some examples of tracking you can use are DoubleClick and Mediamind.

- Integrate measurement into your campaign process (for example alongside planning and targeting). Report regularly on performance against KPIs. Use reporting also to iterate your media plan and allocate budget accordingly.

  It is often best to keep the measurement methodology simple at first but an illustration of basic to more advanced methodologies are:

  - last click (paid, owned, earned);
  - last click (paid, owned, earned) and post-impression (paid, earned);
  - attribution model (paid, owned, earned);
  - attribution model (paid, owned, earned) and panel (brand);
  - attribution model, (paid, owned, earned), panel (brand) and econometrics (non-digital).

- Continuous testing programme (eg targeting, creative, proposition, incentives, media placements). For example, brand terms for PPC such as 'American Express' or 'Argos': many advertisers find that bidding on these terms does not add sufficient incremental value to their campaign to be worthwhile if the brand is position 1 for that term in natural search.

- Refine media measurement over time. The cookie window is important for campaign activity to track last click or post-impression sales. You don't want to be attributing sales, for example, to media that has not driven the sale. By analysing impression and click data you can decide what is right for your brand. Some advertisers have found that limiting their window to 48 hours is sufficient.

  Be aware that the right approach to measurement changes over time. You need to be aware of trends that may impact the effectiveness and appropriateness of your tracking, especially in the digital space. For example:

  - Cookie-based tracking is becoming less accurate due to various factors including third-party cookie-blocking.
  - SEO is becoming harder to accurately measure due to a privacy update that Google implemented in 2011, which has led to a significant number of keywords being attributable in analytics packages.

- The increase in multiple devices being used in a typical consumer journey (eg mobile and tablet) has led to complications with cross-channel attribution.

Due to some of these factors, publishers such as Google started to evaluate alternatives to cookie-based tracking in 2013.

- Other considerations:
  - Keep other stakeholders across the business up to date with changes in measurement. This is especially important for budget holders, eg finance and the board.
  - As mentioned above, a different approach might be appropriate for different business models. For example, a retailer might choose to conduct geographic PPC A/B testing (with city pairings, for example) to evaluate the true incrementality of media across all channels including in-store sales.
  - It is likely you will need to use several data sets as your measurement gets more sophisticated. However, you need to ensure you minimize duplication in how you attribute sales and allocate budget. For example, if you use DoubleClick for PPC, and Mediamind for display, you can set them up to de-duplicate via a master account.

Alex Tait has held senior digital marketing roles at Arcadia Group, American Express and the Post Office, and was chair of ISBA's Digital, Direct and Data Action Group.

Meaningful application of big data for marketers, Andrew Bradford, VP, Nielsen

Fundamentally, the marketer has three main challenges: they need to reach the right people, their message needs to resonate with the audience and ultimately that communication must engender a reaction.

The role of insight is clear: it must facilitate the plan, provide real-time measurement and ultimately allow optimization/refinement, preferably in-flight. Traditional panel-only approaches struggle to provide sufficiently robust insights to plan confidently and refine in-flight. Increasingly, large data is often being combined with even bigger processing to facilitate this.

Measuring online campaign **reach** will provide similar metrics as disciplined (traditional) media – reach, frequency and GRPs – but has to be able to deal with myriad placements across millions of pages over the same time period (daily) as broadcast media – a standard panel approach doesn't cut the mustard here. When I say reach, let me be clear, we're measuring the number of people first and foremost – not the number of browsers. Increasingly, this can be achieved leveraging third-party subscription data. The role of the traditional panel will remain important for the purposes of calibration rather than the source of audience projection. Finally de-duplicating those ratings with television data (BARB in the UK) to provide a daily breakdown of those exposed to TV-only, online-only and, of course, both.

But if we can now measure TV and online GRPs, how do we understand their relative value – how did the opportunity to see **resonate**? In order to allow the marketer to drive performance, these measures must also be available in-flight. In the last 12 months, we have also seen the emergence into the mainstream of neuroscience as a tool for refining the use of creative online. And the final step is to understand the **reaction** to that exposure.

So, a natural progression of needs. In the future, however, we'll be seeing a lot more of this type of data being pulled together. There are two broad approaches for integrating data commonly used currently: fusion between two datasets, usually with fully profiled panellists; or hybridization, where panel data is integrated with census data. We undertake heaps of this type of work. But the outputs do have their limitations. However, increasingly a new solution is available to the marketer. One that offers a number of advantages over integrating multiple datasets: single-source data.

Pulling it all together

We ourselves use single-source databases created and processed by third parties on our behalf, so that privacy can be maintained. These databases match 'watch' data from our own media data with 'buy' databases from a range of sources: our own panels, store data and credit card transaction data. Because a single-source database created from our media panel and this purchase data matches the actual viewing and purchase behaviour of anonymous individuals (to control for privacy), it is possible to calculate precisely the sales lift between those exposed to an ad campaign (and at what frequency) and those not exposed. In the UK we're now providing this type of data to a number of clients trying to understand the impact of marketing communications on purchasing (see Figure 4.1).

FIGURE 4.1 Single-source data

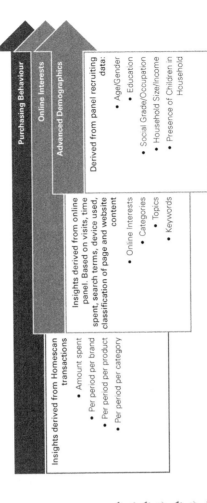

Purchasing Behaviour

Insights derived from Homescan transactions
- Amount spent
  - Per period per brand
  - Per period per product
  - Per period per category

Online Interests

Insights derived from online panel. Based on visits, time spent, search terms, device used, classification of page and website content
- Online Interests
  - Categories
  - Topics
  - Keywords

Advanced Demographics

Derived from panel recruiting data:
- Age/Gender
- Education
- Social Grade/Occupation
- Household Size/Income
- Presence of Children in Household

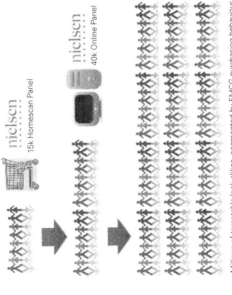

nielsen
15k Homescan Panel

nielsen
40k Online Panel

Millions of targetable look-alikes, segmented by FMCG purchasing behaviour

Besides fast-moving consumer goods (FMCG) data from loyalty cards, the product and service categories for which this approach offers opportunity are those, naturally, for which consumers frequently use credit cards, debit cards, or automatic bill payments from their checking accounts. Such categories most notably include retailers, restaurants – within which casual dining represents a particular opportunity, given the sizeable spend and intense competition for 'share of stomach' in this subcategory – travel, entertainment, financial services, and telecommunications. The growth of online shopping, currently expanding much more quickly than its offline cousin, offers another increasingly attractive opportunity for this approach.

FIGURE 4.2   Using single-source data in the marketing mix

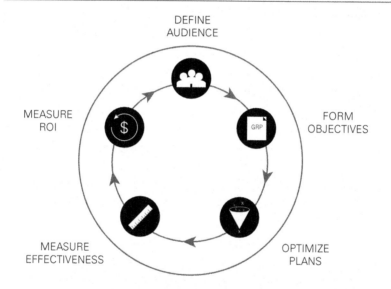

Figure 4.2 shows how single-source data can be used to refine a marketing plan developed using marketing mix modelling for broad allocation decisions. Essentially, once you have defined your audience and developed a plan based on a given number of gross rating points (GRPs), you use single-source data to optimize the plan, measure its actual effectiveness in terms of sales lift, and determine the actual ROI of the campaign.

That result then feeds in to the next cycle, so that your ad budget becomes more efficient each time you move around the circle. It is worth stressing that the key to the exercise is that only single-source can establish a precise campaign-level ROI and thus accountability for the results of the whole campaign.

But here's a great example of how analytics can help even creatively: our Neuro Focus teams can run a 60-second TV creative through a target audience in our labs and monitor second by second what works and what doesn't, and automatically edit the ad down to a 15-second creative with more impact, ready for online distribution.

Considerations

As implied above, single-source data will lead to new ways of doing business in many parts of the advertising ecosystem. Each participant – advertiser, agency, or publisher – will need to come to grips with the skill sets involved in best exploiting this new world. Audience behaviour will be looked at in new ways. Different ways will emerge of aligning media inventory with new audience profiles to maximize efficiency and impact. When the technology and processes, which are still new, are mature, the cycle-time on which advertisers can improve a campaign will shorten. In the past, one had to run a campaign, monitor its effects through analysis of two distinct data sets, and fine-tune accordingly. It seems reasonable to suppose that, as with so many other technologies, this one will eventually achieve the ability to enable modification of a campaign 'in-flight'. That is a long way off – but still shows that, generally, for the technology to achieve its full potential, many steps involved in planning and executing a typical advertising campaign will have to change.

Finally, the promise of an audience that will deliver the best sales lift should not turn marketers' or their agencies' heads too thoroughly: sales lift is a short-term measure, and should not be allowed to crowd out attention to long-term brand goals. The market has already started to move in pursuit of greater advertising precision. Advertisers, agencies and publishers generally understand the transformative nature of this capability; and some players are moving faster than others to take advantage of it. Advertisers who are in the lead are increasing their ability to connect with their key customers. Media companies are getting closer to claiming the full value of their audiences.

Pedro Silva, presidente executivo/CEO, IVC Brazil

The important thing to realize is that the basics of marketing haven't changed that much. Finding new measurements is interesting and adds value, but it doesn't replace the basic Media 101. All the metrics from the pre-internet era are still valid; you just need to understand how people's habits have changed in order to adapt your communications to the new, fragmented environment. And you use the basic metrics of GRP, reach and frequency and you build from there.

The world is changing much faster now and in ways that we can't predict, so as a marketer you have to update yourself very fast. You can't be a guru with a vision; you have to be pragmatic and adapt to the changes as they are happening. For example, we didn't have social networks a decade ago, and we don't know if we'll have them in a decade's time. And mobile phones now permeate everything we do, creating a revolution in developing countries. Twenty years ago, everyone in developed countries had a phone line, but the only people in Brazil who had them were the upper classes. Now everyone in the country has a mobile, and you see young people using their smartphones for everything.

In developing countries, this speed of development also means you're making leaps rather than walking through the changes. Things changed in an evolutionary way in that established markets move much faster, and in bigger leaps in emerging markets. But it's more demanding for emerging markets to keep up because they don't have the resources in terms of the education and the number of people with the right understanding.

But this speed of development also means you sometimes have the opportunity to leapfrog a technology that is in place in established markets. For example, there's an opportunity with hybrid measurement. Panels and surveys are not perfect; they're expensive and they have difficulty addressing the rate of change of devices. They're also having a tough time doing mobile; in the United States they're doing mobile panels, but they're only looking at Android, which is a bias and an important one. So hybrid models merge information from web analytics to improve the accuracy and scope of panel data.

Now it's possible to go the other way and take web analytics and do surveys that complement them and transform them into audience data. There's been work done on pilots in the UK and Brazil, and because mobile panels probably won't be expanded outside the United States very quickly, there's an opportunity for developing markets to come up with something new instead. If there's something that takes too long to develop in mature markets, technologies that are quicker to expand will have the opportunity for a broader reach. That's important for the UK, but it's more important for Brazil because at the moment there is no mobile panel here.

It's also now a boundaryless world; the technology is available to anyone at any time. The huge differences in prices and purchasing are decreasing fast. The cloud means that tools and technologies are becoming available all around the world at the same time, and at the same price. For example, the development of ad viewability technology is happening in Brazil at almost the same time as it is elsewhere.

That leads to tension between the global and national levels. Multinational advertisers tend to apply the same standards around the world; for example, they'll push for the same viewability information in Brazil as in the United States. But media is not global. The top TV channels in Brazil, the top newspapers and magazines, they are Brazilian. And you can say the same about the internet too. So the practices demanded by the multinational advertisers and global agency networks will take time to be adopted by the country's media. It may be less true now than it was with traditional media, but it still applies, and it's true around the world.

So for marketers it remains true that you have to understand your business and its objectives first. You have to have a clear understanding of who you want to talk to. Then you can apply the metrics that best suit that business. Start with GRP, reach and frequency and develop from there. So for branding it's how many times people have been impacted and across which platforms; for e-commerce you want to add click-throughs and conversions. The use of attribution modelling too is something that depends on the nature of the individual business – it's important, but the fact that it's hard to do means that it's more significant when the company is selling more expensive items.

Then the challenge in Brazil is how to influence people across a very diverse country. There's jungle in the north, big cities in the south-east and well-developed countryside in the south, so you have to look at the country in terms of those different environments, and it's important to measure them separately. It's different from the United States, which is much more similar across the country in the penetration of technologies and so on. Los Angeles is very similar to New York and Miami, which is not the case in Brazil. So Brazil is a more complicated market than the United States, even though it's somewhat smaller.

Digital campaign validation, by Scott Joslin, VP International Advertising Effectiveness, comScore

Few industries have seen the level of disruption and high velocity of change that the digital ad industry has experienced in recent years. Just as we've seen tremendous growth in terms of the volume of digital advertising, the landscape itself has also experienced a massive evolution. From new ad formats and placement strategies to new delivery systems and ad technology, it has become challenging for players across the industry to stay up to speed. Add to this the trend towards audience targeting and the shift to viewable impression measurement, which have already turned the US market upside down in what seems like an instant – with these changes spreading around the world, driven in part by global advertisers.

Until recently, digital advertising measurement had not kept pace with the complexity of these changes. The traditional transactional focus had been on measurement of gross impressions delivered, as opposed to those that were actually seen by consumers in a particular target. However, as ad platforms, formats and delivery technologies have evolved, it has become obvious that not all online ads delivered actually have an opportunity to be seen. The result: marketers have been limited in their ability to understand how online advertising performs, especially when compared to other media channels. This lack of understanding resulted in reluctance by many marketers to fully embrace digital advertising.

This reluctance was also fuelled by the conventional wisdom that there was an unlimited supply of online ad inventory. This prompted the digital advertising industry to promote served impressions as a currency. Publishers and their clients reasoned that, if an ad would only be paid for if it was clicked on, then it didn't matter if the ad was never seen, especially since little real cost was incurred in reproducing or delivering the impression. Eventually, the entire industry, even cost per mille (CPM)-based advertisers, coalesced around served impressions as currency.

One damaging effect of the served impression currency is that it increases the risk of buying online ads for brand advertising buyers, because of a perceived lack of accountability – a paradox for a medium that has premised its value on accountability. This is starkly illustrated by the lack of information on whether or not served impressions are actually seen by a real consumer. If an ad is delivered but never seen, then it has zero potential to improve branding metrics or sales at premium prices. Ad buyers dislike not knowing whether a real consumer could actually see 20 per cent or 60 per cent of their purchased impressions. Faced with the non-quantified risk, buyers must naturally discount the value of what they are buying to compensate for the risk they are taking. The result: lower pricing.

To counter this, we need a reality check – digital ad supply is not unlimited if we only count ads that users can see. In other words, ads must deliver an opportunity to be seen by a real person in order to count as a true ad impression. In this environment, non-visible banners would not count. Ads that have not finished rendering would not count. Impressions generated by non-human traffic would not count, nor would ads that are in languages other than those native to the viewer's market.

While the focus thus far has been on ad viewability as a mechanism to introduce accountability, there are additional important factors that affect the value delivered to advertisers. These are:

- Geographic compliance: ensuring that ads are delivered to the appropriate geography also introduces scarcity into the marketplace as it will limit the supply of ad inventory within target geography.

- Brand safety: given the complex daisy chain of ad delivery, the ability to eliminate the real-time delivery of ad impressions shown next to undesirable content is important. Avoiding content that is not going to deliver a positive impact, or that may potentially deliver a negative one, reduces the perceived risk to advertisers. It also lowers the valid supply, although typically by a negligible amount. Moreover, it brings online advertising into conformity with other media that have traditionally had standards and practices to assure brand safety.

- Non-human traffic: in some cases, current impression numbers include counters of various sorts. While counters themselves are not inherently problematic, they can be used to artificially inflate impression counts. In other cases, the activity taking place is more disreputable, including cases where ad impressions are generated robotically or programmatically for the sole purpose of artificially driving up traffic. This artificial increase is achieved by delivering ads to non-human entities such as a fraud server or through using invisible 1x1 pixels on a computer screen. Advertisers do not want to pay for impressions that are not delivered to actual consumers. Publishers suffer because this non-human traffic generates false inventory and harms the reputation of the medium. All types of non-human traffic need to be filtered out of validated impression counts.

Clearly there is a need to move from served to validated impressions as a digital currency. Advertisers want to understand ad delivery to each of these core dimensions, and they also require a holistic, unduplicated view of total campaign delivery. In order to achieve this unduplicated accounting of delivered impressions, advertisers require a simple measure that eliminates all of the wasted time and error associated with merging disparate data sources. Validated impressions offer a more accurate assessment of digital advertising effectiveness. By eliminating the noise associated with non-valid impressions, the likelihood of measuring a higher return on marketing investments is markedly improved.

It should be noted that while there are now multiple approaches for measuring viewability in the marketplace, the definition used in this section is based on comScore's visibility methodology. (The criteria used to determine visibility are those that were established by the 'Making Measurement Make Sense' or 3MS initiative in the United States, which requires an ad to be at least 50 per cent visible for one second or more in order to be considered viewable.)

Digital campaign validation can also provide the ability to measure across media channels. In order for marketers to plan, measure and evaluate media across channels, they require digital campaign delivery measurement that can be translated into traditional metrics, like reach, frequency and gross rating points (GRPs). A central component of comScore's approach to digital campaign validation is the validated GRP (vGRP). The vGRP provides the industry with a cross-media comparable GRP metric that is also meaningful in the context of how online advertising works.

vGRPs are calculated by first removing all ad impressions that did not have the opportunity to make an impact, including those that were not in-view, delivered to the wrong geography, served near brand unsafe content and subject to non-human traffic, and secondly, by converting cookie counts into people to avoid the overestimation of audience. (The average UK consumer has five cookies from a typical third-party ad server in the course of a month. The methodology for measuring people rather than cookies was developed as part of comScore's digital media planning data used in 44 countries.) Similarly, validated target rating points (vTRPs), include an overlay of audience-validated data, providing yet another actionable metric for marketers seeking to plan campaigns across channels.

The internet has promised to be the most measurable medium largely on the basis of measuring served impressions and clicks. We now understand that both of these metrics are deeply flawed, and have effectively shackled the industry in its quest to capture a bigger share of the advertising pie.

With digital campaign validation, the opportunity to truly deliver on the promise is now within reach.

About the contributor

This chapter was prepared with the invaluable help of Alex Tait and Paul Goode, SVP Marketing, APAC/EMEA/LATAM, comScore.

Are customers finding you?

05

OUR CHAPTER PLEDGE TO YOU

In this chapter you'll discover answers to the following questions:

- Why is search important?
- What is a search engine, and how does it work?
- How big is search?
- How do I optimize my website for the search engines?
- What is paid search marketing and how does it complement SEO?
- What is black-hat SEO and why should I avoid it?

Search: *still* the online marketer's holy grail

When the first edition of this book was published in 2009 I called search the online marketer's holy grail. Back then search was essentially the panacea that, if harnessed effectively, would drive sustainable waves of targeted traffic to your website, and ultimately generate more revenue for your business. For many businesses it still is.

During the intervening period social media has continued its remarkable surge in popularity and, with an ever-increasing population of ever-connected smartphones, mobile has grown to deliver on at least some of its latent promise. Both have been grabbing more than their share of the digital limelight, and have shifted the spotlight away from search marketing.

The stats reflect this shift too. In 2010 more US web users visited Facebook than visited Google (Experian/Hitwise report, December 2010). Although Facebook was not able to maintain the top spot, referral traffic from social networks continues to drive upwards while search traffic is flatlining or worse. Shareaholic's latest report, published at the end of 2013, showed organic search traffic dropping 6 per cent year-on-year, while social referrals more than doubled.

That is pretty impressive, but it's important to remember that visitor volume is only part of the equation when it comes to choosing an effective platform for marketing your business. When it comes to getting your information in front of a highly targeted audience at the precise moment *when they're looking to buy your products or services*, search engines still reign supreme. To discount their importance to your online business based on the fickle barometer of online 'buzz' would certainly be a mistake.

In the last chapter we discovered how your company's website forms the hub of your digital world. Your website is much more than a shop window to a huge and growing global marketplace: a well-designed and implemented website is a place where you can interact with your customers, a virtual meeting place where you can do real business, with real people, in real time. The commercial potential is, quite simply, unparalleled.

But if you're going to realize even a fraction of that potential then you need to make sure that people can *find your site*. Even in this age of rampant online engagement, peer recommendation and reviews, the way that the vast majority of people find the things they need online is by typing a phrase into that little empty box on the homepage of their favourite search engine.

On the internet there's really no such thing as passing trade. The chances of a potential customer stumbling across your site while randomly browsing the web are approaching negligible. That means your visitors have to learn about your site from somewhere else: by word of mouth recommendations (online or off), through conventional advertising and branding channels, by following a link from another website or (and still by far the most likely scenario), by clicking on a link in a search engine results page (SERP).

Think about the way you use the internet. Where do you go when you're looking for information, products or services online? If you're shooting the virtual breeze with your friends you head for Facebook or Twitter, but if you're trying to find something specific you're much more likely to head for your favourite search engine, even if you're using your mobile phone. There are relatively few class-leading online brands (such as Amazon.com for books, eBay.com for online auctions, YouTube.com for video) where consumers are likely to remember the web address (URL) to access the site directly. For almost everything else, people use search engines.

Search: still a fledgling industry

Can you remember an internet before search – before Yahoo!, Bing (the search engine formerly known as MSN Search), and Ask... before Google?

Today it feels as though search engines have been with us forever, but Google – the market leader in search by a country mile – was only established in late 1998. In less than 16 years the search company has become a leading global brand to rival the biggest and the best out there, and has changed the way that businesses operate forever.

Google's incredible growth, and the unprecedented rise of search in general, is testament to the practically ubiquitous appeal of online search, both to a constantly growing pool of internet users, and as a marketing vehicle for businesses large and small. To the user, search engines offer a window to the web – a convenient way for them to sift through the literally billions of pages out there to find valuable, relevant information on what they are interested in at any given time. For marketers, search engines offer a unique opportunity to get their products or services in front of online prospects at the exact moment they're looking for them. It is, perhaps, one of the ultimate forms of targeted, prequalified marketing.

The fact that the internet search industry is still a relatively young one, and that it is still growing and evolving so quickly, makes the whole area of search engine optimization (SEO) and paid search advertising an incredibly exciting and challenging one. Because things are changing constantly, you're always shooting at a moving target, and have to tweak your aim accordingly. Search is a fluid and dynamic environment, and no one has all the right answers, because the nature of the questions keeps changing.

The rules have changed over the years, rendering tactics that previously bore fruit (on a very risk reward basis) as obsolete. Ineffective at best – harmful at worst.

Differing tactics have largely vanished with SEO in its most current form. There is only one real tactic that most SEOs see as sustainable long term – build relevance to your site and focus on providing a resource for your customers.

SEO is an amalgamation of factors – the quality of the site's architecture, its content, and the influence of other websites, social channels and endorsements: SEO done correctly needs to satisfy every one of these aspects.

About the engines

Why is search engine marketing so important?

In 2013, US businesses spent a staggering $20.6 billion on search marketing, according to the Winterberry Group. Why spend so much?

Simple: because search engines give those businesses a prime opportunity to put their products, services or brands in front of a vast and ever-growing market of prospective customers *at the precise time* those customers are looking for exactly what the business is selling. That is a pretty evocative marketing proposition – especially when you consider the volumes involved.

During the month of December 2013, in the United States alone, search engines fielded more than 18.3 billion search queries (comScore qSearch). That's more than two and a half searches for every living person on the planet in a single month!

Some important points to note:

- 70–80 per cent of users ignore the paid ads on any given search, focusing on the organic results.

- 75 per cent of users never scroll past the first page of search results.

- Companies that blog have 434 per cent more indexed pages. Companies with more indexed pages get far more leads.

- SEO leads have a 14.6 per cent close rate, while outbound leads (such as direct mail or print advertising) have a 1.7 per cent close rate.

- While this varies between different verticals, a study from Slingshot SEO shows that of Google searches 18 per cent of organic clicks go to the #1 position, 10 per cent of organic clicks go to the #2 position, and 7 per cent of organic clicks go to the #3 position.

How do search engines work?

Before you start optimizing your site for the search engines, it makes sense to know how they work. Not the detailed technical 'nuts-and-bolts' of it all – just a high-level understanding of what makes a search engine tick. Knowing what the search engines are trying to achieve, and how they go about doing it, is at the heart of good SEO.

The mission of search engines

It is important to understand at this point that search engines are interested, first and foremost, in delivering timely, relevant, high-quality search results to their users. You could say it's their prime directive – their reason for being. The search engines are constantly researching, developing, testing and refining ways to enhance the service that they provide – looking to optimize the relevance and quality of the results they serve back to the user on every single query.

The rationale is simple: the better the search experience for the user, the better the reputation of the search engine and the more users it will attract. The more users a search engine has, the more alluring it is to advertisers, ergo the more ad revenue it can pull in.

Putting users first makes search engines richer... and that makes search engine shareholders happy. In that respect the internet is no different to traditional marketing channels like commercial television, radio and print publications. It is the viewers, listeners and readers that these channels look after first – because it's the audience that brings in the advertisers. Without an audience, they have no advertisers, and without advertisers they have no business.

From a marketer's perspective the search engines' constant quest to improve the search experience for users is something of a double-edged sword. Yes, it means that the best search engines have a bigger pool of potential prospects for your paid search advertising and your organic SEO efforts. But equally, the fact that things keep changing makes the process of optimization a continuous, uncertain and labour-intensive process.

Scouring the web

To deliver accurate, relevant, high-quality search results to their users, search engines need to gather detailed information about the billions of web pages out there. They do this using automated programmes called 'bots' (short for robots) – also known as 'spiders' – which they send out to 'crawl' the web. Spiders follow hyperlinks and gather information about the pages that they find.

Once a page has been crawled by a spider, the search engine stores details about that page's contents, and the links both into and out of it, in a massive database called an index. This index is highly optimized so that results for any of the hundreds of millions of search request received every day can be retrieved from it almost instantly.

It is a mammoth task. While no one knows the real number of unique web pages out there, and search engines typically don't publicize the size of their indices, a post on Google's official blog in July 2008 gave some rare insight into just how big the web is:

> The first Google index in 1998 already had 26 million pages, and by 2000 the Google index reached the one billion mark. Over the last eight years, we've

seen a lot of big numbers about how much content is really out there. Recently, even our search engineers stopped in awe about just how big the web is these days – when our systems that process links on the web to find new content hit a milestone: 1 trillion (as in 1,000,000,000,000) unique URLs on the web at once!

Search engines don't index every one of those trillion URLs, of course. Many contain similar or duplicate information, or are not really relevant to search (think of a dynamically generated online event calendar, for example, with links to 'next day' and 'previous day' – in theory you could keep clicking forever, but only pages containing event information are of any relevance in search results), so some don't make it into the index.

We don't know how many pages there are on the web, or, for that matter, how many are stored in the search engines' indices (information that is rarely volunteered), but it's safe to assume that we're dealing with some very big numbers.

The list of results for any given search query, which often contains many millions of pages, is then run through the search engine's complex ranking algorithms: special programs that use a variety of closely guarded proprietary formulas to 'score' a site's relevance to the user's original query. The output is then sorted in order of relevance and presented to the user in the SERPs.

Search engines process a huge volume of searches, scanning billions of items and delivering pages of relevant, ranked results in a fraction of a second. To the user the process seems quick, straightforward and seamless; but there's a lot going on behind the scenes. Google and Bing (which, following a 2010 agreement between Yahoo! and Microsoft, now also powers Yahoo! search results) are running some of the most complex and demanding computer applications in the world.

Optimizing your site for the engines

To many, SEO appears to be something of an arcane art. It is a world that is shrouded in high-tech mystery, a complicated world full of secrets that mere mortals haven't a hope of understanding. But according to leading UK-based SEO expert Jason Duke, of Strange Logic, there are no real secrets in SEO. 'The web is a very open place,' he says. 'If a site is riding high in the search engine listings, then you can, with enough persistence, get to see why it ranks so well. Replicate it, and you can join them – it really is as simple as that.'

TABLE 5.1   Links to webmaster resources for major search engines

Search engine resource	URL for webmasters
Google Webmaster Central	**http://www.google.com/webmasters**
Bing Webmaster Tools	**http://www.bing.com/toolbox/webmaster**
Yahoo! Web Publisher Tools	**http://tools.search.yahoo.com/about/ forsiteowners.html**

Matt McGee, an SEO expert who specializes in advising small businesses (**www.smallbusinesssem.com**), concurs with Jason's sentiments. In an interview on the 'Your SEO Plan' (**www.yourseoplan.com**) blog in December 2006, Matt said: 'SEO is not rocket science... It's simple, but it's not easy. There's a difference!... There's a small set of basic rules that apply to any web page or web site, whether you're a small business or not. Your site has to be crawlable, your content has to be good – and I'd include things like page titles, keyword use, etc, under the umbrella of "content" – and you need quality, relevant inbound links. That applies to everyone.'

One of the best places to start for tips on improving your site's ranking with the search engines is with the search engines' own guidelines, tips and resources for web site owners (see Table 5.1).

Make your site easy to crawl

If you are looking to attract search engine traffic, the last thing you want to do is make it difficult for search engines to index your website. Make sure your site design doesn't present unnecessary obstacles to search engine spiders.

Spiders are interested in text, text and more text. They don't see the graphics, clever animations and other flashy bells and whistles that web designers routinely use to make sites look pretty. In fact, over-reliance on some of these things can even hinder spiders, potentially preventing some sites from being indexed at all.

While some 'window dressing' is obviously important to make your site appeal to real people when they arrive, to get enough of them to your site in the first place it is vital that your design doesn't unwittingly alienate search engine spiders (see Table 5.2). Make sure your site works for both, and that each page includes relevant text-based content; avoid flash-only sites and frames, which are difficult for spiders to crawl effectively; and make sure that every page on your site can be reached via a simple text-based hyperlink.

TABLE 5.2 Spider traps: web design features that can hurt your search engine visibility

Website feature	Why it's bad for your SEO
All flash website	Difficult for spiders to crawl. While search engines have improved their ability to index text-based content within flash files, excessive dependence on flash is still a bad idea for both SEO and usability.
JavaScript navigation	Spiders often don't activate JavaScript code, so unless you implement an alternative they may struggle to reach other pages on your site via script-based navigation. Make sure you have at least one *regular, text-based hyperlink* to every page on your site.
Frames	Frames are notoriously difficult to implement effectively from a user experience perspective, are very rarely necessary, and often cause indexing problems for search engine spiders.
Image maps and other non-text navigation	Some spiders may have problems following these links. If you use image maps for navigation on your pages, make sure you have *alternative text-based hyperlinks* leading to the same pages.
Dynamically generated pages	Less of a problem than it used to be, but some spiders can have trouble with very long dynamically generated URLs that contain too many parameters (?W=XYZ). Try to configure your site to use 'Search Engine Friendly' URLs where possible, or at least restrict dynamic URL parameters to a maximum of three.
AJAX	See notes for JavaScript above.

Words are the foundation for SEO

The starting point for effective SEO is knowing what the people who are looking for your products, services or information are typing into that little box on the search engine homepage. Known as keywords or keyword phrases (which consist of two, three or more keywords), these form the foundation of your SEO efforts. Effective keyword selection should always be the very first thing that is carried out as it permeates every aspect of SEO activity. Keywords are used to differentiate site architecture and will also inform the content marketing strategy. Search engines are becoming smarter at understanding not only the meaning but also context of search, and semantic search is likely to become increasingly important in the future, with the focus on keywords gradually declining. Nevertheless, finding and using the right keywords in content will be a key factor in successful SEO for some time to come.

Choosing effective keywords

So how do you go about choosing the right keywords for site optimization? Well, a good place to start is with the people you are hoping to attract. Knowing your target audience is a critical component of any marketing campaign – and it's the same here. Put yourself in your prospect's shoes, sitting in front of your favourite search engine looking for information on the product or service you're selling. What would you type into the box?

These are your 'seed' keywords. They give you a starting point to work from. Take these keywords and play around with them. Imagine the various combinations of search terms your prospects might use to find your site. Type these into the engines and look at the results. Examine the sites that are ranking highly for your chosen keywords. Analyse them and try to work out how they are achieving those rankings.

You can also use a wide range of automated keyword suggestion tools such as the free tools provided by Google AdWords (**http://bit.ly/GoogKWTool**) and on the SEO Book website (**http://bit.ly/UDMSEOBook**); or Wordtracker (**www.wordtracker.com**) and Trellian's (**http://bit.ly/KWDiscovery**) keyword tools, both of which offer a free basic service with paid upgrades for a more comprehensive version. These tools typically provide insight into the search traffic volumes for the most popular phrases relating to seed keyword phrases you provide.

There are a lot of different keyword research tools and services available on the web... perhaps the best way to research your options is to look for things like 'keyword research tool' or 'keyword suggestion' in your favourite search engine.

Analyse the competition

Other tools on the web can provide you with insight into how your leading competitors are doing in terms of search engine traffic for particular keywords. Services on sites like SEO Toolset (**www.seotoolset.com**) and Compete (**www.compete.com**) can provide information on which keywords are driving traffic to your competitors' websites from the major search engines, and which of your competitors' sites are ranking for which keyword phrases – all of which can inform the choice of keywords you want to optimize for.

While automated tools are a good guide, don't underestimate the value of people as a source of inspiration for keyword selection. 'Use the automated tools to assist,' advises Jason Duke, 'but please remember that although automated tools are brilliant, nothing is better at understanding the minds of people than people themselves.'

That's good advice. What you believe people will search for and what they actually type into the search box are often two very different things. Get a group of people together – if possible, representative of your target market – and start brainstorming keywords. The results will probably surprise you.

I have my initial keyword list, now what?

After analysing your keywords and phrases, and examining the competition, you have probably got a list of target keywords as long as your arm. What do you do with them all?

The first thing you want to do is narrow your initial list down to a more manageable size. What constitutes a manageable size will depend on your situation – on how much time, money and resources you have available for your SEO effort. Remember, there's nothing wrong with starting small: optimize a few pages for what you believe are your main keywords, monitor the results on ranking, traffic and conversion for those pages. That will give you a solid foundation from which to build your optimization efforts, and your SEO expertise.

To whittle your list down to size, start by eliminating all of the words or phrases that are too general. Broad single-word terms such as 'shoes', 'mortgages', 'bottles' or 'computers' tend to be both very difficult to rank for (because they are high-traffic terms that can apply equally to a huge number of sites across the net), and at the same time are far too generic to drive valuable targeted traffic to your site.

Suppose you're an independent mortgage consultant based in Killarney, County Kerry, Ireland. If you choose to optimize a page based on the keyword 'mortgages' you will find yourself competing with a raft of mortgage providers, mortgage advisers, mortgage brokers, mortgage industry news sites... etc, from all over the world. Even if (and it's a big if) your page does make it to those coveted elevated positions in the SERPS for that keyword, the chances that people searching for the term 'mortgages' will be looking for an independent consultant in County Kerry are slim at best.

Phrases such as 'mortgages in Killarney' or 'mortgage consultant Kerry', on the other hand, are potentially much less competitive, and generate much lower search volumes, but are much more valuable to your business, because the people who search on those terms are far more likely to be interested in the products and services you offer.

In other words, the more general a keyword, the less likely it is that your site will contain what the searcher is trying to find. Effective SEO isn't just about generating traffic volume; it's about finding that elusive balance between keyword search volume and keyword specificity that drives the maximum volume of *targeted traffic* to your site.

'Your target keywords should always be at least two or more words long', explained search guru Danny Sullivan in a 2007 article for Search Engine Watch (**www.searchenginewatch.com**). 'Usually, too many sites will be relevant for a single word, such as "stamps". This "competition" means your odds of success are lower. Don't waste your time fighting the odds. Pick phrases of two or more words, and you'll have a better shot at success.'

Single keyword searches used to be the norm – but not any more. Search users are using more sophisticated search queries to narrow down the results they get back. These days two, three or even more words are becoming increasingly common. Exploiting that trend in your choice of optimization keywords can yield real dividends.

Long-tail versus short-tail keywords

Keywords in SEO fall into two broad categories. Short-tail keywords are simple one- or two-word phrases that are typically very general in nature and attract a large volume of individual search requests. Long-tail keywords, on the other hand, are more complex queries that contain more words, and are much more specific in nature. Individually they attract a much lower volume of search traffic than their short-tail counterparts, but cumulatively these long-tail type queries account for the lion's share of internet search traffic.

Martin Murray, head of Google's small and medium business channel for EMEA, sums it up like this:

> In any keyword domain there are a small number of highly trafficked keywords or phrases and a large number of low-trafficked keywords or phrases. Often, the keyword domain approximates to the right-half of a normal curve with the tail of the curve extending to infinity. Low-trafficked keywords are therefore also known as 'long-tail keywords'.
>
> The highly trafficked [short tail] keywords have the following characteristics: highly competitive, consist of one or two words, have a high Cost per Click and may have low conversion rates as they tend to be quite general. Examples from the accommodation sector might include 'hotel', 'London hotel' or 'cheap hotel'.
>
> Low-trafficked [long tail] keywords are not so competitive, often consist of 4, 5 or more words, have a lower Cost per Click and can have a higher conversion rate as they are quite specific indicating that the searcher is further along the online purchasing cycle. Examples might include 'cheap city centre hotel Dublin', 'stags weekend hotel temple bar Dublin' or 'business hotel with gym and spa Wexford'.
>
> Effective search marketing campaigns tend to put a lot of effort into discovering effective long-tail terms, particularly for use in sponsored listings (PPC) campaigns.

Successful keyword research should ultimately allow the marketer to find and focus on phrases that satisfy:

- volume – the number of people actually using that term to search;
- competitiveness – the number of other sites competing for the same phrase relevance;
- profitability – based around the products or services with the best margin.

Typically it makes sense to take a balanced approach, and work with a mixture of general short-tail keywords and more specific long-tail keywords as part of your organic SEO effort, while focusing on highly specific long-tail search terms is likely to yield a higher return on your investment for pay per click (PPC) campaigns (see later in the chapter).

Tracking the effectiveness of keywords has become more difficult since Google began to encrypt the referring terms, which now show as 'not provided' in analytics platforms. Keyword research therefore needs to be managed using other methods such as historical SEO data, webmaster tools, paid search data and site search data.

Focus on one page at a time

The list of keywords you are left with is very important. It essentially provides you with an SEO 'template' for your website. One of the key things to remember when you are approaching SEO is that you will be optimizing your site *one page at a time*. While you will look at some site-wide factors as part of your SEO effort, SEO isn't a straightforward 'one-size-fits-all' operation, and each of the existing pages on your site will need to be optimized independently. It is also highly likely you will want to create new pages to maximize your potential search engine exposure for as many of your chosen keyword phrases as possible.

Think about it: when a search engine presents results to a user, it is not presenting whole sites, it is presenting the individual pages that, according to its algorithms, best match a user's query. That means each individual page on your website gives you an explicit opportunity to optimize for specific keywords or phrases – and that's important.

'Each page in your website will have different target keywords that reflect the page's content', says Danny Sullivan. 'For example, say you have a page about the history of stamps. Then "stamp history" might be your keywords for that page.'

Jason Duke of Strange Logic also emphasizes the importance of optimizing individual pages for specific keywords: 'These [keywords] become the structure for your site, with a page for every topic. Laying these foundations and allowing them to grow according to what you, your team and your visitors think is the key to successful opportunities to rank.'

Your goal, then, is to isolate the important keywords and phrases in your particular market, and then to ensure your site includes individual pages with unique, relevant content optimized for a small number (ideally one or two... no more than three) keyword phrases. The more individual pages you have, the more opportunities you have to get your business in front of your prospects in the SERPs... and at the end of the day that's what SEO is all about.

Give each page a unique theme

Each website page should have a unique, specific theme. This will help to determine the 'key' words that it should be optimized for. Whether this is a homepage, category page, product page, guide or blog post, keeping each page focused makes optimization much more specific as well as delivering users the content that they are expecting to see.

Choose your page <title>s carefully

There is a small but very important HTML tag that lives in the header section of the code on each of your web pages. It's called the 'title' tag, and the text it contains is what appears in the title bar at the top of your browser window when you visit a web page. It's also, crucially, the text that appears as the 'clickable' blue link for a page when it is presented to users in the SERPs.

This means that what you put in the title tag is incredibly important for the following reasons: 1) The title tag is one of the most important on-page factors used by the search engines to rank your page. At this stage most, if not all, SEO experts agree that appropriate use of the title tag is a key factor in ranking well in the SERPs, and advise weaving your primary keyword(s) for a page into the title tag whenever possible (see Figure 5.1). Just remember not to sacrifice readability for your human audience; 2) The title is the first glimpse of your content that a search user will see. Giving your pages concise, compelling and informative titles will entice more users to click through to your page when it appears in search results.

Give each page a unique meta-description

Another HTML tag that used to be very important for SEO, but is now pretty much obsolete, is the meta-tag. Meta-tags contain information that is accessible to browsers, search engine spiders and other programs, but that doesn't appear on the rendered (visible) page for the user. This meta-data

FIGURE 5.1   Screenshot showing title tag and meta-description as they appear in HTML source code, and the same page as it is rendered in the Firefox browser, showing the start of the same title tag in the active tab

was once used extensively by search engines to gauge what a page was about – especially the once obsessed-over meta-keywords tag.

These days, however, the tag that was once the staple of SEO, has become more or less redundant in terms of influencing a page's ranking in the major search engines. Engines rely principally on their increasingly comprehensive ability to analyse the *actual content* of the page – the words the user sees – and on incoming and outgoing links, to help them determine a page's relevance to the submitted search query.

There is, however, one HTML meta-tag that is still worth including as part of your SEO, and that is the meta-description tag. As with most things in search, the opinion of leading experts in the SEO community is divided as to just how valuable the meta-description tag is in terms of search engine optimization. While it is widely acknowledged that the tag does little, if anything, to improve your page ranking, it can help to boost your click-through rate (CTR) when your page does appear in the SERPs.

Depending on the query and the page content, leading search engines will often use the contents of your meta-description tag as the descriptive 'snippet' of text that appears below your page title in the SERPs. A well-written description for each page can, in theory at least, entice more users to click through to your page when it is returned in search results.

Use of the meta-description text by search engines is inconsistent. The rules applied vary from engine to engine, and even between different types of query on the same engine. However, having compelling, informative meta-description tags is something that search engines encourage, certainly won't hurt your rankings, is beneficial to users, and may well boost traffic to your site.

Use HTML mark-up for page headers

The actual difference that using specific HTML mark-up for page headings (eg <h1>, <h2>, etc) makes is marginal. However, the heading of a page should summarize its content and will therefore determine the types of keywords that it will be optimized around. Using HTML heading mark-up won't do any harm and will also provide users with a snapshot of content when they arrive at that page.

Make navigation easy for visitors and search engines

Search engines use a site's structure to determine the relative importance of pages within it, so pages linked from the main navigation are given a higher priority than deeper, secondary or tertiary-level pages. The words used within the navigation are also key for engines, allowing them to determine the themes of linked pages – so it is important to use specific terms rather than generic, non-specific terms such as 'products', 'services' or 'solutions'. CSS based drop-down navigation systems can help to provide flexible, search engine friendly links to internal site categories and pages.

Both users and search engines benefit from the use of breadcrumb navigation when exploring website structures. For users, breadcrumb navigation provides a quick and easy way to determine exactly where they are within the site and navigate up a site structure easily. For search engines, breadcrumb links provide an overview of the site's structure and direct access to related pages.

Tag visual content for search engines

Page-specific images make sites much more appealing for visitors, and search engines are becoming much better at recognizing the content of photos. However, it is still important to properly tag and describe visual content for search engines and visitors. This includes adding an ALT description to all key images and, if relevant, a caption. This is vital for linking images as their ALT tags act like anchor text, so are given much more weight than for non-linking images.

Enhance search engine listings

Structured data mark-up is a way of providing additional meaning and context to the search engines about the content of a page, so they can create 'rich snippets' that enhance its listing on the SERPs. The main standard for structured data is ratified by **www.schema.org** and can be applied to a huge variety of data: for example, reviews, locations, people, events and products. When properly tagged, structured data can enhance search engine listings with star ratings, dates and additional information that benefits users and can also improve click-through rates. It is worth exploring the information contained in Google's Webmaster Guides as well as Schema.org to see which data types within a site can be tagged to enhance the user experience.

Another way to enhance search engine listings is through Google Authorship. When a connection is established between an author and the content they create through Authorship, Google displays the author's profile picture, name and a link to their Google+ profile (see Figure 5.2).

FIGURE 5.2   Screenshot showing Google Authorship

WordPress › Google+ Author Information in Search Results (Free ...
wordpress.org/.../**google**-author-information-in-search-results-w... ▾
by Florian Simeth
25 Oct 2013 - A) Set up **authorship** by linking your content to your Google+
profile. Create a Google+ Profile (http://plus.**google**.com); Follow this link to
open ...

Content – the most important thing on your site

Content is the single most important thing on your website: period. Unique, relevant, informative content is what sets your site apart from the competition. It is the reason users want to visit you, why other sites will want to link to you and, of course, why search engines will want to suggest your site to their users in search results.

The term content, if you take it literally, encompasses everything on your website. It includes all the visual elements on the site – the flashy graphics, animations, videos, banners, etc – that the search engine spiders can't see, and of course all of the text, which they can. In the context of SEO though, when we talk about content, we're really talking about the text on each of your web pages.

When writing content for your site the key thing to remember is that you are writing it, first and foremost, for a *human audience*, not for search engine spiders. Yes, your pages need to be 'search engine friendly', but the spiders should *always* be a secondary consideration: put your human audience first.

Frankly, if your copy doesn't engage real, live people when they arrive – address their needs right from the start – then investing time and resources to attract more search engine traffic is pointless. If your content doesn't deliver, visitors will leave as soon as they arrive. Remember, on the web you don't have a captive audience. The user is in control... one click, and they're gone.

Your copy needs to be relevant, it has to be interesting, and above all it has to provide the answers the user is looking for. It needs to do all of this quickly, in a concise, easily scannable way (see the section on content in Chapter 3 for more on creating good web copy).

Content and the search engines

Search engines have evolved rapidly, and are now in what is considered to be their third generation. Each generation has become much 'smarter' than the last at interpreting the actual visible content on a page, and judging its relevance to the user. Today's generation of search engines, unlike their predecessors, don't rely on meta-data to judge the content of a page, they analyse and interpret the actual content presented to the user. And they're getting better all the time at doing it.

Ultimately all of the mysterious 'voodoo' behind search engine ranking algorithms is about analysing and prioritizing your content. There are all sorts of criteria that contribute to the process – some known, many guessed at, and no doubt some that we'll never know. At the end of the day though, they all combine to measure just two things: the relevance and authority of your page content in the context of what the user typed into the search box.

Search engine optimization for sustainable high ranking, therefore, hinges on the production of great original content that appeals to real, live people.

Keywords in content

The subject of keywords in content is something that generates a lot of debate in SEO circles: where to place them, when and how often they need to appear on the page and lots more besides. As with most things SEO, opinions tend to vary significantly on the subject.

Our advice: don't worry too much about it. If you're writing copy about a specific set of keyword phrases, there is a high probability you'll use those keyword phrases and related phrases organically in your writing, and will achieve a natural balance. That's exactly what search engines are looking for. Focus on writing compelling copy that addresses the needs of your target audience while keeping your target keywords for that page in mind, and the search engines will do the rest.

'Just make sure that your chosen keyword or phrase is contained in the title tag and URL, and then simply make sure your content's on topic', advises Jason Duke:

> Don't worry about any other 'on page' SEO such as keyword density, meta tags, this trick or that trick, as it's all so 1999!
>
> Search engines are now more than intelligent enough to understand the semantic relationships between words and phrases, so trying to assist them with certain keyword densities is a fruitless effort. Leave them to their algorithms, and simply enjoy the rewards that their efforts can deliver to you and your website.

There is no magical number of words per page or number of times to use your phrases in your copy. The important thing is to use your keyword phrases only when and where it makes sense to do so for the real people reading your pages. Simply sticking keyword phrases at the top of the page for no apparent reason isn't going to cut it, and it just looks silly.

Links – second only to content

The critical importance of links in securing a high page ranking is one of the few things that has universal consensus in the world of SEO. Popular opinion maintains that nothing, but nothing, is more important than high-quality inbound links from 'authority' websites in achieving high rankings in the search engine results.

But wait a minute... if nothing is more important than links, why did we just say in the heading that links are second only to content? Simple: because creating outstanding content is the most effective way of attracting high-quality inbound links from authoritative online sources. And there's no doubt that those are the links that have the biggest impact on your search engine rankings.

Why are links so important?

Search engines need to determine two things when they attempt to fulfil a user's search request – they need to decide which pages in their index are relevant to the user's query, and then they need to rank those pages in terms of quality and importance. And therein lies one of their biggest challenges, because a search engine algorithm can't read the content and assess its quality the way a human can – at least, not yet.

Instead the engines have to rely on other criteria, and one of the main things that indicates a page's perceived importance to a search engine's ranking algorithm is the quantity and quality of references – or links – to that page from other web pages. Each link to a page is, if you like, a vote of confidence for that page. The more links that point to an individual page (and globally to the site as a whole), the higher the collective vote of confidence for that page (and/or site) becomes, and the more important the page is deemed to be by the search engines.

But of course it's not quite that simple.

Votes from different pages carry more or less weight depending on the perceived importance/quality of the source page, the type of link, the anchor text used in the link and a host of other factors taken into account by the search engine ranking algorithms. When you consider the tangled skein of interconnecting links that make up the world wide web, you begin to appreciate the complexity inherent in assessing the relative importance/quality of all of those pages in relation to one another.

Fundamentally though, what it boils down to is that incoming links in general are a good thing, and play a critical role in determining your search engine rankings. The more links you have pointing to your site, the higher your perceived authority – but there's a caveat. For 'votes' to be counted, the incoming links have to pass certain search engine filtering criteria. Those that fall outside the engines' criteria (generally any link that is designed to hoodwink search engine's into assigning higher rankings rather than to guide site users to a relevant page – check the search engine guidelines for more information) are either ignored (ie their votes are not counted) or, more seriously, can have a negative impact on your ranking.

While all incoming links that satisfy the search engines' criteria will influence your ranking in a positive way, it makes sense to try and maximize the value of your incoming links by focusing your link-building efforts on quality links over quantity. Attracting high-quality, natural links from authority sites with subject matter that is aligned with the content on your site is the real key to high rankings. That's not easy, but the way to get those kinds of links is, of course, producing outstanding content that high-authority sites will want to point their users towards.

Links from authority sites are probably the single most significant factor in boosting your site's overall rankings in the SERPs. A single link from, say, the CNN.com or BBC.co.uk homepage could be worth more to your site in terms of ranking and exposure than countless links from smaller, relatively unknown sites. Authority sites, by their very nature, also tend to be high traffic sites, and you'll inevitably garner some direct traffic as people click through to your site via the link.

The flip side of this, of course, is that links from authority sites are notoriously difficult to secure, while links from smaller, less well-known sites generally take less effort. It's a case of swings and roundabouts, but in practice your aim should be to get as many inbound links as possible from sites with as high a perceived authority level as possible.

The role of internal and external links

Internal links and external links are both important for boosting the ranking of individual pages within your site. First let's define exactly what we mean by internal and external links.

External links: these are links that reside on pages that do not belong to your domain – in other words, links from other websites.

Internal links: these are the links that reside on pages that belong to your domain or subdomains – in other words, links between pages on the same website, or pages that reside in subdomains of the primary domain.

All of these links are important. Links from reputable external sources boost your site's perceived authority with the search engines, which in turn helps your more popular pages to rank higher in the SERPs. Internal links give you a way of distributing the 'authority' accrued by your more popular pages (like your homepage, for example) to other important pages that you want to rank for. Internal links can also help to group pages of related content. For example, using a 'related posts' list helps to make site content more engaging, and encourage visitors to explore the site rather than bounce off a page as soon as it has been visited.

Getting good links

There are a huge number of ways that you can encourage people to link to your site. But building quality natural links isn't easy, and it takes time. It depends on creating high-quality content, and building a reputation for excellence (or notoriety – which can work well for links, but might not project the right image to your customers) in your chosen field, which in turn encourages other website owners to link to you.

There are, of course, some quicker, easier ways to secure incoming links, but such links tend to either be of poor quality (hence of little SEO value), or violate search engine guidelines. Search engines take a dim view of anyone trying to artificially manipulate search results. Remember, they are trying to deliver the most relevant, highest quality results to their users – and see any attempt by a less relevant or lower quality site to leapfrog up the rankings as 'search engine spam'.

Harvesting links purely for the purpose of boosting your site's rankings in the search engines is frowned upon, and while it may work in the short term, it's a risky strategy at best that will ultimately harm your rankings, and may even result in your entire site being blacklisted and removed from the search engines' indexes altogether. If you're trying to build a sustainable, long-term online business it simply isn't worth the risk.

For sustainable long-term rankings, focus instead on building high-quality links through ethical means, concentrate on your content, and build your site with your end user in mind. Exploiting search engine loopholes and 'clever' tricks to artificially boost your rankings isn't really search engine optimization, it's search engine manipulation, and that will ultimately backfire. Working within search engine guidelines may mean that it takes a lot longer to achieve the rank you're looking for, but in the end it is generally better that way.

Link-building tips:

- **Generate truly valuable content that other sites will want to link to:** these one-way unsolicited links are by far the most valuable kind.

Search engines love them, and see them as a genuine endorsement of one site by another. As your site becomes more visible, the content will organically attract more links, which in turn will improve your visibility, attracting even more links. When it works, this process is self-perpetuating, leaving you free to concentrate on quality content, while the links look after themselves.

- **Let people know your site is out there:** people can only link to your site if they know it is there. Promote your site at every opportunity, especially in places where you know there are other website owners. Use the medium to your advantage. Online communities, forums, social networking sites and e-mail lists all offer great opportunities to get your site URL out in front of people who can link to it. Blogs are another source of potential links – some blogs are incredibly popular, and bloggers are noted for their affinity to linking. Try submitting a few poignant comments to high-ranking blogs in your sector (do this responsibly; aim to add real value to the discussion rather than simply promoting your site – see Chapter 7 for more on using blogs to promote your site).

- **Create your own blog:** a blog can be an incredibly powerful promotional and link-building tool, if used wisely. If you have strong opinions, or a high level of knowledge in your industry, and you are happy to write regular posts, setting up a blog is easy and can be a great way to increase both visibility and incoming links.

- **Network, network, network:** use your network of contacts both online and offline to promote your site and encourage people to link to it, and pass it on to their own network of contacts in turn. If people look at your site and like what they see, they may well link to it.

- **Ask the people who link to your competitors to link to you:** use tools such as Moz Open Site Explorer, SearchMetrics, LinkDex or MajesticSEO to find out who is linking to your main competition for your selected search keywords. Approach those sites and ask them if they would be willing to link to your site too. After all, if they link to your competitors, why wouldn't they?

- **Encourage links within content and with descriptive anchor text:** links within content are preferable to links on a page that just lists links. Surrounding content helps to put a link in context, both for the user and for the search engines. You should also encourage descriptive anchor text that, if possible, includes one or two of your chosen keywords.

- **Submit your site to high-quality directories:** getting your site listed in high-quality, well-respected online directories such as the Open Directory Project (**www.dmoz.com,** which is free) and Yahoo! Directory (**dir.yahoo.com,** which charges an annual fee for commercial listings) can be a great way to get your link-building started. These links will help both search engine spiders and that all-important human traffic to find your site. As leading directories are also considered 'authority' sites by the major search engines, links from these sites will also help boost your ranking.

- **Use link bait:** link bait is anything that will entice incoming natural links from other websites or users. Link bait can be an interesting or controversial article, a downloadable document or report, a plug-in that improves the functionality of a piece of software or useful widgets (small snippets of code) that other website owners can embed into the sidebars and content of their pages that include a link back to your landing page. Link bait is really ANYTHING that could entice someone else to link to your content. Be creative! Just stay within the search engines' published guidelines.

- **Offer to swap links with a select few relevant, high-quality sites:** these are called reciprocal links. Although they are less useful than they used to be in terms of SEO value, they can still be used effectively in moderation. While the power of reciprocal links to boost your rankings has been diluted, they do help to establish relevance and authority in your subject area – just be sure that you link to relevant, high-quality sites, and only swap links with a few of them. As a rule of thumb, you should *never* – just for the sake of a reciprocal link – link to a site that you wouldn't genuinely recommend to your site visitors.

Submitting your site URL and sitemap

Submitting your site URL, strictly speaking, isn't necessary any more. If you have followed the advice above, and have managed to secure some inbound links, it won't be long before the spiders find you. That said, all of the major search engines offer a free submission process, and submitting your site won't hurt. If you want to kick-start the indexing process, then by all means go ahead and manually submit your homepage and one or two other important pages.

The other thing you can do that will help search engines to crawl all relevant pages on your website is to submit an XML sitemap that adheres to the sitemap protocol outlined on **www.sitemaps.org**, which defines a sitemap as follows:

> Sitemaps are an easy way for webmasters to inform search engines about pages on their sites that are available for crawling. In its simplest form, a Sitemap is an XML file that lists URLs for a site along with additional metadata about each URL (when it was last updated, how often it usually changes, and how important it is, relative to other URLs in the site) so that search engines can more intelligently crawl the site.
>
> Web crawlers usually discover pages from links within the site and from other sites. Sitemaps supplement this data to allow crawlers that support Sitemaps to pick up all URLs in the Sitemap and learn about those URLs using the associated metadata. Using the Sitemap protocol does not guarantee that web pages are included in search engines, but provides hints for web crawlers to do a better job of crawling your site.

The sitemap protocol was originally introduced by Google in June 2005 to allow web developers to publish lists of URLs for search engines to crawl. Google, MSN and Yahoo announced joint support for the new protocol in November 2006.

Submitting a sitemap won't do anything to up your pages' rankings, but it will provide additional information that can help search engines to crawl your site more effectively. It is one more thing you can do to improve the odds, so ask your webmaster, web developer or SEO to include a sitemap for your site, and to either manually submit it to the major search engines, or to add an entry in your robots.txt file (a file that sits in the root directory of your webserver that contains instructions for automated crawlers) that lets them pick it up automatically.

Local SEO

Any business that gets some or all of its customers or clients locally should consider local SEO. That could be a local restaurant, retail outlet, doctor, dentist or lawyer, but it could just as easily be a local ad agency. If you have a physical address in a city and expect people to go there, you should be doing local SEO for that location.

While all of the factors that apply to regular SEO also impact local SEO (on-page factors, links, content, indexing, etc), local comes with a few unique elements. The first and probably most important is that for local SEO you need to create and claim a local profile on Google (and other platforms as desired). Your local listing is what will usually show for localized search results.

The second most important thing is called a NAP citation, which is any place online that uses your company name, address, phone number. Google views NAP citations in the same way as regular SEO views links – citations from authoritative and relevant sources can help improve your ranking. While Google is very smart, it is important that all citations use the same format as far as possible. Don't abbreviate in one and not the other (St versus Street, for example).

Third, you need reviews. Lots and lots of reviews (preferably really good ones). The quantity and quality of reviews left for your business on your Google Places page is one of the most important local ranking factors.

The three biggest factors in local listings appear to be the number of citations, the number of reviews (primarily on your Google Places listing, although other places do count), and how positive the reviews are overall. From what we've seen, positive reviews will trump citations, so persuading your customers and clients to recommend you on your Google local page is the single most important thing you can do.

And start all over again....

Now you have your site optimized, it's time to sit back and start reaping the rewards, right?

Unfortunately not! The ever-changing nature of the search environment means that there is no magic bullet in SEO. It's not a one-size-fits-all discipline, and it never ends. You have to work hard to find the right blend of targeted keywords for your particular business, operating within your particular market at the current point in time. You have to optimize your pages based on those keywords, and deliver compelling, high-impact content. You have to attract incoming links.

Then you have to measure, monitor and refine continuously, tweaking and tuning your optimization efforts based on changing conditions in the marketplace, the search engines and your customers. Take your foot off the gas, and that high ranking you've worked so hard to achieve will gradually (and sometimes not so gradually) start to slip away.

Optimization is a dynamic and iterative process – and if you want sustained results it needs to be ongoing. In this section we have barely scratched the surface of the wonderfully dynamic, often frustrating but potentially incredibly rewarding world of search engine optimization. To learn more, check out some of the free and subscription-based SEO resources online such as SEO Book (**http://bit.ly/UDMSEOBook**), visit **www.gogadm.com**...

or just 'Google' it. After all, it's reasonable for you to expect the best people to advise you on your SEO to be up there near the top of the SERPs.

Advertising on the search engines

Paid search marketing, pay-per-click (PPC) advertising or search engine marketing (SEM) as it is also known, has in a very short space of time transformed search from what was essentially seen as a 'loss leader' activity into what is probably the digital world's biggest cash cow. PPC advertising is the principal way in which the search engines generate revenue... lots of revenue. According to figures released by the Interactive Advertising Bureau (IAB), paid search revenue for the United States came in at US $16.9 billion for 2012, a figure that accounted for just over 46 per cent of total online advertising spend.

What is paid search engine advertising?

Paid search marketing refers to the paid-for advertising that usually appears alongside, above and occasionally below the organic listings on the SERPs or on a partner site. These are usually labelled with something like 'sponsored links' or 'sponsored results' in order to make it clear to users that they are, in fact, paid-for ads and not part of the search engine's organic listing.

Typically, you pay each time your ad is clicked, hence 'pay per click' or PPC. PPC is the most common form of paid search marketing but you can also buy ads on a 'cost per thousand' (CPM) basis.

It's no surprise that the biggest players in the pay-per-click arena are the leading search engines: Google AdWords and Microsoft Search Advertising (which also serves ads on the Yahoo! network). You will also find a number of smaller PPC search programmes out there targeting niche areas or serving particular verticals. Explore your options, because depending on your business they may offer better opportunities to reach local, industry specific or specialized niche markets than the larger players. By and large, though, when we're talking about paid search advertising the 'big two' are where the action is for most online businesses.

How does paid search advertising work?

When a user enters a search query into the search engine, the engine returns a list of organic search results. It also determines which ads to show that are relevant to the search query. These ads, which sit adjacent to or above the organic listings, used to be small, unobtrusive text-based ads, but now may come with enhanced listings that include images and other data such as price and merchant name. While high ranking in the organic listing is the ideal that most webmasters are striving for (because it's 'free' and because users see organic results as impartial: they trust, and therefore click on, organic listings in preference to paid ads), optimizing a page to rank in organic search results can be difficult, and getting a consistently high and sustainable ranking takes a substantial amount of effort and a lot of time.

Time without traffic, of course, is a missed opportunity for your online business, and that's where paid search advertising comes in. By agreeing to pay the search engines a fee per click for your ads to show up as sponsored result when a user types in your chosen keywords, you can put your site in front of your prospect in the SERPs almost immediately. When the user clicks on one of your ads, you get a new visitor and the search engine bills you for the click: everybody is happy, at least in theory.

PPC keywords are bid on by advertisers in an auction-style system: generally the higher the bid per click, the higher the ad's placement in the SERPs. Most PPC systems also employ a 'quality' quotient into their ad placement rankings, based on the popularity of the ad (its click-through rate, or CTR) and the perceived quality of both the ad content and the landing page it points to (eg Google's AdWords Quality Score).

Why use paid search marketing?

There are a lot of reasons to use PPC search marketing. Here are just a few:

- **Generate traffic while you're waiting for your SEO to kick in:** it can take months to get your site to the top half of the first page of organic search results through SEO. PPC ads can get your site in front of your audience almost immediately.

- **Highly targeted ads means a better chance of conversion:** you're not broadcasting your message to the masses as you would be with a display ad or banner ad – your search marketing ad will only appear in front of users who have prequalified themselves by typing your chosen keywords into the search engine in the geographical regions you have selected.

  It can be an incredibly effective way to advertise. You only pay for your ad when a prequalified user clicks on it and is taken to your site. If they don't click, you don't pay. Providing your keywords are highly targeted and your landing pages convert well, it can generate a very healthy ROI. Some of the specific benefits of PPC advertising are:

– **Full financial control:** there is no minimum spend, you can set maximum monthly budgets on an account-wide basis or on individual campaigns, and you specify the maximum amount per click that you are prepared to pay for each ad.

– **Full editorial control:** you are in complete control of every aspect of your campaign – from the title and ad copy, to the keywords and keyword matching option to apply, to the URL of the page you want users sent to.

– **Testing, tracking and tweaking on the fly:** there are tools that allow you to run real-time comparison tests to see how differences in your ads affect your click-through rate, and a host of reporting options that let you track your campaign and tweak it to achieve better results.

– **Improve your reach:** target different keywords to those you rank for in the organic search, and broaden your reach for those more specific long-tail keywords that yield small volumes high-value traffic.

– **Transcend the boundaries of the SERPS:** for even broader reach you get to select whether you want your ads to appear only on the search engine's own sites, on their advertising affiliate sites, or even on specific affiliate sites of your choosing.

Sounds great, how do I get started?

Unsurprisingly, the search engines have made setting up PPC campaigns really easy. There are automated wizards to guide you through the sign-up process, and plenty of tools to help you establish, monitor and optimize your campaign. It's all very slick, and from a standing start you can have your first ad appearing next to search results and driving traffic to your site in under 15 minutes.

But hold your horses... just because you can, doesn't necessarily mean that you should. Rushing headlong into your first PPC advertising campaign might yield great results for you 'out of the box', and then again it might not. As always, it pays to do a bit of preparation first.

Choose your keywords wisely

Look for longer keyword phrases that are likely to be less competitive and will send highly-targeted traffic to your site. Ideally you should aim for phrases that generate a healthy amount of search engine traffic, without attracting a lot of bids from other advertisers.

Keywords are the foundation blocks for any successful PPC account. To ensure maximum return on investment, a list of relevant keywords must be researched that correctly represents the products and services offered by the website. The presence of these keywords will ensure that when a user enters their search query into the search engine, a quality ad will be triggered and a sale captured.

There are different types of keywords that can be used within an account:

- Brand keywords: including variations, eg Croud, Croud Marketing, Croud PPC – great converting words.

- Product-specific keywords: search engine marketing agency, PPC account management – essential in the buying cycle.

- Generic keywords: SEM, SEO, PPC – high-volume keywords and typically high CPCs too.

- Long-tail keywords: low volume but often excellent conversions.

- Misspellings: search mraketing, account managemant – often less competition, so lower CPC.

- Negative keywords: a negative keyword is a search term that the advertiser does not want its advertisement to appear against. For example, if you sell cruise holidays you might add '–tom' as a negative so you don't show on searches for 'Tom Cruise'.

It is important to build a relevant keyword list with the correct mix of the different types of keywords, so that adverts can be displayed to capture users based on all the different types of search behaviour at different stages of the buying cycle.

Match types

Match type selection can massively affect CPCs and 'quality score', and needs careful planning. Google has led the way with match types so we detail their policy below. To ensure the largest audience is reached by the keywords it is possible to apply different match types that will make the keyword work harder.

FIGURE 5.3 Keywords: an example of 'exact match'

Example		
Exact match keyword	**Ads may show on searches for**	**Ads won't show on searches for**
[women's hats]	women's hats woman's hats	buy women's hats women's hats on sale

Exact match

When keywords are added on this match type the advert will only ever appear following a search for this particular keyword (see Figure 5.3).

Phrase match

With 'phrase match', the advert can show when someone searches for the advertiser's exact keyword, or the advertiser's exact keyword with additional words before or after it. Using phrase match, the advertiser appears not only when the exact phrase is the search term but also when phrases are searched for which contain that particular phrase. The advertiser's ads won't appear for similar phrases or when the words are ordered differently (see Figure 5.4).

Broad match

By adding keywords on broad match, a business's ads may appear in response to the specific search itself, the search term with other words before or after it and for the keyword phrased in a different order and with words in between the keyword. Google may also elect to display advertiser's ads against 'related keywords', which may not even include the search term in question (see Figure 5.5).

Since the main engines provide advertisers with three different match types, and since 'broad match' is often likely to display the advertiser's ad against other keywords that the advertiser wasn't expecting, but which the engine deems to be relevant, there are ways in which an advertiser can control the searches that their advertising appears in response to.

Broad match modifier

This is a process whereby an advertiser, within Google, adds a 'plus sign' to the start of a particular keyword. Doing this ensures that any of the searches

FIGURE 5.4   Keywords: an example of 'phrase match'

Example

Phrase match keyword	Ads may show on searches for	Ads won't show on searches for
women's hats	women's hats buy women's hats woman's hats Women's hats	girls hats womens baseball hats

FIGURE 5.5   Keywords: an example of 'broad match'

Example

Broad match keyword	Ads may show on searches for
women's hats	women's hats buy ladies hats womens caps hats for girls womans hats Buy red hats for women

carried out by users must include this word or words in order for the advertisement to appear. Unlike broad match keywords, modified broad match keywords won't show the ad for synonyms or related searches. For this reason, it adds an additional level of control to broad matching.

A few points to keep in view

Three key things to remember when advertising on the search engines:

- **Optimize your ads:** your ads need to entice users to click on them if you're going to get traffic. Think carefully about your title and ad copy. Remember you want targeted copy that will appeal to people who are *ready to buy* – so be specific. Generating clicks that don't convert here *will cost you money*!

- **Converting clicks into customers:** once you get the clicks, you need to turn your new prospects into paying customers as often as you can. It is your *conversion rate* that will make or break your PPC campaign. Don't direct traffic from your ad back to your homepage. Send it instead to a page directly related to the text of the ad they have just clicked on – a product page might work, but better still would be a specific *landing page* tailored to reinforce your PPC campaign. Remember, if you fail to convert your traffic into revenue, all your PPC campaign will do is haemorrhage cash.

- **Measure everything and test, test, test:** the best way to learn is to start small, track your campaign carefully and study the metrics (see Chapter 4). Try out different ad combinations, different landing pages, different keyword combinations and measure how the changes affect your CTR, your conversion rate, your cost per conversion and, ultimately, your bottom line.

Mastering the intricacies of PPC advertising could take a lifetime, but the basics are straightforward enough, and the best way to learn is to dive in and start using it. You'll also find plenty of resources to help you, both in the search engines' advertising sections and in the online marketing community. A great place to start is the free online webinars in the Google Learn Classroom (**www.google.com/ads/learn**) and Bing's resources for advertisers (**http://advertise.bingads.microsoft.com/en-us/how-to**).

What are the downsides?

There are surprisingly few if you manage your campaign carefully and stay on top of your spending and conversion rates. The biggest one is that as bigger businesses continue to wake up to the potential of search marketing, and funnel more of their advertising spend online, the cost per click of more competitive keyword phrases is being pushed ever upwards. Highly competitive keywords can soon get prohibitively expensive for smaller advertisers, but by getting clever with your use of long-tail keywords there are still plenty of opportunities to reap real rewards from PPC advertising.

The key thing to remember is that you have to pay for every click whether or not you convert – so it is important to keep track of the metrics and make sure you're getting value from your investment.

Top 10 tips for paid search marketing success

1 Define your goals and objectives before you start any paid search campaigns.

2 Target your search account to your website – create individual ad groups around products and services you have pages for.

3 Keep keywords in each ad group to a minimum and ensure they are all thematically relevant – ideally less than 25 keywords per ad group.

4 Write bespoke creative for each ad group and always run with three or four variations of messaging so you can test which works most effectively for your business.

5 Think carefully about match types: don't put everything on the default broad match option unless you know what you are doing.

6 Include as many negatives as possible and look to add these at an ad group level.

7 Decide carefully about whether to use in-house skills or an agency, and complete proper due diligence.

8 Focus always on the 'quality score' and the user experience. Setting up search badly hits your pocket very hard, and costs much more money than is necessary.

9 Keep a close eye on competitors and the search landscape – their messaging and keyword coverage gives you an indication of what will work for you!

10 Optimize, optimize and optimize the account – this needs to be done regularly in order to get the best out of performance.

Integrating SEO and paid search

In a constantly changing market, using paid search unassisted or relying totally on the power of SEO will never fulfil the total potential of a brand's online performance. Where SEO has always been effective is in its long-term viability as a low-cost acquisition model. PPC, on the other hand, offers instant gratification – the main reward of a successful integration of PPC and SEO is measured in conversions.

Use PPC to inform the viability of targeting terms for the SEO strategy. With Google continuing to encrypt referring search terms in ever greater numbers, there is no keyword level tracking available to any analytics teams, therefore PPC data is becoming the only accurate way of testing keyword conversion rates. PPC conversion data will underpin all SEO keyword research.

PPC creative is also the best way of testing click-through rates. As standard best practice is to rotate three or four pieces of creative to increase the click-through rate, the best performing is a natural fit for SEO descriptions.

If a page has a higher-than-average bounce rate, this is an alert to Google that the page is not relevant for that search term and will not only see wasted paid-for clicks but a gradual downgrading of that page's authority, By monitoring analytics closely we can be sure to spot these issues and bring in the SEO team to improve on page factors and content.

Mobile search

Consumer behaviour has fundamentally shifted as a result of mobile technologies, and established industries have been totally disrupted by the velocity of change. Consumers are leading the way, and businesses that fail to place mobile at the heart of their business strategy, are going to struggle to keep up.

Nick Hynes, co-founder and CEO, Somo

Over the last seven years, every year has been the 'year of mobile', but now mobile search is most definitely here and it is consuming more and more marketing dollars every month – in the four weeks to the end of December 2012, eBay made a sale on mobile every second.

One of the most keenly anticipated aspects of the Enhanced Campaign rolled out from Google during the second half of 2013 had to be the 'Cross–Device' tracking functionality, part of the 'Estimated Total Conversions' insight that will soon include data on calls and in-store visits.

For years, advertisers have understood that multiple devices are involved in a user's conversion cycle, and to have a closer understanding of the process is key to maximizing the potential for their online activity. The problem has been simply that previously marketers haven't been able to align the data.

Now, when a user is signed in to their Google accounts across multiple devices (mobile, tablet, desktop etc), Google can record the user journey to a point of conversion from clicks from each different device and then use this data to provide an 'estimated total number of cross device conversions'.

What this will do is give advertisers far more insight into the role of various devices in the conversion cycle and better data to optimize to for accounts. The undoubted outcome will be an increase in mobile-device targeting, as advertisers are able to attribute better and understand mobile's involvement in the overall key business-performance metrics. One thing is for certain – the importance of mobile will continue to grow at astonishing rates!

Search marketing has always been about serving the right ad to the right audience at the right time. Now, with today's searcher moving continuously across platforms – from mobile, to tablet, to desktop – it's also about serving the ad in the right format on the right device. Search is focused on responding to demand in a time-critical way, but the level of optimization required to do that successfully has massively increased. Mobile search is an increasingly competitive landscape, and one that's growing at a phenomenal rate – this year it looks like more than half of all mobile ad spend will come from paid search.

Nick Hynes, co-founder and CEO, Somo

Black hat, the darker side of search

The SEO methods explored earlier in this chapter are methods that adhere to the search engine's own guidelines (or at least they did at the time of writing – but guidelines can change, so it is important to keep up to date: check the links to the webmaster resources earlier in this chapter for the latest information). Generally referred to as 'white hat' SEO, these techniques are seen as legitimate optimization of a site to align it with the needs of the site visitor and simultaneously make the site content accessible and easy to index by the search engines.

But there is another side to SEO – an altogether darker and more sinister side, where less ethical practitioners attempt to exploit every trick and loophole they can find in order to 'game' the engines, increase their rankings and drive traffic to their sites. Dubbed 'black hat' SEO, search engine spamming or spamdexing (spamming the indexes) when discovered, offending sites are quickly banned from the search engine index.

But the black hat SEO isn't worried by bans or penalties. For a black hat, banishment from the search engines comes with the territory. They are not interested in building quality sites with sustainable high rankings – they're looking for short-term gains from high-traffic to ad-laden sites. By the time one batch of sites has been banned they have already moved on to the next. Black hatters typically have many sites running on many different domains across a variety of hosts, all exploiting loopholes in the system to artificially boost their rankings and generate advertising revenue.

Why should I care what colour hat these guys wear?

On one level, you shouldn't need to. The battle that is raging over artificially inflated rankings in the SERPs is between the black hatters and the search engines. It is up to the Yahoo!s, Googles and Microsofts of this world to wage that war.

Wherever there is a system in place you will find people – often some of the most innovative and resourceful people out there – attempting to exploit that system for their own gain. You will also have some equally resourceful people on the other side trying to stop them. It's human nature, and it's not going away any time soon.

Essentially, black hatters are simply taking the principles of SEO we discussed earlier in this chapter – creating a list of keywords, building pages, getting links – and pushing the boundaries to the extreme. Instead of a manageable selection of keywords for which they can create unique and engaging content, black hatters typically create lists of hundreds or thousands of keywords and stuff their pages full of keyword-rich bunkum created by automated content-generation tools. Instead of building links naturally, they use automated 'bots' to spam posts stuffed with links into blog comments, guest books, forums and wikis all over the web.

Black hats typically are not interested in you or your site – unless it's as a possible repository for link spam in your blog, guestbook, forum or wiki (and that can generally be avoided by implementing security features on your site that require human intervention to post). What is perhaps more significant is that by pushing their spammy sites up the SERPs they are artificially pushing down more legitimate sites like yours, making them less visible to searchers and potentially affecting your traffic and revenue.

Some common black hat SEO techniques

- **Keyword stuffing:** repeating keywords over and over again on a given web page. This is less successful now as search engine algorithms are better at distinguishing this gobbledegook from properly written content.

- **Cloaking:** a technique that uses code to show one search-engine-friendly page to the spider, and a completely different page to a human visitor. The engines hate this as it makes it impossible for them to gauge the quality of the content a user is seeing. In early 2006 Google blacklisted car manufacturer BMW's German website **www.bmw.de**, dropping it from its index for employing a cloaking page.

- **Invisible text:** essentially text that is the same colour as the background of the page – result, humans can't see it, search engines can. This is like keyword stuffing – but with the cloaking element of showing different content to the search engine bot and the human visitor.

- **Doorway page:** these are highly optimized web pages whose sole purpose is to send traffic to other pages either through an automatic redirect or by simply being full of links.

- **Spam page:** a page with no meaningful content that is full of ads from which the webmaster makes money if someone clicks on them.

- **Interlinking:** the practice of setting up multiple websites on a given topic and linking backwards and forwards between them purely in an attempt to increase their rankings in the search engines.

- **Buying and selling links to help boost search ranking:** buying and selling links purely to manipulate your search engine ranking is frowned upon by the search engines. In early 2011 leading US retailer JC Penny hit the headlines when it was seriously penalized by Google after the *New York Times* revealed an extensive link-buying programme implemented by the company's outsourced SEO agency.

- **Buying expired domains:** buying up expired domains that contained high-ranking pages to try and garner some of the old site's inbound 'link-juice'.

This is just a small selection of the techniques that black hat SEOs use to boost their rankings and drive traffic. There are many more. As a rule of thumb for your own site, if what you're doing *adds genuine value to the end user*, you generally have nothing to worry about. If, on the other hand, you're implementing something to artificially manipulate your search engine rankings you could be venturing into grey – or even black hat – territory. If you value your domain's long-term reputation, be very careful.

When you come across these sites while browsing the web they can be irritating, and having to deal with spam in any medium is infuriating, but for the most part your business doesn't need to worry too much about the black hats who are doing their own thing to their own websites.

But there is another, more sinister aspect...

Negative SEO

Far more worrying, potentially at least, is the concept of negative SEO. Some black hat SEOs have started peddling commercial services, not to increase their client's rankings in the SERPs but to damage the ranking of their competitors – or even to get them banned altogether.

Dubbed negative SEO, it is still uncommon, but is certainly something that webmasters and online marketers need to be aware of. Google, the leading search engine, maintains that there is 'almost nothing a competitor can do to harm your ranking or have your site removed from our index'. But that '*almost*' has got people worried.

In June 2007 *Forbes* magazine brought the subject of negative SEO out of the shadows of the search community and presented it to a mainstream audience. In the *Forbes* article, two SEOs admitted to journalist Andy Greenberg that they use negative SEO, and revealed some of its implications.

'I understand the rules of search', SEO Brendon Scott said in the article. 'And once you understand the rules, you can use them not just constructively, but also destructively.' He went on to claim that he could reduce a competing site's visibility to searchers, or even make it seem to disappear from search results altogether.

Negative SEO was spawned, ironically, from the efforts of Google, Yahoo! and other search engines in order to filter out the spam generated by black hat SEO and keep their search results relevant to their users. As part of the battle against spam, the search engine algorithms identify 'spammy' tactics and penalize the offending site's rankings accordingly. If there are enough, or severe enough, transgressions to the search engine's guidelines, the site could be thrown out of the index altogether.

Some of the negative SEO tactics that could have a negative impact on a site's rankings include, but are far from limited to:

- **DOS and 404 errors:** the attacker initiates a denial of service attack (DOS) to swamp the target domain. Once the target domain is down, the attacker then employs numerous methods to encourage search engine spiders to visit the site. If the spiders arrive and receive a 404 (not found) error, those pages will typically be de-indexed. Once the server recovers, the website is up and running, but is no longer appearing in the search results.

- **Redirection:** the attacker redirects to the targeted pages from 'bad neighbourhood' sites such as porn sites, link farms, etc. The targeted pages can end up being removed from the search engine index through association with spammy domains.

- **Link bomb:** the attacker links to the targeted pages from blatant link farms or free-for-all link sites, using anchor text with irrelevant or spam-like keywords. They then submit those link-farm pages manually to the search engines, and get as many spammy sites as possible to link in to it. Search engines flag the target site as spam and remove it from their index.

- **Duplicate content:** the attacker copies content from targeted pages and duplicates that content on disposable 'bad neighbourhood' domains, embedding spammy keywords such as porn, pills, casinos, invisible text and other spam flags, this *may* result in both sets of pages being removed from the index.

- **Black social bookmarking:** the attacker sets up multiple accounts with social bookmarking sites, and tags targeted sites excessively with irrelevant and spammy terms such as porn, gambling, pharmaceutical, etc. As a result, the target site may be penalized heavily or even removed from the search engines index once the social bookmark pages have been spidered.

(Source: Fantomaster, formerly at **www.fantomaster.com**)

NB. We in no way condone any of these tactics, and are listing them here merely to illustrate the potential real-world threat of negative SEO for digital marketers.

Negative SEO is potentially a very real threat – but for most websites not a very probable one. It pays to be aware of the possibility, and if you are concerned that your competitors might employ such tactics it at least gives you a heads-up on the sort of things that you should be looking out for.

If you truly believe that your website is under attack through negative SEO, your best bet is to hire a specialist consultant to help you combat the threat in the short term. They will typically help you to identify the nature of the attack, where it is coming from, and help to implement a security plan that will shield your site against future attacks.

Bringing in the pros

While SEO and PPC campaigns can certainly be managed in-house, if you lack specialist search talent and want to fast-track traffic to your site, then bringing in a professional search marketing consultant can pay real dividends.

If you decide to bring in an external consultancy to help with your search marketing, do your homework and choose wisely. There are many excellent SEOs out there who will do a great job of promoting your business online, but equally there are unscrupulous companies looking to exploit the uniniti-ated. Not all SEO companies are created equal, and it is an unfortunate fact that some of them will stray into less than ethical territory to secure high rankings quickly... making them and their services look good in the short term.

The good news is that, having read this chapter, you are now armed with the knowledge you need to engage positively with your prospective search marketing partner, understand what they are telling you, and to discuss your SEO requirements with them in some detail.

Here are a few things to bear in mind when you engage with an SEO professional:

- Make sure you're dealing with a reputable company that has a strong track record to back up their claims.

- Ask to see case studies and get references from previous clients.

- Check their own site – has it been optimized? Does it adhere to search engine guidelines?

- Look and listen for any hint of the black hat techniques listed above. If there is any doubt about the ethics and integrity of the company, walk away. It's your domain they will be playing with, and it's not worth risking your reputation with the engines.

- Once you have engaged an SEO company, don't just leave them to it. You need to keep abreast of what your SEO company is doing on your behalf – after all, it's your site.

Universal search – more opportunities to rank

Universal search is a term coined by Google to describe a fundamental change in the way it presents its web search results. The search company introduced universal search in mid-2007 for Google.com users, and continued rolling it out to other Google domains (.co.uk, .ca, .ie, etc) through 2008. Billed by commentators as one of the most significant and radical developments in the history of the search industry, universal search (or blended search, as it is also known) takes results from Google's specialized (or vertical) search engines (Google News, Google Books, Google Local/ Maps, Google Video, Google Image, Google Groups, etc) and slots them into standard web search results in order of relevance.

Google's then Vice President of Search Products & User Experience, Marissa Mayer, explained it succinctly in post on the official Google blog (**http://googleblog.blogspot.com**) in May 2007: 'With universal search, we're attempting to break down the walls that traditionally separated our various search properties and integrate the vast amounts of information available into one simple set of search results.'

As you would expect, other major search engines were not far behind, and both Yahoo! and Microsoft's Live Search introduced similar blended search results soon after Google. For users, this development is a huge boon. Instead of having to manage and navigate multiple specialized search tools, users can now enter their search query in one convenient location in order to find results across multiple platforms.

But what does all this mean for search marketers? Essentially, there are two ways of looking at it. On one level it is a potential threat, in that for any given keyword phrase your pages now have to compete with results for news, video, maps, discussion groups, images and a host of other sources in order to get those coveted top SERP rankings. On the other hand, if you produce the right sort of content and submit it to the relevant places, universal search offers additional opportunities to rank for your chosen keyword phrases.

Universal search doesn't change any of the SEO advice we provided earlier in the chapter – but it is something to be aware of as you optimize your pages, and it offers additional avenues to get your content in front of your target audience. As the title of Marissa Mayer's blog post says, even with the roll-out of universal search 'the best answer is still the best answer' (see Figure 5.6).

Shifting goalposts – search innovation and the quest for relevance

Search engines by their very nature are always innovating in their quest to deliver that optimum search experience to each and every user who types in a query. The pace of search innovation can be frustrating for search marketers, as it keeps 'shifting the goal posts'. Just when you think you've got this search thing 'sussed' along come the leading search engines with a development that changes things again.

Here's the thing... the search engines don't care a hoot about upsetting your finely honed SEO campaign. Remember the prime directive we discussed right at the start of this chapter? Search engines are striving to deliver the most relevant, valuable content to their users, improving their user experience and retaining or increasing their market share.

To that end, the leading search engines constantly 'tweak' their ranking algorithms, refining the way they assess relevance and authority based on content, links and other factors. This constant tinkering with the nuts and bolts of how search engines assess relevance has always been a challenge

FIGURE 5.6   Universal search results page on Google.com for the search term Darth Vader

for search marketers, but more recent developments, aimed at delivering tailored search results to each individual user, have caused quite a stir in SEO circles.

Personalization: search results tailored to individual users

Back in 2007 Google started to roll out the personalization of search results for users who were signed in with a Google account (the feature was available even earlier to users opting in through the 'Google Labs' interface in their account settings). What it meant was that Google would start taking the search history of users into account when assessing the relevance of search results.

Let's say, for example, that you searched for 'Mustang' while signed in to your Google account, and you had recently been searching and clicking on results for car-related stuff. The search engine might reasonably assume you want information relating to the Ford Mustang car rather than, say, the Wikipedia page for the mustang horse.

Then, in late 2009, Google really shook things up by extending similar search personalization to all users, whether they had a Google account or not (again, users could opt out, but by default the feature was turned on). The move sent the SEO world into turmoil, and instantly rendered as pretty much meaningless the coveted SEO goal of 'being number one in Google' for any given keyword phrase. Now, my number one search result could be different to your number one search result, which could be different to everybody else's number one search result.

Ultimately, search personalization served to move the focus of SEO away from a race to the once coveted positions in the top of the SERPS, and shifted it back to where it really should have been all along: delivering great content that adds real value for users, and making sure that search engines are aware of that, and monitoring and measuring success based not on your position in the SERPS, but on the actual number of targeted visitors referred to your visitors by the search engines. That, after all, is what sustainable SEO is really all about: harnessing the power of search engines to help you deliver outstanding, relevant content to your target market.

Search gets social – integrating updates from online connections into search results

In late 2009 Microsoft fired the first silo in the battle to make search more social by announcing deals with both Twitter and Facebook to include real-time status updates in its Bing search results. Google followed suit by announcing a similar deal with Twitter for its own real-time search, and by introducing a feature it called 'Social Search' into its main web-search offering.

When a web user is signed in to their Google account and conducts a web search, Google now incorporates publicly available content created or recommended by a user's online friends and connections across Google's range of products and other publicly available web services.

That means that along with regular web results, users who are signed in will see relevant content that their online 'friends' have shared publicly on YouTube, Picasa, Flickr, Twitter, on their blog, in their Google Reader and in lots of other places online.

The rationale, of course, is that old search engine mantra of relevance. The web is becoming increasingly social, and people are more willing than ever to share information, opinions and experiences. We also trust the recommendations of people we 'know' online and, by incorporating content from our extended online network into search results, search engines are betting we will find those results more relevant, useful and personal.

What does social integration into search mean for search marketers?

On the surface, having recommendations from a search user's online social connections appear in the standard web SERPS may seem like bad news from a search marketer's perspective. It means that there is yet more content competing for those limited spaces on the first page of the SERPS for any given search term. Then again, if you are creating compelling, useful and... that word again... *relevant* content for your target audience, the stuff that is being recommended in those social search results could easily be yours.

Social search emphasizes the need to get out and engage with your customers in the social arena, to create useful, compelling content that is worth sharing, and to build enduring relationships with the people you want to do business with. The integration of a social element into search results is growing in importance, and while there are privacy concerns and other stumbling blocks that need to be overcome, ultimately the search engines' obsessive quest for relevance is turning search into a very personal experience.

The Knowledge Graph and conversational search

The Knowledge Graph was officially launched in May 2012, and has significantly changed the SERPs and the way that users process and digest information. It displays information in entities rather than on a query level. Google understands that when you search for 'Brad Pitt', for example, you could be looking for information about his past or upcoming films, his biography, or his date of birth, so it shows you all this information based on what it determines is your intent. If you follow this search with the query 'who is his wife?' Google has already decided you are talking about Brad and will show you results for Angelina! For local searches, for example searching on a town or city, we now see a carousel at the top of the SERPs, inviting us to click and explore 'things to do in the city'.

What does this mean to business? We're back to content again because with the Knowledge Graph, Google is giving users the option to stay within the SERPs for longer, as they scan information based on their search.

Looking forward

Both the increasingly widespread adoption of high-speed internet access in the home, and the ever-increasing capability and market penetration of mobile digital devices, are opening up a slew of new digital media opportunities for marketers the world over. The rise of social networking sites, and the word-of-mouth and viral marketing opportunities that they offer (see Chapter 6), may in time dilute the prominence of SEO and paid search advertising in the digital marketing mix. Likewise, as ever-increasing numbers of web users develop a 'feel' for where they need to go to find the things that they want online, or access branded content directly on the move through dedicated smart-phone applications, they are likely to rely less on search for certain things.

As the ways that we interact with the web change, though, search engines are developing to move beyond strings of text typed into little boxes. We reveal so much about ourselves through online search, and Google is increasingly using our data to become less reactive, less keyword driven, and instead to be able to anticipate our needs before we are even aware of them. Search is becoming smarter, more conversational, more context-aware.

While the significance of search may wane for a proportion of people and for certain applications over time, given its current level of importance for both internet users and digital marketers, the propensity of major search engines to innovate and adapt, and the fact that new people are going online and discovering the value of search engines every day, search looks certain to remain a cornerstone of digital marketing for some time to come.

About the contributor

Our thanks to Ben Knight, founder and operations director at digital marketing agency Croud, for his contribution to this chapter.

CASE STUDY   The Entertainer

The Entertainer has 90 stores in the UK, and stocks thousands of products online. With 30 years' experience in the retail industry, they understand perfectly what kids want! With a winning combination of fair prices and excellent customer service, they are quite popular with mums and dads too.

Location

UK

The challenge

Drive online sales and volumes cost-effectively, ensuring a high-quality user experience at all levels and robust coverage across its range of over 5,000 toys.

Target audience

Toy consumers.

Action

- The focus of the strategy was product-listing ads.
- Granular product targets were created to provide maximum control of product-specific visibility (type of toy etc).
- The account structure was mapped to a feed to ensure visibility was tied to stock availability.
- Specific bids were then applied for each of the product targets.
- This allowed micromanagement of bids and performance.
- Bids were reviewed frequently in order to distribute investment in line with performance and maximize cost-effective sales volume.
- Based on performance trends, these bids were then adjusted in order to make the most effective use of the budget available.

- Negative keywords were researched frequently in order to maximize relevancy at a product level.

Results

- Over its first week, product-listing ad activity increased overall non-brand orders by 90 per cent.
- CPCs across the initial period were sustained at a very low rate of £0.01.
- The activity also increased additional but important wider user actions by 73 per cent, such as 'e-mail me when back in stock' requests.
- Product-listing ad activity was so efficient that its 'cost of sale' is in line with brand activity.

Links to campaign

- http://www.croud.co.uk
- http://www.thetoyshop.com/

About the creator

Croud's mission is to make digital marketing accessible to all advertisers, regardless of their size and budget. Founders Luke Smith and Ben Knight realized that the traditional agency model makes digital marketing unnecessarily more expensive and doesn't give all businesses the proper service they deserve. In September 2011, they began to deliver cost-effective digital solutions for clients using only the best marketing talent; thus Croud was born. Croud recognized the evolving employment landscape; that the age of Cloud computing and remote working has offered the ability for digital experts to work flexibly but with the same quality control needed for success. To deliver this unique offering to a wide range of clients, we have built our own technology: **Croud Control**. Our platform allows all our work to be managed effectively by our **Super Croud** experts in HQ.

Understanding social media

06

OUR CHAPTER PLEDGE TO YOU

When you reach the end of this chapter you'll have answers to the following questions:

- What does the term social media really mean?

- How is it changing the digital marketing landscape?

- Why should I get involved?

- How can I harness the power of social media to reach and engage with my target audience?

- How can consumer input help me to do business more effectively and refine my products and services?

- What are the social media rules of engagement?

Join the conversation

Do you listen to your customers... really listen to them? Do you take their opinions, ideas and criticisms on board, and allow them to inform your business decisions? If you do, you're ahead of the game. Historically, marketers have focused on delivering a particular message, to a predefined target audience, with the aim of eliciting a specific response. Consumers were sometimes consulted in the process, of course – through market research, consumer surveys, focus groups and the like – but by and large the marketing tended to be 'show and tell' in nature, the consumer's role that of a passive recipient of information peddled by the marketer.

Now, thanks to the increasingly interactive nature of the internet, and a shift in the way that people are consuming media, all of that is changing. Consumers are talking, just as they always have, only now they are talking online to more extensive groups of their peers. The conversations they are having seamlessly transcend geographical, temporal and cultural boundaries. The web is abuzz with a billion conversations, and that presents exciting opportunities for marketers who are brave enough to engage.

Marketing too is evolving rapidly to become more of a conversation than a lecture. Progressive marketers realize that to be heard in today's interactive world, they need to participate in that conversation... and, of course, if you want to get the most out of any conversation, you have to spend part of your time *listening*.

Listening is not a trait that marketers are traditionally renowned for, but to truly embrace the opportunity presented by Web 2.0 and beyond, we need to sit up and take notice of what our online customers and prospects are telling us about our brand, our industry and the world in general.

Through blogs, wikis, social bookmarking, online discussions, social networks, peer review sites and other online media, we have the potential to foster a much more productive and meaningful relationship with our customers, to gain powerful insight into their perceptions of our products, services and brand, and allow them to contribute and collaborate in our businesses in ways that were never possible before.

Understanding social media demands a paradigm shift for the marketer. We have to realize that our target audience is, in fact, no longer an audience at all. They are now active participants in a constantly evolving debate; as online marketers it is a debate in which we can't afford to sit on the sidelines.

What is social media?

Social media is the umbrella term for web-based software and services that allow users to come together online and exchange, discuss, communicate and participate in any form of social interaction. That interaction can encompass text, audio, images, video and other media, individually or in any combination. It can involve the generation of new content; the recommendation of and sharing of existing content; reviewing and rating products, services and brands; discussing the hot topics of the day; pursuing hobbies, interests and passions; sharing experience and expertise... in fact, almost anything that can be distributed and shared through digital channels is fair game.

In a webcast for Search Marketing Now (**www.searchmarketingnow.com**), Xoogler (ex-Googler/former Google employee) and leading social media commentator Vanessa Fox described it as follows: 'There are all kinds of ways that people talk online, and Social Networking really is anywhere people are talking online. From a corporate perspective what you're most interested in is where people are talking about you, talking about your products, and talking about the topics that you care about.'

A huge range of websites now leverage elements of social media to engage with their audience, and some, including a number of the highest profile sites to emerge in recent years (the Facebooks, YouTubes and Twitters of this world), base their entire business model around the burgeoning popularity of online social media, user participation and user-generated content (UGC) (see Figure 6.1).

FIGURE 6.1   The proliferation of social media sites on the internet today is making it incredibly easy for like-minded consumers to connect with each other. They're talking about everything... things that are important to you and your business. It's time to join the conversation!

Social media is nothing new

One of the biggest misconceptions about social media is that it is a new phenomenon. Online social interaction has been around since the very beginning. In its crudest form social media predates the web by some two decades. Primitive dial-in bulletin board services (BBSs) and online communities such as Compuserve and Prodigy allowed users to post messages online for other members to read and respond to, UseNet newsgroups (early internet discussion groups) allowed like-minded participants to exchange views about all sorts of topics ranging from brain surgery to budgerigars, while e-mail discussion lists did the same. Internet relay chat (IRC) introduced real-time chat into the mix, and browser-based forums and chat rooms brought the discussion on to the web. Social media, one and all.

What has changed over recent years is the reach and penetration of these social media technologies, their adoption into the everyday lives of a mainstream audience, and the proliferation of user-generated content and peer-to-peer interaction that is resulting from it. In the past, online discussion was generally restricted to early adopters: technologists who felt comfortable interacting over the net, and who had the technical skills to fathom clunky, often unwieldy user interfaces to accomplish their goals. Today, though, anyone can participate through slick, well-designed browser-based user interfaces that adopt conventions that everyone is comfortable with. It's easy, it's convenient and it's incredibly powerful; not because of the technology, but because of how that technology nurtures the connections between people.

Social media is naturally compelling

The proliferation of social media is a natural extension of increasing levels of internet usage and the penetration of always-on broadband access. As more people head online, and start weaving the internet seamlessly into the fabric of their daily lives, it is only natural that they bring with them the very human need to interact and belong. We are biologically programmed to be social and gregarious creatures. The need to interact with other people is hard-coded into our DNA; it is part of who and what we are, and that is as true online as it is off. That's one of the main reasons why so many of us find social media incredibly compelling.

Social media is nothing to be afraid of

Compelling it may be, but for many marketers the thought of venturing into this openly interactive, anything goes, consumer-championed world can be daunting, even scary. The rules here are not dictated by marketers, but by consumers – media-savvy consumers who can spot marketing hype a mile away, and want nothing to do with it. It's a dynamic, unpredictable world, and if you get things wrong you risk the very real prospect of a backlash that will travel throughout the network in the blink of an eye.

Worrying? Possibly, but at the end of the day you have to remember that social media is just about people talking, connecting and sharing with other people. Marketing as an industry is (or at least should be) also all about people: understanding them and communicating with them. As a marketer, is the prospect of talking with the very people you want to connect with really such a frightening prospect?

With or without you – why it's good to get involved

But, we hear you cry, how can I hope to control this open conversation? You can't – so don't even try. What you can do, however, is choose to participate in that conversation, and strive to have a positive influence on its direction. That is fundamentally what social media marketing (SMM) is all about.

One thing is certain: your customers are already talking to each other online; they are talking about your industry, your competition, your company, your brand and other topics that are relevant to what you do. The conversation is happening, regardless of whether you choose to get involved or not. Surely it's better to be aware of what is being said, to listen, engage and foster relationships with these communities, rather than wondering from the periphery.

Effective social media marketing is about leaving the sledgehammer approach to product promotion at home. Stop beating your prospects over the head with the cudgel of marketing hyperbole, and instead work to develop your skills in the subtler art of consumer engagement. Find out what people are interested in, what they are talking about, and then provide useful information, advice and content for them. Talk to them, not at them, and above all, *listen to them*. If you manage to do that effectively, then social media can have an incredibly positive impact on your organization's online profile (see Figure 6.2).

FIGURE 6.2   Why it's important for your business to get involved in social media

- Deeper engagement with customers
- Get insights not available any other way
- Your customers are online already

Just how deep you choose to steep yourself in the social media marketing game will depend a lot on your business, your customers, your goals and your overall digital marketing strategy. But there really is something out there for everyone. Here are just some of the potential benefits of engaging with your customers through online social channels:

- **Stay informed:** find out what your customers really think. Get invaluable insight into their perception of your products, services, brands, industry and more general topics of interest. Knowing your customers is the key to effective digital marketing – and engaging with them on a social platform can be incredibly revealing, without being intrusive.

- **Raise your profile:** by engaging proactively through social media you appear responsive, and can build your reputation as an authoritative and helpful player in your field of expertise.

- **Level the playing field:** focus groups, market research surveys and other offline methods of gauging consumer sentiment are expensive and can be well beyond the means of smaller businesses. Now, any organization can immerse itself in the social web to discover what consumers are talking about and how they feel, with little or no financial outlay.

- **Influence the influencers:** often the people who are most active in social media circles will be the element of your target market who can be classified as *influencers*. While small in number compared to the market as a whole, these influential individuals have already gained the trust and respect of their online peers, and fostering their good opinion can have a disproportionate impact on your broader online reputation.

- **Nurture brand advocacy:** by engaging positively with people who already have a positive attitude to your brand, you can nurture passionate brand evangelists who will voluntarily advocate your organization through online social media. And your greatest brand advocates may well sit inside your business – encouraging your employees to actively participate through social media can exponentially expand your reach.

- **Pass it on:** one of the most powerful aspects of social media is its capacity for viral propagation. It is the online equivalent of word-of-mouth marketing, except that online the word can travel further, faster. Whether it's a video on YouTube, a high-profile news story about your company, a post on your blog that is picked up and distributed by your readers – if it hits the right note, suddenly it's everywhere, and your profile soars. If you get it right, there is no more effective way to promote your business.

- **The wisdom of the crowd:** you know what they say, two heads are better than one. Well, hundreds, or even thousands of heads are better still. Smart companies realize that by harnessing the collective intelligence of online communities they can find answers to some of their most challenging business problems. Getting input from online communities using social media is affordable and effective. As well as helping to solve real business dilemmas it can also help you to make more informed research, design and development decisions, based on what customers actually want. Now there's a radical concept!

Different forms of social media

Social media websites come in a wide variety of 'flavours', which are all broadly based around the premise of personal interaction; creating, exchanging and sharing content; rating it and discussing its relative merits as a community. The content can be links to other websites, news articles or blog posts, photographs, audio, video, questions posed by other users... anything, in fact, that can be distributed in digital form.

Most social media websites don't sit neatly into a single category; they tend to mix a range of social components that transcend the discrete boundaries people try to define for them. Still, given our human propensity for filing things into nice, neat boxes, there are several generally accepted groupings into which most social media sites sit with relative comfort, based on their primary function. The following list is a taster, and is far from exhaustive. Start looking, and you will find plenty of social media sites/components out there that don't fall neatly into any of the categories we outline below, some that span multiple categories and others that defy categorization altogether. All of which demonstrates the dynamic, constantly evolving nature of the space. As the saying goes... we live in interesting times.

Social media submission sites

The first sites to allow users to tag and share content they liked were book-marking sites such as del.icio.us (**www.delicious.com**), which allow users to 'save' bookmarks to their favourite web resources (pages, audio, video... whatever), categorize them using tags (labels that help you to identify and filter the content you want later) and share them with their online friends. The concept is much the same as adding a page to your browser favourites, just taken to the next level.

Social bookmarking sites have declined in popularity and been largely superseded by social media submission sites, such as Digg (**www.digg.com**), Reddit (**www.reddit.com**) and StumbleUpon (**www.stumbleupon.com**). These sites are rather like social bookmarking sites, but instead of saving personal bookmarks for your own future reference, you actively submit links to content you 'like' for the online community to rate and rank. The more people who 'vote' for a particular content item, the higher up the rankings it rises. Submissions that get enough votes end up on the site's homepage, which can drive significant traffic spikes to the site in question.

As well as the votes, of course, there also tends to be a lot of discussion and debate on these sites, which means they can offer tremendous insight into the way people think and react.

What's in it for marketers

- **Find out what people are interested in:** you can use social media submission sites to gauge what type of content in your particular field people find compelling. Look at the content that is floating to the top. Ask yourself why it is so popular. What is appealing about it, and how can you draw on that to make your own content more compelling?

- **What's the *buzz*:** as well as what's 'hot' on the sites, there is a lot of discussion going on around popular content items. The more popular an entry gets, the more people see it and the more debate there is. Examine what people are saying – look at reviews, comments and discussions; find out what people like, what they don't like, and use that insight to inject that elusive 'buzz' quotient into your own content.

- **Amplify your exposure, traffic and online reputation:** having articles and other content ranking highly on these sites can give you a tremendous boost in traffic. However, they also give you the opportunity to raise your profile and perceived authority within your online community. By contributing constructively, submitting relevant and interesting content, and joining the debate surrounding on-topic content you can boost the community's overall perception of your brand – and by extension your power to influence others.

Forums and discussion sites

Online forums and discussion sites have been around since the early days of the internet. Broad, general discussion groups such as Yahoo Groups (**http://groups.yahoo.com**) and Google Groups (**http://groups.google.com**), where anyone can sign up and start their own online or e-mail discussion community on any topic under the sun, are still popular, and you'll find a tonne of other discussion sites focusing on general, industry specific (vertical) and niche communities covering every topic imaginable.

What's in it for marketers

- **Get closer to your customers:** checking out what consumers are talking about in forums is a great way to find out what makes them tick. The more you can learn about your customers, the better prepared you will be to engage with them in a meaningful way.

- **Raise your profile:** contribute to the discussion, offer help and advice, demonstrate your expertise. Pretty soon people will start to respect and trust your contribution to the community – and that can do wonders for your online reputation and profile.

- **Nip bad things in the bud:** by participating in forums you will be able to spot potentially negative comments or conversations relating to your business or brand, and be proactive in resolving them before they escalate (more about this in the next chapter). What's more, if you're already participating as a valued member of the community, you may well find others jumping to your defence.

- **Targeted traffic:** traffic shouldn't be your main reason for joining a discussion forum – blatant off-topic promotion, and linking to your own sites for the sake of it, is frowned upon, but most forums allow (even encourage) one or two links in your signature (a short snippet, usually a few lines, that is appended to the bottom of every post you submit to a forum). Make sure you follow the forum rules on this, but by including links in your signature you give other people on the forum a convenient way to find your site(s), and to discover more about you and your company. Many will click through for a closer look, particularly if you make regular, valuable and relevant contributions to the forum.

Media sharing sites

Media sharing sites are incredibly popular. Pinterest (**www.pinterest.com**) which lets people save and share images and videos grouped around topics (or 'pinboards'), has reached 70 million users since its launch in 2010. Sites such as Instagram (**http://instagram.com**) and Flickr (**www.flickr.com**) allow communities of members to upload, share, comment on and discuss their photographs; YouTube (**www.youtube.com**), Blip.tv (**www.blip.tv**) and Vimeo (**www.vimeo.com**) *et al* do the same for video content; and a host of other social media sites support alternative media types: Slideshare (**www.slideshare.com**), for example, is a site that allows people to upload, share and discuss their presentation slides with the world.

The sites typically allow you to make content publicly available, or restrict access to the people you specify, to send content to your 'friends' and even to 'embed' (seamlessly integrate) the content in your blog post or website for others to find it, distribute it and discuss it.

To match our ever-shortening attention spans, the current trend in media sharing is towards the micro. In January 2013, Twitter launched its Vine app (**https://vine.co**), which allows users to create, share and comment on six-second looping videos. Vine has proved popular, gaining 40 million users within eight months. Instagram responded in mid-2013 by expanding its service to support videos with a slightly more generous limit of 15 seconds. And going even further, messaging app Snapchat lets people send pictures and videos that self-destruct up to 10 seconds after being seen – the ultimate in disposable content!

What's in it for marketers

- **Find out what turns your target market on:** by analysing the popularity of items on content submission sites, and reading the user comments, you can gain insight into your target market's likes and dislikes, and can incorporate that into your own content creation.

- **A ready-made vehicle for content distribution:** these sites are the ideal vehicle for rapid distribution of your own digital media content. In fact a whole micro-discipline of digital marketing has evolved around YouTube and viral video content. Hit the right buttons with your audience, and who knows, maybe your video clip could become the next 'The Man Your Man Could Smell Like' from Old Spice (**http://bit.ly/UDMOldSpice**) – with 47,544,000 views... and counting.

Reviews and ratings sites

Reviews and ratings sites do exactly what the name says: they allow users to review and rate companies, products, services, books, music, hotels, restaurants... anything they like. They can be stand-alone review sites, such as Epinions.com (**www.epinions.com**) (see Figure 6.3) or Reviewcentre.com (**www.reviewcentre.com**); or a review component added to a broader site, such as the product rating and review facilities on e-commerce sites such as Amazon (**www.amazon.com**).

You'll also find specialist industry specific review sites covering many vertical markets, like TripAdvisor (**www.tripadvisor.com**), which focuses on travel; or RateMyTeachers (**www.ratemyteachers.com**), which allows pupils and parents to rate and comment on their educators.

FIGURE 6.3 Epinions.com allows consumers to submit and share independent reviews of the products they use every day

What's in it for marketers

- **Advertising:** most review sites rely on advertising to generate revenue, and therefore offer advertising opportunities for businesses either directly or through advertising and affiliate networks.

- **Insight into what's good, and what's bad:** even if people are not rating your business directly, you can still get valuable information on these sites on what's working for consumers and what's not within your particular industry. If you run a hotel, for example, you can see what are people's main gripes, and what they particularly appreciate... then apply that knowledge to your own business.

- **Find out what people really think:** if consumers are posting reviews about your business, that sort of feedback is pure gold – reinforcing what you are doing well, and pointing out areas where you can improve. It's market research... for free.

- **Demonstrate good customer service:** by monitoring reviews and responding in a constructive way to negative feedback, you can show good customer service in a very visible way.

Social network sites

These are your archetypal social media sites – the Facebooks, MySpaces, LinkedIns and Google+. These are the sites that people automatically think about when you mention the words social networking. They are – to paraphrase Facebook's opening gambit '*social utilities that connect you with the people around you*'. They basically let users build up a group (or several discrete groups in the case of Google+ Circles and Facebook Lists) of 'friends' with whom they can share things in all sorts of ways – from videos, to articles, to games, to groups and causes, to.... well, if you haven't got one already, sign up for a profile of your own, and you'll soon get the idea.

Huge numbers of people use social networking sites, and those numbers are growing all the time as those people invite all of their friends and contacts to join them. Today Facebook heads the social networking pack with nearly 1.2 billion active monthly users. The numbers are staggering when you consider that Facebook was only created in 2004, and that it wasn't opened up to the general public until April 2006. Facebook is currently the second most popular site on the internet, behind only Google, according to its Alexa Traffic Rank (**www.alexa.com**).

There have been signs of late that Facebook may be peaking. While it is still growing in developing markets, it is reaching saturation point in some developed markets such as the UK. A Pew Center report published at the end of 2013 showed that the biggest growth is now amongst the over 65s, who are joining to keep in touch with their friends and family. At the same time, Facebook use amongst teens and young adults appears to be stagnating or even dropping, as they move to new platforms out of sight of their parents and grandparents.

Social network sites are popular because they offer users the ability to find and connect with people they already know in novel, convenient ways; to rekindle old acquaintances, and reinforce new ones. They make the process of communicating with a large network of people easy and painless. You post information to your profile and it is instantly available to those of your friends who are interested. You can broadcast information to all of your friends simultaneously, or choose who you want to share specific content with.

Talking to a room full of software developers in San Francisco in 2007, Mark Zuckerberg, Facebook's youthful founder, summarized the company's mission thus: 'At Facebook we're pushing to make the world a more open place, and we do this by building things that help people use their real connections to share information more effectively.' That pretty much encapsulates the social networking phenomenon that is gripping the online world today.

What's in it for marketers

- **Advertising:** social networks are increasingly opening up to paid advertising and offer flexible advertising options, usually based on the PPC model, for businesses looking to target their ads based on the profile information of users and/or particular actions. While the targeting angle is a compelling one, and social network audiences are large… it's important to remember that most users visit social network sites to *socialize*. They're not really in 'buying' mode, and the jury is still out on how effectively social network advertising converts. It's something to consider, certainly, if it's a good 'fit' for your business, and you have a clearly defined audience that is interested in your product or brand, but be cautious: consider the context in which your ads will be seen and seek to engage, entertain or inform rather than just sell, and track your results carefully.

- **Improve your online exposure/reputation:** social network sites usually allow organizations to set up their own profile or page.

Members of the network can then become 'fans' or 'like' these pages. Your page is essentially a business hub within the network, and it can be a great way to build a community around your brand and monitor what consumers think about you, find out more about them, and to offer valuable content. Having a presence on these networks, keeping your content up-to-date, relevant and valuable to your audience, and responding positively to the feedback you receive, is another great way to boost your online reputation.

- **Nurture social evangelists:** your social network can be a great place to attract brand advocates and to recruit and nurture brand evangelists. People on social networks love to share. Find the people who are passionate about your industry, your brand, your products – reward them with valuable information and content... then watch as they put all of their passion, zeal, and social media acumen to work promoting your brand to the rest of their social network. And don't forget that your greatest brand evangelists may sit inside your organization!

Blogs

In the space of a very few years the widespread popularity and adoption of the blog (an acronym of weB LOG) as a medium of self-expression and communication has caused one of the most fundamental shifts in the history of modern media. Suddenly, anyone can be a publisher.

Barriers to entry have come crashing down, and free, easy-to-use blogging platforms have liberated millions of individuals, giving them access to a global audience. Setting up a blog can take as little as five minutes of your time on a free hosted service such as Blogger (**www.blogger.com**) or WordPress (**www.wordpress.com**), and setting up a blog on your own domain and hosting service is only marginally more complicated.

People all over the world are using blogs to report local news, vent their frustrations, offer their opinions, share their visions and experiences, unleash their creativity and generally wax lyrical about their passions. And the world is listening, and answering.

The blogosphere (the collective name applied to the global blogging community) is *the* home of internet buzz. If something is worth talking about online (and often even if it's not) it will be written about, commented upon and propagated through the blogosphere. There are, of course, millions of blogs out there that simply don't make the grade – but they don't get an audience. The best blogs float to the top (largely through online word-of-mouth, effective search engine ranking and the effect of the social media submission and social bookmarking sites we have already mentioned).

It is not just private individuals who are blogging, of course – the blog is becoming an important tool in the business marketing arsenal too, adding a personal element to the bland corporate facade, helping companies to reach out and make human connections in an increasingly human online world.

Bloggers read each others' posts, they comment on them, they link to each other prolifically, and the best of them have a massive following of avid and loyal readers. These readers go on to elaborate in their own blogs on what they have read, and spread the word through their own online social networks.

If you choose to do only one thing in the social media space, then get to know the popular blogs in your industry. Who are the people behind them, what are they writing about, what turns them on (and off), which topics generate the most comments? Prominent bloggers tend to be the biggest online influencers of them all – you need to be aware of them, build a relationship with them, and leverage that position where possible in order to help spread the word.

Never underestimate blogs. Their simplicity belies an unprecedented power to mould and influence online opinion. As a digital marketer, blogs and bloggers can be your salvation... or your damnation. Treat them with the respect they deserve.

What's in it for marketers

- **Potentially massive exposure:** traditional press releases to your local media outlets are all very well, but get your story picked up and propagated by prominent bloggers and you'll get more online exposure, traffic and inbound links (think SEO) than any traditional press release could ever hope to achieve (for more tips on getting online press releases picked up by bloggers, see the Online PR section in Chapter 10).

- **Consumer engagement:** use your own corporate/business blog to add your voice to the blogosphere. Show your customers a personal side to your business, give them valuable information they can use, provide answers and improve their overall experience of dealing with your company. Try not to use your blog as a vehicle for blatant product and brand promotion, but rather as a platform to offer your readers a personal insight into your company and brand. Sure, product announcements, and press-release-like posts are fine, but look to add value with genuinely useful content too. You could offer your opinions and insight into industry news and events, comment on and link to other blogs that are discussing relevant issues, or get your resident experts to post 'how-tos' on getting the most out of your products. Engage with the online community, and they will engage with you in turn. The more you give of yourself, the more you'll get back.

Podcasts

Podcasts are, in many ways, just the rich media extension of the blogging concept. A podcast is simply a series of digital media files (audio or video) distributed over the internet. These can be accessed directly via a website or, more usually, are downloaded to a computer or synchronized to a digital media device for playback at the user's leisure. They tend to be organized as chronological 'shows', with new episodes released at regular intervals, much like the radio and television show formats that many of them emulate. Users can usually offer their feedback on particular episodes on the accompanying website or blog.

Whatever your area of interest you'll find podcasts out there covering it... and podcast portals such as Podcast.com (**www.podcast.com**), Podomatic (**www.podomatic.com**), and Apple's iTunes (**www.apple.com/itunes**) offer convenient hubs to find, sample and subscribe to podcasts of interest.

What's in it for marketers

- **Listen and learn:** leading podcasters in your industry will very probably be talking about things that are relevant to you as a business and to your customers. Podcasters also tend to be social media enthusiasts – influencers who have their finger on the digital pulse of their audience. You can harness their understanding of the online community in your particular space by analysing their podcasts, and the comments and feedback from their audience, to feed into your own digital marketing efforts.

- **Do it yourself:** podcasting is easy to do – but can be difficult to do well. At its most basic, all you really need is a digital audio recorder (your computer and an attached headset will work fine), some editing software and a place to post your files once they're ready. Depending on your business, your audience and your goals (back to strategy again), podcasting may well offer you a valuable additional channel to reach your market. It could also help position you as a progressive digital player in your industry.

Micro blogging

Micro blogging has become popular with a mainstream audience (and hence with businesses, brands and the mainstream media) in a very short space of time. Its rapid rise in popularity is thanks in no small part to widespread adoption of the best known micro-blogging platform, Twitter, by well known celebrities, and the voyeuristic compulsion of millions of fans to check out what their idols are doing 24/7.

In May 2007 there were approximately 111 micro-blogging services online around the world. Today (January 2014) while there are still other services out there such as Tumblr (**www.tumblr.com**), by and large when we talk about micro blogging from a marketer's perspective Twitter (**http://twitter.com**) really is the only show in town.

Twitter is essentially a short-message broadcast service that lets people keep people up-to-date via short, public text posts of up to 140 characters long. Leading social networks, like Facebook and LinkedIn, also offer similar micro-blogging functionality within their 'walled garden' networks through the 'status updates' feature.

At first glance, micro blogging may seem a bit pointless. After all, what can you really say in the Twitter-imposed limit of 140 characters? Well, think about SMS text messages on your phone – for a long time there was a 160 character maximum limit, and billions of people managed to communicate effectively with them every day.

The true value of micro blogging isn't necessarily in the individual posts, it is in the collective aggregation of those mini-posts into more than the sum of their parts. When you receive frequent, short updates from the people you're connected to you begin to get a *feel* for them, to develop a better understanding of what they are all about, and to feel a stronger connection with them. Twitter can offer an immediate and surprisingly accurate barometer of public opinion on the web.

What's in it for marketers

- **Your finger on the digital pulse:** as a marketer, micro blogging platforms give you access to high-profile thought leaders in your industry. The most progressive among them are likely to use micro-blogging services to post snippets about what they are doing, how they are doing it, links to new online resources and thoughts on developments at the bleeding edge of the industry. By 'following' these thought leaders you can harness that valuable intelligence, and use it to inform your own marketing decisions.

- **Understand the influencers:** follow the influencers in your industry, and influence them in return. Identifying influencers is easy – they will be the most active participants talking about topics relevant to your business with the most followers. You'll be amazed at how much insight can be provided by following the micro-blogging streams of a group of industry influencers.

- **Communicate with your customers:** why would you want to micro-blog to your customers? Well, some very high-profile companies do (including Dell, the *New York Times*, ITN News, the BBC, South West Airlines and British Airways, to name but a few), not to mention prominent politicians (Barack Obama, for example, was prominent on Twitter during the 2008 and 2012 presidential campaigns), and other high-profile public figures. In a world where e-mail has become increasingly noisy, offering a micro-blog feed provides beleaguered consumers a convenient alternative way to subscribe to your updates without adding yet another newsletter to their cluttered inbox.

- **Raise your online profile:** micro blogging offers you yet another opportunity to get in front of your online audience and establish your expertise. Be forthcoming, answer questions, provide interesting snippets of news and advice, direct people to useful blog posts, articles and other resources... yours and other people's. Help people, learn about them, listen to them, and give your online reputation another boost.

- **Generate traffic:** Twitter thrives on sharing links to interesting content, so letting your followers know when you publish your latest blog post, white paper or video can help drive significant traffic to your website.

Wikis

Wikis are online collections of web pages that are literally open for anyone to create, edit, discuss, comment on and generally contribute to. They are perhaps the ultimate vehicle for mass collaboration, the most famous example, of course, being Wikipedia (**www.wikipedia.org**), the free online encyclopedia.

At the time of writing (January 2014) Wikipedia reports that it has a staggering 4,426,000 English language articles in its database, with over 2.6 billion words. To put that number into context, it is nearly 60 times as many words as are contained in the *Encyclopedia Britannica* (**www.britannica.com**), a leading commercial publication and the next largest English language encyclopedia. Despite criticisms from some quarters over the accuracy of some of its articles, and the perceived authority of the information it contains, according to independent web-tracking company Alexa (**www.alexa.com**), in January 2014 Wikipedia was ranked number six globally in terms of on-line traffic, more than 5,000 places above its commercial rival *Encyclopedia Britannica*.

The name 'Wiki' originates from the Hawaiian word for quick... although it is sometimes also used as what has been dubbed a 'backronym' (a sort of reverse-engineered acronym) of 'what I know is'. And essentially, that's what wikis do – they let large communities of people collaborate to share their knowledge, experience and expertise online. Wikis are created by, and policed by, the community. Because of their open nature, inaccurate or misleading information can find its way on to a wiki, but if the wiki is active and vibrant, inaccuracies are usually picked up quickly and eradicated by other community members. So wiki articles are constantly evolving, and tend to become increasingly accurate and authoritative over time as the community grows, and tend to be updated with new information as it becomes available.

What's in it for marketers

The concept of using wikis as a marketing tool is still a new phenomenon, and their value may not be as readily apparent as some other forms of social media. However, they are a powerful collaborative tool, and with collaboration between companies and their customers in the ascendancy, look out for increasing use of wikis by innovative organizations in the not too distant future.

- **Build a strong collaborative community of advocates around your brand:** wikis can be a great way to encourage constructive interaction and collaboration between people inside your organization and people outside it (your customers). Consumers begin to feel ownership and connection with a brand that encourages, facilitates and values their contribution. That ownership evolves into loyalty, then advocacy: powerful stuff from a marketing perspective, especially when you consider these contributors will often be online *influencers* who will go on to sing your praises on other social media sites.

- **Harness the wisdom of the crowd:** how much talent, knowledge and experience do you have inside your organization? Probably quite a lot – but it pales into insignificance when compared to the massive pool of talent, experience and expertise you can access online.

Retired experts, up-and-coming whizz-kids, talented amateurs, undiscovered geniuses... they are all out there. Wikis give you a simple, powerful and compelling way to draw on and capture some of that collective intelligence. Why not harness a wiki, for example, to help refine the design of your products, come up with your next great marketing campaign, define a more efficient business process, produce and/or augment product documentation, develop a comprehensive knowledge base... or anything else that might benefit from a collaborative approach.

What's next for social media sites?

New social media sites are constantly springing up and fading away, and keeping on top of this ever-changing environment can be daunting. While there are signs that Facebook may be peaking, at the time of writing (January 2014) its Instagram photo-sharing site is the fastest growing social network, while messaging apps like Snapchat are also gaining rapid popularity, particularly amongst teens. You will find advice and guidance on current developments in social media platforms at **www.gogadm.com**.

As social media sites mature, there is growing pressure on them to demonstrate they can actually make money – particularly for those sites such as Facebook, LinkedIn and Twitter that are now public companies with shareholders. We are already seeing more of a push towards advertising, and Facebook – in its latest algorithm change at the end of 2013 – reduced the reach of organic fan pages, putting pressure on brands to spend money on ads. It appears that the era of social networks as 'free marketing' may be coming to an end.

Social media dashboards – all your updates in one place

The proliferation of social media platforms today can make it a pretty daunting task to keep track of what's going on between all of your different social media accounts. Luckily, it's easy to consolidate your various social media streams and updates in one convenient location using tools dubbed 'social media dashboards'.

Dashboard software takes a variety of forms, from desktop-based applications to web-based services and mobile applications that let you keep track of and update your accounts on the move. Tools such as HootSuite (**www.hootsuite.com**) and Tweetdeck (**www.tweetdeck.com**) have evolved quickly from straightforward Twitter clients into fully integrated social media dashboards that incorporate multiple social media accounts spanning different platforms. You'll also find 'enterprise' class social CRM software... which essentially do the same thing.

Ultimately, these dashboards give you a convenient place to monitor all of your social media activity in one place, and the best of them offer built-in statistics and measurements, scheduled updates, keyword monitoring and more. If you're new to social media you will probably start off on the website of the service you want to use. Over time, though, most marketers will find an integrated social media dashboard invaluable.

The rules of engagement

Social media, then, offers a wealth of opportunity for consumer engagement and building brand awareness, but in such an open and dynamic space it is critical to consider carefully what you are doing. Social media is consumer driven, and the very characteristics that make it such an enticing proposition for marketers – the interconnected nature of online consumers, and the staggering speed at which information traverses the network – can just as easily backfire.

The 'rules' of social media are really about applying a bit of common sense to what are essentially human relationships. The key thing to remember is that this is *social* media – people are going online to interact and exchange information and content with similar, like-minded people. They are unlikely to be interested in your latest sales pitch, and they are certainly not interested in promotional hype. They want interesting, fun, informative, quirky, addictive... whatever turns them on.

When it comes to social media, you're not just sending out a message, you are inviting a response, and what you get might not be quite what you are expecting. You need a plan to engage in social media marketing, but you also need to be flexible and respond to the community:

- **Draw on what you already know:** you already have a wealth of knowledge about your customers – who they are, what they like to do, where they hang-out online. Okay, so one of the main reasons you're getting involved in social media is to get to know them a little better – but the point is that you're not going into this blind. Use that knowledge: apply what you already know about your customers, your business and your brand to your social media strategy. As you learn more, refine what you're doing accordingly.

- **Don't jump in unprepared:** have a clear plan before you start – know who you're trying to engage with and what you want to achieve. Define ways to gauge and measure your success, with frequent milestones to help keep you on track. But remember to be flexible, and modify your plan as necessary in response to community feedback.

- **Look, listen and learn:** before you engage in social media marketing, spend some time 'lurking' (hanging around without contributing). Familiarize yourself with the different types of social media sites that you plan to target. Go and use the sites, read the blogs... immerse yourself in the media. Look, listen and learn. Just like in real life, every online community is different. Familiarize yourself with the various nuances before you dive in.

- **Be open, honest and authentic:** nowhere is the term 'full disclosure' more appropriate than in social media. Don't go online pretending to be an independent punter extolling the virtues of your brand. You will get found out, and when you do your company will go 'viral' for all the wrong reasons. There are some high-profile examples of companies getting this spectacularly wrong, with disastrous results. Never pretend to be someone or something you're not.

- **Be relevant, interesting and entertaining:** everything you do should add value to the community, as well as moving you towards your business goals. Be helpful, be constructive, be interesting and entertaining – join the conversation, offer valuable, authoritative and considered advice. Make a real effort to engage with the community on their terms, and you will usually find them more than happy to engage with you in return.

- **Don't push out a 'spammy' message:** don't join social media sites just to submit a tonne of links and push information about your own products, or flood the community with posts on why your company is the best thing since sliced bread. It smacks of spam, and adds nothing to the conversation. At best the community will ignore you... at worst, well, we're back to the negative viral effect again.

- **Respect 'rules':** if the site you're frequenting has policies, guidelines and rules – read them and abide by them.

- **Respect people:** always be respectful to your fellow community members. That doesn't mean you always have to agree with them; healthy debate is good in any community. When you do disagree, though, always be polite and respectful of other people. They have as much right to their opinion as you do to yours. Don't make it personal.

- **Respond to feedback:** if users give you feedback, this is invaluable. Let them know that you appreciate it, that you are interested in what they have to say. Be responsive, and show them how you have used that feedback constructively.

Adding social media to your own site

Remember, social media is not the exclusive province of specialist social and community websites. You can integrate social media components into your own website and begin to harness the collective talent and intelligence of a vibrant community of users. Perhaps the most obvious example is Amazon's reviews and ratings system – emulated around the web – which allows consumers to review the books and other products that the site sells.

Another area where social media really comes into its own is in allowing your consumers to collaborate with you. Forums such as Dell's IdeaStorm (**www.ideastorm.com**), for example, which allows customers to suggest and vote on features they would like to see implemented in the computer manufacturer's product line-up. It is like a next-generation business suggestion box and focus group rolled into one. The ideas that get the most votes from the IdeaStorm community rise to the top of the heap, much the same as items on social media submission sites such as Digg. The top ideas are then evaluated by the company and selected to go into production.

Through IdeaStorm, Dell's customers are having a direct, positive and tangible influence on the design and development of Dell products (see Figure 6.4). The consumer feels more involvement and connection with the brand, while the company enjoys an improved reputation in the community and ultimately delivers a better end product to its customers. It's a classic win-win scenario.

Then, of course, there are customer support forums – where the community can answer each others' queries about your products and services. People get quick answers to their questions, and over time you build an invaluable, search-enabled knowledge base of solutions to common problems.

FIGURE 6.4 Dell IdeaStorm is a great example of a company harnessing the collective intelligence and creativity of consumers to inform real business decisions. This ultimately fosters consumer buy-in and delivers what customers want

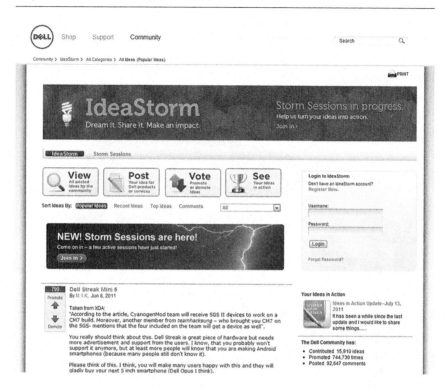

Because consumers are responding to each others' queries, you improve the overall customer support experience, while reducing the burden on your own support resources... again a win-win. There are literally hundreds of ways to use social media to harness the collective intelligence, experience and latent talent of your customers and the broader online community. Imagination, openness and a willingness to engage with and learn from others is all that it takes.

Whatever social media strategy you choose to implement, remember that even when you host social media components on your own sites, the same rules of engagement apply: be open, be honest, be considerate... and most of all *listen* to your customers, hear what they have to say and *respond* in a proactive and positive way.

Welcome to the conversation; welcome to the future of marketing!

CASE STUDY   Bennetts Bike Social

Bennetts are the UK's No 1 bike insurance specialist. With more than 80 years' experience in the insurance industry, they currently provide bike insurance cover to over 200,000 riders across the UK and are the most recommended bike insurance brand.

Location

UK.

The challenge

Price comparison websites entered the bike insurance market in 2007 providing an easy route to market for new providers, and eroding the core performance of the more traditional, direct-led providers. As a premium brand, Bennetts' brand awareness had declined 14 per cent, direct sales had halved, and the brand was no longer deemed to be 'standing out' in the bike industry.

A completely new brand strategy was required to return the brand to health and achieve its growth and profitability aspirations.

Target audience

Motorcycle rider, primarily looking for bike insurance.

Action

- Independent brand tracking by Ipsos Mori highlighted the insight that 74 per cent of consumers looking for bike insurance would go directly to a price comparison website as opposed to a direct brand such as Bennetts. Standing out as a specialist provider on aggregators proved impossible – a brand is simply a logo, feature list and price point – nothing about the brand's unique assets is communicated to consumers. Bennetts needed to acquire more business directly and to achieve this we needed to increase the frequency of interaction with the brand.

- Bennetts placed the biker at the heart of everything we do, with the commitment to spend our direct marketing budget on bikers and their community. Social media was used as the linchpin to the new strategy.

- The brand already used 'unowned' social media platforms (eg Facebook, Twitter and YouTube) to position Bennetts as the 'go to' brand for industry news, views, gossip and rider updates, and we were already often first to break the news of the most exciting changes in racing, thanks to our well-placed sources around the world.

- We created 'money can't buy' experiential promotions via Biking Dreams (where Bennetts enable a biker to undertake a once-in-a-lifetime experience, such as meeting their biking hero, or having a VIP visit the Ducati factory in Bologna) and promoted these across all social media channels, endorsing the brand's commitment to bikers in order to drive recall and advocacy of the brand by having the winners blog, status update and tweet about their amazing experiences – and to share these with the biking community. These were fully integrated to all Bennetts' assets such as Bennetts: LIVE – our highly successful national and regional events programme.

- Bennetts also developed full customer servicing across both Facebook and Twitter, delivering on our commitment to being 'easy to do business with'.

- The brand then took social to a totally new level by launching our own network – a UK first, Bike Social, designed and built specifically for bikers – a site for bikers to own and get the most from their biking lifestyle and community. This site overcomes the risks of a purely 'unowned' strategy of data ownership, lost SEO benefits and consumer privacy. The site brings together all 'unowned' social media activity whilst empowering the biking community to contribute content such as photos, routes, clubs, events via blogs, forums and message boards.

Results

Key objectives of the new brand strategy included:

- significantly increased direct sales;
- improved brand metrics on every key metric: most strongly around awareness and 'a brand supporting bikers and their community';
- 50,000 Facebook fans, 5,000 Twitter followers and 2 million YouTube views;
- reduced advertising spend as a result of brand advocacy across the biking community;
- reduction in complaints by offering customer service via social media networks;
- two successive years of record direct sales and on track for a third;
- number one brand across 10 key factors including 'specialist brand', 'is part of the biking community' and 'does more for bikers than any other brand';
- brand awareness up 20 per cent;
- complaints down 65 per cent and 'No 1 for Customer Service' crown stolen from a competitor;
- over 107,000 Facebook followers, more than all competitors and also major bike brands including Honda, Silverstone and Triumph. Reflects 10 per cent audience penetration versus a financial services industry average of 0.2 per cent;
- over 12,000 Twitter followers and 4.4 million YouTube views;
- over 650,000 visits to Bike Social without any advertising;
- £1.2 million reduction in PPC spend via enhanced natural search performance (spent on bikers instead who advocate the Bennetts brand throughout the community. Top three search terms moved from positions 13, 13, 11 to 3, 3, 4 in less than one year;
- word-of-mouth recommendation for the brand doubled YOY.

Bennetts are on a journey to becoming the true biking brand and our success trajectory is expected to continue, further widening the space between our market leadership and our competition. The evolution of this radical strategy is expected to deliver:

- the top ranking on natural search (fully eliminating PPC spend);

- continued record sales volumes;

- 500,000 bikers regularly interacting with Bike Social; 28 per cent of returning visitors come EVERY DAY!;

- new revenue streams – brand appeal across all things biking, not just insurance;

- elimination of marketing spend that does not benefit bikers and their community.

Links to campaign

- http://www.bennetts.co.uk/

- http://www.bennetts.co.uk/bikesocial/clubs/

About the creator

Hannah Squirrell is Director of Marketing and e-Commerce for Bennetts, the UK's No 1 for motorbike insurance. She is responsible for the delivery of Bennetts' business plan across marketing, e-commerce and aggregation to enhance its market leadership position and continue to deliver exceptional growth.

Hannah has extensive experience of developing and implementing multichannel brand-marketing strategies across a number of businesses. She was a founding member of the Capital One marketing team, where she was instrumental in managing its media strategy and marketing channels. Hannah then joined a Top 5 London independent advertising agency where she set up and managed the digital function working across brands such as Tesco, 3M, Haven Holidays, Thorntons and Avon Cosmetics.

Understanding e-mail marketing

07

OUR CHAPTER PLEDGE TO YOU

When you reach the end of this chapter you'll have answers to the following questions:

- What is e-mail marketing and how can it benefit my business?

- How can I make sure my e-mail marketing campaign won't be seen as spam?

- How can e-mail marketing tools help me?

- How can I use technology to manage my customers?

- How can I write effective copy for my e-mail marketing campaign?

- What are the main design considerations when crafting an e-mail?

- How can I test a campaign's success?

The new direct mail

E-mail marketing is one of the most powerful elements in your digital marketing toolbox. It lets you communicate easily with your customers on a personal level through a universally accepted digital medium. Choosing the right approach for your e-mail marketing communications is, of course, key. Unsophisticated mass-marketing techniques, or anything that smacks of e-mail spam, is likely to be ignored, that's if it makes it to your prospect's inbox at all.

Think of the junk mail that arrives through your letterbox every day. Most of it gets thrown out, unread and, in many cases, unopened. A scene in the 1991 Steve Martin comedy *LA Story* depicts the main character, Harris Telemacher, watching a never-ending barrage of junk mail pouring through his letterbox. He nonchalantly kicks a waste-paper basket under the unwanted stream of promotional bunkum and continues eating his breakfast. While exaggerated, it is a scenario that many of us can empathize with – and an apt analogy for what is happening with electronic mail today.

Naturally, as e-mail started to become integrated into our business and personal lives, so the mass marketers turned their attention to the new medium. Junk paper mail became junk virtual mail. But whether it is online or in the 'real world', if your business becomes associated with streams of junk mail (or spam) it will destroy your credibility. People will either ignore your electronic missives, or will filter them out before they even arrive.

Despite the proliferation of spam, and the fact that most people's inboxes today are bursting with irrelevant and unsolicited messages, e-mail can still be used as a beneficial and effective marketing tool that delivers real value, both to your customers and to your business.

Customers will still open your e-mail

The truth is, many customers will welcome regular e-mail communications from your business, in the same way as they may welcome the occasional traditional or 'snail' mail offering a money-off voucher for their favourite store. They will open an e-mail containing a newsletter or promotion from you, as long as they recognize your brand, they're expecting to receive communication from you, and are confident it will contain something of value to them. The key is to make these messages relevant and interesting for your chosen audience; fail in that, and unfortunately your message is destined for the virtual recycling bin.

E-mail marketing can be a tricky field to navigate effectively. You have to simultaneously respect your customers' right to privacy, protect your brand, and ultimately maintain your value proposition over time. It is very easy for your carefully cultivated e-mail prospects to unsubscribe from your mailing list, and once you've lost them, they're probably gone for good.

What exactly is e-mail marketing?

E-mail marketing is a fusion of marketing savvy and imaginative copy. In its simplest form, it's an e-mail sent to a customer list that usually contains a sales pitch and a 'call to action'. This could be as simple as encouraging the customer to click on a web link embedded in the e-mail. Some examples of e-mail marketing campaigns could include:

- a hotel promoting a special summer discount;
- a recruitment company informing business clients about a free seminar;
- a gadget store offering a money-off code to be used at its online checkout;
- a fitness centre offering members a special printout voucher that entitles the bearer to bring a friend along for free;
- a beverage company encouraging people to download a game that integrates into the user's Facebook profile.

You can also use e-mail when you don't have anything specific to market, as a mechanism to maintain consumer engagement, strengthen brand perception and add credibility to your business. In fact, even in the Web 2.0 world of blogs, social networks and RSS feeds, e-mail newsletters are still incredibly popular, and offer a very effective way to get your brand out in front of your list of prospects on a regular basis. Examples might include:

- an accountancy firm keeping in touch with its clients by informing them about changes in tax legislation;
- a weekly newsletter from a public relations company that contains interesting snippets of industry news and web links to longer articles;
- a daily digest or breaking news alert from an online newspaper;
- a young adult book publisher using e-mail marketing to promote free and exclusive screen savers, ring tones and wallpapers to its young readers.

Because e-mail is an incredibly cost-efficient communications medium, when used effectively it can deliver an excellent return on investment (ROI).

E-mail marketing tools

When it comes to managing and sending your marketing e-mail, you probably won't want to rely on your standard desktop e-mail client to do the job. While it's a perfectly feasible approach for very small lists, as more people subscribe to your e-mail offering it will quickly become cumbersome and unmanageable.

What you need instead is one of the many custom e-mail marketing systems out there. These can either be software that you install on your local machine, software you run on your own server, or a software-as-a-service (SaaS) offering hosted by an online service provider. These systems let you manage your e-mail list, craft your design templates for your messages and, most importantly, help you to track your e-mail campaigns (see Figure 7.1).

FIGURE 7.1 E-mail marketing specialists like Benchmark Email (**http://bit.ly/UDMBenchmark**) offer scalable hosted e-mail solutions to help you manage every aspect of your e-mail marketing campaigns

Some of the functions that e-mail marketing tools can provide (and this is not an exhaustive list) include:

- Easy-to-use tools that let you create and work from e-mail templates without having to be a technical expert.
- Testing tools that allow you to check your message will make it past major spam filters.
- Tracking tools that show how many people have ignored, opened or responded to your e-mail (more about this is mentioned in detail towards the end of the chapter).

- Personalization tools that let you modify the content dynamically to individuals or specific target profiles on your list.

Customer relationship management

It is no good using e-mail marketing tools if you don't know who you're sending your e-mails to. Customer relationship management (CRM) is a business concept that has been around for about 25 years. It is the art, if you will, of keeping your customers happy and maintaining an ongoing personal relationship with them. Let's say you run a small grocery shop in an equally small neighbourhood. Over time you'll get to know your regular customers, their likes and dislikes, and what other products they might be interested in trying, etc. Larger businesses struggle to maintain that sort of personal connection with consumers, and that is where CRM comes in.

For instance, if you keep a record of the products or services that a customer has bought from you in the past, what they've looked at on your website, how often they've contacted you – you can merge that data with the relevant demographic details, then, using CRM technology, you can track and anticipate what those customers are likely to be interested in. The result? Relevant, targeted marketing that is much more likely to convert.

When it comes to e-mail marketing, CRM can help you segment your list, allowing you to focus highly targeted campaigns to the customers most likely to respond. You can fine tune your e-mail offering and align it with your customers' purchase history. The possibilities are virtually endless.

If your business already uses CRM systems for more traditional marketing, then you should be able to incorporate that data into your e-mail marketing strategy. Some CRM systems cater for e-mail campaigns as part of their feature set, while others integrate with your chosen e-mail marketing solution.

We'll talk about technology where appropriate as we progress through the chapter but ultimately, e-mail marketing tools will only prove effective if you, as a digital marketer, spend time developing the right e-mail strategy for your business, and execute it in the right way.

Before you start

Before you begin planning your e-mail marketing campaign, there are a number of things you need to consider from practical and legal perspectives.

Building your e-mail list

As we mentioned earlier, people won't respond to seemingly random e-mail communications: they won't even open them. So before you can do any e-mail marketing you need to build up a list of customers who *want* to receive e-mail communications from your business. The best way to do that is to encourage them, whenever you get the chance, to opt-in to receiving your e-mails.

Your website is the hub of your digital marketing world (see Chapter 3), and is a natural place to ask people to sign up for your opt-in mailing list. All you need to do is place a simple, prominent form on your site encouraging visitors to sign up for the latest updates, direct to their inbox. If they like your site and value your content, many will welcome the opportunity to hear from you by e-mail with regular news, special offers and occasional one-off promotions.

Use your extended web presence to encourage sign-ups, too. Embed a newsletter sign-up form on your brand's Facebook page, for example, and encourage sign-ups by linking to your sign-up page from the occasional Twitter update. You could also use your e-mails to encourage readers to introduce your newsletter to their friends... and perhaps even offer an incentive for them to do so. There are lots of ways you can harness broader digital marketing principles to help you build your list organically... get imaginative!

If you're in a hurry to build a list and send out a campaign quickly, another option is to rent an e-mail list from a specialist marketing company, but be careful. You need to make sure that the organization providing you with the list is a member of your country's Direct Marketing Association or similar, and that they tick all of the boxes in terms of their anti-spam and privacy policies. People on these lists should have opted in to receive e-mail offers from third-party companies or 'partners' – if they haven't, then any mail you send them is essentially spam, regardless of your impeccable intentions. You will also need to check that no one on your rented list has already unsubscribed from your own mailing lists. If they have you'll need to remove them before you send out your campaign.

Another way to attract opt-in is when a customer completes some kind of transaction on your website, such as purchasing a product, downloading a white paper or requesting additional information. By making an e-mail address a mandatory component of the transaction, you can add to your e-mail list. Legalities vary here, but in many countries, including in the UK, it is fine to send marketing e-mails to people once they have completed a transaction with you, as long as you have given them the option to decline.

This is referred to as a 'soft opt-in'. And remember, every marketing e-mail you send out must provide the recipient with a straightforward way to unsubscribe from your list – an opt-out, if you like.

Legal requirements

Another crucial factor is, of course, to be familiar with the law in your jurisdiction. Sending out unsolicited e-mail to random consumers will breach spam legislation in most Western countries. Anti-spam laws are there to enforce ethical e-mail marketing practices that respect customer data and privacy. Legitimate businesses will follow the laws, but spammers are hard to trace. They will typically use underhanded techniques to harvest e-mail addresses and send large volumes of unsolicited e-mails.

Back in late 2007 spam accounted for an astonishing 95 per cent of all e-mail traffic. Things have improved slightly since then, and according to the Kaspersky Lab Spam Statistic Report published in November 2013, e-mail spam had dropped to 68.3 per cent of e-mail traffic. But that's still a ludicrously high volume of spammy e-mail.

China is the biggest source of spam globally, contributing 22.2 per cent. The top three countries – China, the United States and South Korea – together account for 55 per cent of the world's spam traffic according to Kaspersky Lab.

The practice continues because: 1) it costs very little to send a marketing e-mail to millions of people on a list; 2) even the tiniest conversion rate turns a profit for the spammer; and 3) most spam can't be traced, and originates outside the relevant jurisdictions.

Just in case you hadn't picked up the vibe, we'll spell it out: SPAM IS BAD. It is almost certainly against the law in the country you're operating from, and what's more it annoys the very people you're hoping to connect with: your future customers. When you're just starting out, and don't have much of an opt-in list, it can be tempting. Don't do it!

Anti-spam legislation in the United States and Europe

US law

In the United States, the CAN-SPAM Act (Controlling the Assault of Non-Solicited Pornography and Marketing Act) came into effect on 1 January 2004. The Federal Trade Commission has a fact sheet, accessible at **www.business. ftc.gov/documents/bus61-can-spam-act-compliance-guide-business**, outlining legal requirements for businesses sending e-mails. The main points include:

- Recipients must be able to 'opt-out' of receiving future e-mails, and such actions must be processed within 10 business days.
- The source of the e-mail must be traceable.
- Subject lines must not be deceptive.
- Your full postal address must be included.

Apart from being fined up to US $16,000 for violating any of these terms, there are additional fines for using spammers' techniques, including automatically generating e-mail addresses or harvesting them from the web.

European law

The Privacy and Electronic Communications (EC Directive) Regulations 2003 is the overriding anti-spam legislation. You will find that individual countries will interpret the law in their own ways, and you need to take data protection legislation into account, too.

In the UK, you can download a fact sheet for marketers from the Information Commissioner's Office website at **www.ico.org.uk**. These clearly outline, in Q&A form, what digital marketers can and can't do with e-mail. As we have mentioned, having the recipient opt-in to marketing messages is crucial (but don't forget the 'soft opt-in', which means that once you've collected contact details from someone who has bought a product or service from you, or expressed an interest, then you can go ahead and market to them as long as they have been given an easy way to opt out).

Logistical problems

Sometimes the mail just doesn't get through. There are a variety of reasons why your e-mails may not arrive in your customers' inboxes. They may have been inadvertently/incorrectly categorized as spam by the ISP (Internet Service Provider), or filtered into a junk-mail folder by a web-based or desktop e-mail client. Spam filters are so aggressive these days that people may not see much spam in their inbox, but an overzealous spam filter can sometimes intercept legitimate mail too. For the customer this seems great, but it does mean that they can be missing out on potentially useful and informative e-mails – like your latest newsletter!

In e-mail marketers' jargon, when a legitimate e-mail is blocked by a spam filter it is called a 'false positive'. These false positives can be a real setback to your e-mail marketing endeavours. Even discovering that your opt-in marketing e-mail is being blocked can be a tricky proposition, and resolving the problem can be difficult, especially when you feel you have followed the rules to the letter.

Your best bet is to try and avoid the spam trap problem from the beginning by making sure your e-mails don't look and read like spam. If your e-mail software has an option to test how well your message will fare with spam filters, use it, and change anything that it flags as potentially suspect. You should also make sure that all of your e-mail can be traced back to a valid IP address from a reputable host. If you do that, there's no real reason for your e-mails to be blocked.

An organization called the Spamhaus Project (**www.spamhaus.org**) works to track and block spammers. On their website there is information on why legitimate e-mails can sometimes be blacklisted, and what you can do to resolve the problem.

E-mail formats

Another reason your e-mails may not be seen is that you're sending them out in a format that your recipients' e-mail clients – the software or website used to read and reply to e-mails – doesn't recognize. This is not as much of a problem as it used to be, because the adoption of internet standards has improved significantly, and pretty much all of the e-mail clients today will seamlessly handle rich text or HTML e-mail, unless the user has specified otherwise.

When you send out your marketing e-mail, you can normally choose to send it in its most basic plain text form (with no formatting). You can be fairly certain that all of your prospects will be able to read it, but it is hardly the most aesthetically pleasing experience. One step up from plain text is rich text format, which allows you to format the text with font sizes, colours, bold and italics, and allows recipients to click on web links. This looks better than plain text, and can be very effective for simple informational newsletters.

The most sophisticated e-mails are built using HTML (the same code that developers use to build web pages). This essentially means that your e-mail can look exactly like a regular web page, complete with images, web links and all the rest. Images are not usually sent with the e-mail, but are usually pulled in from a webserver when the e-mail is viewed. HTML e-mails can tie in with the look and feel of your website, providing a consistent look and great brand continuity when your prospects click through to your landing page.

For most e-mail marketers HTML is now the standard format for sending mail, but it's important to remember that many e-mail clients (and web-based e-mail such as Hotmail and Gmail fall into this category) automatically block external images for security reasons until recipients override the setting either for an individual message or for all messages from a particular sender. It makes sense, therefore, to do two things: 1) make sure that your e-mail message works even without the images (ie ensure your value proposition and call to action are clearly outlined in the text); and 2) encourage your readers to automatically allow images from your address for future e-mails.

Generally you won't need to worry about sending different versions of your e-mails to different customers. An internet standard called MIME (Multipurpose Internet Mail Extensions) means that messages today go out in 'multipart' format. This means that your recipient's e-mail client will be able to view the message in the best way it can, and if a recipient has set their client to receive text-only e-mails, then that's what they will see.

Planning your campaign

As with any part of your digital marketing strategy, to get the most out of your e-mail you need to define who you are targeting, why, and what you want out of it. Do you want to generate more sales? Or are you looking to maintain a relationship with your customers by keeping them up-to-date with the business? It's important to be specific here, and to make sure that your e-mail marketing strategy feeds into your overall business goals.

Digital customer relationship management (CRM) can help you to segment your customers, and to target specific groups with tailored e-mail offerings if that makes sense. You can also deliver personalized content to them, and wherever possible you should endeavour to personalize all of your e-mail marketing as much as you can. At its most basic, this involves using your prospect's real name in your e-mail messages, but more sophisticated software will allow you to pull in specific dynamic content based on a particular customer profile. For example, an e-mail from an airline could highlight the number of frequent flyer points a customer has left to spend before they expire, or an online bookshop could recommend new books based on a customer's purchase history.

Focus on great content

Good e-mail design is important, and it makes a lot of sense to establish some brand continuity between your e-mail templates and your website design. Every aspect of your digital marketing campaign should, of course, work seamlessly together. But *always* remember that your e-mail content is paramount. Your template design should complement, rather than compete with, your e-mail content for your readers' attention.

In general you aim to make your e-mail copy punchy, scannable, snackable and engaging – much like effective web copy. Long, sales-letter-style e-mails tend to be less effective, but remember that it very much depends on your business and your audience. Use your judgement, your knowledge of your business and your customers, and craft your message to suit. Test your content regularly, and tweak it to yield optimum results.

Above all, remember that crucial call to action.

When and how often?

You should think carefully about the frequency of the e-mails you send out to your list. Send mail too infrequently and you drop off your customers' radar, but send them too often and you start to irritate them. People don't want to be bombarded with marketing e-mails... even the ones for which they have opted in.

Sometimes it can be hard to predict how often you should send out marketing e-mails, and when, in fact, is the best day or time to send them. That's another reason why it is so vital to track and analyse every aspect of your e-mail campaign. If you notice people suddenly starting to unsubscribe from your lists, ask yourself why. Are you sending out e-mails too often, or has a change in format prompted the exodus? Whatever it is, keep a close eye on your campaigns and the data they generate, and when things do go awry, try to rectify the problem as soon as you can. If you don't, you risk your e-mails being perceived as spam, and that can do more than just damage your e-mail campaign – it can have a serious impact on the broader online reputation of your business.

Lessons from your own inbox

You can learn a lot about what works and what doesn't in e-mail marketing by taking a closer look at your own inbox. Examine the array of newsletters and marketing e-mails you've signed up to receive. Do any of them jump out at you and scream 'read me'? Why?

What is it about a particular message that makes you want to open it? Are there any e-mails you've signed up for that you actively look forward to receiving? Are there some that you never open?

Analyse the marketing e-mails in your own inbox, deconstruct them, and apply what you learn to your own e-mail marketing campaigns. As your e-mail campaigns evolve, you will naturally start to find what works best for you... after all, no one knows your business or your customers like you do.

E-mail marketing dos and don'ts

Sean Duffy, a leading UK-based e-mail marketing expert, shares his dos and dont's for the six key areas of successful e-mail marketing.

There are six core areas that represent the essential stages of e-mail marketing at its best. They are delivery, content, timing, testing, legal and measurement.

Delivery

There is no point in looking at e-mail marketing until we address how to miss the junk folder and land in the inbox. The messages you are sending are, of course, going to be legitimate and opted-in, but unfortunately they share many characteristics of spam e-mail such as the large volume being sent in a short period of time, and the sales-focused copy with words like 'free' or 'offer'.

Over the years ISP's and spam filters have tried many ways of trying to distinguish between spam and legitimate e-mail. First they looked at the content of the e-mail and, in particular, keywords used. However, spammers quickly learned to get around this by changing 'viagra' to 'v1agra' or hiding their text within an image.

Therefore, there has been a shift to looking at the reputation of the sender instead. If the server sending the e-mail has a history of a high number of complaints or invalid addresses then the ISP is more likely to block the e-mail. Yet even this was not enough, as spammers moved on to switching servers very quickly. Therefore, ISPs looked to change the emphasis so that new servers found it harder to get e-mail campaigns delivered than an established server with a good reputation.

All of this has made e-mail delivery a complex area and helped create further growth in the e-mail service provider (ESP) industry. For only a few pounds per month, ESPs help take the majority of the burden off you, allowing you to concentrate your time on creating quality e-mail campaigns.

Do:

- Keep your lists clean. ISPs will look at the amount of bad addresses you are sending to, and complaints your e-mails are generating from their customers as to whether you deserve your e-mail to be delivered.

- Be relevant with your e-mails. Just blasting your database with non-targeted offers will lead to higher complaints, as well as having other detrimental effects on the success of your e-mails.

- Use an e-mail service provider – even if you have limited budget there are providers who will manage the send from their white-listed servers for a few pounds per month, thus taking the burden of looking after all the technical aspects required to get good delivery rates.

Don't:

- Just think that using an ESP will guarantee good inbox placement. An ESP will help out with providing the technical infrastructure to achieve good delivery rates but only you are in control of your sending reputation.

- Add to your list any e-mail addresses that you can get hold of. Sending unsolicited e-mails, or sending to old lists, will cause delivery issues.

Developing content for e-mail

When thinking about developing content for an e-mail it is useful to think about the context of your customer checking their e-mail account. Increasingly the inbox is becoming overcrowded, with more than 180 billion e-mails sent and received each day in 2013, according to the Radicati Group. This allows for less time per message, which means you need to stand out amongst the clutter, and grab their attention when they do open your e-mail.

In addition, there is also the longer-term impact of getting your content right or wrong. Those brands that are trusted by the customer and have provided relevant e-mail content previously are more likely to be opened than those sent by brands whose messages have failed to send anything that inspired or was relevant. Your customers will learn to know which brands' e-mails are not worth their precious time to open.

Do:

- Write punchy short copy. E-mail users tend to scan an e-mail to see if there is anything of interest, so you need to grab their attention. Writing long copy may work in a direct mail letter, but the way people read e-mail is different.

- Focus your effort on the top of the e-mail, which is visible when opening. This is known as 'above the fold'. If you don't engage them here then they won't scroll to find something else in the e-mail.

- Be relevant. This is common sense, but if there is nothing of interest in the e-mail they don't need to respond. Worse still, if the customer develops a perception that there is never anything relevant to them in your e-mails, then even when there is, the chances are they will ignore the e-mail. Either send different versions to different segments, or utilize dynamic content where whole areas of the e-mail are tailored to the customer's preferences or past purchases.

- Craft your design so that your key messages still jump out even when the e-mail client does not download images without the recipient first clicking.

Don't:

- Worry about certain keywords or content getting your e-mail blocked. The days of the word 'free' causing your e-mail to land in junk are over. What is important is your reputation as a sender with ISPs.

- Include any attachments, JavaScript, Flash or video. It won't work and will cause many of your e-mails to be blocked as ISPs consider this to be a security concern.

Timing and frequency

When is the best time to send an e-mail? How often should I e-mail my customers? These are probably two of the most asked questions in e-mail marketing. Of course the answer to either of these is not simple. The best time to send an e-mail is not as important as the quality and relevance of the message. There are plenty of examples of e-mail campaigns that perform extremely well no matter what time of day.

Second, how often to send to your database should really be geared around how often you have something valuable and relevant to say. This will not be the same for each segment of your database. New customers should get a welcome programme, defected customers might get an incentive to come back and make a purchase, or you might want to follow up on those who requested a brochure – in order to convert them to a purchaser. E-mail marketing is not just e-mail newsletters.

Do:

- Only send when you have something of value. Don't get fixated by needing to maintain a certain frequency.

- Time e-mails around the customer life cycle, not just when you have an offer. Instead of treating everyone the same, think how you can improve conversion rates, encourage loyalty and reduce defection through 'triggering' special e-mails at key times in your relationship with the customer.

- Send an e-mail before they forget who you are. After putting the effort into getting website visitors to part with their e-mail address, don't leave it a few weeks till they get your first e-mail. By then the relationship between you and the customer is likely to be colder, and therefore it is more difficult to engage with them through e-mail.

Don't:

- Presume that additional e-mails will always generate more revenue. A long-term effect of too many e-mails will lead to your subscribers switching off and ignoring your messages, reducing the revenue generated from e-mail.

Testing

One of the greatest strengths of e-mail is the ability to get a message out to your customers in minutes. This presents a danger and an opportunity when it comes to testing.

First, the danger is to skip necessary but tedious pre-flight checks through the desire for speed of delivering the e-mail. E-mail has a certain complexity, which means your e-mail may not display as you intend, or it may get caught in spam filters.

Then the opportunity. Due to the speed to create a campaign and collate the results, marketers can test different versions to samples of their database. This takes the guesswork out of what type of subject line or call to action creates the most opens and clicks.

Do:

- Try different A/B split tests to prove what works best. Ensure that you send to a minimum of 1,500 per test, otherwise the results are unlikely to be reliable.

- Test in different e-mail clients and webmail providers to make sure the e-mail arrives in the inbox, looking exactly how you intended. Alternatively, use an application such as Litmus.com, which does all of this for you.

Don't:

- Test more than one thing at a time when split testing, otherwise you won't know what caused the change in results.

- Send your e-mail without having sent yourself a test as an e-mail. E-mail systems can mangle text and break links as they are not as strong as your browser at handling HTML.

Legal and ethics

The law around who you can send marketing e-mails to does vary from region to region. In Europe the privacy legislation is also implemented differently in each member state. In the UK marketers are required to get consumers to opt-in to receive e-mails. However, they can operate on an opt-out basis with corporate customers. This means they can send e-mails until the receiver tells them to stop. With all types of e-mail marketing an option to easily unsubscribe through a link or e-mail address must be included in each message, and actioned promptly.

While it is important to understand the law, just ensuring you don't end up in court is not enough. There are many examples of brands pushing the law – whether it be making it difficult not to opt-in, or indeed difficult to opt-out. This is self-defeating, however. If someone does not want to be on your list there is no point in keeping them. It can cause deliverability issues as more recipients use the 'report as spam' button – and damage to your brand can also occur.

Do:

- Make it clear on your data capture forms what they are opting into, what they will receive and how often.

- Make it easy to unsubscribe, and honour those unsubscribes.

Don't:

- Think that just because you are within the law that your data capture policy is ethical. In reality, spam is defined by what the recipient thinks is spam, not what the law courts say.

Measurement

E-mail marketing campaigns can be fully tracked to enable you to see who got the e-mail, who opened the message, clicked or purchased an item. This presents marketers with a wealth of data in which actionable decisions can be made to improve their e-mail marketing.

Do:

- Track opens, clicks and conversion activity. Every ESP enables you to do this and even Google Analytics will allow you to track how many sales can be attributed to a specific e-mail campaign.

- Report trends, not just specific e-mail campaigns. This enables you to identify if you have declining performance and to project what would happen if that trend continues.

- Analyse per segment of your database. The more you break down the reporting information, the more insight it will give into where your e-mail marketing is and is not working. For example, how do new customers perform compared to existing customers? Is there a difference between gender? What content does each segment prefer? All of this will then lead on to ideas as to how you can improve underperforming segments.

Don't:

- Just measure short-term metrics of what happened in that campaign. You need to take a long-term view. Here is an example. If you average 15 per cent open rates, is it the same 15 per cent each time? If so, why are the remaining 85 per cent so inactive? Now you have identified those people it provides a huge untapped opportunity.

- Be happy with industry benchmarks. Just because your competition may average 12 per cent open rates and 3 per cent click rates does not mean you should settle for these. Those brands that put the time and effort into making their e-mail marketing programme relevant and timely usually improve on the benchmarks by at least 50 per cent.

Sean Duffy, formerly principal e-mail marketing consultant at E-mailcenter, a leading e-mail service provider based in the UK.

E-mail design

Many of the same usability principles that apply in website design apply equally to the design of an effective HTML e-mail template. You will want your message to display consistently and effectively across as many platforms as possible. People will be viewing their e-mails using different screen widths and formats, and will be using all manner of different e-mail clients to display your messages. Make sure your template degrades gracefully (works well without images, and is viewable and makes sense using the lowest common denominator in e-mail formats: plain text), and test your templates thoroughly on as many different platforms as possible in order to make sure they work (or use a service such as Litmus.com to take some of the pain out of cross-platform e-mail testing).

When working on your e-mail design, think in terms of 'above the fold' – just like with a newspaper folded in half, the top of your e-mail should capture the recipient's attention immediately and encourage them to read on. Don't force them to scroll through pages of text before they reach your 'once-in-a-lifetime' never-to-be-missed offer. Get to the good stuff early, and leave less important stuff/supporting information for lower on the page. Also remember that e-mail clients often show a short 'preview' of the message body below the subject line in the inbox. Use this: engage prospects with those first couple of lines and entice them to open your message.

Your design should reflect your corporate identity and branding, and should extend through to the landing page that the e-mail links back to. Consistency and continuity is key here, and a seamless experience between your e-mail and your website promotes trust, and crucially, improves conversion.

Use rich media judiciously

By and large you should avoid rich media (flash, video, audio, interactive banners, etc) in your e-mail marketing. Rich media can be really useful in augmenting the content on a web page, but it rarely adds value to e-mail communications, and often has the opposite effect.

While it is possible today to embed all sorts of interactive content into HTML e-mail templates, you need to think very carefully about why you are doing it. Does it really add value and enhance your message? Will your e-mail still degrade gracefully and work for people who have rich media content disabled, or whose e-mail software can't handle it? Would your rich media content be better employed on the landing page that your message sends people to, rather than in the body of the message itself?

Apart from the inherent distraction risk of rich media content, there is also the issue of your message being routinely blocked by corporate firewalls and e-mail security systems that view active content in incoming e-mail as a potential security risk. This means that if people are signing up to your mailing lists from a work account, or your target market consists of business users, there's a good chance they will never see your all-singing, all dancing, multimedia-infused masterpiece.

Attachments are another thing that tend to be a bad idea in e-mail market-ing. Avoid sending out PDFs or (worse) MS Word documents with your marketing e-mails. By all means tell your subscribers about your new brochure or latest white paper, but don't include it... instead link to a landing page on your website with more information and the option to download the file if they choose to. It's a simple, effective and much more user-friendly alternative than sending unsolicited file attachments to thousands of e-mail addresses – and has the added bonus of potentially encouraging incoming links to your landing page, delivering SEO benefits and the prospect of new e-mail sign-ups. How's that for a win-win?

Remember, mobile users read e-mail too

More and more people are accessing their e-mail... including your e-mail marketing missive... on their smartphones and tablets while on the move.

That presents a challenge for the e-mail marketer. Think about small display sizes... users may not see your entire subject line, for example, and small display size may affect the way that your carefully crafted e-mail looks. Think about mobile users when you are designing your message: try to ensure it will work on a smaller display, keep your key content to the top right of the e-mail, and make sure it works in text-only form too.

With a small display you have less room to manoeuvre... so be sure to 'hook' the reader early with killer content.

Writing killer e-mail copy

While the design and look of your e-mail is important, it's the copy that is going to galvanize people into action. Beneath the gloss and the sheen, you need to write compelling, engaging copy to get results.

First, it should be instantly obvious that the e-mail is from you. Use your company or brand name in the 'e-mail from' field – and make sure it matches the brand that the user signed up for. It's important that people recognize instantly that this is an e-mail they've opted in to – or they may inadvertently flag your legitimate message as spam (using the 'report as spam' button that is integrated into many e-mail clients today). That not only means that future messages from you will be relegated to that particular user's spam folder, but if it happens too often, may ultimately have repercussions for the deliverability of all your e-mail.

Crafting the e-mail subject line is one of the most important steps in writing your e-mail. The subject is the one piece of creative copy that you know your prospect is going to see *before* clicking through to open your message. It is your one chance to engage and enthral them... to entice that click.

Great subject lines should be catchy, but they also need to instantly communicate the value proposition of your message. Why should the prospect open your e-mail from a list of tens or potentially hundreds of messages landing in his or her inbox every day? Your subject line should answer that question.

Don't try to be too clever with your subject line – clever subjects can be ambiguous, and ambiguous e-mails rarely get read. Your subject needs to be descriptive, yet compelling, which can be a tricky combination to pull off... but if you manage it you'll see your e-mail open rates soar.

For the main body of your content you need to ensure you are talking your customers' language. Always remember to keep your target audience in mind, and write accordingly. Remember that people are busy, and e-mails need to get to the point relatively quickly to hold attention and interest.

Make sure your value proposition and call to action are crystal clear, and that key elements of your message (including links back to your website) are easily scannable and stand out from the body of your copy.

Keep text short and punchy, and avoid lengthy paragraphs (unless you're a particularly skilled and engaging writer, and you know that longer copy works for your particular audience... *there are always caveats*). Long paragraphs can be unwieldy unless they are exceptionally well written. They are difficult to write well, and when written poorly are even more difficult to read. The result: people don't read them. Short copy is easier to get right, will lend your content life and energy, and will help zip readers through your e-mail quickly.

Keep the tone of your copy friendly and approachable, and tailor the language to your audience. Yes, this is a business communication medium, but formal corporate prose is the last thing people want landing in their inbox. Keep things light and conversational, engage with the reader on a personal level (address the individual, not the crowd). You may be sending to a list of thousands, but to the reader it's one-to-one.

Proofread everything at least twice... and then get someone else to read through it too. Read it in plain text and in its final HTML form. Make sure your content is accurate not only in terms of spelling and punctuation, but also in terms of the detail. Double check things like prices, dates, contact details, etc. Then, when you're ready to click send, check them again!

E-mail delivery

Making sure your e-mails are delivered to the people on your list is another crucial element in your e-mail marketing. It's good practice to send out your e-mail to a few 'test' or 'seed' e-mail addresses of your own in order to make sure everything is arriving in the inbox as you expect it to before sending it out to your entire list.

Keeping your mailing list 'clean' is vital, and you should endeavour to honour unsubscribe requests as soon as they arrive. Many of these will be handled automatically by your e-mail service provider/e-mail software, but you should also monitor for unsubscribe requests through other channels (think other company e-mail addresses, social media, etc) and remove them manually where necessary.

If you find mail to certain addresses on your list are bouncing regularly (ie messages are undeliverable), investigate why. If the address is dead, purge it from your list (but don't remove addresses immediately... e-mail downtime is a fact of life, and occurs more often than you might think). Most e-mail service providers allow you to specify a bounce limit beyond which they will automatically purge addresses from your active lists and move them to a separate bounce list. You can then view them and either delete them or reinstate them as part of your routine list housekeeping.

If a lot of your mail starts to bounce, it's worth checking to see if a particular ISP or webmail provider is blocking your e-mail. If it looks like that is happening, it's important to contact your e-mail service provider immediately to try and get the situation resolved.

When you send out your messages you should be prepared for a rush of incoming replies. Automated 'out of office' autoresponders and 'unsubscribe' requests will start to arrive as soon as your e-mail message hits people's inboxes, so don't be surprised to see them. This is probably the main reason you want to choose a dedicated (but monitored) e-mail address as the 'from' address for your campaigns.

One other thing worth noting here is that if you're starting with a small list, and want to use your desktop e-mail software to send out a few exploratory marketing e-mails to get your toes wet, *please* make sure you use the BCC (blind carbon copy) field, rather than the regular 'To' field for your list of e-mail addresses. If you don't, everyone on the list will see everyone else's e-mail address... and we're betting that's not covered in your privacy policy!

Measuring your success

Analysing the success of your first campaign can provide valuable data that can shed light on how you progress and evolve future campaigns.

You can use e-mail marketing tools to analyse:

- approximately how many people opened the e-mail (called the open rate);
- when people typically opened your e-mail;
- what links people tended to click on (the click-through rate);
- the percentage of people who opened the e-mail who then went to click through to the website (the click-to-open rate);
- who never opens their e-mails;
- the types of e-mails with the best conversion rates;
- track e-mails that regularly bounce;
- how many people unsubscribed from your lists;

- which e-mail clients/providers (if any) blocked your messages;
- how frequently a series of e-mails is opened by a particular subscriber.

Target your campaigns

The more data you have on your subscribers, the more you can split and segment them into niche groups that you can target with more specific campaigns, as long as your set-up can support it.

If you have a complex business with a wide array of different customers, investing in a sophisticated CRM system will let you build an even more detailed profile of your customer base and of their purchasing behaviour. By linking their customer account (if they have registered on your website) to other databases within your business, and 'mining' customer data from a variety of sources, you can get an increasingly granular view, and can target ever more relevant messages to particular segments of your e-mail lists.

Test your techniques

To gauge the success of a potential e-mail campaign, you can also run A/B split tests with groups of subscribers. This simply means sending two (or more) versions of an e-mail that communicates the same message in different ways (using a different subject line, for example), and monitoring to see which one is more effective. Based on the results, you then send the most effective version of the message out to your entire list.

Here we asked Simon Bowker, Teradata eCircle's Managing Director for the UK and a leading practitioner of e-mail marketing, to provide a point of view and some advice for digital marketers.

Measuring e-mail success

Simon Bowker, Managing Director of Teradata eCircle UK, shares some invaluable insight and advice for e-mail marketers...

The 'MarketingSherpa 2013' benchmarking report showed that consumer e-mail marketing programmes record an average ROI of 114 per cent. However, digital marketing is no longer about e-mail versus SEO or website design versus social media; serious brands understand there is no such thing as a single solution. Integration between e-mail, social, SEO and analytics has never been more important.

Research that eCircle conducted with Neilsen shows that the combination of display and e-mail marketing campaigns significantly increases ad recall and the propensity to buy. It is vital that businesses understand exactly what are the aims and objectives for their e-mail marketing. There are a number of important questions marketers should ask before starting a new e-mail campaign. For example, is there an existing database or do you need to purchase data from another source or create a mechanism to get your customers signed up to e-mails? Will your e-mails target customers effectively at different times in their life cycle?

It is possible to analyse e-mails in a number of different ways. Marketers need to ensure that the best possible ROI measurement tools are linked to the aims of the campaign. One of the most basic figures that every e-mail marketing campaign is assessed on is open rates. Different e-mails will generate very different responses. However, your first contact with a new customer, or the welcome e-mail to a new subscriber to your newsletter, tend to be some of the best read. This means that your subject line and starter offers are extremely important and should not be neglected.

To begin an effective e-mail campaign you need to do more than just capture e-mail addresses. The more information you collect at the sign-in process, the better the opportunity to personalize and target the e-mail content, which ultimately increases the chances of your e-mails being read. Segmentation is fundamental to ensuring that your e-mail campaign is targeting the most appropriate audience. By dividing your database, it allows you to send more thorough, focused, targeted and personalized e-mail communication, leading to a higher positive response rate. To help you make the choice about which way to segment your data, it is helpful to consider the different types of segmentation models that can be applied – these include profile-based segmentation (age, gender, geographic location, key dates) and behavioural-based segmentation (analyse click behaviours and browsing, or purchase, history).

Leading on from segmenting your database, the best approach to target your different segments needs to be determined. On a basic level, segmentation can be implemented in order to test different subject lines, depending on who the e-mail is being sent to. Although simple, it is still an effective way to use segmentation, due to the high level of impact that a subject line can have on the opening of an e-mail, and it helps to gain further insight into visitor behaviour and to increase conversion rate. A/B split testing is when you have two versions of an element (A and B) and a metric that determines the most successful. To establish which version is better, both versions are tested simultaneously to measure which version was more successful and which performs the best.

The number of customers clicking-through from your e-mails onto your website is another important metric. According to Silverpop's '2013 E-mail Marketing Metrics Benchmark Study', the average click-through rate is below 5 per cent. To increase this you have to keep two things in mind: segment your database into appropriate target groups and ensure that you are sending your subscribers targeted and relevant content.

To really gain insight from both the click-through and open rates you should look to find a ratio between these two figures. If you divide the click-through rate by the opening rate, you will gain insight into the success of your campaign from the addressees who opened the e-mail. This indicates whether readers considered the content interesting or whether you need to look at ways to optimize it further. The key metric for all e-mail campaigns is the conversion rate that analyses the number of recipients who have carried out a specific action – eg purchase, download or registration – in relation to the broadcasted volume of e-mails.

Analytics

The process of integrating the different strands of marketing analytics can be daunting. However, the good news is that the best e-mail service providers (ESPs) will be able to provide you with a 'plug and play' solution, which will join your e-mail and web analytics packages seamlessly.

Before making significant changes to your digital marketing strategy it is often worth considering an e-mail audit to assess exactly what stage you are at now, and gain a better understanding of which parts need improving. Broadly speaking, this should cover six core areas: strategy, segmentation and personalization, layout and content, list growth, automation and efficiency, and analysis.

E-mail service provider's technology should give you direct access to critical information such as impressions, clicks, open rates and bounces. With the additional support of specialist web analytics companies you can also drill down much deeper into your customers' behaviour to see click-through rates from specific sections of the e-mail, revenue and orders from a campaign, and conversation rates.

Information gathered from the analytics packages can then be fed back into your database and used to enhance future campaigns.

For example, if you can identify customers that have clicked-through from the campaign but have not purchased, you can then target these people with an automatic abandoned basket campaign – reminding them to return to their purchase or offering them suitable alternatives. Results from abandoned basket campaigns are typically very high, with 25 per cent open rates and clicks of 15 per cent.

The future of e-mail marketing

Everybody is always talking about the next big thing and the future of e-mail, but marketers should really be concentrating on what's happening *now* and how their customers are interacting with them *today*. How many marketers are actually taking advantage of all the marketing tools at their fingertips (advanced e-mail applications, web analytics, social media, social commerce, recommendation engines, mobile applications and so on) to work towards a common goal right now? Not many. The process of understanding our customers in the 'moment' and tailoring our relationships to support that interaction will evolve our tools and techniques for communicating with them, so that our transition into the 'future' will be a natural event.

However, we have begun to see a number of trends emerging since early 2010 that are affecting the way we communicate. The rise of the mobile has seen consumers increasingly access their e-mails on the go and have technology on them at all times, creating a link between the online and offline worlds. The increase of mobile access to e-mail has had a serious impact on the content and format of e-mails, as different devices vary the way that e-mails appear.

As the use of social media and online networks continues to grow and develop, it is increasingly important to integrate campaigns seamlessly. Consumers do not necessarily differentiate between how the brand communicates on e-mail or Twitter, so brands must maintain a high level of consistency between the channels. According to iContact's 'Small and Midsize Business E-mail Marketing Survey 2013', 64 per cent of businesses integrate their e-mail marketing and social media marketing, so while some brands are recognizing the need for a co-ordinated approach, there is still room for improvement.

Data is the oil of digital marketing and will continue to grow in importance. Understanding your database and being able to pull out very specific segments to target, whether these are new customers or lapsed customers who appear to have lost interest, will need to become increasingly more sophisticated in order to make sure that you continue to send relevant, targeted e-mails that ensure the success of your e-mail campaign.

User-generated content and true e-mail dialogue between customers and businesses is also more focused than ever. With the increasingly available and affordable technology that can be easily integrated with existing systems, we expect to see adoption of user-generated content across the board from small- to medium-sized enterprises up to multinational companies.

E-mail – a vital component of digital marketing

The real beauty of e-mail marketing is that it lets you deliver your message directly to an individual who actually wants to hear from you. Compare this to your website, which is necessarily more generic (to appeal to a broader audience) and needs to work harder to attract and retain a visitor's attention.

While e-mail marketing is just one of the many ways of connecting and maintaining a relationship with your customers, and is perhaps getting a bit long in the tooth compared to the young and dynamic social media channels that are emerging, it nevertheless remains a stalwart of the integrated internet marketing strategy, and when executed properly can be incredibly effective.

CASE STUDY   Help for Heroes

Help for Heroes is a charity set up in the UK to help soldiers who have been injured, need support and also supports affected families.

Location

UK.

IN SUPPORT OF

HELP *for* HEROES

CHARITY NO
1 1 2 0 9 2 0

The challenge

To create a way to consistently stay in touch with Help for Heroes' 500,000 subscribers.

Target audience

Help for Heroes subscribers.

Action

- Help for Heroes stay in touch with their subscribers in three fields: charity, retail, and events and challenges.
- Events and challenge headlines are primarily used to send mailings about keeping supporters informed.
- Retail headlines usually cover direct sales of a range of Help for Heroes branded merchandise, which now includes over 500 items.
- Events and challenges headlines encourage people to take part in and organize events to support the charity's work and also encourage fundraising.
- In order to fulfil the necessary three fields dotMailer set in place their Microsoft Dynamics software, this enabled Help for Heroes to create a new, seamless, e-mail marketing initiative.
- The Help for Heroes templates also underwent a redesign, including the development of new and exciting graphics.
- The Help for Heroes mailing list was integrated into the Microsoft Dynamics software to give them the ability to send out e-mails quickly and more efficiently.
- Analytics were also built in so that help for Heroes could track receiver's actions, including open, forward and click-through rates.

Results

- Dramatic cost-saving for the charity and to keep overheads as low as possible.
- Ability to streamline all Help for Heroes operations.
- Response rates have improved significantly.
- Much more time-efficiency throughout.

Links to campaign

- http://www.helpforheroes.org.uk
- http://www.dotmailer.com

About the creator

Established for over 15 years and the UK's largest and fastest-growing e-mail service provider, dotMailer is the trusted e-mail marketing partner of huge success stories including DHL, Dove Spa, Odeon, London & Partners, ITV, Reiss, Renault Trucks and Nationwide Building Society.

dotMailer is transforming the way that organizations and brands do e-mail marketing.

The tools they have to hand have changed the game – empowering marketing teams to take their e-mail marketing to the next level and beyond.

Quote

Ben Henson, IT change manager for dotMailer said: 'Being able to refine mailing not just by content but by targeting them directly towards those people we know are most likely to respond is going to have a profoundly beneficial effect on the success of e-mail. We've already seen that the linking of MS Dynamics and dotMailer offers huge potential for streamlining our operations and reducing costs.'

Understanding mobile marketing

08

OUR CHAPTER PLEDGE TO YOU

When you reach the end of this chapter you'll have answers to the following questions:

- What is mobile marketing?
- What is the potential for mobile marketing?
- How do I go about setting up a mobile marketing campaign?
- What can mobile marketing do for my business?
- What are the top tips for building a successful mobile marketing campaign?
- What role do mobile apps play in an increasingly mobile marketing world?
- How significant are location-based apps and mobile gaming?
- What are the privacy issues surrounding mobile?

Mobile – market size and rate of growth

In November 2009, the Mobile Marketing Association updated its definition of mobile marketing to the following:

Mobile Marketing is a set of practices that enables organizations to communicate and engage with their audience in an interactive and relevant manner through any mobile device or network.

Over the past decade or so, mobile marketing has gone from being a fairly broad advertising term to referring to a rather specific type of marketing. Once used to describe any form of marketing that made use of a moving (mobile) medium (things such as moving billboards, roadshows and other transportable outdoor advertising), today it refers to a completely different form of advertising: reaching out to connect and interact with consumers through their mobile electronic device of choice.

As with other forms of online marketing, mobile marketing in its various guises has evolved rapidly in a relatively short space of time, fuelled by consumers with a hunger for anything that can help them streamline their congested, hyper-connected lives. As lifestyles evolve to become ever more generic, global and portable, the lure of the 'always connected' mobile device gets ever stronger.

According to a Gartner study published in January 2013 mobile ad spend worldwide was set to reach US $11.4 billion in 2013, jumping to a massive $24.5 billion by 2016. 'Smartphones and media tablets extend the addressable market for mobile advertising in more and more geographies as an increasing population of users spends an increasing share of its time with these devices,' said Andrew Frank, research vice president at Gartner. 'This market will therefore become easier to segment and target, driving the growth of mobile advertising spend for brands and advertisers.'

Gartner cites the growth in smartphone adoption and mobile media tablets as a major driver in the growth of mobile advertising budgets, and while the vast majority of mobile users don't currently own a smartphone, that is set to change over the coming years. In February 2013 the International Telecommunication Union (ITU) estimated that there were 6.8 billion mobile subscriptions worldwide, equivalent to 96 per cent of the global human population. While the majority of handsets are so-called 'feature handsets' (non-smartphones), sales of smartphones overtook feature phones for the first time in 2013, and are expected to continue to grow rapidly.

A Portio Research study from 2012 revealed that a total of 7.8 trillion SMS messages were sent in 2011. Portio estimates that SMS messaging will peak at 8.3 trillion messages annually in 2015.

Meanwhile, OTT (over-the-top) messaging traffic from apps such as WhatsApp, Facebook Messenger, and Apple iMessage is growing exponentially. Portio expects cumulative OTT messaging traffic to exceed 100 trillion messages from 2013 to 2017. These are ludicrously huge numbers.

'Messaging is still king', states Portio. 'We want to be absolutely clear about this. Messaging still dominates [mobile operators'] non-voice revenues worldwide.' Estimates predict that mobile messaging services will generate

US \$1.17 trillion in worldwide service revenues over the five-year period from 2013 to 2017 inclusive.

Another study, this time by Ovum in November 2013, shows that by 2018 application to person (A2P) messaging traffic will reach 2.19 trillion messages. What is A2P messaging? It's simply automated messages from an application rather than a person. It is widely used in financial services, advertising, marketing, business administration, ticketing, television voting etc. When your mobile operator sends a text to your phone to say your latest bill is available online, or your credit is running low... that's an A2P message.

But what does that mean in mobile marketing terms?

Despite all the hype surrounding mobile web access, search, apps, smartphones, tablets, location-based services and everything else... for the time being, at least, messaging is very much at the heart of the mobile marketing industry. But things change quickly, more so in mobile than perhaps any other branch of digital marketing, and marketers around the world would do well to prepare for a future dominated by mobile access to online information and services.

The steady rise of mobile has become *the* main event in the digital marketing arena over recent years. Mobile has, of course, been the 'next big thing' for what seems an eternity, but with the continued growth of smartphone adoption (increasing by more than 30 per cent year-on-year), the convergence of mobile computing, improved connectivity, and development of the cloud, mobile is finally rising to realize its potential.

Mobile internet adoption is increasing at a rate that is eight times that of the equivalent for desktops 10 years ago. More than half of all new internet connections now originate from mobile devices. We are in the midst of another fundamental shift in the way that people access digital information and services – when most marketers are still reeling after the last one.

Don't ring the death knell of desktop and laptop computers just yet, though; for many things (writing this book for example) a 'proper' computer is still likely to be a better choice than a mobile device. But there is little doubt that the scope of their utility is diminishing, and as people get used to accomplishing more and more with the devices in their pockets, they will turn to their computers less and less.

And not only are consumers using mobile devices more frequently to connect to the internet, but they are increasingly using a variety of different devices and form factors, moving back and forth between smartphone and tablet.

As marketers, we need to adapt to this shift in communications technology and learn once more to engage with our audience through their current medium of choice, and optimize their experience, however they choose to connect.

Mobile – Web 2.0

The widespread adoption of internet-enabled mobile devices gives consumers access to timely, relevant information and services wherever they happen to be. It lets them interact with their network of online contacts and share experiences, images and content – any time, any place, anywhere. That takes the paradigm shift that is the interactive Web 2.0, and raises the bar to another level entirely.

With mobile you have to deliver personalized, relevant and exciting content, participate in a two-way conversation rather than one-way messaging, and really listen to and engage with your customers. When you reach out to a person's mobile, you essentially reach into their personal space. There's something immediate and intimate about it. That's a powerful combination for the marketer, but it is one that comes with a lot of responsibility. It's a position that is easy to abuse, and the potential repercussions for your brand reputation could be huge.

From the consumer's perspective, if you're delivering marketing-related content to their personal mobile device then you had better 'wow' them. Give them a flawless user experience, efficiency and convenience, and respect their privacy and personal preferences. Make it *relevant*, make it *useful*, make it *entertaining*. As with the rest of digital marketing, the days of using mobile as a one-way broadcast medium for spammy one-way marketing messages are coming to an end.

We're entering mobile's next generation, and it's time to engage! (Apologies for the *Star Trek* reference... we couldn't resist.)

Mobile marketing – a game-changing channel, or just another conduit?

Mobile marketing *is still* marketing on the internet. The net *is still* the net, regardless of the device you use to access it. Social media *is still* social media no matter what device you use to share your content; the world wide web *is still* the world wide web, whether you're accessing a mobile-optimized version of a site or belt-and-braces desktop version, e-mail *is still* e-mail no matter how you choose to pick up your messages.

That's good news... it means that all of the information you've read so far in this book... by and large... also applies to marketing for mobile devices! The real differentiators with mobile today are the immediacy of having access to information and services wherever you are, the additional functionality afforded by the hardware in modern mobile devices (such as GPS sensors, motion sensors and touch screens), and the way these combine to alter user perception, expectation and ultimately the potential utility of your marketing message.

As with everything in digital, it is the human element of the mobile equation that makes it so powerful, the technology is the bit in the middle that helps that human connection to happen in new and more interesting ways. You may recall earlier in the book – way back near the beginning – we mentioned that digital marketing has little to do with understanding technology, and everything to do with understanding people. Well, it's the same thing with mobile.

Mobile works because it makes people's lives easier, it's portable, it's accessible, it's always on and it lets people tap in to the information they've come to rely on 24/7. It's in our pockets, it's the last thing many of us check before we go to sleep at night and the first thing we reach for in the morning.

If you understand people – specifically your customers – and how they integrate their mobile devices into their lives, then you already know how your business can reach out to them across the mobile internet. Making it happen is just logistics.

'Show and sell' is dead, welcome to the world of 'utility and entertainment'

A great example of a brand embracing the 'utility and entertainment' aspect of mobile to maximum effect was the 'Axe Wake-Up Service', a campaign that ran in the mobile marketing capital of the world: Japan.

Research showed that 70 per cent of Japan's urban male youth (the brand's target market) used their mobile phones as alarm clocks. All Axe did was to use this generic consumer behaviour as a platform, and built a campaign around it (see Figure 8.1).

Axe simply launched a service that allowed the consumer to visit Axe online, enter their mobile number and set a wake-up call time. A young, attractive woman would then make the wake-up call, even appearing by videophone if the customer desired. Naturally, the campaign reminded the customer to spray on a little Axe to smell great. The brand took an existing consumer behaviour, and offered a useful and entertaining solution that built upon it in a fun and engaging way. The result: a runaway success!

FIGURE 8.1   The Axe Wake-Up Service campaign – entertaining and useful... the essence of effective mobile marketing

AXE FRAGRANCE BODYSPRAY

AXE WAKE-UP SERVICE INC.

AXE started a wake-up call service for happy awakening in the morning.

A branded utility contents with which everyone can receive a wake-up call easily by booking from the PC/mobile site.

We tried to approach targets through the service in the morning, when we want our targets use AXE the most, to encourage them steady use of AXE every day.

>> LAUNCH "AXE WAKE-UP SERVICE INC."
* This is a demo of the morning call booking.
* Bookings cannot be made outside of Japan.

HI, this is AXE WAKE-UP SERVICE INC.

♦ VIDEO PREVIEW

So what can mobile marketing be used for?

The answer to that question could take up an entire book... and then some. Because mobile is essentially a new, exciting and convenient way for people to access online information and services, elements of your mobile marketing can be employed to achieve many of the same business goals as any other form of digital marketing. You can use mobile to:

- build awareness of your brand, product or service;
- foster and nurture conversations with your online community;
- gather valuable insight into consumer behaviour;
- take iterative customer engagement to the next level;
- harness the wisdom of the crowd;
- drive lead generation and new business;
- establish loyalty programmes, competitions and rewards;
- build a deeper and more personal brand experience;
- target your market more effectively based on demographics, geography and behaviour;

- retain more customers and reduce 'churn';
- listen and learn;
- ... the list could go on and on, but you get the idea.

With massive uptake of internet-connected mobile devices accelerating all the time, marketers need to start taking mobile seriously as a fundamental component (if not the principal component) of their digital marketing strategy. The potential of mobile is profound... and the impact of mobile marketing is only going to grow.

Mobile: evolution on steroids

Innovation, and the very human desire for something newer and better, is driving the rapid evolution of the mobile device. We're never content with the status quo. Last month our all-singing-all-dancing smartphone was the bee's knees... but today, well today we really *need* that shiny new tablet. You know, the one that is so achingly cool we don't even need to turn it on to impress our friends. Next month a new version of our phone will hit the shelves – sleeker, brighter, faster.... It's all happening so damned quickly.

When you break it down it's not really that different to the evolution of biological systems – it just happens much, much faster. Darwin's survival of the fittest theory still applies, but instead of waiting hundreds of thousands of years for new species to evolve, in the mobile ecosystem we have new mobile devices evolving in a matter of months.

Manufacturers introduce new features and form factors in their mobile devices all of the time in a bid to capture and retain a share of this burgeoning new market. If those features resonate with people (are truly useful, fun or, ideally, both), then the positive selection pressure of people handing over hard-earned cash pushes the retention and enhancement of those features; if they don't, they die. Over time this leads to the iterative refinement and development (the evolution) of devices that are ideally suited to their particular niche in the digital ecosystem.

Full circle: from tablet to tablet

In the beginning there was the stone tablet: Flintstone marketing at its best. Today the tablets we have to play with are a bit more functional, and weigh substantially less. But are tablets here to stay, or are they a passing fad?

Indications are that they're here to stay: according to Adobe's Digital Index, in 2013 global websites saw more traffic from tablets than from smartphones, while analyst firm Canalys predicts that sales of tablets could overtake portable PCs in 2014.

Tablets are interesting because they're not really portable in the way that your mobile phone is portable. It's still mobile – but it's not something people have with them 24/7 like their phones.

They're also not fully fledged computers in the more 'traditional' sense of the world. You still won't find many people sitting down to write a 10,000 word business report, or create a complex financial spreadsheet on their iPad.

Tablets sit somewhere in the middle ground. The bigger screens and intuitive touch-interface means that tablets excel as media consumption devices: watching online video, catching up with a TV show you've missed, accessing blogs, websites, social media, video-calling your gran, playing games and running apps are all quick, convenient and intuitive on a tablet. They are also fantastic for doing simple online tasks quickly: things like online banking, ordering a birthday gift for your mum on Amazon, subscribing to a new podcast, quickly checking your e-mail or discussing a TV show you're watching with your peers on Twitter.

For more complex tasks you will still typically boot up the laptop... but for convenience and instant gratification, if there's one available, you'll reach for a tablet every time. There is little doubt that tablets are here to stay, and with competition hotting-up, the constant pressure to innovate will drive their continued evolution. Tablets will become more capable, and as more of us acquire the habit of using them we'll do more things online with them. Which of course means that as marketers we have to factor the rise of the tablet into our online strategy.

How big are tablets going to get?

No, we're not talking screen size... we're talking market size.

Various reports from industry behemoths such as Morgan Stanley and Cisco suggest that there could potentially be up to 75 billion internet-connected devices by 2020. To put that number into perspective, we passed the 10-billion device milestone in 2013, according to analyst firm ABI Research, and the number keeps growing apace.

Gerd Leonhard, from the aptly named Futures Agency in Switzerland, concludes that 'tablet devices will become the way many of us will read magazines, books, newspapers and even attend live concerts and kick off an era of mobile augmented reality with content being bundled into mobile service contracts to be consumed on any mobile or tablet device'.

However the future of mobile marketing evolves, tablet devices are likely to play a significant role in that evolution. They span the divide between mobile phones and full-blown computers, are already the quintessential device for multimedia consumption and are getting more capable with each iteration. Tablets are here to stay.

Mobile user experience

As consumers increasingly interact with brands via a variety of different mobile devices, understanding the different requirements for mobile channels and making sure customers have a good experience, no matter how they choose to connect, will be critically important for marketers.

In Adobe's '2013 Mobile Consumer Survey' the company highlighted some key best practices and recommendations for mobile channels:

- Reduce the number of touch events to conversion – research shows that the fewer steps customers have to go through in order to make a purchase, the more likely they are to buy.

- Design for mobile interactions – focus on touch-driven controls rather than mouse clicks and keyboard controls. Use mobile display controls, like swipe, pinch and zoom, and make interaction and navigation buttons simple and large.

- Optimize for speed – even a one-second delay in mobile page load equals a 7 per cent drop in conversion rates. Incorporate dynamic media content and responsive design that adjusts to fit device type and network.

- Make content 'findability' easy – the majority of mobile customers start with search, so optimizing the site search function is crucial.

- Integrate analytics from the beginning – being able to directly measure visitor behaviour is important in understanding the effectiveness and ROI of mobile channels.

- Prioritize tablets – Adobe's Digital Index shows that websites get more traffic from tablets than smartphones, and tablet users typically spend more per online purchase.

- Optimize social media channels for mobile – check that customers can click through to offers in social media channels from their mobile devices.

- Link mobile advertising campaigns to mobile websites – ensure landing pages are optimized for mobile and don't just route mobile users to a desktop home page.

The rise and rise of mobile advertising

It's been a while coming but in 2013 we could finally say that this was the year of the mobile. Thanks to the innovation of the likes of Steve Jobs, bringing fresh thinking to smartphone design, the mobile phone is now so versatile that many people couldn't live without it.

Wherever you are – watching TV at home, travelling to or from work, or just out and about – mobile devices are becoming the method of choice for connecting to the internet. Just think how often you reach for your phone to play games when you're travelling, check your social networks for updates, or pick up your e-mails.

Let's consider some of the facts:

1 In September 2009, just 0.2 per cent of all UK web traffic originated from a mobile device. By February 2013, smartphones and tablets accounted for one-third of all UK page views, a staggering rate of growth.

2 The huge market penetration of smartphones in the UK (32 per cent at December 2010, forecast to be 75 per cent by 2014), better connectivity through increased Wi-Fi networks/3G services and unlimited data plans and the roll-out of 4G networks throughout 2012 to 2015 are the key drivers behind this growth.

3 Mobile advertising in the UK doubled its share of the online advertising market between 2012 and 2013, and was expected to pass £1 billion in 2013.

4 Mobile advertising in the UK is forecast to grow to £5.2 billion by 2017.

5 The UK's internet advertising market is now worth over £6.2 billion in 2013, a 44 per cent share of the overall UK advertising spend. Mobile advertising in comparison with £1 billion is only 8 per cent of this figure.

While advertising spend on mobile media is still relatively low as a proportion of all ad spending, advertisers are sure to follow the crowds. And the crowds are flocking to mobile.

So, for advertisers why is mobile media so powerful?

A smartphone is the owner's mini personal computer, always with them and always connected. It allows them to send and receive e-mail, instant messages, surf the web, find out the weather, play games, watch TV, even make phone calls and text too! Built in GPS means they'll never get lost and can always find a local restaurant, petrol station or ATM. Whether it is looking for a bite to eat or how to repair a puncture, there's always an app for that. Used in the right way this is hugely powerful for advertisers. Mobile advertising allows advertisers to target people on the move or at home and capture them when they're most receptive.

In a nutshell, advertising to consumers via their mobile device is the future and brands that are quick to learn how to use this highly innovative medium will be the ones to win the mind share of the public.

In 2011, for the first time, standardized key metrics for measuring advertisements were established for the mobile interactive industry. Developed in a joint effort by the Interactive Advertising Bureau (IAB) and the Mobile Marketing Association (MMA), and with the assistance of the Media Rating Council (MRC), the 'Mobile Web Advertising Measurement Guidelines' provide a framework to govern how ad impressions are counted on the mobile web.

In 2013, the IAB, MMA and MRC announced updated guidelines, covering not only mobile web advertising but also ads within mobile applications. The measurement guidelines for mobile applications and mobile web advertising will help marketers to assess accurately the delivery of ads within mobile websites and apps, and offer a clear way to count ad impressions, assuring them that their advertising messages are reaching mobile consumers.

More than anything, the guidelines demonstrate the mobile industry's commitment to its marketing partners to create a transparent and consistent business environment for buying and selling ads, to establish actionable guidelines that work across a complex industry, and to encourage the continued growth of mobile advertising.

These kinds of developments are encouraging. We still have a long way to go but there are exciting times ahead for everyone involved in the mobile advertising industry today.

CASE STUDY   Accor Hotels

Accor is a world leader in hotels and services. Accor's free iPhone application allows users to find their ideal hotel, leveraging geolocalization and intuitive map search. Users can add the hotel contact details to their contact lists, find current promotions, book their hotel and check their current reservations.

With the introduction of their iPhone app, Accor and their agency turned to Google's AdMob to help them boost downloads upon the launch of their app and increase the number of mobile bookings. Accor's priorities for their campaign were threefold:

- Reach target audiences in core markets, including Australia, Germany, France, Italy, the UK and the United States.
- Maximize the ranking of their app within their target App Stores in both the travel and overall categories.
- Drive cost-effective downloads of the app.

Solution

Accor used geotargeting to reach the millions of iPhone and iPod touch users in AdMob's network globally. Their ads appeared in many of the most popular local iPhone apps and sites. AdMob's cost-per-click iPhone ads enabled easy discovery and downloads of the app by consumers, taking users from the ad directly to the App Store download page with just one click.

Accor worked with PureAgency who managed the campaign on their behalf. Monitoring cost per acquisition in real-time through AdMob's robust reporting and with their own download measurements, PureAgency was able to ensure optimal results.

Results

The campaign achieved their objectives in each of their target markets. Within the travel category, the app moved up to become one of the highest ranking apps in each App Store; highlights include France becoming the #2 app, Italy #4, UK #11, and the app reaching #29 and #30 in the overall App Stores in France and Italy respectively. Accor firmly believes that if they had continued their advertising spend it would have pushed them into the top 10 rankings in these markets as well.

Throughout the two-week campaign, Accor was extremely pleased with the results that their campaign received:

- click-through rates of 1.30 per cent on average;
- conversion rates (clicks resulting in app downloads) of 5 per cent on average;
- approximately 300,000 visits to their apps download page.

Some conclusions

To deliver on this continuing growth, we need to overcome many of the existing challenges to mobile advertising uptake. Delivering the tools, capabilities and features that guarantee greater transparency, measurability, relevance and, crucially, profit will be the trigger that brands need in order to fully embrace mobile.

As consumer adoption of smartphones and tablets reaches critical mass, brands now realize that they need to move beyond using mobile as just another channel for consumer engagement, to develop a fully comprehensive mobile strategy around marketing, advertising and increasingly around mobile commerce. This is where many in industry believe that the true tipping point will lie in driving these predicted volumes of growth.

As consumers spend more time engaging with smart devices, their willingness to purchase through these devices is increasing. Yet, the availability of transactional m-commerce sites and apps still needs to catch up with consumer demand. As m-commerce technology evolves and delivers an increasingly seamless user experience, the propensity of consumers to buy through mobile will be instrumental in persuading brands to spend greater chunks of their budgets on the channel. This is the real opportunity for marketers to get their hands around.

The realization of the importance of having a mobile strategy, the right tools and appreciation of delivering measurable consumer engagement and ever more sophisticated mobile technology will mark the coming years as a turning point for mobile advertising.

Location, location, location

The fact that your mobile *always* knows where you are can be a bit disconcerting, but there's no denying that it's also an incredibly useful feature. Using maps on your mobile device always comes in handy to quickly find out where you are, how to get to where you want to be, locate a nearby Thai restaurant that your friends recommended, or find the nearest cinema showing the film you want to see.

But what about taking the utility of knowing *where* people are, and using it to help them make the most of what is available around them, discover cool new locations, locate friends who happen to be nearby or avail themselves of the latest offers from local businesses? Welcome to the world of location-aware applications and location-based services. These apps use your mobile's built in GPS or triangulate your position based on data from the mobile phone masts that your device is connected to, and use that data (with your permission, hopefully) to do all sorts of clever things.

The real opportunity with location-aware applications from a marketing perspective is that it offers businesses with bricks-and-mortar premises the opportunity to deliver real-time information, offers and incentives to people *who are physically in the area*. Location information is something that marketers can leverage to make the information they provide to prospects more *useful and relevant* than ever... and that will always drive higher conversion rates.

Check-ins checking out?

The first location-based applications, like FourSquare (**www.foursquare.com**), Gowalla and Facebook Places relied on users making a conscious decision that required action: they needed to physically 'check-in' at locations using software on their mobile device.

Over time, check-in profiles built up. Users were awarded points, badges and 'mayorships' as their 'status' grew and they checked-in to locations regularly. All of this, of course, was designed to reward repeated use of the service, encouraging people to 'check-in' wherever they went, and ultimately establish a habit that would endure beyond initial experimentation with the 'shiny new toy' of location-based social media.

Ultimately, though, the act of checking in has proved to be one of the biggest challenges facing location-based models, because there is no intrinsic value to the process for users. Facebook, after acquiring Gowalla in 2011, has since retired Places and relegated location sharing to a status update tag. While FourSquare continues with the check-in model for now, it is trying to combat user fatigue by making the check-in process simpler.

Instead of requiring people to manually check in to receive relevant information and promotions, marketers can now use mobile phone technology to automatically detect when someone is nearby and send messages to them, provided they have agreed to receive them, of course!

Mobile gaming

Mobile gaming has been described as the wide-open battleground of the entertainment industry. While the likes of Facebook and Zynga dominate social games, and big publishers such as Xbox, Sony and Nintendo rule console games, the global smartphone games market is still patently up for grabs.

Mobile games are huge because mobile devices are... well, mobile! You have your mobile with you 24/7. Sitting in a doctor's waiting room with time to kill? Waiting for the bus home from work? Waiting in line at the supermarket checkout? What are you going to do? Almost invariably, if you have one, you'll whip out your smartphone.

Some people will update their social media status, some will check their e-mail, others might read their favourite blog, and even check in using their location-based service of choice to check out local offers. But many will fire up the latest and greatest mobile game.

There are millions of mobile games spanning the gamut of mobile devices and mobile platforms. And where there are games, there's an audience, and where there's an audience there are opportunities to promote. Brands are already delivering promotional messages *within* mobile games and even *sponsoring entire games* in order to drive consumer engagement.

With potentially billions of users in the mobile market, mobile gaming could well grow to become the single largest gaming market of them all. Smartphone games have been growing fast since 2007, when the iPhone was introduced, and tablet games followed suit with the introduction of the iPad in early 2010. Mobile games are now the fastest-growing segment of the video games market, according to Gartner, with revenues set to nearly double to US $22 billion by 2015. Successes like that of Rovio's now legendary 'Angry Birds', which has been downloaded more than 200 million times, mean that mobile game companies can attract tens of millions of dollars in investment capital.

The games market today is dominated by consoles, with mobile games accounting for a relatively small but rapidly expanding slice of the pie. Few doubt that the growth will continue, as emerging digital markets in Asia embrace the smartphone revolution, and mobile devices become the primary connectivity and entertainment device of choice for a massive chunk of the human population.

But it's not all a bed of roses in mobile gaming. Established mobile game developers such as Digital Chocolate have warned that a glut of games being released on major smartphone platforms means that game developers will find it very hard to make money. They point out that in many cases average revenue per game doesn't even cover development costs. A rash of poor games can ruin the market for everyone, making it more difficult for consumers to find what's 'good' and generally tainting the gaming experience on mobile platforms for everyone. At the time of writing (January 2014) there were 185,815 active games in the App Store, with around 80 new games submitted every day.

Increasingly, consumers like to try before they buy, and while paid-for downloads made up roughly 70 per cent of gaming app revenues at the end of 2013, by 2017 free-to-download games funded by in-app purchases are expected to account for around three-quarters of revenues.

But it's not just about the numbers, either. Savvy mobile marketers need to remain neutral in their assessment of the market and, of course, platform agnostic. The winning platform for your business is not necessarily the one with the most apps, it is the one that retains and engages the attention of your particular target market.

CASE STUDY   Kiip – virtual gaming, real-life rewards

Two hundred million minutes a day. By now, that's an extremely conservative estimate of the amount of time that people spend flinging birds at pigs. In many respects, Angry Birds has become the flagship title and the single biggest story in the app ecosystem to date. However, it is just one game among thousands that are attracting people's attention during their downtime.

Mobile gaming is massive – and with it comes numerous opportunities for brands to connect with a new, engaged audience. Kiip is one new company with a unique twist on mobile advertising. They offer real rewards for virtual achievements. In an era where up to 80 per cent of traditional mobile ads are 'clicked' through by accident, Kiip offer a new way to get an audience's attention in a good way.

Rewards are tied to achievement moments – finishing a level, completing a task, levelling up or getting a new high score. Their algorithm learns how good you are and tailors rewards accordingly. Most importantly, it doesn't disrupt the gaming experience – the rewards are delivered using a simple HTML5 overlay that disappears if you don't want it and never pulls you away from the game. By tying in with achievements moments, which provide a natural break in gameplay, Kiip ensure that they don't annoy developers and gamers alike.

So far, the results have been impressive. Their official launch came in April 2011. They are already working with major US brands such as Dr Pepper, Popchips, Sephora, 1–800 Flowers and many others. An EMEA launch is planned for autumn 2011. To date, campaigns have achieved double-digit redemption rates across the board. Perhaps more surprisingly, they have yet to hear a single complaint from a gamer or developer – while brands are reaping the rewards associated with developing quality engagement with their customers by rewarding them rather than simply pushing a banner ad at them.

A combination of quality offers, smart behavioural economics and partnerships with established and up-and-coming games developers should ensure that gamers start to see a lot more real-life rewards for their in-game achievements over the coming months and years.

Mobile applications

Mobile applications are quite a simple concept. They are just pieces of software that are pre-installed on your mobile phone or are available to download from the internet. They are nothing new. There have been mobile applications available for multiple handsets for years now – ranging from games to currency conversion tools to more complicated applications allowing you to broadcast live video and audio from your phone.

As technology advances rapidly we are moving from a push model to one of pull. People no longer want information they don't really need shoved down their throats. Today's consumers want to be in control; they decide what they want, when they want it and how they want it delivered... and the result is modern mobile apps.

App stores and the explosion of mobile applications has been little short of revolutionary. 'I've never seen anything like this in my career in software', was how Apple founder and CEO Steve Jobs described the initial success of the iPhone App Store – and once again it seems Mr Jobs was right on the money.

Every major media outlet in the world has run pieces on the success of the App Store. The phrase 'there's an app for that' peppers headlines and conversations around the world. The *New York Times* heralded the revolution in mobile applications as a 'new gold rush'.

There are now more than 1 million applications in the App Store (and counting) – with hundreds of thousands more available across Android, Blackberry, WebOS, Windows 8, Symbian and myriad alternative operating systems in the market. In late 2013, Apple announced that more than 60 billion apps had been downloaded from their App Store since its launch, with 10 billion downloads in just the previous five months.

The subsequent launch of a variety of tablet devices has generated yet more app-related hyperbole, and with the launch of Chinese-made sub-US \$100 handsets running Google's Android operating system, and a serious push from Amazon and all of the major smartphone manufacturers, we live in interesting times for mobile marketers.

The hard reality is that there are a significant number of different application platforms available to brands, agencies and marketers. Choosing the right platform, talking to the right audience, and breaking through the noise generated by the sheer volume of applications released on a daily basis is an incredible challenge. At the time of writing, Apple's App Store and Google Play are neck and neck. There are now about 950,000 Android apps available, compared to just over 1 million for the Apple App Store. And while Apple still leads on revenues, Google Play now generates more downloads than the App Store.

Over the last few years, we have seen apps released by nearly every brand on the planet. Users like branded apps. Research by Admob, one of the biggest mobile advertising networks in the world, found that 70 per cent of iPhone users surveyed had downloaded a branded app.

Some of the download figures for branded applications are enormous. Barclaycard released a Waterslide app, which tied in with a successful UK television ad campaign, and which was downloaded more than 9.5 million times. Lighter manufacturer Zippo was one of the first companies to release an app – a simple interface that allows you to 'flick' a lighter on your screen and produce a flame. That simplicity has been rewarded with more than 6 million downloads. Audi's A4 Driving Challenge, where players take a new Audi A4 round a track, has topped 4 million downloads.

The difficulty for brands and developers is how to measure the success of these applications (see the 'measurement' section later in the chapter). Download numbers are a possible metric, but they don't tell the whole story. Engagement is key.

Research by New York-based app analysis company Pinch Media has shown that only 20 per cent of users return to a free application after one day. After 30 days, fewer than 5 per cent are engaging with the app.

The key seems to be giving people something that adds a level of value or engagement. North Face, the outdoor equipment manufacturer, had more than 300,000 downloads of its snow report app in 2009. The app was simple enough: it gives people the weather forecast for multiple ski resorts worldwide, along with details of what time the ski lifts open, webcam feeds and more. While the headline figure of 300,000 downloads may not be as impressive as Zippo's or Barclaycard's, North Face brand manager Nate Bosshard has said that users 'utilize the service several times a day, sharing reviews, checking weather, and updating Twitter feeds regularly'.

The outcomes can be impressive as well. Audi generated more than half a million visits to the A4's website from its iPhone driving application. Kraft's iFood Assistant carries recipes and how-to videos, and not only does it generate revenue for the company (it costs US $0.99), but it is also responsible for a sizeable mailing list, with 90 per cent of app users registering at Kraftfoods.com.

The real key for brands and agencies is not to get caught up in the idea of building an application for the sake of building one. Surely, it is far better to follow the lead of pioneering companies such as North Face (or Smirnoff Vodka who, rather than build their own mobile applications, opted to sponsor the *Time Out London* application): build something useful, promote it using all available channels, and you could find your app being hailed as the next big success story.

Top tips for building a successful app:

1 Plan, plan, plan: scope the app well in advance.

2 Do your research.

3 Understand the business model around the app (free/paid).

4 What problem is it addressing?

5 How will the app be marketed? Who are the target profile/ demographic?

6 How will you measure success? (not just downloads)

7 Focus on design, user interface (UI) and user experience (UX) – the best, most popular applications are simple, effective and look good.

8 Think about content – are you building an entertainment app that will amuse people for 30 seconds before being deleted? Or are you building a utility that people will use on an ongoing basis – like the North Face example above?

9 Think about the device – problems occur when brands try to shoehorn existing content on to a mobile device. Instead of thinking about the limitations presented by screen size – think instead about the options in terms of the device you are targeting.

Measuring mobile

The old adage, you can only manage what you measure, certainly rings true for most marketers in this ROI-driven world. A number of recent white papers have tried to shed light on the measurement of mobile marketing, customer loyalty and engagement. Surprise, surprise... the overriding message is that, when it comes to evaluating the success (or otherwise) of your mobile campaign, there is really no substitute for timely, accurate and independent tracking and measurement.

While we are still some way off a standardized set of metrics for measuring mobile campaign success, white papers and the introduction of guidelines by organizations such as the IAB and MMA help to offer a consistent overview of the mobile marketing landscape, and facilitate knowledge transfer in terms of measuring mobile campaigns across the industry. Together they offer some fairly good signposts that help us to decide what we need when choosing our mobile analytics solution.

What insights does mobile analytics deliver when measuring mobile marketing?

Mobile KPIs

We looked at KPIs for general web-based analytics in Chapter 4, and the basic premise with mobile is exactly the same... a KPI gives an instant snapshot of how your campaign is doing. As with other elements of your digital marketing, measurement and analysis of your mobile metrics is invaluable. It allows you to instantly gauge how well your mobile strategy is working, and to adapt it to deliver better results.

Some examples of popular KPIs for mobile campaigns might include:

- total downloads;
- total app users;
- new users;
- frequency and duration of visit;
- bounce rates;
- segmentation by device type;
- CTRs.

Successful digital marketing is all about iterative refinement... constant tweaking based on interpretation of real data to deliver more effective marketing creative that drives conversion. It is exactly the same with mobile campaigns. By using real data, and the insight it provides, we can focus our efforts (and our finite marketing budget) where it will yield maximum results.

Some of the variables to watch in your mobile campaigns might include:

- User segmentation – it is important to understand which users are interacting with your campaign and taking the actions you want. Are there trends or patterns based on the users' country, device type, platform or other variables?

- Timing – look at the timing of your campaigns in different regions... do some times yield better returns than others? Understand what times of day are likely to deliver higher conversion rates with your particular audience.

- Advertising channel – based on your analytics you can identify which advertising channels deliver the best results across your mobile portfolio, and reinvest your budget accordingly. The key here is to ensure an independent and viable comparison across all your mobile advertising channels.

According to research carried out by specialist UK-based mobile analytics company Bango, 83 per cent of brands do not use mobile specific analytic tools, and 27 per cent of brands failed to implement any sort of analytics for their mobile campaigns. That's throwing away a massive opportunity to improve the ROI that they see from their mobile spend.

We know from the statistics presented at the beginning of this chapter that mobile marketing is growing fast, yet the Bango survey shows that brands are missing a beat when it comes to utilizing real data to enhance the performance of their mobile campaigns. Accurate and comprehensive data, and effective reporting, help to keep campaigns focused, deliver enhanced ROI, and ultimately drive brands to achieve more success with their mobile marketing campaigns.

Mobile privacy

If the holy grail of mobile marketing is accurate and effective measurement, then its arch-nemesis must surely be privacy. Privacy concerns are rife across the web, but are more prevalent than ever when you're talking about a device that most of us carry around with us all day, every day: a device that knows exactly where we are, when and for how long.

How much data do consumers *really* want to share with marketers anyway? From a marketer's perspective the more data we have about a prospect, the more effectively we can deliver useful, relevant, timely information to them exactly when and where they need it. That all sounds great for the consumer too... and it is, as far as it goes. That old chestnut 'when advertising becomes useful it ceases to be perceived as advertising' was never truer than when somebody's mobile phone helps them find a local Italian restaurant that six of their friends recommended over the last few months.

There are plenty of 'win-win' examples like that. Essentially that's what mobile marketing at its best is all about. But things are intensely competitive in the mobile arena, and there is a line in the ever shifting sands of the digital marketing landscape beyond which mobile marketing becomes intrusive rather than informed. Defining exactly where that line is... that's the tricky bit.

Most responsible marketers realize that sending mobile advertising without the relevant permission or consent causes more harm than good. The mobile equivalent of e-mail spam is only going to turn consumers off in an era when you really need to be engaging in a productive and enduring relationship with them.

For mobile marketing to work, consumers need to have confidence that their privacy will be protected. If they don't, it doesn't really matter how well crafted, imaginative or cool your next mobile campaign is. Without consumer consent and buy-in it's really not going anywhere. Successful mobile marketing needs to be *permission based*, it needs to be *relevant and useful* (or entertaining) and it needs to be part of a broader mobile engagement strategy that extends beyond the initial 'blip' of campaign-based marketing.

As with many other areas of digital marketing, the legal framework in which we operate has struggled to keep pace with innovation and change. The law is playing catch-up as it tries to deal with issues such as unsolicited mobile advertising, behavioural targeting, and the use of personal identification and location-based information without the user's explicit consent.

Many mobile telecommunications regulations across the developed world are woefully outdated, particularly when it comes to unsolicited commercial communications. The result is a flood of fast-tracked legislation and regulation aimed at assuaging consumers' fears that governments around the world are not taking their privacy seriously. The danger, of course, is that rapid-fire reactive legislation is often poorly thought out and ends up stifling innovation and simultaneously disrupting the user experience – which is bad for marketers and even worse for consumers.

What impact all of this legislation and regulation will have on the evolution of mobile marketing remains to be seen, but when the dust settles, if user's privacy concerns have been allayed, at least somewhat, then that's good news for mobile marketers. While regulation and legislation by their very nature give us more hoops to jump through, ultimately it has to be better than the anarchy that would otherwise prevail. If unscrupulous marketers are allowed to fuel consumer paranoia about privacy, then people will simply stop engaging with *any* form of mobile advertising, no matter the source. That would be bad news for everyone.

There are undoubtedly some very serious consumer protection issues that marketers need to be aware of as mobile takes off. Some of the key legal elements that mobile marketers should carefully consider include the following:

Disclosure

Marketers should clearly disclose the terms of any offer. With the growth of mobile applications, the spotlight is being centred on how transparently mobile marketers disclose the terms of things such as in-app purchases. The limited space on mobile screens can present challenges when it comes to full disclosure, but marketers need to find creative ways to make sure that consumers see material terms before they part with their money.

Privacy

Mobile companies are increasingly coming under fire for not adequately disclosing their mobile data-collection practices to consumers. As we have already discussed, there is a huge push around the world to bring legislation up to date in the mobile privacy arena. Now is the time for marketers to put their house in order in terms of mobile privacy. Keep an eye on legal developments in your jurisdiction/ those of your customers, and pay attention to how new mobile privacy proposals may ultimately affect your mobile strategy now and into the future.

Consent

Consent or permission is another key area, and one that is likely to become more critical as mobile commerce and payments take off. Issues such as how to ensure that the person making a mobile transaction is, in fact, authorized to do so, will be at the forefront.

Many companies using mobile as a direct communications channel to their customers have been caught out for failing to get consent before sending promotional text messages. In some cases settlements reached into the millions. Make sure you get a consumer's permission before contacting them on their mobile.

Mobile data

As with privacy, a lot of interest is now being paid to our behaviours and the data trail that we are leaving behind on a daily basis from all our activity on mobile devices. According to the 'Ericsson Mobility Report', mobile data traffic is expected to double in 2013, with a compound annual growth rate (CAGR) of around 50 per cent between 2012 and 2018, driven mainly by video. Video accounted for 31 per cent of mobile data traffic in 2012, and is expected to account for around half by 2018. Web browsing makes up 14 per cent of mobile data traffic, social networking 10 per cent, and file sharing 8 per cent, according to the report.

Futurists (now there's a job title we'd love...) are also predicting that new 'open' environments will lead to a new generation of mobile devices with even more sensors capturing ever-increasing streams of data about our movements in the physical world – including things such as temperature, noise, location and even smell!

Add sensor data to user data, voice data and other data sources and it's easy to see how that data could be used to build a picture of individual behaviour that is scarily close to the mark. It poses some tough questions. How will all this potentially valuable and personal data be filtered? Who is going to own it? Where is it going to be stored? How is it going to be secured?

The mobile cloud

Having weathered the economic storm of the last few years, mobile network operators are now eagerly seeking out new revenue opportunities, and they're looking to the cloud. There is a lot of energy and investment currently flowing into 'mobile cloud' projects and mobile companies and other players in the mobile ecosystem are betting heavily on the trend of services and applications being hosted in and delivered from the cloud.

The proliferation of smart mobile devices of all types fuels massive demand for data to power social networking, sensor-based interaction and video and digital entertainment. This demand is resulting in an exponential need for computational muscle, storage and bandwidth, which in turn is driving the development of new cloud-based applications and platforms.

A Morgan Stanley study from September 2010 found 41 per cent of mobile peak-hour traffic is due to 'real-time entertainment', most of which is video. Considering that YouTube adds approximately 100 hours of video to its archive every minute, that's hardly a surprising statistic, but when it comes to coping with that ever-increasing demand it does present significant challenges.

Behind the scenes, the industry is moving from a rigid model of individual servers or designated banks of servers towards a much more scalable and dynamic model that can respond almost instantly to changes and shifts in computational demand. The dynamic scalability of cloud computing is essential to modern mobile developers as they strive to improve user experience through lower latency, increased throughput and reduced costs.

How is 'the mobile cloud' different from 'the cloud'?

Ask 10 different tech experts that question and you will get 10 different answers. Often, the term 'mobile cloud' is simply used to indicate that the most common device being used to access a particular service is mobile, although as the mobile cloud evolves you can expect subtle differences in terms of security, back-end infrastructure, application design and other variables tailored to the particular demands of mobile access.

A report from Yankee Group analyst Brian Partridge entitled 'The Mobile Cloud: Unlocking New Profits' from 2011 sheds some light on possibilities and challenges for the mobile cloud and suggests that it has the potential to change how we work, transact, socialize and entertain ourselves in every conceivable way. Yankee Group defines the mobile cloud as a 'federated point of entry enabling access to the full range of capabilities inherent in the mobile network platform', which sounds very grand, but essentially means that you can access every available mobile service from a single point: your mobile device of choice.

Many solution providers in the mobile space have been actively working on assembling the networks, skilled people and real world experience they are going to need to deliver new and exciting managed services. Essentially these operators are looking to offer a one-stop-shop for enterprises, brands, mobile marketers, content and application owners, network owners, solution providers and developers. Their services aim to seamlessly integrate multiple networks into one convenient commercial offering, bringing the world of the internet and mobile together and unlocking the potential of the operators' entire networks, including infrastructure and, of course, customer data.

Downstream, all of this impacts the end-user experience. As network operators strive to improve the overall experience for developers, brands and service providers (their customers), that in turn filters down, allowing them to make more relevant, engaging and affordable services available to consumers. It's another one of those win-win situations that seem to crop up constantly in digital.

The mobile cloud is the future – that's something most experts agree on – but at the moment the reality for many of us still falls far short of the promise. Always-on, always-connected devices tapping into the boundless capacity of the amorphous cloud *only works when you actually have a high-speed data connection*. If you live in the middle of a major city you're probably fine, but venture a bit further afield and that all-promising cloud quickly becomes an impenetrable fog as your device switches to a legacy mobile connection and everything slows to a crawl.

'There's no point having beautiful shiny products, or the best content playing on the best mobile device or tablet if you have intermittent connectivity,' cautions Torsten de Riese, former Digital Director for NBCUniversal in EMEA. 'That's still the case even in developed countries, not just in the developing countries. I live in London and struggle to connect to my iPad in many areas.'

De Riese warns that we shouldn't get ahead of ourselves. No sooner are we adjusting to the latest tranche of mobile products and services, powered by mobile cloud solutions, than the rapidly evolving industry heaps another dollop of innovation on our heads. 4G connectivity is slowly being rolled out, with the promise of better coverage and higher bandwidth, but it is important for marketers to remember that not everyone has access to the same connectivity, products, experience or expectation.

It is vital to keep in mind your particular audience and the technology and platforms they use as you develop your mobile strategy. 'Mobile devices are going to create a different working "sensation" for individuals,' de Riese predicts. 'When you can do things like connect your social network to your car, all sorts of behaviours will change. There will be a different paradigm for how we use and think of mobility.'

Further exploration

We have only really scratched the surface, and looked at a high-level snapshot of the mobile marketing landscape. Getting into the detail would go far beyond the scope of this volume. The years ahead promise to deliver more innovation, change and rapid development in the mobile space.

Mobile marketing is finally coming of age. With the gradual introduction of sophisticated new technologies, marketers are beginning to track results and manage mobile metrics in ways similar to those used for the web. Some critics argue that the medium is still not reaching its full potential: of course it's not... even in terms of digital marketing it's still a baby... but it's growing up fast. In this chapter we hoped we have shared some of the boundless scope and potential that makes mobile marketing so exciting. Mobile is already a significant layer in the digital marketing mix, and over time will grow in importance as more people turn to their mobile devices for the information, answers, products and services they need every day. Whether mobile marketing is a good fit for your business is up to you to decide... but the potential of mobile is certainly worth exploring.

Some other areas of mobile that fall beyond the scope of this chapter, but may be worth a quick 'Google' include:

- SMS and short-code mobile marketing;
- mobile payments;
- mobile commerce;
- QR codes;
- augmented reality;
- mobile mapping;
- mobile banking;
- mobile health.

Building a multichannel marketing strategy

As mobile increasingly becomes the preferred method for connecting with the internet, savvy marketers who ready themselves for the new multichannel world can take advantage of opportunities to get closer to their customers than ever before.

The intimate nature of mobile – always close and always on – can provide a wealth of data about our habits and movements – perhaps more than some of us realize or would want! And with consumers increasingly willing to purchase through their smartphones and tablets, there are already signs that smart companies can reap success through targeted marketing campaigns.

Mothercare is using mobile, for example, to provide relevant promotions by pinpointing a customer's location, sending details of their nearest store and identifying special offers available to them. It is also building longer-term relationships with new customers through its mobile app, which provides week-by-week advice to pregnant mums.

TUI Travel has also seen success with its MyThomson mobile app, which provides information and planning tools to support holidaymakers, from the moment they book their travel to the end of their holiday, and allows them to share their experience through social networks. MyThomson became the most popular travel app on the Apple App Store shortly after launch and had over 180,000 downloads within a few months of release.

Mobile is a unique channel, with differing needs for different device-form factors and connections. It can no longer be thought of as an add-on to a marketing strategy but needs to be integrated fully into the overall marketing mix. People expect a positive experience no matter what device they're using – nothing kills a mobile web experience like a pesky pop-up!

The year of the mobile is finally here. Make sure you're ready!

CASE STUDY   Dubizzle.com

The Dubizzle.com site attracts over 6 million unique visitors and 200 million page views per month.

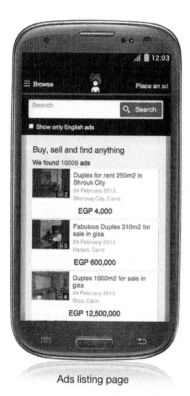

Ads listing page

Ads creation page

Location

Dubizzle.com is one of the most popular and largest classified advertising sites in North Africa and the Middle East.

The challenge

- Reach a new market of smartphone and tablet users.
- Reduce cost and increase reach.
- Increase the quality, quantity and engagement of site traffic.

Target audience

Consumers in the following markets:

- Algeria;
- Bahrain;
- Egypt;
- Jordan;
- Kuwait;
- Lebanon;
- Oman;
- Qatar;
- Saudi Arabia;
- Tunisia;
- UAE.

Action

- Dubizzle.com sought the help of Google Ad Words to help them increase traffic to their website.
- The mobile site was then edited so that users could quickly find what they were looking for, using a responsive format that resizes automatically for each device.
- They saw this as a very big opportunity to reach the new market of smartphone and tablet users.
- Mobile and tablet users represented 23 per cent of all of Dubizzle's traffic, which went up by 4 per cent over weekend periods.
- Google Ad Words were chosen as Dubizzle had the view that mobile users were likely to be serious buyers.
- Due to this, mobile users were given the option to browse ads on sites, place their own ads and send messages to sellers about items they may be interested in.
- They also enabled a click-to-call functionality, which connects them directly with the seller.
- A function was created that allowed mobile users to take pictures of the items they were placing on the site, and upload their listings directly from their smartphones.

Results

- Increased click-through on mobile search by up to 14 per cent.
- High-quality traffic increased conversion rates by up to 300 per cent.

Links to campaign

- www.dubizzle.com
- www.google.com/think/ad-types/cross-media.html
- www.google.com/think/products/mobile-ads.html
- www.google.com/think/products/search-ads.html

About the creator

Google Mobile Ads: we help customers to reach audiences on-the-go. Mobile ads appear on mobile devices in Google search results, on content websites, in apps and video. We work so you can use them to put your business in front of people as they use their smartphones and tablets throughout the day.

Quote

Nadia Zehni, Search Marketing Manager at Dubizzle, said: 'Having a responsive design site is a very big opportunity to reach a new market of smartphone and tablet users. The volume and quality of traffic from mobile advertising have been crucial in helping us achieve our goals, Smartphone and tablet traffic to the site has tripled since this time last year, and paid traffic has grown sevenfold.'

Understanding performance marketing

Recognizing opportunities for strategic partnership

In the context of digital marketing, 'strategic partnerships' are most often defined by a deal between two (or more) parties where the desired outcome is a win-win for all concerned. Ideally a strategic partnership should be about synergy: all parties should come out of the relationship with more than any of them could have achieved alone.

One way to visualize a strategic partnerships is in a bricks-and-mortar 'retail' context: suppliers rent space in high-traffic department stores in order to sell their products or services to customers who visit that store. The store brings in the traffic, the supplier sells their wares, the customer gets more choice... everybody wins.

Almost exactly the same process occurs online. A website that attracts large volumes of traffic will seek out long-term partnerships with suppliers to rent space in sections of their website; at the same time, online retailers or 'e-tailers' are looking for additional online 'venues' to peddle their wares. When they come together in the right circumstances you have all the ingredients for a mutually beneficial strategic partnership. Of course the 64-million-dollar question in all of this is agreeing the balance of risk.

Online strategic partnerships usually go something like this

A large portal with 1 million visitors per day sells inventory (space) on its site to a travel company to advertise its products and special offers. In that scenario, the burden of risk is entirely with the travel company – they are paying to advertise on the portal's website in the hope of attracting new customers. But wait a minute, isn't that just a form of online advertising?

Yes, except that, in order to mitigate some of the risk, the travel company may negotiate with the portal to lower the cost of rental in exchange for certain incentives. The incentive could be exclusive products or offers for the portal's users (increasing the perceived value of the portal site, attracting and retaining more visitors).

With a tangible mutual benefit on the table, there's a good chance that the portal site will be temped to reduce the required advertising investment in return for:

- guarantees for their users in relation to special offers – possibly around exclusivity;
- a revenue share of business accruing from the campaign, which can be tracked using page tags and analytics software;
- a long-term deal that can guarantee portal owners a healthy ROI.

Because portal owners now have a vested interest they also agree to do some editorial and PR around the advertising to build up the partnership.

Hold on though... doesn't that smack a little of sponsorship? The burden of risk is still almost completely with the e-tailer. While there may certainly be some value in the 'exclusivity' element of the deal it still doesn't feel balanced, because on the basis of no 'business being transacted' the only real loser is the merchant – in our case the travel company. And if it's a long-term deal that doesn't bode well for them.

A strategic partnership should be clearly balanced on both sides with risk being shared throughout. Just because a portal has millions of users and a premium for advertising space on their site doesn't mean they are going to be worse off by adopting a revenue-share approach rather than one that consists of guaranteed cash. That view may not be the one regularly peddled by portal owners around the world... but nonetheless, it is true!

Surely the aim of the portal owner should be to maintain and grow traffic to their site, ensuring the content is up to date, up to scratch and that they offer users something of real value? In that respect, they are like good old-fashioned media. How, then does it suit users if the site offers a series of exclusive offers backed by marketers and ultimately paid for by the highest bidder? In a word, it doesn't... but it is a practice that has been rife among websites who, understandably, have been focused on using every trick in the book to maximize advertising revenue on the site, often enticing marketers with that tired old formula of advertising masquerading as editorial (or special offers) in an effort to bolster advertising opportunity.

Tips on entering into strategic partnerships

Our advice to marketers seeking strategic partnerships with high traffic websites is as follows:

- Do not enter into long-term arrangements without fully testing the site first. This is the real beauty of digital marketing – the ability to test before you invest.

- If you do decide to go for a long-term deal, make sure this is going to be of ongoing interest to the end users. Vary the content, change your offers regularly, use seasonality or other features to mix things up. You don't want to end up with the same message, day in, day out – except, of course, when it works!

- Talk to the site's other strategic partners – find out how long deals have been in place and how they value the association. Ask them how they go about tracking performance etc. If possible, find out which strategic partnerships they no longer run on the site, and what happened. Marketers can be quite guarded with this kind of information, so you may not get it – but if you can overcome their reticence the information can be invaluable.

- Agree how performance will be measured from day one, and ensure your advertising and promotional messages are fully 'tagged' to track all necessary data – remember it's not about clicks its about actual conversions.

- Be prepared to disclose profit margins; seek to build a close, transparent relationship with the site, a relationship where both parties fully understand the commercial realities and the mutual benefit involved. A little bit of patience and commitment upfront will certainly help to establish realistic expectations.

What is performance marketing?

This section covers performance marketing, an increasingly popular channel for brands within the digital marketing mix. In previous editions of the book I referred to this area as 'affiliate marketing' but like all things digital, the term has steadily evolved to be now more commonly referred to as 'performance'. I am also very fortunate to have collaborated with Andrew Copeland on this chapter. This is the third time we have worked together over the last few years and in my opinion, no one understands more than Andrew about this subject:

> Performance marketing is a relatively new term applied to an already established branch of digital marketing. Previously called 'affiliate marketing', the industry has rebranded itself to ensure that it delivers in name what it delivers in practice.

> Performance marketing, unlike other digital disciplines, is not a single medium or method of marketing. It is a way of utilizing any and all digital channels to market a brand's products or services but where the brand only pays for the results achieved.

This may sound quite vague at this point but the workings of performance marketing will become clearer as we progress through the chapter.

Definition

Wikipedia does not have a decisive definition for performance marketing (the industry rebrand is that recent). It does have a definition for performance-based advertising though, which provides us with a good starting point:

> Performance-based advertising is a form of advertising in which the purchaser pays only when there are measurable results.
>
> **(http://en.wikipedia.org/wiki/Performance-based_advertising)**

Overlay the definition of affiliate marketing and you start to get a flavour of what performance marketing is trying to achieve:

> Affiliate marketing is a type of performance-based marketing in which a business rewards one or more affiliates for each visitor or customer brought by the affiliate's own marketing efforts. The industry has four core players: the merchant (also known as 'retailer' or 'brand'); the network (that contains offers for the affiliate to choose from and also takes care of the payments); the publisher (also known as 'the affiliate'); and the customer.
>
> **(http://en.wikipedia.org/wiki/Affiliate_marketing)**

By combining these two definitions, we can create our own definition for performance marketing:

> Performance marketing is a type of performance-based advertising in which a business rewards one or more of its partners for carrying out some form of advertising or promotion of the business's products or services, which results in a customer taking an action. The action is prescribed by the business, allowing them to ensure their advertising spend is delivering actual, measurable results.

History

Performance marketing has been around since the dawn of the internet. Okay, not quite but very close. The first performance marketing programme (affiliate marketing, back then) was launched in 1994 by PC Flowers & Gifts. To put that into context, that is just three years after the invention of the web and a full two years before Larry Page came up with the idea for Google!

Early performance marketing programmes were very simple in their objectives and payment metrics. Partners (affiliates) were predominantly paid on a cost-per-click model (paid a small amount for each prospective customer who clicked through to a brand's website).

However, these metrics quickly evolved to the cost-per-acquisition (CPA) model we know today, where brands pay partners a commission or revenue share for each sales completed by a referred customer. The first major brand to launch a CPA-based programme was Amazon, who launched their Amazon Associates programme in 1996... a programme still going strong today.

Today's performance marketing programmes couldn't look more different from those of their early predecessors. While they continue to run on the same principle of paying for a prescribed action, the 'actions' are far more numerable and complex. It is not uncommon to find an individual perform-ance marketing programme paying for multiple actions. These could range from something as simple as a click to something as complex as a social media share or a positive review.

Introducing the players

So how does it work? In order to understand that, you need to understand the different players in the game and how they interact. There are four main categories of participants in performance marketing programmes and we'll review them individually.

Brands/advertisers

Performance marketing is used by a wide variety of businesses. Due to the diverse mix of active publishers (covered later), any business looking to promote its products or services can find a route to market. Typical advertisers could include retail brands, travel companies, financial institutions and even dating websites. What all of the advertisers who use performance marketing share is an understanding of the value that the channel can bring and the reduction in risk that it can offer.

Publishers

Publishers are the websites that actually run the advertising on behalf of the advertisers and that receive a commission once a consumer completes the required action. Performance-based publishers come in all shapes and sizes. In fact, some of your favourite websites are likely to include an element of performance-based advertising.

Performance publishers could include price comparison websites, cashback websites, websites promoting vouchers and discounts, review sites, blogs, paid search specialists... you name it, they could all be performance based.

As you can see from the list above, performance marketing publishers encompass almost all areas of digital. This is the primary reason why performance marketing is defined by how brands pay their publishers rather than the actual type of activity undertaken. Normally, performance-based publishers concentrate on mechanisms to help consumers make a decision to complete an action, such as a sale, as they will only be remunerated once the action is undertaken.

Networks and tracking providers

While there is a distinct difference between networks and tracking providers, it is important they are defined together as they share many similarities.

A network is essentially a middle-man. Networks operate the tracking systems that allow advertisers to track consumer actions and assign commissions to the relevant publisher. On the one hand, advertisers sign up to the network for a period (usually no less than 12 months) and the network provides advice on how those advertisers should be running their performance marketing activities. On the other hand, publishers voluntarily sign up to the network to gain access to the list of advertisers and voluntarily run their advertising. The network provides the tracking, billing and payment facilities as well as advice to both parties.

Tracking providers also provide tracking, billing and payment facilities but, generally, not the advice. More often than not, tracking providers license their systems for advertisers to use themselves. Essentially, a software service. It is up to the advertisers to implement their own performance strategies, find their own publishers and manage their own performance marketing activity.

Typically, advertisers who want a small or controlled performance marketing programme or who have the expertise to run a full programme in-house will use a tracking provider. The vast majority of advertisers will use a network, as they receive the advice they need and can dedicate less internal resources to their performance marketing programmes.

Agencies

Media agencies may or may not be involved in the process, depending on what they have been contracted to do for a particular client. Traditionally, media agencies have concentrated on other areas of digital, leaving the performance marketing activities up to the advertisers to run themselves, or advising advertisers to contract specialist performance agencies to work alongside them. However, recent trends have seen many of the top media agencies setting up internal performance marketing teams to provide a full-service offering to their clients.

So how does it work?

For simplicity, Figure 9.1 shows a 'do it yourself' performance arrangement, where the web merchant is running their own performance programme. Things can get a little more complicated when a performance network acts as an intermediary between merchant and consumer, but the basic premise remains the same.

In its simplest form, performance marketing works something like this: advertisers work with networks or tracking providers to track consumer activity resulting from promotion by publishers.

FIGURE 9.1 How basic performance marketing works

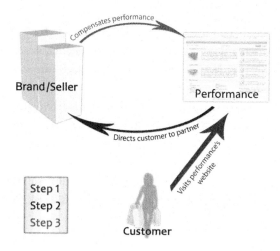

Looking at this process in a little more detail helps to make things clearer:

- **Advertisers work with networks or tracking providers**
  As a first step, advertisers will need to set up their performance marketing programme. We'll go into this in more detail later in the chapter. However, for now, let's define this as advertisers needing to provide a network with the commercials, creative and brand messages needed to engage with consumers.

- **To track consumer activity**
  As part of the set up, advertisers will need to integrate a small piece of tracking code onto their websites, which tells the network or tracking provider when an action has been undertaken by a consumer.

- **Resulting from promotion by publishers**
  Once the set-up is complete, publishers are able to join the programme and gain access to all of the promotional collateral for a particular advertiser. They then use that collateral to promote the advertiser to their user bases. The network or tracking provider tracks the use of the collateral and the consumer engagement and action, recording commissions against the individual publisher accounts when consumers complete the necessary actions.

Why brands should use performance marketing as part of the marketing mix

In this section, we focus on why brands should use performance marketing if they are not already doing so. We review the benefits, investigate a few of the considerations that brands should take into account, and get some tips on what to look for.

On the face of it, performance marketing seems like a no-brainer and is something all brands should get involved with. In the main, this is true. However, there are a few important questions that brands need to answer before jumping in with both feet.

But first we'll look at the benefits that brands can enjoy should they get their performance marketing plans right and develop a successful programme.

Benefits

The benefits of performance marketing are too numerous to mention so I have selected five that should resonate with the vast majority of advertisers. Rather than focus on the creative, marketing-related benefits, I have selected very business-centric benefits, which will aid many marketing managers to sell the concept of performance marketing into pretty much any department in their respective companies.

In this section, the assumption is that the advertiser has contracted a network to help with their performance marketing activity. I've made this assumption as this is how the vast majority of brands currently work in the space. There has been a shift in recent years for larger, more experienced companies to migrate their programmes to a tracking provider and manage their publisher relationships in-house. However, this is not the norm just yet.

The five selected benefits of performance marketing are as follows:

- **Reduced risk**
  Possibly the primary benefit of performance marketing is the reduced risk that advertisers can enjoy when it comes to budget expenditure. Many other marketing channels require upfront commitment with the promise of success. Performance marketing, on the other hand, requires the promise of budget commitment *once success has been achieved*. This is a very important distinction as it is the cornerstone of the performance marketing industry.

  With advertisers paying commissions once a customer has completed a desired action, brands can rest assured that their marketing budget is being used to maximum efficiency. If customers don't complete the actions, the advertisers don't pay anything, making performance marketing possibly the least risky marketing method available. This is also the reason why performance marketing is a very effective method of advertising for small or niche brands who may not have substantial marketing budgets. With smaller budgets, advertisers need to ensure that every penny is being used to maximum effect. Protecting the pennies and ensuring they are only paid out for a valuable customer interaction makes sense... not just for the smaller brands but for larger brands too.

It is for this reason that you will find most household brand names running performance marketing programmes.

- **Test and learn**
As we have already discussed, brands can enjoy a significant reduction in expenditure risk when using performance marketing to promote their businesses. This allows them to be more imaginative with their performance marketing activities.

I have often referred to performance marketing as a sandbox, much like the ones you play in as a child. Here, brands can build things up, add to them if they're working, tear them down if not – and all the while be safe in the knowledge that they are not overreaching on the expenditure. After all, they only pay when things work and consumers interact.

Advertisers are therefore able to seek out and implement ways of promoting their products that are far less established than they would otherwise like. They can test new ideas, new marketing messages and ways of interacting with customers without risking some of that precious marketing budget on something that doesn't work.

If some of these new ideas work well then they're able to integrate them into their other marketing channels with confidence, allowing them to continually improve all marketing channels through the use of performance marketing.

- **Access to innovation**
For advertisers who choose to run their performance marketing activities through a network, they gain the added benefit of having a partner who is continually adding to their pool of publishers. Any network worth their salt will have their finger on the pulse of the digital marketing ecosystem and be searching out cutting-edge publishers to broaden their offering.

Brands benefit from this in two ways. First, they can test any new, untried marketing methods in a low-risk environment. Marketing budgets are often set once per year and it can be very difficult to fence off funds for trying new things, especially when you don't know what those new things are or how much return you'll see from them. Using performance marketing to try new areas of digital allows brand owners to guarantee a return on their marketing investment, making it much easier to secure budget through the channel.

Second, they can be sure that their network (provided they've picked the right one) will be actively seeking out the next big thing, meaning brands don't have to. Being in a position to make use of the latest trends in digital without having to invest significant manpower is very appealing and commercially sensible. In-house marketing teams are very often time poor and don't have the resources to continually keep abreast of industry progress. Having a trusted partner who can do this for you ensures that marketing teams can focus in the right areas.

- **'Free' brand exposure**
By paying on consumer action, brands can push the payment point further down the purchase funnel. However, in order for publishers to entice consumers to interact with a brand's advertising, they still need to promote that brand and ensure that consumers are exposed to the brand message.

  As with any form of advertising, not all consumers are going to relate to the message or interact in the way the brand wants, at least not immediately. However, there may still be value in these consumers, maybe just not right now. Many brands spend a huge amount of budget on branding activity (display, offline etc). In the performance channel, unlike many other channels, the exposure that a brand gets prior to a consumer interacting with it is essentially free, as there is no cost for a consumer who doesn't interact in the way the brand has prescribed.

  This important by-product of the way that publishers are remunerated in the performance industry is a major reason why the industry is gaining traction with advertisers of all sizes. After all, everyone loves a freebie.

- **Significant reach**
We have already looked at the variety of publishers in the market and how they come from all areas of digital. This creates a significant

opportunity for advertisers as they are in a position to leverage any type of digital promotion through one programme of activity.

Most networks have thousands of publishers on their network all looking to promote the right brands or offers to consumers. This offers brands immense reach in a very short space of time if they can offer publishers what they need.

For most advertisers, contacting and contracting this volume of publishers themselves would be impossible. However, through the use of a network, advertisers have access to a ready-made directory of possible partners.

If you are an advertiser who has an international presence, a partnership with the right network could be very lucrative as the network could provide both local and cross-border publisher opportunities much quicker than you could identify them yourself.

Considerations

As with anything in business, there are considerations that need to be taken into account before jumping in with both feet. Performance marketing works well for most advertisers in most industries. However, individual companies will have their own objectives, constraints and budgets and a full review should be conducted to ensure that performance marketing is the right fit.

Here we look at five of the most common considerations advertisers should take into account before beginning their performance marketing programmes:

- Cost

  Cost is the obvious starting point and is often the most difficult element of performance marketing for advertisers to get their heads around. Unlike other areas of marketing, it is very easy to calculate the cost of an individual consumer interaction but very difficult to calculate the cost of the performance programme as a whole.

  This is because, while advertisers get to set their own commission levels and negotiate their network fees, there is no intelligent way to predict the volume of consumer interactions they are likely to achieve. Get the publisher commercials and marketing message wrong and there will be no cost as there's no consumer interaction. Get them right and you could have thousands of interactions, each with an associated cost.

  It is for this reason that most brands don't account for performance marketing costs from their marketing budgets. Rather, they account for it as a cost-of-sale. In this way they can factor the cost into each consumer engagement to ensure that each one is profitable while leaving their marketing budget free for other areas of promotion.

So, advertisers need to consider what they can afford to pay for each consumer interaction in order to retain profitability, factor in cashflow considerations and ensure that, should they succeed with their performance marketing activities, they have the funds to pay their publishers promptly and maintain a healthy margin.

- Competition
  Once advertisers have calculated their costs and can ensure profitability, they will be in a position to benchmark themselves against their competition. The first consideration when evaluating the competition is investigating whether any competitors are even active in the space. In the absence of competition, advertisers need to determine whether their competitors are absent for good reason and performance marketing may not be effective or, hopefully, if there is an opportunity to be first to market. This latter is a distinct possibility, as performance marketing is only now making it into the mainstream marketing press and so is still a relatively unknown area of digital.

  A more likely scenario is that multiple competitors will be active in the space and it is against these other performance programmes that advertisers will need to benchmark themselves. It is tempting for advertisers to compare themselves based on non-performance metrics but it is important to compare the performance programmes based on their specific merits.

  Advertisers should initially look at the commissions offered by their competitors, as this is where publishers will naturally focus once a programme is live. If the market rates are significantly higher than expected, advertisers should think carefully about whether they have other unique selling points that will entice publishers to their programmes. It is possible to be successful in the performance space while paying low commissions but many other factors need to be in place to achieve this.

  Once commissions have been evaluated, advertisers should then look at the collateral supplied to publishers by their competitors. This is often an area of opportunity and, with some careful thought, advertisers can quickly identify areas here where publishers are missing some key consumer messages.

As long as advertisers are able to identify a unique message that they can provide to publishers, and can compete on commercials, there is a very strong opportunity for a successful performance marketing programme.

- **Resource and expertise**

Performance marketing is not a hands-off route to market. In fact, it is one of the most relationship-heavy, hands-on marketing methods.

Brands should take an objective view on just how much resource is available internally to look after the performance marketing channel. If advertisers have an agency running their digital campaigns, this evaluation is even more important, as adding a new channel may incur significant costs.

Should the resource be available, attention should then be turned to the level of expertise that resource has. This will impact on the level of service needed from a network or aid in deciding whether the use of a tracking provider is a viable option.

If there is a high level of performance marketing expertise within the team, advertisers may be able to negotiate lower rates with networks if the advertiser is able to assume more of the workload. Conversely, if advertisers need to rely heavily on their network for knowledge and education, more network hours will be required.

Having a solid understanding of the skills at an advertiser's disposal is crucial in ensuring that the performance marketing programme is correctly supported as, without the correct resource, few programmes achieve the success they could otherwise have enjoyed.

However, if the right balance is struck between internal resource, network expertise and sufficient account management time, even the most inexperienced marketing teams can run very effective performance marketing programmes.

- **Service level requirements**

Once a thorough review of available resource and expertise has been conducted, advertisers will have a clear picture of the type of support they are going to need from their network or tracking provider.

The challenge is in matching their support requirements to vendors to find the right fit. Tracking providers are less of a concern as, generally, advertisers only opt for a pure-play tracking provider if they have substantial internal resource and experience.

When negotiating with networks around account management time, the level of service required should be very clearly outlined in order to ensure advertisers are not left short. Networks should act as an extension of an advertiser's marketing team and aid in achieving the goals of the business. In order to do this effectively, advertisers need to ensure that their networks are providing sufficient account management resource to manage any aspect of the performance marketing programme that the advertiser is not able to service themselves.

- **Delivery capabilities**
  You wouldn't hire a member of staff for an important position if they didn't have the required experience. The same rules apply to running a performance marketing programme. When selecting a network or tracking provider, it is crucial that whomever is selected can demonstrate experience in delivering positive results for clients in the same or similar industries.

  This is particularly important when considering which network to work with as there are so many options available. Depending on which industry an advertiser is active in, it is highly recommended that advertisers review at least three networks to ensure that the correct fit is achieved. Some networks specialize in particular industries, such as finance, and pride themselves on industry-specific areas such as compliance. Other networks may focus more on the retail sector and have better publisher tools allowing for a more creative performance programme. Whatever the requirements, finding the right partner, with a proven track record in delivering results, is an important part of the set-up process.

  Additionally, in recent years there has been an explosion of advertisers who either have international operations or ship their products internationally and so are looking to attract overseas consumers. If an advertiser's business has an element of cross-border activity then it is imperative that they select a partner or partners who can deliver in each geographic area.

  Depending on where business is being conducted, advertisers may be able to identify a single partner who can provide international coverage through a single platform. However, brands should also consider market share and local knowledge when reviewing whether performance marketing will work in all territories. The performance marketing industry is an established area of digital in most developed markets. However, as the industry is relatively new, small markets tend not to be as advanced and may require a different strategy to deliver results.

During the review process, brands should look at the basics, such as whether a platform can handle local currencies and languages, as well as the more detailed market situation in order to determine what their performance marketing plans should be.

Many advertisers use different platforms in each market to leverage the local knowledge of their partners. While this approach creates a slightly steeper learning curve, as advertisers need to learn different systems, it can lead to bigger returns as a result of working with specialists in each market.

10 questions every brand should ask

While by no means a definitive list of questions, we hope the questions listed below – a basic cheat-sheet for any advertiser who is looking to begin a performance marketing programme – will help to answer some of the important questions that brands need to consider:

- Do I have the time/resource to manage a time-intensive method of marketing?
- Are any of my competitors using performance marketing?
- Are their performance marketing programmes successful?
- What can I offer that is different from what is already in the market?
- What level of commission can I afford to pay and is it competitive?
- Do I know how to run a performance marketing programme or do I need help?
- Who are the providers I should be speaking to (networks/service providers)?
- Is there a standout specialist for my industry?
- What markets do I want to be active in?
- Should I use a single partner or local specialists?

How to get the most out of your performance marketing activities

Once the decision has been taken to start a performance marketing pro-gramme and a network or tracking provider has been selected, the next stage of the process is to set up the actual programme.

This is a crucial part of the process, as the effort put in here will have a direct impact on the initial success of the programme. It is imperative that the programme is set up correctly from day one in order to help publishers gain confidence in a brand's commitment to the channel. First impressions count!

How to set up a performance marketing programme

There are three main elements to the set-up of a performance marketing programme: the commercial structure, the technical implementation and the marketing collateral. The elements are interlinked yet each play different roles in the running of a performance marketing programme. In this section we'll look at each one individually and then put them together to show the final implementation.

The commercial structure

The commercial structure of a performance marketing programme is possibly the most important element to consider. The commercials will determine how appealing the final programme is to publishers and provide a base for comparison against competing programmes.

Before setting up the commercials, advertisers will need to have decided on the user action that is desired. For the purposes of this section, we'll assume that the advertiser is a retailer and that the user action is a completed sale of a product.

In the retail world, publishers are usually paid a commission in the form of a percentage of purchase price. The exact amount of commission will vary per transaction but the percentage will remain constant. How much an individual advertiser will be able to pay publishers is determined very much by their margins. However, once a commission has been decided on it is strongly advisable to get your network's opinion on whether it will appeal to publishers. Networks have access to far more data than any individual advertiser, and can much more easily benchmark a proposed commission structure against competing programmes.

Once the commissions have been decided on, the next important decision to be made surrounds reporting. Each network or tracking provider has their own unique reporting capabilities. Additionally, depending on a client's needs, they will each have more or less complex custom reporting available. Deciding on the level of visibility needed at this stage is crucial, as many reporting requirements result in changes to the technical implementation needed later. By missing off a critical piece of data at this stage, advertisers will create more work for themselves later when they try to make changes to their technical implementations. While changing structure is generally a straightforward exercise, it is much simpler to get the requirements right up front.

Once the commissions and reporting requirements are set, the network can set up the commissions within their platform and pass the commercial and reporting requirements to their implementations teams who will translate these into a technical requirements brief.

The technical implementation

The technical implementation will be led by the commercial structure and reporting requirements. However, a basic implementation will take the form of having to implement a small amount of tracking code into the advertiser website. In the case of our retail example, it is likely this code will need to be included on the sale confirmation in order to track completed sales.

The implementation of tracking code is usually done by a webmaster or development team so it is tempting for the marketing team to want to take a back seat until the work is complete. It is highly recommended for the marketing teams to gain at least a basic understanding of what is being implemented as this will ensure they are well aware of what consumer activities are being tracked and, ultimately, what they are paying for.

For advertisers with multiple digital channels, it may be worthwhile at this stage to discuss more complex features such as container tags and analytics integration to ensure that the performance marketing programme is integrated into the marketing mix from the start.

Once the technical implementation has been completed on the advertiser side, the network or tracking provider will complete a round of tests and should provide the advertiser with example reporting to ensure that what has been implemented is as the advertiser would expect.

Additional items such as product feeds will also be discussed in order to ensure that publishers have access to up-to-date product and pricing information once the programme goes live.

The marketing collateral

This element of the set-up can be completed while the technical implementation is under way, as it should rely heavily on any technical expertise. This element is very much sales and marketing related but with a slight twist. Unlike selling a product to a consumer, the sales collateral and marketing material needed for a performance marketing programme needs to sell the advertiser's virtues twice.

First, items like a programme description, a clear explanation of the commission structure, advertiser company stability etc are needed to sell the performance programme to publishers. This is a crucial first step as, unless the marketing collateral entices publishers to join the programme and promote the products, the programme will never get off of the ground.

Second, assuming advertisers grab the attention of publishers, the advertiser needs to provide publishers with the marketing messages that appeal to consumers. It is important that advertisers remember that publishers are not experts in the advertiser's industry nor do they know the advertiser's business. Any information that can be provided to publishers to help them sell the advertiser's products or services should be shared. Additional items that will be required at this stage will include sets of banner create, textlink suggestions and high-performing keywords that publishers can target.

Once all three of these elements have been completed, an advertiser should be in a position to launch their performance marketing programme with confidence. They will be sure that, once sales start coming in, they are paying the right amount, have the right visibility and are providing the right collateral to continually help their publishers drive more business for them.

Programme set-up checklist

Here is a brief set-up checklist that will help ensure that an advertiser has all of their bases covered:

- Are commissions set at a level where each sale is profitable?
- Do I need to pay different commissions for different products and have these been set up?
- Have the reporting requirements been defined?
- Do these match with the advertiser's internal business reporting?
- Has the tracking been implemented to track the data the advertiser needs?
- Has the tracking been implemented at the right point in the purchase journey to track the right consumer action?
- Has the advertiser provided enough creative collateral for publishers to use?
- Has the advertiser provided live product information?
- Is the programme description strong enough? Will it entice publishers to join the programme?

- Has the advertiser provided enough information for publishers to promote the business to consumers with confidence?

- If the answer to all of the above questions is 'yes' then the chance of success will be high.

Setting goals and KPIs

Now that we have a performance marketing programme set up, the next stage is ensuring that the results of the activity are in line both with company objectives and industry benchmarks. With this in mind, it is now time to set some goals and begin to monitor important KPIs. In the first few months of a performance marketing programme, the KPIs are unlikely to be record-breaking sales numbers.

Rather, initial focus should be put on publisher recruitment and traffic generation through the performance channel. Whereas with some other channels that allow for instant results, performance marketing requires more of a patient start as publishers learn about the programme, analyse the benefits in comparison to other programmes in the market and ultimately begin promoting the products or services to consumers. Depending on the time of year and the level of competition, this may take a little while.

During this initial recruitment period, your network's experience is vital. They should be able to furnish you with a list of their top publishers and provide regular updates on progress on getting them on board. Getting publishers up and running is the most important aspect at this early stage.

Once publishers do start joining the programme, though, the focus needs to change to activation as it is very common for publishers to join programmes to plan for a future promotion, resulting in a long list of inactive publishers. A rough guideline should be 20–25 per cent activation rate, and if an advertiser is achieving this, they can count themselves successful. Again, the network should be helping here but this is the time for brands to really get hands on with their performance programmes and begin building relationships with their publishers.

At this point the goal should be publisher activation and the KPI should be traffic generated to the site (let's not worry about conversion just yet... remember that the branding element is free).

After four to six weeks, assuming all has gone according to plan, brands can start to look at conversions and optimization of publishers. This is the time where brands should be looking at providing their network with quarterly targets (set in conjunction with the network to ensure they are achievable). Targets should include a number of metrics. Conversions will naturally be the most important but traffic, impressions, number of new publishers recruited, conversion rate per publisher, etc should all form part of the monitored KPIs for the programme. After all, they are all valuable elements and all of these stats need to grow for the programme to continue to add value.

As business needs change, so should the goals and KPIs of a performance marketing programme. The best programmes continuously evolve to keep in line with the wider business strategy. The key is to communicate with both the network and publishers and really bring them into the decision-making process. Some of the industry's best performance marketers are not great at marketing. They are however, fantastic at communication.

Top five tips to publisher success

Information is best when you hear it directly from the source, so here I've asked Oliver Jones, Partnerships Director at Yieldify (**www.yieldify.com**) for his top five tips on how to get the best from your publisher partners:

1 Use the resources available to you. Get to know your account manager and key contacts within the network you have chosen. Remember that they have won your business and are there to help. If you are starting a programme from scratch and don't have much experience of the industry, ask your account manager for advice on promotions, communicating to publishers, setting and achieving your objectives and any extras the network may be able to offer you. There might be resources for them to build you banners or creatives and set up links and automated reports. Use their expertise to find the intelligent insights behind your stats and results.

2 Set clear goals and objectives for your programme with KPIs to measure your achievements throughout each month. This will help you to spot any issues, correct them quickly and prevent any hiccups from happening again. Whether it be acquisition of customers, sales, e-mail database growth, lead generation or increased registrations, organization and planning in advance really are the keys to success. Create a promotional calendar to run alongside your set objectives. You can give this to your publishers to plan ahead. Doing this will establish a steady return from your programme.

3 Make sure you set a competitive and appropriate commercial performance model that caters to the different publishers you may want to work with. A tiered commission structure is a great way to incentivize publishers to promote your company. Paying higher rates to the publishers that drive more business to your site will motivate them to promote your company more and put more resource into working with you.

4 Keep an open mind. The industry as a whole is growing constantly, with many new and exciting publishers entering the space, many with different technologies available to help achieve your own set of objectives. Be sure to explore the market and keep your finger on the pulse. From traditional voucher code and cash-back publishers to on-site retargeters and basket abandonment partners, they can all help you grow your business in different ways. Be open to testing each solution to find out which works best with your business model. The performance commercial model allows you to do this with minimal risk as you are only paying commissions on performance.

5 Build strong relationships and stay in touch with your key publishers. Regularly talk to your top partners and arrange face-to-face meetings to review performance. A little effort goes a long way – and remember that this is a team game where you, your network and your publishers are working towards the same goals.

Embracing innovation

In this chapter, we have repeatedly mentioned the variety of publishers who are active in the performance marketing industry. This is of massive benefit to advertisers but can also come with some challenges. Most notably, how do advertisers evaluate such a diverse mix of publisher opportunities and identify the right ones for their business?

The first step is for advertisers to come to terms with the fact that there are likely to be times when they simply don't understand the publisher's proposition. That's okay. It is also the start of a potential opportunity. If a way of promotion crops up that an advertiser has never heard of, then it stands to reason they're not currently using it.

However, before diving into the detail of individual publisher opportunities, it is crucial that brands understand how each publisher works and the impact that their activity will have on other marketing channels.

Often, new publisher ideas slot in seamlessly alongside existing activity. Additionally, new innovative technologies can actually improve the performance of other channels. In a small number of cases, performance publishers can actually replace the performance of another channel.

All of these are good things but brands need to understand the impact of these activities to ensure that they are planning ahead effectively.

How performance marketing can enhance other marketing channels

Let's look at two examples of how performance marketing can improve the results or coverage a brand gets from another channel. Take paid search as an example. Most brands will bid on their brand terms and other highly searchable, high-converting terms that will drive consumers to their website. More often than not, this activity is not conducted through the performance channel, with advertisers either using specialist paid search agencies or conducting the activity themselves.

However, if a brand also discounts some of its products or offers voucher codes to loyal customers, it is doubtful they will be bidding on discount terms, eg brand + voucher code. This is because deal-savvy consumers generally prefer to find discounts through specialist discount websites. Research has shown that consumers don't believe they will get the best discount directly from the brand.

So if an advertiser isn't bidding on these discount terms, they are losing traffic by not being visible. In steps the performance marketing publisher. Most of the large discount code sites also offer additional paid search services, specializing in the brand + discount code space. In exchange for a strong discount offer, they will also normally conduct paid search activity on these terms for free (or at least as part of the agreed exposure and commission package). In this way, the advertiser can increase the exposure they get through paid search, provide consumers with the user experience they want and not increase their costs, as it is all still paid on a CPA.

Now let's take a channel that isn't distinctly marketing, SEO. SEO is often viewed by brands as a free channel, as consumers visit their site from natural search results that don't incur a cost. So, depending on the strength of the SEO work, a brand will attract a certain number of customers each month. Then, depending on a few other factors, a certain percentage of those customers will convert, providing a conversion rate for the site.

Usually, conversion rates are between 1 per cent and 10 per cent, depending on the site and the advertiser industry.

So how can performance marketing help?

Well, there are publishers out there who specialize in conversion optimization rather than new traffic generation. Take the guys at SaleCycle (basket abandonment remarketing) or Yieldify (onsite retargeting). Their technologies are designed to maximize the return from each individual customer by using technology to intelligently communicate relevant product offers to consumers before they move off to a competitor.

By improving the number of conversions from existing traffic, the advertiser's conversion rate improves, making SEO (or any other channel) more effective. Yes, there is a cost involved in using a performance marketing publisher to achieve increased conversions, and some of those conversions would have happened naturally anyway. However, the increase in conversion far outweighs the cannibalization of any existing conversions.

These are just two examples of how performance marketing can be employed to great effect when looking at existing traffic and conversion maximization.

Summary

- The performance marketing industry is growing faster than any other form of advertising and brands should seriously consider entering into a performance programme if they haven't already.

- The industry offers numerous benefits at very low risk and, with the variety of publishers in the market, brands can keep at the forefront of digital without investing large amounts of resource.

- Other marketing channels can benefit from the integration of performance publishers and overall conversions can be improved very quickly.

- While performance marketing may not be as well-known as other areas of digital, it can offer significant gains if implemented correctly.

Common pitfalls of performance marketing

Everyone makes mistakes. New entrants into performance marketing are no different and, as with anything digital, what works for one company may not work for another so there is bound to be a bit of trial and error involved in establishing your performance marketing programme. However, there are a few common pitfalls, which we'll hopefully help you avoid:

- **Focusing on actions rather than costs** – or 'Bambi syndrome' as some in the performance industry like to call it. This sometimes happens when a new entrant into the market realizes the true power of performance marketing. They see the number of sales rocketing, but forget to stay focused on the bottom line. It is not uncommon for a new programme to offer huge commissions to get off the ground by attracting top affiliate partners, but at some point commission rates will need to come down or the campaign will run at a loss.

- **The 'our message is timeless' effect** – you've worked hard, your launch content is outstanding, your creative elements are top-notch and affiliate partners flock to your campaign. Success! But don't sit back. The hard work is only just beginning. You'll need to keep the various elements of your campaign fresh to keep affiliates interested and recruit new partners. A common mistake is for companies to take their eye off the ball when their collateral is working for them. By the time they realize performance is slipping, it's too late to come up with something new and their hard-won partners have moved on to the new 'best' merchant in the space.

- **If I brand it, they will come** – being a big brand doesn't guarantee success in the performance market. In fact, being a huge brand – the biggest brand – doesn't guarantee success. Your brand strength will help you to be recognized by affiliate partners, but don't get lulled into relying on your brand equity. Affiliates won't feel obliged to promote you – they will assess your offer on its merits, and will only choose to partner with you if your offer stacks up.

CASE STUDY   Number One Shoes

Number One Shoes strives to provide their customers with 'the right shoes at the best price and a huge range – and something new each week!' Fashion is their passion and their huge range caters for all desires, tastes and needs.

Comment

Smart performance marketing drives rapid customer-database growth.

Location

New Zealand.

The challenge

To cost-effectively utilize any and all online channels to aggressively grow Number One Shoes VIP e-mail database.

Target audience

Footwear consumers in New Zealand, primarily women.

Action

- The key aspect of this campaign was to focus on the new customer acquisitions.
- The way to do this was through 'The Number One Shoes VIP Club', which allows customers to hear about special offers, the latest trends and new-season footwear.
- By growing this database, it provides Number One Shoes with an important, cost-effective sales channel.
- FIRST digital marketing used performance media, display advertising, paid search marketing and social ads to help maximize the return on ad spend with real-time bidding.
- They also measured the value of impressions with A/B and multivariate testing, and analysed data to get a complete understanding of consumer behaviour.
- Performance marking tools included Google AdWords, Google's online advertising tool; Marin Software, and Brandscreen, a real-time media-trading technology.
- By using these tools they were able to gain visibility into marketing effectiveness, respond quickly to changing market conditions and consistently deliver ever-improving financial results.
- By FIRST applying their media technology to get the 'Number One Shoes' brand out to the wider community, they were able to reach and engage their customers.

Results

- Delivered 14,000 + new e-mail records in six months.
- Generated new customer records at half the CPA goal.

Link to campaign

- www.numberoneshoes.co.nz/

About the creator

FIRST use a proven digital marketing framework to help companies gain and maintain a competitive advantage by developing a digitally led sales and marketing strategy and culture within their organization.

Digital is a big deal. For many companies, placing digital strategies at the heart of their business can be a turning point in sustained profitability and growth. Marrying digital design, technology and marketing, as a multidisciplinary digital agency, we deliver campaigns and creative that targets, captures, engages, convinces and converts consumers.

We do this through the application of a proven digital marketing framework, a 360-degree approach to a brand's online presence that gives our clients a digital marketing blueprint to success. This contemporary framework is built around four spheres of capability.

Quote

Fiona Jenks, Online Strategist for Number One Shoes said:

FIRST has proven in a short period of time their expertise lead in generation. They have used a number of different online performance channels including Kiwi Surveys, Facebook as well as Google AdWords to build our e-mail database with New Zealand customers that we can now communicate with on an ongoing basis. They achieved the cost per lead KPI that was set and we're also getting some great recommendations around conversion rate and optimization and Google Analytics. Very happy to be working with the FIRST team.

Understanding online public relations

OUR CHAPTER PLEDGE TO YOU

In reading and absorbing this chapter you will:

- Understand the issue of reputation and the wider PR context.

- Know how the digital and social media revolutions have changed PR and online reputation management (ORM) – and how they have not.

- Identify the key online PR and ORM channels.

- Learn from leading clients and practitioners what success looks like – and how to avoid those fails, too.

Welcome to the new world of online PR and reputation management. Whatever you take from these pages, I suggest you don't read this chapter in isolation. That's because as any brand owner with marketing, customer service, PR, digital and customer-relationship marketing departments will tell you, the lines are blurring between the disciplines – with social media acting as the glue. A PR professional is now just as likely to be managing a brand's entire digital strategy as a niche communications brief.

Perhaps you're reading this because you are starting a business or running a small- to medium-sized one. You may be your own IT director, chief finance officer and sales manager. It's tempting to put PR at the bottom of this list, but that would be a mistake: public relations is about communicating with your customers, investors and influencers – a stakeholder group without which you wouldn't have a business – and this chapter is about giving tips to help you do so.

PR's defining essentials remain the same – understanding your audience, having a communications strategy, deciding on coherent messages and crafting stories well – but social media has fundamentally changed the game. Public relations has always been about two-way conversations, but the advent of the social web provides even more opportunities to listen and converse.

Google – judge and jury

The rapid growth of social marketing, compounded by increasingly sophisticated search habits, has big implications for how you manage your brand and reputation online. Every transaction begins with a search: Google is usually the first port of call for anyone considering a business or personal prospect, followed closely behind by a trawl through Twitter's search engine. A prospective transaction can sometimes end there too: Google's own study into how business-to-business (B2B) companies are researched found that more than half (or 57 per cent) of buying decisions were taken before a face-to-face meeting had occurred. An unflattering headline or ill-considered tweet can derail a potential piece of business or, worse still, sow the seeds of poor brand reputation, whether justified or not.

This shift is why I will use this chapter to set out the tried-and-tested rules of PR and reputation management, and then highlight the ways you need to adapt your approach in the age of social. To help you cut through the clutter created by the rapid momentum of technological and media change, you'll be reminded of PR's time-honoured truths as well as the significant developments that can make the internet work *for* you, not against. I'll finish by asking PR's great and good to give their one tip for online PR and reputation management success.

And one thing is certain: digital silence is not an option for your business. We are increasingly operating in an inbound 'pull' rather than a 'push' marketing economy and that change requires us to accentuate the positive truths about our businesses and ourselves. The rise of Google, Facebook and YouTube as the world's largest search engines underscores the importance of maintaining a good online reputation and ownership of your brand. So before Google gets to cast its verdict, the job of PR and ORM is to present your business in the strongest possible light.

Online – it's where PR lives now

Some might say the term 'online PR' is already outdated – that online PR and reputation management are one and the same thing – in the same way that the terms 'social media' and 'digital' are now interchangeable. The UK's Public Relations Consultants Association neatly sidesteps placing too much emphasis on channel, with the following definition of PR:

> Public relations is all about reputation. It's the result of what you do, what you say, and what others say about you. It is used to gain trust and understanding between an organisation and its various publics – whether that's employees, customers, investors, the local community – or all of those stakeholder groups.
>
> Public relations professionals use many different techniques as part of their PR campaigns: from media relations and lobbying, to speaking at conferences, to online viral campaigns, to sponsorship – and more. PR isn't always about short-term campaigns, such as product launches. It can encompass longer-term strategic aims, such as brand building and working with local communities.

However we label it, these days you can't afford *not* to have a PR plan that lives online: in 2006, 16.2 million people in the UK were using the internet every day, according to the Office for National Statistics. Since then, this has soared to 35.7 million – representing 73 per cent of the population. Another statistic paints an even more granular picture: web users spent an average of 1 in every 12 waking minutes each day online in the first six months of 2013, according to the most recent Internet Advertising Revenue Report, conducted by PwC on behalf of the Internet Advertising Bureau.

The continued consumer migration to digital channels requires your business to change not just the channels it uses, but the *way* it promotes itself and protects its image. While event-driven, one-off campaigns still have their place, the emphasis now is on continuous story-telling that contains multiple narratives: in other words, strategic, content-led online reputation management should be central to any PR you undertake.

Five essentials of traditional PR and reputation management that you (still) need to know

The discipline of PR has migrated from the age of Gutenberg (the man who introduced the printing press to Europe in the 15th century) to the era of Zuckerberg (who needs no explanation to readers of this book), but the fundamentals are the same: take your brand or company's core values that you want to promote, and knit together creative concepts with brand message, while identifying the influencers who will take these forward to your target market in an objective manner. As ever with PR, the challenge is planning how to control the messages when the medium is not always paid for.

Those core steps are listed below.

Start with strategy and an understanding of your audience

It would be foolish, not to mention costly and time-wasting, to embark on PR without having established your goals for such activity. Perhaps it is big-picture stuff about positioning your brand in a certain market, or at a more micro level, the launch of a new sub-brand product or service. Whatever your goals, PR should always support your company's wider marketing efforts. If marketing hasn't done this already, start by doing an internal audit to identify core strengths as well as vulnerabilities, and messages you want to consistently deliver. If your business has a consumer insight function, use the information they have collated in order to create an audience profile.

Your strategy will also revolve around how *exactly* you achieve your goals. For instance, as part of Skype's bid to extend usage of its internet calling service to different devices, it wanted to change the social media conversation from technology to user-based stories and used its Skype Blog Network to do so. It won international recognition with a SABRE award for its efforts.

Know the influencers, understand their pressures, gain their trust

The stakeholders who have always formed and assessed reputations – journalists, customers, prospects, investors, financiers – are still the group you must seek to influence. These days you need to do so online as well as through traditional channels.

Effective PR relies on knowing your stakeholders and developing them as a network of influencers who can absorb your message and carry it forward. The PR–journalist relationship, for instance, was and remains a value exchange: you give them ideas, they give you coverage. If your business is, say, to sell beauty products, you need to identify the key beauty journalists and bloggers and, more especially, gain knowledge of how these writers work. How do they get their news stories or subjects for longer features? What time on what days do their deadlines fall? Do they work on an exclusives-only basis? What is a good time of the day to call or e-mail them? And, if you connect with them, do you have something relevant to say?:

- Follow and engage with journalists on Twitter and connect with them on LinkedIn. Align some of your social content to their sectors and interests, and enter into a conversation with them. They won't know you exist unless you engage with them.

- Don't forget to make face-to-face contact. If there are trade shows, conferences and other industry events you know are attended by journalists, bloggers and other stakeholders relevant to you, make sure you are there also to press their flesh and put a face to your name. This will make them more receptive to your next call, e-mail or Twitter direct message.

- Store and jealously guard all this intelligence in a spreadsheet that contains details of the journalists and bloggers covering the sector in which you operate.

The humble press release – it still works

A quick way to get word out about your business is via the tried-and-tested press release. A release is just that: a means of getting information out to interested parties. Because of the need for online content to be 'discovered', some argue that press releases need to be even better written than those designed for print. However, the fundamentals remain the same:

- Pitch a story, not your product or service, and make sure it's worth reading.

- Write the release in a journalistic fashion, with the story first, and the detail later. Remember the 'inverted pyramid' rule of news writing (also applies to website copy too) with a hierarchy of important information. Your press release should be cut-able from the bottom up.

- Don't forget to include your boiler plate of factual information at the end of the release, together with contact details.

As a way of saving time, ask yourself three questions before you start to write your release:

- **Why** is this release being written and how will it help your business?

- **Who** is this copy for? Should you tweak the release, depending on the sites, bloggers or publishers you're aiming at?

- **What** is the measure(s) of success for your release? How do you want and expect its readers to respond?

Though it has become popular to predict the demise of search engine optimization, you must still apply its core rules when writing releases or blogs. There are myriad free sources as guides: try copyblogger.com or Google's own Webmaster tools. For understandable reasons, Google doesn't like its rankings to be manipulated, or its Webmaster Guidelines to be flouted, and so in October 2013 the search giant released the fifth edition of Google Penguin, its web spam-hunting algorithm. See searchenginejournal.com for a list of Penguin's do's and don'ts.

Compile a distribution list of all the relevant publications in your sector and, to maximize exposure, send your release to specific press release distribution sites, some of which charge for placement but promise wide dissemination and targeting: **www.prweb.com**; **www.clickpress.com**; **www.businesswire.com**, to mention just a few. Global resource PR Newswire is one of the oldest of such services and has a useful 'Frequently Asked Questions' section at **http://www.smallbusinesspr.com/why-pr/faqs**.

Creativity that gets cut-through: surprise and delight your audience, and make it as simple and low-cost as you like

The media through which you create promotional buzz today may have changed, but the creative principle remains the same. Try and go for the 'wow' factor that earns attention and inspires conversations about your company or brand, be it on a large or more niche scale.

To be guaranteed of reaching your audience, a creative idea must work across multiple media and therefore doesn't start with a decision over which particular channel to use. 'We tend to get way too wrapped up in the execution side of PR and ORM,' cautions Graham Goodkind, chairman and founder of Frank PR. 'It's not about the mechanic or the channel: it's all about the idea. That's what we should all be thinking about from the off.'

With the internet airwaves now so busy, the threshold for making even the smallest of ripples on the web is high. This places huge importance on creativity and the ability to resonate with consumers in a memorable, emotive and engaging way.

So far, so challenging. But the good news is that PR creativity at its best centres around a simple idea. Take, for example, Royal Mail's 'Gold Post Boxes' campaign, devised by Eulogy! and its social media agency Onlinefire in partnership with Royal Mail to mark the launch of the postal service's 'Gold Medal Stamps' campaign in 2012, the year of the London Olympics. I cite it here as an example of 'a creative, quick-win, low-cost idea that achieved blanket coverage', as Travelodge communications director, Shakila Ahmed, described it to UK industry bible *PR Week* (21 March 2013).

CASE STUDY Royal Mail gold post boxes

Royal Mail Stamps
@RoyalMailStamps

Follow

Wonder where we take our #GoldMedalStamp images from? Here's @GregJRutherford's Gold winning long jump in context pic.twitter.com/CSDFCooa

Reply Retweet Favourite ••• More

29
RETWEETS

4
FAVOURITES

The challenge

It takes a special occasion for Royal Mail to issue commemorative stamps and the London 2012 Olympics and Paralympic Games were just that. The ambitious task that Royal Mail set itself was to celebrate each and every gold winner with their own stamp, printed the night of their win and delivered to post offices the next day. The PR challenge was to put Royal Mail – which was a licensee of the Games, not a sponsor – at the heart of the greatest sporting show on earth in a credible and relevant way that would resonate nationally, and perhaps even overseas. The campaign also needed to remind consumers of Royal Mail's position in local communities and, of course, to promote sales of the stamps themselves.

Laura Trott @
@LauraTrott31

Follow

My sister just sent me this.. love it!!!
pic.twitter.com/JILMRKuw

 Reply Retweet ★ Favourite ••• More

146
RETWEETS

52
FAVOURITES

Laura Trott's sister
with gold postbox

Target audience

UK consumers and national and international media.

Action

Eulogy!, Onlinefire and Royal Mail's group communications team looked at Royal Mail's famously red post boxes and had the creative brainwave of painting them gold in medal winners' localities in order to raise awareness of the Gold Medal stamps. As the stamps were being printed overnight, the relevant post boxes were being painted too.

It was pure PR gold dust that brought Royal Mail's efforts to life for consumers at a grass-roots level. As Team GB clocked up gold medals and the painting of post boxes began happening the length and breadth of the country, this simple idea ignited conversation about Royal Mail while delivering regional, national and international coverage for every Gold Medal stamp and each gold post box. A new website, **www.goldpostboxes.com** was built to encourage public interaction, while Onlinefire tweeted every step of the stamp creation process, making it feel tangible and bringing consumers closer to this aspect of the Games.

Mo stamp with positive feedback

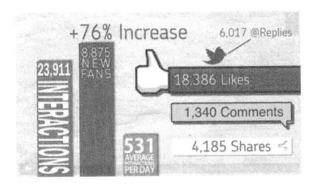

Royal Mail Facebook
social media results

Results

- Royal Mail more than doubled its Gold Medal stamps sales target.

- The PR campaign's creative concept tapped into the pride felt by local communities towards their medal-winning athletes. The post boxes became tourist attractions and created talking points, offline and online, up and down the UK. This helped drive the brand's story online, as people uploaded their photos to goldpostboxes.com.

- Onlinefire's social activity supported the campaign by creating an unprecedented level of dialogue between Royal Mail and its consumers. Over the course of the London 2012 Olympics and Paralympics, from 27 July to 9 September 2012, the agency's Twitter and Facebook work resulted in a total of some 23,000 interactions (likes, comments and shares) with the Royal Mail Stamps & Collectibles Facebook page, the only Royal Mail presence on the platform. The page got 8,875 new fans, a 76 per cent increase on its pre-Olympics base, during the period of the Games.

- Stamps, all of a sudden, were cool again and Royal Mail found itself the only non-Olympics sponsor invited to take part in the victory parade in September 2012.

- The campaign gave Royal Mail its mojo back and made consumers think of Royal Mail's place at the heart of the community in a very different light. 'When have you ever seen Royal Mail standing up this confident?' Fraser Chisholm, Royal Mail's head of media propositions, declared to a gathering of senior marketers in late 2012.

- The campaign was chosen as one of 2012's most memorable, as nominated by industry luminaries in *PR Week*'s 'Power Book'.

Damage limitation: when crisis strikes, be proactive

The annals of great PR and crisis management, before the advent of the internet and after, have one core success element in common: taking control of the agenda. In the pre-internet era, this was best evidenced by Johnson & Johnson's reaction to the Tylenol tampering crisis in 1982 – which was text-book fast, decisive and comprehensive.

A more up-to-date example of good crisis management is from January 2013, when Tesco faced a reputational challenge of epic proportions as the brand most associated with the discovery that beef products sourced from Irish suppliers contained horsemeat. Below are the lessons from how it weathered the crisis:

It starts with us.

What's been happening lately has made us
look at the way we do things.
Made us realise that we need to do our bit
to change the way our food industry works.
We need to do our best by our farmers.
Work together to make the food we sell
as good as it can be.
We're already paying our dairy farmers
above the market price for their milk.
But we can't stop there.
We need to move faster, try harder.
We're rolling up our sleeves,
building better, stronger relationships with our farmers.
We're offering longer contracts
to those who want them,
so that they have the support
to concentrate on what they do best.
This is it.
We are changing.

TESCO

For anything you want to know, go to www.tescofoodnews.com or call us on 0800 50 5555.
Twitter: @ukatesco Facebook: facebook.com/tesco

What we found.
And what we're doing.

Two weeks ago, we apologised to you, our customers,
because three of our frozen beef burger products were found to contain horsemeat.

We promised to find out exactly what happened and then come back and tell you.

Here's what we now know.

Our frozen burger supplier used meat in our products that did not come from the list
of approved suppliers we had given them. Nor was the meat from the UK or Ireland,
despite our strict instruction that they only use beef from those two countries.

This supplier will no longer supply any products to any of our stores.

But we, Tesco, are responsible for the food that we sell.

We have an expert technical team in place, with stringent tests, checks and controls,
to look after the quality of our food. In this case, it wasn't enough.

So we're taking action. We will now introduce a comprehensive system
of DNA testing across our meat products.

These checks will set a new standard for all supermarkets.

We want you to know that we will do whatever it takes to ensure the quality of our products.
And that when something is not on the label, it's not in the food.

For more information contact customer service by phone: 0800 50 5555; or go to www.tescoplc.com
Email: customer.service@tesco.co.uk Twitter: @uktesco Facebook: facebook.com/tesco

Our responsibility and our promise.

From the moment we were made aware of traces of horsemeat in our processed meat products, we have been working to get to the bottom of the issue.

We told you we would do whatever it takes to ensure the quality of our products. This is what we are doing:

We are reviewing our approach to our supply chain and building a thorough traceability system that includes DNA testing.

We will let you follow the progress we're making with our testing programme, and which products have been tested, at www.tesco.com/food-concerns.

We will make sure that you won't lose out as a result of the testing process. From today, if a product is withdrawn from sale, we will provide you with a better alternative for the same cost.

We have a responsibility to take the lead on this issue. The improvements we make will help set new standards for the industry.

What matters most to us is the trust you, our customers, place in us.

Our promise is to keep doing all we can to make sure you have confidence in the quality of every product we place on the shelf.

This will not mean more expensive food. It will mean that you can expect nothing less than the highest possible standard.

It's what you expect of us, and it's what we demand of ourselves.

For more information contact customer service by phone: 0800 50 5555; or go to www.tescoplc.com
Email: customer.service@tesco.co.uk Twitter: @uktesco Facebook: facebook.com/tesco

What burgers have taught us.

The problem we've had with some of our meat lately is about more than burgers and bolognese.

It's about some of the ways we get meat to your dinner table.

It's about the whole food industry.

And it has made us realise, we really do need to make it better.

We've been working on it, but we need to keep going, go further, move quicker.

We know that our supply chain is too complicated.

So we're making it simpler.

We know that the more we work with British farmers the better.

We've already made sure that all our beef is from the UK and Ireland.

And now we're moving on to our fresh chickens.

By July, they'll all be from UK farms too. No exceptions.

For farmers to do what they do best, they need to know they've got our support.

We know this because of the work we've been doing with our dairy farmers to make sure they always get paid above the market price.

We know that, no matter what you spend, everyone deserves to eat well.

We know that all this will only work if we are open about what we do.

And if you're not happy, tell us.

Seriously.

This is it.

We are changing.

TESCO

For anything you want to know, go to www.tescofoodnews.com or call us on 0800 50 5555.
Twitter: @ukitesco Facebook: facebook.com/tesco

1 Respond quickly to show you are in control, as a slow response can be as bad as no response at all. The scandal broke on 14 January 2013 when the Food Safety Authority of Ireland revealed it had found traces of horse DNA in frozen beefburgers sold in Tesco and other retailers. It took a full day for Tesco to issue its first statement, when it announced on 15 January it had withdrawn the products from sale. In the social economy, reaction times are compressed and brands must adjust to this. (In December 2013 NatWest was quick off the mark when it sent its first communications tweet 1 hour and 20 minutes after its systems meltdown saw millions of customers of RBS, NatWest and Ulster Bank unable to withdraw cash or make payments.)

2 Apologize sincerely. Tesco's communications were couched in a sincere tone from the outset; apologies appeared on 16 January on Facebook, Twitter, tesco.com and in the national press.

Company leaders must be front and centre as spokespeople, nowhere more so than online. Tesco's initial statement on the crisis was from group technical director Tim Smith. As the drama unfolded into February, chief executive Philip Clarke used the tesco.com video blog to confront the reputation issue head on: 'Nothing is more important to Tesco than the trust our customers place in us,' he said. 'And that trust depends on the quality of the products we sell.'

3 Produce online content to control the agenda and create an alternative to the content being created by the media and other critics. In mid-February, for instance, the tesco.com website announced a new 'farm and factory' website would make the management of its food supply more transparent to consumers.

4 Never, ever make light of a crisis. A Tesco tweet on 17 January, announcing the retailer's social media team was off 'to hit the hay', was inappropriate and flippant. Tesco apologized as users posted hundreds of jokes on the web.

5 Accept responsibility for where you are at fault and do not apportion blame. A Tesco press ad entitled, 'What burgers have taught us' was deemed a statement too far; it was banned by the UK's Advertising Standards Authority for implying there were issues with meat standards across the whole food industry. Tesco defended the ad, saying it was trying to show that it was taking the horsemeat issue seriously and to demonstrate it was listening to customers.

Nonetheless, the grocer's handling of the crisis was considered deft overall. Google the word 'Tesco' and the word 'horsemeat' does not appear in the first 10 pages of results, and those beyond. There is no sense that Tesco has manipulated search engines – but by understanding them and creating content that addressed consumers' issues directly, providing alternative content to the media's coverage, it showed it is possible to take control of the agenda in the social media era.

Four new rules of PR and reputation management you need to know

Integrate your idea and manage reputation from top down, and across media

We've seen that, regardless of the social media revolution, the essence of PR is still about creating a brand idea that not only engages consumers, but your entire stakeholder group. Such ideas require integration across an ever-widening set of channels: ranging from paid media (advertising), shared media (social), to produce-earned media (traditional PR) and your owned media (blog or website).

CASE STUDY   Bristol-Myers Squibb's melanoma exposed

The challenge

To alert men – often a difficult group to reach with health messages – about the benefits of early detection of melanoma.

Target audience

Adult males.

Action

BMS and its agency Ogilvy PR/New York drew up a campaign in the United States that reached its male audience through sport, with a strong call to action that drove awareness and encouraged early detection. To hit its target market, spokespeople from the NFL (the National Football League in the United States) were appointed to tell personal stories of skin cancer in order to raise awareness; a website was created hosting educational video and details on local screenings; gamification was used through a football-themed game called Football Avenue; and a mobile examination facility was located at highly attended NFL events. Finally, the NFL's digital reach was harnessed through Facebook and Twitter.

Result

- After attending events, 81 per cent of respondents said they were more knowledgeable about melanoma.

- Some 42 million people were reached through NFL digital entitles.

- The campaign achieved 176 million media impressions and garnered several industry awards.

Get to grips with content marketing

The expansion of social media and the explosion in demand for content are perhaps the two biggest – and strongly interlinked – evolutions in PR since the 2012 edition of *Understanding Digital Marketing*. Simply put, content marketing is about telling a story. Ask yourself: are you ready to tell yours? Start by thinking back to the stories that have impacted you. Did you feel informed, connected, moved to react? Then, think about your influencer group: what stories are likely to resonate with them?

You might ask why you need to go to the effort of creating great content. As search engines tighten their ranking algorithms against manipulation, they continue to reward and prioritize high-quality, popular content. In other words, good content inspired by audience insight helps your search engine ranking, so try to gain an understanding into what your audience's passions are.

If you have a website, you need to think like a media owner, producer and distributor of content to promote your business:

- **Share it:** to take advantage of earned media, it is vital that your content is easy to share. If you're targeting magazine or newspaper brands, think about how editors operate these days – they have fewer resources and yet are judged on levels of site traffic and engagement. So invest in content with the potential for sharing: original articles and blogs, infographics (good for telling a databased story better than words can), images and video that keep readers dwelling for longer. Content must be win-win-win: in other words, content that enhances your own website and draws in readers, which is of a high enough quality to appeal to time-pressured editors/publishers of trade and business websites, all the while gaining your company great visibility and credibility.

- **Bespoke it, in real-time:** it's very easy, and kind of lazy, to take content from other channels such as TV and plonk it on social. And it won't necessarily work, unless perhaps you have an emotive blockbuster of an ad such as John Lewis's Christmas campaign. Social has its own set of content tools, as Simon Veaney, director of social media communications at American Express, points out. 'Use Instagram or vine videos, and challenge yourself to keep it short – under 200 characters is ideal, even if the platform does not dictate a word-count like Twitter,' Veaney advises. 'Remember your audience is viewing your message in the moment and likely on a mobile device, in real-time.'

- **And don't forget a call to action:** make like direct marketers and insert calls to action that invite user participation; have a poll and ask readers to cast a vote or create a video competition and request entries – anything to get users to join in the conversation around your brand.

    There is a wealth of free guides to get you started: the contentmarketinginstitute.com site has good advice and case studies for B2B businesses; sites such as slideshare.net, support.brightcove.com and LinkedIn feature useful advice for beginners.

Break down the 'inattention' barrier

Undivided attention is a thing of the past. Passive viewers of marketing/ advertising content have become active engagers and sharers of content. With a pick of hundreds of TV channels, many with a social layer attached, gazillions of YouTube videos, and Facebook/Instagram/Tumblr sites full of entertaining content to choose from, attention spans are diminishing. The onus is on you to be attention-grabbing with whatever content you create and, increasingly, creative cut-through is coming via an ingenious use of social media, user-generated content or a memorable experience.

With advances in technology, the borders of creativity have become non-existent so that you can do quality creative very quickly and it doesn't have to cost the earth. All you need is Photoshop or an equivalent (see 'A–Z of online PR and reputation management tools', page 290) and a smartphone – and you can create engaging content. You start with an idea, create a video, spend a minimum amount of money to seed that video (see 'Don't bank on free media', below), and some time later you will have generated YouTube views, quality links and hopefully registered supporters and coverage in relevant external media.

As outlined above, always keep insight into your desired audience and your goals at the heart of your planning, in that order. Then choose your channels. As shown in the case study box, a campaign by UK bank NatWest ticked all these boxes, as well as providing that 'surprise and delight' factor for recipients.

CASE STUDY   NatWest's 'Be Uniproof'

NatWest Help ✔
@NatWest_Help

🐦 Follow

@KingJords Hi Jordan here's a video which will help goo.gl/C1YdoT DR

2:53 PM - 19 Aug 2013

〰 Vine @vineapp

 **NatWest Help** ✅
@NatWest_Help

@Shikirki Good stuff Paddy, don't forget to check out all
our vine videos, here's my favourite: bit.ly/1cJDB1I. :) PW

6:04 PM - 16 Aug 2013

꙾ Vine @vineapp

The challenge

UK bank NatWest has long courted students in an attempt to recruit them early in
their careers and develop their lifetime loyalty and value. However, this audience
is known for its high 'unattention' thresholds and the bank needed an appropriately
creative solution to cut through.

Target audience

Students aged 18–20 who had just received their A level results and were about to
embark on college life at the start of the 2013 academic year.

Action

As part of a wider advertising and social media campaign called 'Be Uniproof',
NatWest used micro video app Vine to broadcast a series of nine short, witty and
visually arresting videos with deliberately quirky production values – the content

of which ranged from tips on doing your own laundry to simple ways to be financially savvy at university. It promoted the videos as part of the #BeUniproof trend on Twitter, with an @NatWest_Help handle for students to ask questions about managing their finances.

Results

Undisclosed.

Don't bank on free media

It was a comfort to think of social media as being 'socialist' in nature, compared with the commercial beast of paid platforms such as TV, radio, outdoor and print. But no longer: as social platforms mature, grow more mass market and go public, their business model has evolved and it means you now have to consider paying for exposure.

And while the way your content is being found on Facebook, Twitter and Instagram may be less organic these days, it is reasonable that people should pay for wider reach or more refined targeting. If your brand has, say, 10,000 fans, with a small amount of media spend you can go beyond the 10,000 to a much wider group or a more targeted demographic. Social networks have sophisticated platforms that allow you to specify the audience – demographics such as age, region, interests – for advertising, but also to promote your content posts in an increasingly cluttered environment.

The key messages here are: first, that you understand how to promote your content – sites such as socialbakers.com will help explain the mechanics – and that when you're drawing up your promotional budget, ensure you include spend to do so. For Facebook's guide on targeting audiences, see facebook.com/business/ and for Twitter's own version, go to business.twitter.com.

With all these tips in mind, a content-driven PR strategy can become the pivot around which you build an inbound marketing campaign and protect your reputation, allowing your PR efforts to move from pushing a new product or service and instead to create that gravitational pull necessary to generate influence and convince your audience. Now we turn to industry luminaries to crystallize the points in this chapter by distilling down their own experiences.

If I could tell you one thing...

Armed with years of experience at PR's coalface, industry experts give their one tip for managing your business reputation online:

Positive ORM isn't a sticking plaster fix
Steve Barrett, editor-in-chief, *PRWeek*

A positive online reputation is not something that can be applied or fixed after the event, like a sticking plaster. Rather, it is the result of tapping into a deep well of engagement with stakeholder groups including internal staff members, customers, investors, and the media. By allying this engagement to a smart social strategy, brands and corporations can avoid demolishing their reputation in 140 characters.

Your reputation, online or not, is still all about relationships

Paull Young, director of digital, charity: water

Your online reputation, and indeed digital marketing in general, is all about relationships. And every relationship (whether with your best friend or a brand you love) requires both sides to give benefit to each other. Focus on the customer experience and building trust with your stakeholders, and your online reputation will be fine. Ask not what your customers can do for you, but what you can do for your customers.

Start with the idea, not the channel

Graham Goodkind, chairman and founder, Frank PR

We tend to get way too wrapped up in the execution side of PR and ORM. If I had a pound for every time a client has asked for a Twitter, Facebook or social media idea...

It's not about the mechanic or the channel: it's all about the idea. That's what we should be thinking about from the off. Start with a blank sheet of paper and try to come up with a great idea. Forget about how or where you're going to do it for a few minutes. Focus on conjuring up that nugget of brilliance that is going to make something eminently shareable and then the rest will come naturally. You'll be able to apply it to the channel you need after that. But not before.

Google and social – your most important ORM tools

Colin Byrne, CEO UK and EMEA, Weber Shandwick

Don't underestimate the role social media plays – and will continue to play – in shaping online reputation for brands. Its tentacles extend far beyond those increasingly powerful channels and now influence Google search engine results – the single most important source for shaping business's reputation in a digital age.

Social media isn't just tactical: it's strategy

Alastair Campbell, journalist, broadcaster, political aide and author, and former director of communications and strategy for Prime Minister Tony Blair between 1997 and 2003

> *Because its messaging can be so short and snappy, social media looks tactical, and that is how many people in public life use it. But used properly, it is a powerful strategic tool.*

... and you have no choice but to get involved

Richard Stephenson, director of corporate affairs, AXA

> *The biggest misconception of social media within large companies is that the decision to participate is their own. You may well be broadcasting and marketing but you are also being spoken about, by your customers, your colleagues, your stakeholders and your prospects. Ignore them at your peril and remember that listening is just as important, if not more so, than broadcasting.*

Be human on social media, with a dash of humour

Nicola Green, director of communications and reputation at O2 (Telefónica UK)

> *Understand that when you're on social, it's as if you are in your customer's front room and respond with humanity and maybe a bit of humour.*

Be fast, be authentic

Peter Cross, communications director, John Lewis

> *Be true to who you are. In the heat of our Christmas 2013 campaign, we noticed that a certain US computer scientist with the Twitter handle @johnlewis, was receiving hundreds of misdirected tweets congratulating him on his Xmas telly ad. As soon as this hit our radar, we contacted 'the other' John Lewis for handling the onslaught of tweets with such care and good humour. Whilst it would have been tempting to milk the opportunity, it was far truer to our brand to be thankful and low key.*

PR is more real-time than ever

Simon Veaney, director of social media communications, American Express

Make it social, make it shareable. Make it quick. Too many PR professionals and marketers take content from other channels and think it will just work in social. It won't. Use Instagram or vine videos, and challenge yourself to keep it short – under 200 characters is ideal, even if the platform does not dictate a word-count like Twitter. Remember your audience is viewing your message in the moment and likely on a mobile device, in real-time. Does your message carry the urgency to cut through? If not, you need to adjust your approach. And quickly.

Facilitate engagement: don't stifle it

Jackie Brock-Doyle OBE, group CEO, The Good Relations Group and former director of communications and public affairs, London Organizing Committee for the Olympic and Paralympic Games

Sometimes you have to trust and create the environment for people to do the right thing, not shut them down. If you are authentic, people will know and they will repay your trust.

During dress rehearsals for London 2012's Opening Ceremony, there was a concern about how in this age of instant news, the entire show might be leaked by being broadcast on a handheld device.

Our solution was to trust the UK public to do the right thing by encouraging commentary, but within defined parameters. We created the Twitter hashtag #Savethesurprise and a personal announcement from our artistic director directly to the stadium audience asked everyone to share their experience but not to spoil the surprise by telling them what is in the show or post pictures. Two dress rehearsals later, while the odd posted picture had been withdrawn on the wrath of fellow tweeters, the PR benefit of over thousands of tweets about how great the show would be could not have been generated in a more authentic or powerful way.

Entertain and open the doors to your world
Steve Martin, CEO, M&C Saatchi Sports & Entertainment

Almost every brand wants to engage with their audience online to create a favourable reputation. The best way to do this is to entertain that audience, be very real and transparent. Lose the marketing speak and talk to them like you would a friend. Not just as a one-off but continually. Adidas did this beautifully during the 2012 Olympics with their award winning 'Take the Stage' campaign. They opened the doors to their world, showed their athletes away from the track or the pool in a refreshing, newsworthy way and got the tone spot on.

Be generous
David Gallagher, senior partner, CEO, Europe and chairman, Ketchum, London

Be generous with time, attention, credit and opportunity. Not later, when you've 'made it'. Be generous right now. Shakespeare said 'Ill deeds are doubled with evil words', and what was true then is truer now in today's viral, hyper-connected, meme-replicating world. So if I could tell you one thing, it's be generous and if you can't be generous, shut up.

Don't overreact to rude comment
Trevor Morris, visiting professor in public relations at the University of Westminster and former CEO of Chime Public Relations

Reputation is about what you do, what you say and what others say about you. Online can enhance what you do by offering quick, plain English customer service. What you say online – and indeed anywhere – should be clear and simple and not make the mistake of trying to be down with the kids.

What others say about you online can sometimes be rude and hurtful. Don't overreact. Correct factual errors, but don't get drawn into arguments on matters of opinion. You will only amplify the problem.

PR still relies on original, interesting stories
John Rudaizky, CEO, TeamGSK, WPP

In an always-on world of robo-charged, social-media-driven content creation, traditional PR agencies still have the best chance of engaging, managing and creating interesting stories – albeit this now needs to be every minute of every day. Acronyms like 'ORM', 'CRM' and 'CEM' will come and go, but because public relations has always been about engaging audiences through original stories, 'PR' is the one that will outlive them all.

The A–Z of online PR and ORM

The range of tools and disciplines available to create online buzz for your company and to protect it in times of need is expanding at a rate of knots. Here's my guide to the ones you need to know:

- **A is for algorithm.** Few people on the planet know how the algorithms of Google and Facebook work but you do need to know that their goalposts shift on a regular basis. To keep up to date on changes, subscribe to the free e-bulletins of authoritative publishers such as SearchEngineWatch.com and TechCrunch.com. See also 'SEO' below.

- **B is for blogs.** If we had one piece of advice about PR blogging, it would be to 'make it real'. Don't attempt to fool the reader with a sales pitch or by disguising your blog as thought leadership, when it really is a press release or an advertisement. See 'O is for Opinion' below and, for some great examples of corporate (large and small) blogs and tips on how to emulate them, see **www.ragan.com**.

- **C is for content.** Any content you create should not have your company at its main thrust, but rather the needs and passions of your customers, prospects and other stakeholders (see 'I for Insight', below). Be aware of the recent shift from PR's main reliance on words for delivering messages, to visual promotion to help your brand or company be discovered and live online.

- **D is for 'discoverability'.** With torrents of content being created every day, you need to work on curating your output effectively for your audience. YouTube incorporates Google's search engine, so familiarize yourself with Google's own SEO commandments, which you'll find at support.google.com/webmasters.

- **E is for events.** The social media revolution has not eradicated the importance of face time – it has, in fact, made meeting and greeting your stakeholder group even more pivotal. On a grander scale, events can create headlines for your company. There are some excellent guides to getting started with event management at **http://www.facetime.org.uk**.

- **F is for Facebook.** As at September 2013, Facebook said it had 727 million daily active users on average worldwide, with some 80 per cent of these outside the United States and Canada. It is a truly global content channel with reach that dwarfs that of TV channels and newspaper brands. And access to Facebook is extremely mobile: Facebook has 874 million monthly active users who used the site's mobile products, as of September 2013.

  It's important to know the different roles that Twitter, YouTube (see below) and Facebook play in online PR and ORM. Facebook gives you the opportunity to tell a story and be visually appealing, much as you would with any brand website. Its 'big data' and analytical capabilities have also evolved to the point that you can target the people you want, where you want – but for a fee. Recent surveys point to a flatlining of interest amongst teens but, given the size of its user base, you ignore Facebook at your peril. A good place to start is Facebook's own guide to targeting: **www.facebook.com/business/**.

- **G is for Google.** The first port of call for recommendations about a company. It is worth trying to familiarize yourself with how Google's PageRank algorithm – the way Google determines a web page's importance and ranking – operates, so you can develop a content-led strategy that gives you a degree of ownership over how your brand is promoted. For a good starter explanation, check out howstuffworks.com/google-algorithm or visit moz.com.

- **H is for history.** Think of Google as the world's biggest archive on the history of companies and people. The way to avoid an online reputation crisis is not to try and censor history by asking your PR expert to have a story deleted, but rather to avoid activating the crisis in the first place. If there are skeletons in your online closet, counter this with positive content creation that seizes back the PR agenda.

- **I is for insight:** on your customers, prospects and stakeholders. It is vital you start PR with understanding your audience – their likes, interests and passions – so you know where they hang out and what will strike a chord with them. For the uninitiated, try searching the key words 'the Independent Consultants Group' and 'DIY research guide' to find the ICG's clear, uncomplicated introduction to gathering insight.

- **J is for journalist.** Time-pressured, often poorly paid, journalists can be a breed misunderstood by the PR world. You'll achieve real competitive advantage if you can get under the skin of journalists relevant to your sector, trying to match your needs with theirs. While sending cupcakes to newsrooms can get you appreciated, such goodwill is only fleeting. The best gesture is always a great story, given exclusively with as much detail as you can disclose.

- **K is for keywords.** A great PR content strategy should not rely on the practice of spraying keywords throughout a piece of content unnaturally, in an attempt to win SEO rankings. Yet every search still begins with a topic the searcher is looking for – the keyword, in other words, even if someone searches in the form of a question. So as a content creator, you still need to decide the overarching string of keywords that defines your content.

- **L is for listening.** You need to listen to what people are saying about your brand or company online, as well as focusing on what you're saying yourself. Try to understand the conversations your target audience are having, not just about your brand, but in general, and this will help you form a content strategy that appeals to them and will achieve your brand and business aims.

- **M is for media.** Now that it is social media – rather than traditional channels such as TV or press – that offers you mass audience reach, get familiar with the mechanics of social media buying. See 'Don't bank on free media' on page 284.

- **N is for newsroom.** Real-time social marketing has led some brands to set up their own 'brand newsrooms', a term made famous thanks to the 2013 Super Bowl, and Oreo's rapid-response to that event's power outage, the now famous 'Dunk in the Dark' tweet. But if you don't have such deep pockets, you can learn from the mentality that goes with such operations: communications must be relevant, on-brand and add value for the audience.

- **O is for opinion.** If you decide to step onto the PR-driven content stage, be sure to have a point of view – your audience expects it. Your company stands for something – you just need to work out what those values are and how to get them over in an engaging way.

- **P is for Photoshop.** One of the world's most popular digital illustrative tool sets, but its parent Adobe charges for a licence to use its suite. Pilxr, on the other hand, does most of what Photoshop does but is free and cloud-based.

- **Q is for quiet.** With so much content being created by companies, it is tempting to feel the need to be visible, and post content, almost for the sake of it. As in life, do so online: if there isn't anything to say that's worthwhile, either for your brand or your audience, then silence is the best course. Make sure that everything you do adds value and isn't just a token presence.

- **R is for response time.** The social web demands real-time response in PR and a fast response can show that you are in control. Many brands are, in fact, using agencies or setting up an in-house capability to help adopt a newsroom mentality (see above) to crisis management. At a base level, RSS feeds can be a cost-effective way of monitoring online mentions of your company. There is, of course, a plethora of social-media-monitoring tools, as well as those that keep tabs on TV and radio.

- **S is for search engine optimization (SEO).** Don't miss the opportunity to become trusted by prospects long before they are in purchase mode. Bone up on the fundamentals of the Google AdWords keyword tool at simplybusiness.co.uk/microsites/google-adwords and track changes to Google's algorithm at moz.com.

- **T is for Twitter.** The key online reputation management tool in your repertoire for its speed and reach. It also scores highly for its questioning and listening abilities. Use it as your own content distribution platform: at the time of its initial public offering (IPO) in November 2013, Twitter had more than 200 million active users – 60 per cent of them interacting with Twitter via mobile – so the Twitter world is your oyster. Try to observe the following rules:

Best times of day to tweet: 9 am, 12 noon, 3 pm, 6 pm.

Best days to tweet to reach consumers are Saturdays and Sundays.

How to tweet:

- The majority of retweets are for tweets that contain links.

- Engagement is 17 per cent higher for tweets with less than 100 characters.

- Engagement is 200 per cent higher for tweets with image links. For help and case studies, visit **https://business.twitter.com** and follow @TwitterAdsUK and @twitterUKI_SME.

- **U is for uniformity.** An oxymoron in the context of this chapter, but your brand needs uniformity throughout social media whilst always avoiding the 'corporate' or 'not of the people' tags. For the masses, uniformity is absolutely not what they seek from social media. It's a difficult balance to deliver, but, like all risky situations, the upside can be huge.

- **V is for video and Vine.** With 1 billion users per month (see 'Y is for YouTube', below) YouTube is the web's second biggest search engine, proving that video is very much in demand. Need we say more? Well, yes. With smartphone technology getting ever more video-enabled, there is no excuse not to explore. You now have the perfect short video tool, Vine, owned by Twitter and capable of creating very engaging content, as we saw with NatWest's BeUniproof campaign (see page 282).

- **W is for writing.** In the world of 140 characters, it may seem that writing skills are diminishing as a communications tool. The truth is the opposite: as any journalist will tell you, short copy can be much harder to pull off than long and there is an art to writing memorable tweets. In general content terms, great writing can give your company or brand a voice on the social web. Avoid waffle – it doesn't scan well and has little value. Go to **www.fastcompany.com** for an excellent guide to writing tweets and to copyblogger.com for its must-read tips: 'copywriting – 101'.

- **X is for x-factor.** In other words, that sparkle, buzz, excitement and point of difference that a PR campaign, backed and amplified by a community, can deliver like nothing else in our marketing armoury.

- **Y is for YouTube.** The Google-owned video site says that 1 billion users watch 6 billion hours of content on its site every month – a stunningly large audience. The channel has long moved on from being focused on videos of cute pets and kids and silly pranks. It is being increasingly used as a platform for professionals to showcase campaigns and business messages. YouTube incorporates Google's search engine, which has its own set of rules to help get your videos discovered, so you need to learn how to tag and describe them. After that, like all the mass media social sites, the targeting of your content on YouTube must be paid for. Econsultancy provides a clear and useful guide to using YouTube for business and targeting at **http://bit.ly/1cFDcw1**.

- **Z is for zest**. The *Oxford Dictionary* defines zest as 'great enthusiasm and energy', a 'quality of excitement and piquancy' and something you use as flavouring. Frankly, I couldn't find a more appropriate description of the best way to approach online PR and ORM, and one I have sought to encapsulate in this chapter.

How not to do online reputation management

By Brooke Zimmatore, Massive PR (published: 17 May 2013)

InShare5

Developing a truly effective system by which one can control their online reputation management is like designing and testing a new bridge structure. You have to work out the engineering pitfalls, try it, then get back on your feet and pave the path to a workable technical and stable system that gives the result you need so that it works 100 per cent of the time.

Online reputation management is a science, with procedures and actions that balance on the edge of a pin. If not done right it all comes crashing down with no results, or worse, negative results. What we are talking about is really black hat online reputation management, on which we will go into more detail.

The 'quick fix'

It still amazes me how many people get tied into the 'quick fix' schemes offered by shiny new companies who **talk about BIG things** for little money. 'Setup 500 social profiles for just $100!' or 'Get 50,000 real Facebook likes for just $1,000!'. Buying thousands of backlinks, thousands of Twitter followers and many other cheap, black hat methods.

Short-sighted is the executive, business owner or SEO company who buys into this. If there were a quick fix for online reputation damage then everyone would be doing it. And if it was effective it would be as expensive as it is valuable.

The no-no's of online reputation management

Let's set aside ethics for a moment and just take this bridge analogy used above. If you build a bridge out of cardboard and styrofoam you will have a disaster the moment someone puts pressure on it. The same goes with your online reputation:

- **Creating fake reviews**: fake reviews will become your Achilles heel. The search engine giant Google has announced that fake 'glowing' reviews will be taken down if detected – and they have entered into their search algorithm many factors to determine this.

  Fake reviews can also be embarrassing and have a very negative effect on your company. Many review websites do a quarterly or annual inspection of the quality of their **user reviews** and if they catch you out it can be quite a hit on your brand.

- **Using black hat SEO to build links**: a sure-fire way to get yourself **sandboxed** by Google and undo all of your hard work is to try to build 'quick links' through spam techniques. You will find many companies offering you thousands of backlinks for abnormally low rates. Watch out for these as they may seem to give you a temporary boost, but one by one, websites practising in black hat link-building will be found and penalized.

- **Content cloaking**: Google makes it clear in their **Quality Guidelines** that the website that viewers see in front of them should be the only content that exists on that page. Trying to enhance your page for keywords without showing it to the viewer will get you nowhere. Google understands page structure and code and can see if your text is the same colour as a background or if you are using JavaScript or small HTML boxes to hide a lot of content.

- **Buying social followers**: not only is this pathetic, but is also indicative of the brand's ability (or lack of) to communicate. Have you ever seen someone who has fake friends in real life? Remember that guy who had the nice car and people pretended to like him? Well, when he got in trouble no one was there to help because he had no real friends. The same goes with social media. In a moment of crisis, you will feel very lonely when one rogue journalist, blogger or ex-employee decides to defame you all over the place.

Real followers are achieved through real interaction only. This applies to all social networks and even general business. Proactive reputation management and crisis management requires the building of loyal followers.

- **Lying in a public arena:** one of the first laws of PR is you never lie. Yes, there will come a time when you will not want to answer a sensitive question pointed at weaknesses in your existing set-up, structure or organization. But a skilled PR or representative, whether online or offline, will know how to deal with that without lying. Trying to boost your reputation with fake reviews, false statements, lies in the press etc will eventually destroy it. When you start attracting a lot of attention, the lies of the past will creep up and bite you. So always be honest in representing yourself.

Quality is the only way

In the end, the answer is simple. The easy way is never the best way, so focus on quality publications, communication and services. Do this in great quantity and you will establish a powerful online reputation and be able to maintain it in a moment of crisis.

Quality is never an accident; it is always the result of high intention, sincere effort, intelligent direction and skilful execution; it represents the wise choice of many alternatives.

William A Foster

Understanding content marketing

OUR CHAPTER PLEDGE TO YOU

When you reach the end of this chapter you'll have answers to the following questions:

- Why do I need to create content for digital marketing success?

- How does content strategy influence my entire digital strategy?

- How is content used by PR, social and search teams?

- What do I need to think about when creating digital content?

- How can I share the digital content I am creating?

- How do I calculate ROI and set KPIs for my content?

Why content? – an overview

You cannot talk about digital marketing without simultaneously talking about content. Today we live in a digital landscape where content is everywhere. You are nothing online if you do not create content. Content in its myriad different forms is the currency that digital marketers use to engage, interact and influence their customers. Content is one of the few marketing channels that allows marketers to contact their potential customers along all phases of the customer cycle, during research, purchase and review.

Content works. In this chapter we show you why content works, how it works and how it sits within an overall digital marketing strategy. We show you how content can be used to make your brand innovative, win new customers and influence your target audience. We also demonstrate how content can work for any brand, big or small, and how to come up with the ideas that can really invigorate your content marketing. Ultimately we show you that the size and scale of digital means that content is now at the heart of everything you do online. It increasingly powers search, social, PR and paid-for advertising, too. As digital marketers, it means that we have to take content seriously; you can get away with not being the best at creating it yourself personally, but you do need to know where to find the best content, how to formulate strategy and how to use that content to build engagement.

The growth of content marketing in the digital age

Content marketing is not new: it has been around for over a century in many different guises. John Deere, the tractor maker, created and published its own magazine, *The Furrow*, as far back as 1895. Michelin, the tyre manufacturer, began producing a maintenance guide filled with travel and accommodation recommendations for French motorists in 1900; Nike published and promoted a 19-page booklet entitled *Jogging* in 1966, practically inventing the sport of running in the United States – and selling a lot of their trainers to boot (excuse the pun) in the process. Content marketing worked. The distribution method for this content in the pre-digital age was direct mail. Content, in the form of ideas, product information and reviews, was what many mail order customers wanted to read. In the days before Google consumers needed information in order to make their purchases. Millions of these purchases were based on branded content that they read via direct-mail marketing material.

Content marketing works and will always work because it offers value to a potential customer; it fills their immediate requirement for information; it engages them and it does not use coercive methods to 'sell' to them. Done right, it is a very powerful brand-building and business-building tool.

Content marketing worked then, and in the digital age it works just as well, if not better. So why the increase in content?

There are a number of reasons why content marketing has seen a resurgence in digital marketing circles in recent years. One of the overriding reasons behind the growth of digital content marketing is because 'now they can'. The barriers to entry for a business or brand to become a publisher are effectively nil. The start-up cost of becoming a publisher – creating content for your blog and/or social media profiles – is next to nothing. Self-publishing platforms such as Wordpress make it easy – and free – to set up. The biggest investment is time. In the digital age, all brands can become publishers with ease. Not for them the costly printing and distribution process of days gone by.

Content marketing is also growing because, as mentioned above, it works. No matter what the size of your business. Content is a strategy being adopted by leading brands such as P&G, Coca-Cola and Amex, as well as by smaller businesses and even one-person entities. Coca-Cola – one of the biggest brands on the planet with colossal marketing budgets – has put content at the core of its 'Content 2020' advertising strategy mission:

> All advertisers need a lot more content so that they can keep the engagement with consumers fresh and relevant, because of the 24/7 connectivity. If you're going to be successful around the world, you have to have fat and fertile ideas at the core.

But for every Coca-Cola investing in content there is a small business capitalizing on it too. A survey by Ad-ology Research in November 2012 found that small businesses in the United States spent an average of 6.9 per cent of their annual marketing budgets on content marketing – more than they were spending on actually advertising on these social media sites. The findings suggest that small businesses are investing in the creation of engaging content and publishing it via social media sites, rather than actually advertising on these sites. Why are they doing this? Essentially because it is cost-effective: just 11 per cent of small businesses surveyed in the United States for BusinessBolts.com spend more than $500 per month on content marketing.

Search

One of the biggest reasons for digital marketers to embrace content comes down to Google. When you dominate the digital landscape as heavily as you do when you are Google – where you have entire industries basing their businesses around what you do – any change is going to be noticed. But the Google Panda (2011), Penguin (2012) and Hummingbird (2013) algorithm updates, of which there have been several tweaks and updates in the intervening years since, entwined search engine optimization (SEO) with content like never before. We will not go into too much detail about the updates here, as these are covered in the chapter on Search (Chapter 5). But essentially Google is looking to give value in search results for sites with better content. Google guidelines recommend that sites should: 'Create a useful, information-rich site, and write pages that clearly and accurately describe your content.'

This has led to the entire SEO industry embracing content in a way that they never did before. Most SEOs pre-Panda paid lip-service to content. They knew they needed it, but didn't value it. They paid for dirt-cheap, poor quality content, often sourced by non-native writers; or worse still spun one article into 1,000 other versions that made no sense at all, but did the job for their link-building needs. This no longer works. Google identifies the quality of the content and has downgraded, or de-indexed the really poor websites that host the spun content, essentially making redundant these ways of working for SEOs worldwide. Today, search teams value good content and are increasingly updating and revising their business models to become more content focused.

'We don't have massive paid search budgets, and rely a lot on good SEO, and our content is what helps us rank', says Graham Charlton, editor-in-chief of Econsultancy.com: 'Simply by smart use of anchor text, good internal linking and quality and shareable content we can rank very highly for some competitive terms.'

CASE STUDY   How content is used in search – East Coast

The challenge

In 2011, British train operator East Coast Main Line awarded Amaze with a brief to handle its SEO, as a core part of a wider digital account.

First, East Coast Main Line has been through two franchise owners since developing its platform and website in 2007, leaving the brand with an extremely weak online presence. Additionally, because East Coast's brand name changed almost overnight, no promotional activity was undertaken before the sale and, consequently, no one knew their new brand name or where to find them.

Not only was the brand hidden from a customer perspective, there were also many technical issues that were affecting the stability and visibility of the site. Search real estate had also been sporadically managed, resulting in uneven distribution across several domains and all search rankings had disappeared.

Essentially, East Coast had to start from scratch in 2011 and the challenge for Amaze was to develop, manage and optimize the company's digital presence with the aim of selling more tickets online and delivering customer service through digital channels.

The approach

Unsurprisingly, search is the leading online revenue driver for East Coast. Upon receiving the brief in 2011, 73 per cent of all sales were completed through this channel and user search data shows that organic search drives 62 per cent of all revenue. SEO therefore became a crucial element for the wider design and build project, for which the ultimate objectives were as follows:

- Improving overall functionality and aesthetics of the site, thereby increasing visits, revenue, conversion rates and return customers.

- Overhaul the digital ecosystem, bringing it into line with broader search developments using all available functionality.

- Increasing the value of the visits to the site by raising the quality of the content available and encouraging registrations to the loyalty programme online.

The new SEO strategy, by its very nature, had to support these larger objectives and in doing so would also guide aspects of the new website functionality and other content we were implementing. A successful SEO strategy would also have to go hand-in-hand with on-site technical changes and, since a large proportion of the organic keyword revenue was with brand keywords (more attributable to paid search efforts), maximizing generic keyword visibility across the site through our technical enhancements was crucial.

The first priority was to conduct a thorough technical audit of the site, identifying issues affecting its stability, which in turn impacted search visibility. With the majority of revenue generated through the website (and with this figure set to increase year-on-year), it was critical that the website was technically robust and easy for customers to use.

Once smaller technical fixes from the audit had been deployed, the project could take a more user-focused turn. This process began with a comprehensive research and discovery phase in the fourth quarter of 2011, which informed the overall digital solution, including the development of an SEO strategy.

The SEO campaigns delivered across four key areas. Below is a selection of the tactics we employed within each area:

1 Technical and architectural strategies:
   - Redirect old domain names to new domain (focusing all assets together).
   - Reduce server errors to improve response for search robots and users.
   - Decrease unused URLs to improve domain crawling.
   - Correctly manage duplicated content so all pages are unique to Google.

- Remove error pages and implement 301 redirect tactics.
- Implement internal linking improvements and an automated XML sitemap generator to improve site indexation.
- Fix site performance issues that were increasing bounce rate.

2 Content strategies:

- Keyword research to identify significant content gaps on the site.
- Creation of a focused organic search strategy working with four content groups:

  a) brand ('East Coast');

  b) destination ('trains to London');

  c) generic ('train tickets');

  d) generic long-tail ('cheapest advance rail tickets').

- Upon establishing target keywords and producing optimized site content, we used the keywords as a focal point of a broader search strategy, starting with destination-specific landing pages to attract searches such as 'trains to London', whilst reserving the home page for brand and generic searches such as 'train tickets'. (Prior to content optimization, the main point of access was the homepage, causing poor user experience for users seeking specific content).

3 Offsite optimization strategies:

- Work with East Coast leisure and PR team and social media channels to create strong back links to site.
- Implement a broad internal linking strategy to complement landing page strategy.
- Blogger outreach and press-driven link acquisition.
- Increase search visibility through the use of rich media (videos and images).

4 Click-through and site conversion strategies:

- Add quick links to footers, providing increased click-through to landing pages.
- UX improvements such as a 'live fare feeds' for one-click booking enquiries and implement 'destination ready' fare search boxes for each individual destination page.
- Streamline rewards site to improve customer retention.

The results

After the first year of working with Amaze, East Coast has seen a number of fantastic results from an SEO perspective. The results given span between when the first strategies were implemented in April 2012 until the first quarter of 2013.

During this period, visits to the revised site quadrupled per month, smashing the targets originally predicted. In addition to this, registrations to the rewards scheme have also increased, consistently 200 per cent higher than previously.

Rankings for keyword terms such as 'train tickets', 'trains to London' etc have also significantly increased – showing considerable movement in SERP rankings across the target keyword list, typically up from the bottom of page 2 to the top of page 1. In turn, this has increased both visibility and revenue for East Coast.

Overall organic search revenue has increased by almost 20 per cent across the period, proving that the implementations are not only driving customers to the site, but also that they are being converted into revenue once on the site. Organic search transaction value has also seen a notable rise across the period.

Quote

At East Coast, SEO activity forms an integral part of our digital approach. Since they started working with us, Amaze has delivered some fantastic results in both increased visibility of the East Coast brand and a 20 per cent increase in organic search revenue as a result of the ongoing activity.
Emma Passey, Digital Manager at East Coast trains

Campaign credits

- Tom Rowlands / SEO Campaign Manager / Amaze
- Paul Carysforth / Head of Media & Analytics / Amaze

Social

Social media has also played a key part in the growth of content marketing. Social media sites such as Facebook, Twitter, LinkedIn, Pinterest and Instagram, as well as Google+ and YouTube are where the majority of on-line users spend their time. This is typically the first place they go to online

– and the last place they check out of before bed. Invariably on these sites it is content that they are consuming: shared links to videos and editorial by their friends and contacts. Many people like to follow their favourite brands online too. All brands, big and small, know they need to engage with their customers via social media. But how do you engage with your customers without content?

The answer is you can't. There are only so many times you can send customers to your website home page or tweet another discount code. That's not engagement, that's old-style marketing. And it doesn't work with social media. In order to succeed with social media, brands have to have something worthwhile to offer. Interruptions to the user experience are seldom rewarded. At best they are ignored and are therefore irrelevant; at worst they can really damage your brand. Enter content and a coherent content strategy.

'Good content is social currency, without it a brand has nothing to share,' says Omar Kattan, chief strategy office for Dubai-based content marketing agency Sandstorm Digital. 'Effective content in a social setting is content that is based around the brand's story. It must also fulfil the brand's overarching business objectives and help drive customers down the leads funnel to induce a purchase, sign up or enquiry. Successful brands manage to place their customers at the heart of this story so that they are able to relate it to their lives and will therefore be in a better position to buy.'

CASE STUDY   Littlewoods: how content is used to feed and drive social media

Objective

Category: social content

Agency: Dot.Talent

Project: Littlewoods Live

Client: Littlewoods.com (Shop Direct)

URL: **http://www.littlewoodslive.co.uk**

Overview

Littlewoods.com was looking for new ways to engage its existing customer base to retain loyalty while attracting new shoppers through increased brand awareness. Any activity had to demonstrate clear ROI and generate sales.

Strategy

Online shopping has increased year-on-year, however, one clear weakness exists for online retailers. With no shop floor, they have much less influence on 'how shoppers feel about my brand'. Digital marketer's dot.talent were tasked with overcoming this hurdle. Recognizing limitations in both TV advertising (high cost) and viral stunts (short-lived hype), dot.talent needed to arrange something very special to re-create a long-term sense of shared experience that would help Littlewoods.com retain its customers' loyalty, year after year. With a growing audience on the Littlewoods.com social media profiles, and celebrity brand ambassadors with equally large social media followings, the focus turned to making the most of these existing online audiences.

Method

On 13 June 2012 a Facebook and UK retail first was launched – a live one-hour celebrity-fronted show, broadcast live on Littlewoods.com's Facebook page. The social TV-show format centred on room makeovers and viewer decorating dilemmas. Dot.talent created an interactive platform, taking real-time questions from viewers via the Facebook application, which streamed the show. The presenter, Laurence Llewelyn-Bowen, called viewers live on air and spot prizes were awarded for the best comments posted within the application.

The Facebook widget / application was created using OpenGraph, which broadcast viewer activity to viewers' networks of Facebook friends, massively increasing the secondary audience and driving more viewers as the broadcast progressed. This was further enhanced by a 24-hour targeted Facebook advertising buy – to coincide with the broadcast. As the Littlewoods.com Facebook fan base increased, so too did the target base for the ads.

Mobile optimized, the Facebook widget/application evolved pre-, during and post-broadcast, giving viewers fresh content that they could view on any device via the Facebook page.

Outcome

- Week 1 sales increased 292 per cent. Littlewoods.com visitation increased 289 per cent.

- Facebook reach grew from 150,000 to 4.5 million due to a combination of Facebook OpenGraph integration and targeted Facebook ads. Likes of the Facebook page increased 10 per cent.

- Streaming on smartphone and tablet devices rose from 28 per cent in episode 1 to 51 per cent in episode 3.

- The Christmas special saw 2,223 consumer comments in just 60 minutes. This is on par with Twitter volumes around UK primetime lifestyle TV shows.

- Comments and interaction provide a unique 'focus group' around the broadcasts, with viewers sharing insights into their purchase behaviour.

- Littlewoods.com Facebook fans have also become part of the broadcasts themselves, testing products and appearing on-screen to talk about their experiences.

- 2012 episodes also included Gadgets with Suzi Perry as well as a Christmas special with Myleene Klass and Laurence Llewelyn-Bowen.

Relation to objectives/cost-effectiveness

- Littlewoods Live is a supplier-funded broadcast, effectively turning Littlewoods.com into a media owner on its own Facebook page.

- Footage is re-edited and placed on Littlewoods.com's YouTube channel.

- The press loved the story of this Facebook first, and Littlewoods.com has benefited from coverage with a value of £250,000.

- Beyond all the stats, the biggest achievement of Littlewoods Live has been to show that, despite the demise of high-street shopping, the right approach to social media activity can engage online shoppers so they become as involved and rewarded by their relationship with a retailer as they ever were.

What skills do you need to be a good content marketer?

Digital marketers are asked to do a lot. Not only are digital marketers expected to be up-to-date with everything new that comes along in digital, they are then expected to be able to plan and manage a myriad different number of campaigns to accompany these new innovations too. And increasingly they need to be able to come up with content. It's a tough ask. As with all marketers, in order to be a good content marketer you need to have a combination of great organizational skills, meticulous attention to detail, creativity and analytical acumen.

Essentially you need to be creative enough to develop great ideas, have the wherewithal to be able to create that content, and then you also need to be able to carry out analysis on what works, dive into the stats and use technology to analyse results. Content marketers in many respects need to be left-brain obsessives who love to live and breathe data; and on the other side creative right brainers with a journalist's nose for an interesting story.

Content strategy

Why do I need a content strategy?

Content strategy is the planning and development of how you intend to attract and engage with your chosen audience via content. It is vitally important for any success when it comes to your content marketing. Plan first, create content later.

If you don't put a proper content strategy in place, the likelihood is that your content initiatives will fizzle out. It is hard to evangelize to others within an organization – and create buy-in – without a conceptualized content strategy in place. There is a lot to think about at this stage of your content development.

It is easy to be overwhelmed when tasked with creating a coherent content strategy for your business. For success it is important that you break everything down to basics. Start at the beginning and think about what you want to say, who you want to speak to and what you want to achieve from the outcome. Think like a publisher, but back-up your thoughts with real digital-marketing data. Create a strategy that focuses on customer and business needs.

Remember that content marketing is one of the few marketing channels that can work along the entire customer journey – so you need a strategy that speaks to your customers at all points along this cycle. This is where data analysis comes in. This is where a content marketer's ability to digest data and look at trends combines with creativity to formulate an overall content strategy. Before creating your content strategy look at all the data. Look at your site's analytics; what pages convert best into sales; what, if any, existing content is shared and visited. Look at your social media pages and do the same. If you can, create a social listening report, analysing what your target audience likes to talk about online. Look at Google trends to research what people are searching for online. Look at what your competitors are doing or have done for success. Then most of all think about what your business objectives might be.

When planning your content strategy you should ask yourself these questions:

- Who do I want to target?
- Is there a specific topic or niche where we want to excel?
- What do I want those I target to associate with our brand?
- What information are my customers looking for?
- What type of content do my customers look for?
- How can I keep existing customers happy?
- How can I attract new customers?
- What do we like/dislike about competitors' content strategy?
- Is there anything I do not want to highlight about our brand?
- What overall business objective do I want to achieve from my content marketing?

Write a content strategy document

Once you have your content strategy firmly identified it is important that you create a content strategy document. This doesn't need to be a mammoth 90-page blueprint; in fact it should be no more than one or two sides of A4 paper. If you can condense your content strategy to this core, it will have more chance of success and more people within your organization will understand it.

This content strategy document is a simple, but extremely effective content mandate that outlines what, why and how you will go about creating content. Include what key performance indicators (KPIs) you may want to achieve from your content strategy. But you do not need to overcomplicate this document with details around tone of voice, style guides, and dos and don'ts. These are details that can be covered in additional documents.

At this stage it is probably worth noting that this document should be fluid. Your content strategy will undoubtedly change over time. Reviewing your strategy and updating your content strategy document will help ensure that you consistently deliver the content that your customer base is looking for and the results you want to achieve. The first piece of content you create as part of your content marketing initiative should be your content strategy document.

Where does content strategy fit into your marketing: who owns it?

It is important to understand where content fits within your organization. This is a crucial question within large organizations with different departments. Ownership of the content process is key. In the past, content often sat somewhere uncomfortably between web development, SEO, social and PR teams. It was the neglected and ignored ugly duckling that no one wanted to think about. Those tasked with ownership of the content process failed to fully understand it, or grasp its overall importance.

This has now finally changed, but there are many misconceptions about who 'owns' the content process. Is content strategy the responsibility of your SEO team? Or perhaps your social media team? Or maybe your PR or corporate communications team? All of these marketing departments should have input into the process. But your content strategy should come from the top. It needs to holistically cover all of your marketing channels. Your content strategy is not an advertising campaign, a search, social or PR strategy. It is more than that. Given the importance that content plays within all of your marketing channels, content strategy is increasingly becoming the preserve of dedicated content marketers who fully understand the content production process and how content can be used for overall digital marketing success.

The significance of content to your digital marketing strategy means that you cannot shoe-horn content into a specific channel, with an 'and we'll do a bit of content on the side' kind of approach, and hope for any sort of overall success. If you do this you are not 'thinking like a publisher' and giving your customers what they want – you are simply feeding the search and social media beast. And if you work like that you will not create anything original that adds value to a customer buying cycle.

Let's review the various channels in more detail:

- **Search strategy:** content is now at the heart of any search engine optimization strategy. Search engines love unique, quality content that enhances the user experience. Keywords, link building and content gap analysis are important elements of search and are welcome add-ons to your content strategy; but your content strategy should be far more than just a list of keywords, meta-data rewrites, link-building initiatives and landing pages.

- **Social strategy:** content is the lifeblood of any brand's social platform. Whether a B2B approach on LinkedIn and Google+, a consumer angle on Facebook and Twitter, or something that incorporates all social platforms, content is what drives brand engagement. But the content needs to appeal to the right people, as well as the right platform. Social strategy will inevitably feed into your overall content strategy, but it should not rule it. You need a content strategy in place in order to succeed with social media; but you don't necessarily need a social media strategy to succeed with content marketing. Your content marketing strategy should come first, followed by a social strategy that makes it easy for your audience to share the content you are creating.

- **PR strategy:** content marketing is not PR in 'new clothes', likewise content strategy is not identical to your PR strategy. They should share fundamental similarities, such as brand message and voice, but they differ somewhat, often, with their target audience. For example, some PR and corporate communications strategies are targeted towards journalists and government, rather than the consumers they may want to target with content. Relying on your PR strategy to become your content strategy is not always feasible or advisable.

What content should I be creating?

There are many different types of content that you can create. What content you create will depend largely on your brand, your target audience, resources and your budget. But as mentioned earlier in this chapter – content can work whether you are a mega-brand such as Coca-Cola, or a one-person business entity.

Be bold: think Red Bull

At the extreme ends of the spectrum you could decide you want to create amazingly unique and groundbreaking content. Nothing comes more extreme than Red Bull's Stratos Jump in October 2012, which launched Austrian skydiver Felix Baumgartner from space, breaking the world record for the highest altitude skydive ever undertaken. It was a spectacular event and feat of daring. And it was a digital-content marketing masterclass. The event set a YouTube record of 8 million concurrent live streams. During the live jump 2.6 million social media mentions were generated – 74,000 of which were Twitter-related # tags via the #redbull hashtag. The Facebook post around the event has attracted more than 50 million users. At the latest count, the Red Bull YouTube video showcasing the jump has attracted over 35 million views.

After the space jump in October 2012, mentions of Redbull spiked at 550 per cent above the average. Links to their redbullstratos.com jumped from 50 domains in September 2012 to 2,400 in the following month and, in the following year, natural search traffic rose 2,180 per cent.

Why did this happen? 'Google loves the links which come from genuinely interesting content. Redbull Stratos proves content marketing is as powerful as it's reach with the people it communicates with,' says Nick Garner, CEO of 90 Digital, a UK-based online marketing communications agency. 'You don't have to fund a space jump to do the same thing, just make your own jump into committing editorial resource and finding your own unique voice. From that, you will resonate, your site will be linked to and traffic will follow.'

The Red Bull event is a great example of how content can be leveraged to engage and promote your brand in a positive way. The social media channels are simply the distribution tools that content marketers use to promote the great content they are creating. Without great content, the distribution channels become ineffective.

Types of content

While few marketers have the budget to launch a man from space, that doesn't mean that the principles of what works for content marketing success are not the same. Create content that your customers will like and then amplify the reach of that content.

Here's a quick overview of the type of content you may want to think about creating:

- **News and blog content:** this form of content is easy to create and should represent a first tick on your list of content marketing to-dos. It is relatively quick and easy content for almost any brand to create and host on their own website. Covering news that is specific to your industry, or writing tip-style consumer-facing blog posts, preferably published each day, works for a number of reasons. First, you are ensuring your site looks up-to-date: your customers don't want to click on your blog and see that the last post was made eight months ago. Second, search engines like regularly updated, content-rich websites; it signals to them that the site is being looked after and is of relevance to potential searchers. Third, publishing short-form content on your own blog on a regular basis gives you something to promote – and engage – with your customers on social media channels. Just as newspapers and magazines may also carry in-depth features and interviews, they also carry lots of news in brief (NIBs) that they know their readers find of interest.

- **Features, guides and interviews:** longer-form content published to your company blog works in the exact same way as the above shorter-form blog content. You do not need to publish this content on a daily basis and what you create may be as a result of customer service issues that you would like to address, keyword ranking reports, or a change in focus of your overall business strategy. Interviews with key members of a company, for example, can work well to highlight business strengths and 'tell the story' behind a company. In addition to publishing this content on your own company blog, one of the benefits of longer form content is that, when it is really good, it can be used for outreach and amplification purposes too, more of which we come to later in this chapter.

- **White papers:** either working internally on your own private data and analysis or via specialist data and research companies, a great way to create content that your customers may want is to create a white paper. A white paper that identifies major issues within your business sector – and offers your overall company opinion on how to solve it – not only positions your brand as a thought leader that knows it's stuff, it can also be used to generate business leads too. How? Create the white paper as a downloadable PDF and then ensure that anyone who wants to download the white paper has to fill out their contact details. This gives you a new database of contacts that are pre-vetted to be interested in your product or services (because they downloaded a very specific white paper), which you can call upon to build up your business.

- **e-books:** in a similar way to the white paper idea above, extending that idea and creating a relevant e-book that is of relevance to your customer base can work extremely well too. Again, this will establish your brand as a thought-leader and it can be an even more successful way to generate new business leads too. And thanks to digital publishing advances and the growing popularity of e-readers – creating and publishing an e-book is an extremely easy way to go about distributing content. It is an increasingly popular content marketing tactic.

- **Infographics:** a graphical representation of data, infographics are useful at illustrating reams of data that can often be confusing to write down in detail. They are used extensively online by digital marketers. Why? They are highly shareable, that's why. Whether a

B2B business illustration or a more tongue-in-cheek-style infographic such as 'The Cost of Being Batman' (MoneySuperMarket.com), the premise is the same: infographics gain a lot of social shares, drive traffic and generate inbound links.

- **Video:** video content is increasingly important for digital marketing success. While big consumer-facing brands often opt for humour ('Old Spice Man'), or extreme events (Red Bull), with the aim of creating a viral hit, video content works for all brands. Company overview-style videos offer a great introduction to your company for potential customers; Q&As on common customer queries or industry issues, delivered in a concise manner do not only aid the customer cycle – giving customers what they want – they can also be used to promote your brand digitally too.

- **Photographs:** with the increasing popularity of platforms such as Instagram and Pinterest, more digital marketers are turning their attention to the creation of photographic content too. This could be publishing photos of a latest product line; photographs of customers using their products; or something a little bit different.

How much content should you create?

There is no set rule on how much content to create. This will differ depending on your objectives, industry and available resource. But as a general rule, the more content you create – the better. Provided that it is good. Provided that it is planned and based on an overall content strategy. If your resources are tight, putting some available budget into content is better than doing nothing at all. Test what works, optimize – and plan.

Content production

How to brainstorm ideas

As illustrated in this chapter, content marketing relies heavily on ideas. Digital technology now means that we have at our disposal distribution tools that marketers a generation before could only have dreamed of. There are few barriers to distributing your content – provided you plan effectively. Today, invariably the success or failure of a digital marketing campaign comes down to the idea behind it. So you need to come up with ideas – and lots of them.

Many marketers fear making mistakes – or are too scared to share their ideas in case they are ridiculed by colleagues. But if you don't share your ideas, who else is going to? How else are you going to hit upon success?

Coming up with ideas consistently can be tough. This is where brainstorming comes in:

> No idea is so outlandish that it should not be considered with a searching but at the same time steady eye.
>
> Winston Churchill

We could go on about the various techniques that different groups and organizations use to generate ideas, but the best advice we can give is – just think about it. Clear your to-do list and give yourself some time to really think about what your customers want and what your business objectives are. Look at all the data and insights at your disposal and then don't be afraid to roll up your sleeves, shout out ideas and see what comes from it all. Remember there are no bad ideas, just less relevant ones!

Creating a content calendar

After you have written your content strategy overview document, after deciding on what type of content is right for your business and after brainstorming ideas, it is a good idea to plan out your content schedule via a content calendar. An organized calendar will save you time by having a structured time frame to stick to, which eliminates time-wasting activities.

Here are a few tips on creating a content calendar:

- **Seasonality:** think about the key seasons and trends in your business and what content you want to create in the run-up to and during these times of year.

- **Topics:** for each month, pick strong themes that can break down into subcategories. Think about events that you could write about that take place in any given month.

- **Timing:** break down your calendar month by month, then week by week, then day by day. This will increase the structure and regularity to your work.

- **Share:** share your content calendar with your team of content creators, both internal and external, as well as all of your other marketing channels. If you can give your SEO, social, PR and display teams insights into what content you are going to be creating in the future you will have a better chance of achieving a more integrated digital marketing strategy.

Objections to content

'We can't create content ourselves' – answer: outsource content production

The demands on digital marketers are increasing all the time. Analysis of big data, new marketing channels to manage and the 24/7 nature of online mean that few marketers have time to actually create the content that their brand needs for digital success. And, in most cases, they are often not skilled enough to create the specialist content that their brand deserves.

The likelihood then is that you have to outsource some or perhaps all of your content production. This could save you time and money. You have a few options here when it comes to outsourcing content:

- **Freelancers:** you can go through the laborious process of recruiting a freelancer to work on your content. Many organizations operate in this way. The bonus is that you can build up a relationship with a dedicated content creator who ideally comes to understand your content objectives. The downside, however, is that individual freelancers typically have more than one client, which means constantly changing deadlines and periods when they are unavailable (not to mention they do occasionally go on holiday and get ill too). Also, when it comes to scaling-up your content needs, few individual freelancers can cope with volume content requirements on a regular basis. Managing their deadlines, proofing their work and providing feedback all comes down to you. The process can work well, but provided you invest the time to recruit and nurture the right person.

- **Cloud-based content platforms:** there are a growing number of collaborative platforms that service the content requirement needs of brands and their agencies. These platforms are effectively online marketplaces that connect those who need content, with those who can create it. They recruit content creators and take a small percentage of your content fee. They are relatively simple to use and can help you scale your content production easily. But note that in many instances the content creators on specific platforms are of differing levels of quality. Again, your strategy, and managing and proofing the content sent to you, is your own responsibility. Check out Skyword.com, Contently.com and Contentamp.com for more information on these platforms.

- **Recruit a content agency:** as we've set out throughout this chapter, content marketing is increasingly becoming a separate function to your other digital marketing channels. Specialist content agencies are springing up to aid brands in their content marketing needs. The benefits of recruiting a specialist content agency is that you can use their expertise and services to develop your own content strategy, to create a content calendar for your business and to ensure that you are receiving quality content to deadline. You also have someone to brainstorm ideas with to ensure your content is good, and someone to help you champion the cause for content within your organization. The negative side is that some, if not most, of these content-marketing agencies work on a retainer model, which can significantly add to your overall digital marketing costs.

Whatever option you take will have the same immediate issues when it comes to outsourcing content. Before outsourcing your content production there are a few things to think about in order to make the process easier for everyone involved. The most important stage of outsourcing your content creation is the initial briefing process. To really get the benefit from outsourcing you need to be able to communicate what you want to achieve. Again, this illustrates just how important the initial content strategy document can be. It can feel a little bit slow to start off with, but once you are armed with this document you can share it with your content providers and really hit the ground running with the type of content you want to see.

'There are too many compliance issues and sign-off processes for our business to create content' – answer: put a plan in place that makes content possible

One of the objections that come up time and time again when you talk content to certain brands is compliance. For many heavily regulated industries such as financial services and the health sectors there are a myriad different compliance processes that need to be adhered to. This can make content creation a challenge, but it is not impossible. In many of these industries you will find people who use the compliance process as the excuse they need to avoid creating content. Don't let them win. The case for relevant content within these sectors is, if anything, stronger than for other sectors; consumers are looking for valuable content that they know they can trust.

In order to create this relevant content it is important to ensure that all legal regulatory compliance issues surrounding the content you create is met. Create a dos and don'ts list of what content you should and shouldn't create.

Work with your compliance departments to ensure that a workable process is established and a sustainable relationship put in place between content producer, marketers, brand head of digital and compliance teams, while also working towards established KPIs. Given the importance – and the continued importance – that content is likely to play in future digital marketing campaigns, it is best to embrace content now rather than rush to it at a later date.

'There is nowhere on our website to publish content and we have no development resource' – answer: setting up a blog on your own website is easy

This is a common objection raised by those looking into content for the first time. It is, understandably, often a more pressing concern among smaller businesses, where their developer resource is limited. The truth of the matter is that publishing content onto your own website is very easy to set up. Services such as Wordpress allow you to set up a blog on your own site easily – and for free. There is some resource required in making your blog look and feel like part of your overall website, but this shouldn't take up too much of your team's time to get done. Alternatively, there are thousands of specialist Wordpress theme designers who can do the work for you for a one-off fee: it'll cost no more than US $400. Once set up, you are good to begin publishing content at will.

There are also plenty of other ways to get set up, too. Many content services can provide XML feeds directly into your site, for example, which only require a minimal amount of technical input. Again, given the value that content brings to your digital marketing, the amount of investment and time it takes to set up your site to publish content is certainly worth the effort.

Promoting your content

Creating content is just one part of the content marketing process. Once you've created that content, you've got to market it. As already mentioned, content is the currency with which brands engage with their customers online. A natural distribution channel for any content that you create should be social media. We also recommend that all of the content you create is as shareable as possible (social-sharing buttons on your own website content pages, for example) and, when relevant, is published under Google+ Authorship too. But again, much of this will be covered in the search chapter of this book (see Chapter 5).

These are great strategies to amplify the reach of the content you are creating. But in addition to these practices, let's look in a little more detail about some other ways you can go about promoting your content.

Blogger outreach

Bloggers are a key conduit to speaking to your customer base online. Blogger outreach is an incredibly effective way to raise your brand profile, increase your brand reputation and share the unique content that you are creating and publishing. Bloggers tend to have a disproportionate level of influence among their specific online communities; they have highly relevant and large social media followings and work well to promote highly relevant content within their communities. There are, of course, particular ways in which you should go about conducting blogger outreach, much of which will already be covered within this book in the chapters on online PR and reputation management (Chapter 10) and the search pages (Chapter 5).

Essentially you are looking to build a relationship with bloggers through content. This may mean encouraging them to promote your own branded content that you have created that is specific to their particular niche. For example, car brand Fiat, looking to promote the Fiat 500 created a humorous 'Motherhood Rap' video **http://www.youtube.com/watch?v=eNVde5HPhYo**. The video spoke to mums and was an instant hit with the mummy blogging community when promoted via blogger outreach. The mummy bloggers loved the video, shared the content socially and embedded the video into articles they were writing. The result was a huge viral success; the latest YouTube count reveals 4.2 million views and over 19,000 likes. The video was promoted and shared throughout the mummy blogging community and gained additional coverage on automotive, trade and national news titles. Blogger outreach was the channel used to distribute and share the content, but again it was the content itself that was key to the campaign's overall success.

Bloggers are very particular so wherever possible you should look to involve them in the creative process. It is an increasingly common tactic for bloggers to be involved in the content creation process as well as the distribution of that content. This can be as basic as working with them on a specific blog post that is of interest to their readership, asking them to film themselves reviewing a product, or perhaps hosting a content-led competition on their website. Remember that bloggers are publishers; they know what content works best for their communities, and if as a brand you can work with them to create content that works for that community they are only too happy to get involved.

Native advertising

One of the biggest digital marketing trends of recent years, the word 'native' is being used by many companies and services looking to be associated with the trend; it is a phrase that is in need of a clearer definition. Behind the hype is a new, exciting online advertising medium that has content at its core. You cannot talk native without talking about content. Given the proliferation of content marketing, it is natural that new content-based advertising models have developed.

What native means is that the right branded content, distributed to the right audience, can now offer rewards to advertisers that far outweigh anything they can hope to achieve with more traditional forms of advertising alone. This is native advertising, and why it is so exciting.

What is native advertising?

Native adverts are contextually relevant posts that combine paid, owned and earned media into a clearly labelled branded message that is user-initiated. Native placements sit seamlessly into the overall design of the host site so that they look like part of the site, rather than any external element to it.

This is a broad definition of what you should expect to see from a native advertisement. Broadly speaking, native advertising should include these three elements:

- **Content-led advertising:** promoted, fully branded custom content.
- **The advert sits seamlessly in the design and layout of the host site:** the ad doesn't sit in a banner placement or as an overlay that interrupts the site; it looks like something that is part of the editorial of the host site, but it is clearly labelled as sponsored.
- **The advert is user-initiated:** the user has to click to view the ad.

Native advertising offers brands the opportunity to speak to, interact and engage with customers at the places where they congregate online – all in a native environment that is completely user-initiated; the content is what drives the interaction between consumer and brand. Crucially, given the growth in mobile, native advertising works across desktop, tablet or mobile device.

Native is completely SEO friendly – there are no violations of Google guidelines to worry about. Native campaigns are clearly labelled as sponsored. Any sponsored post pages are served via JavaScript and the pages are not indexed via search engines – so there are no duplicate page issues to worry about.

Native advertising typically delivers 5–20 times better engagement than banner ads and it acts as a unique way for brands to increase the reach of the content they are creating. Just some of the companies offering native campaigns globally – in different guises – include Outbrain, Taboola, Nativo, C.A.S.T, Content Amp and Adyoulike; while publishing groups such as Buzzfeed, AOL, Atlantic Media and more also have native offerings. Many more publishers and dynamic ad-tech companies are likely to be working native in the future.

Native advertising is here to stay. In future editions of this book, native will need to have its own chapter.

The future of online content

In a November 2013 interview with *Adweek*, WPP CEO Sir Martin Sorrell explained how digital now accounts for 35 per cent of all WPP business worldwide. When asked about what he would do if he was starting a new business today, he said:

> You'd be more focused on media investment and data investment management and digital. The company would be much more balanced. In other words, it wouldn't be classic advertising agency led. It would be much more neutral. You would be much more respectful of people in the media business. You'd be dabbling in content. Same approach in a way as now, but different focus.

While all of what he said is interesting, the fact that Sorrell specifically mentions content is significant. The head of the largest advertising group in the world believes that content is the future. As we have outlined throughout this chapter, we believe it is too. Content overlaps, aids and is part of everything you do in digital marketing. It is increasingly what your digital marketing strategy and launch campaigns will rely on for success.

If the first 15 or so years of digital were defined by technology, uptake and the creation of new marketing channels, the next 15 years may well be characterized by what we do with all of this technological stuff. How do digital marketers utilize all the tools at their disposal in order to win new audience and reach out to their customers?

Increasingly digital technology will be used to do what humans have always enjoyed: tell and share stories. Some of these stories will be shared and created by brand marketers. There will be more technological advances in the years ahead, but these will increasingly be focused on content – and what it can do for the content that brands are creating and looking to share. It is happening already, but in the not-too-distant future all digital marketing will be content. Content has a very bright future ahead of it. In the beginning there was the word; today we are just at the beginning.

About the contributor

Dale Lovell is Co-Founder and Publishing Director at Content Amp, a UK-based global leader in content marketing and native advertising. In 2010, recognizing the growing requirement for branded content and creative marketing services by brands online, Dale co-founded Content Amp. Today Content Amp works with leading brands and agencies on content strategy, native advertising and earned media digital content amplification campaigns.

Dale has worked in online publishing, content strategy and creative content marketing for over 14 years. As a journalist he has contributed to over 50 leading publications and is a regular commentator within the digital marketing industry in the UK.

CASE STUDY Makino

The challenge

- In 2012, the United States witnessed a renaissance in manufacturing. Makino capitalized on this environment by launching its new marketing campaign, 'Make What Matters', which recognizes and supports manufacturing

professionals who produce the high-quality components/products that we interact with every day. Primary objectives for the campaign were to build awareness, encourage customer engagement and generate sales leads.

- Makino's strategy for the Make What Matters B2B social media programme was to bring the campaign narrative to life through social engagements where audiences can participate in discussions about how US manufacturers are making what matters for their companies, communities and industries.

- The backbone for this social strategy was Makino's extensive library of custom content, which included case studies, technical articles, white papers, webinars, imagery and videos. This content was adapted across Makino's Facebook, Twitter, LinkedIn, Google+ and YouTube communities to drive Web traffic to compelling customer stories and inspire audience members to discuss their experiences with peers.

- This combined impact of audience insights and relevant content created a platform for Makino audiences to be heard.

Target audience

The Make What Matters campaign was aimed at all North American manufacturing professionals in the automotive, aerospace and medical industries, no matter their age, title, or location.

Action

- Social media editorial calendars were prepared on a monthly basis to ensure a steady and continuous stream of new content, with each week strategically prepped to include engaging questions, customer stories, technical advice and industry news.

- Audiences were encouraged to upload photos of themselves with their Makino machines and share what they do to Make What Matters.

- Traditional, magazine-style case study articles were repurposed into smaller, more easily digestible content formats, such as video testimonials, infographics and 'story albums', which used text-overlaid images to share customer stories and quotes.

- The Makino team researched key customers and target accounts to discover their corporate social media properties.

- Those with a presence on social media were followed and monitored by Makino in order to share and promote success stories in the spirit of Make What Matters – an effort that led to reciprocated follows.

- A similar approach was employed for trade and national media monitoring with the intent in order to highlight stories of economic growth in US manufacturing.

- The wide-ranging diversity of content formats has enabled Makino to provide relevant information to social followers across all stages of the purchase decision-making process.

- Those nearing the point of investment were provided with convenient access to 'high-value' content such as webinars and white papers, which required registration-form submission.

- Their registration data was then added to Makino's database for direct marketing communications and sales force follow-up.

- To grow social audiences and increase exposure within specific industry segments, Makino deployed several paid social programmes, including promoted content and pay-per-click (PPC) advertising.

Results

- The Make What Matters campaign successfully achieved its goals of building awareness, encouraging engagement and generating leads.

- Since its launch, traffic to Makino's website grew by nearly 18 per cent over the previous year, resulting in over 1,000 new leads (a 200 per cent increase).

- Several marketing efforts have been directly tied to sales of more than US $1 million in equipment and services.

- Organic search represented nearly 65 per cent of overall site traffic to Makino's official website, making it the primary driver for digital leads.

- Paid search efforts delivered impressive results as well, with an 89 per cent increase in goal conversion rate and a 44 per cent increase in overall click-through rate.

- Makino's social media properties experienced explosive growth in followers, engagement and social sharing.

- The official Makino Facebook page saw a 669 per cent increase in page 'likes' and a 5,541 per cent increase in Facebook post engagement.

- Similarly, Makino's Twitter audience grew by 46 per cent, with a 173 per cent increase in retweets and a 150 per cent rise in mentions.

- YouTube subscriptions grew by 95 per cent, which led to a 128 per cent increase in video 'likes' and over 4,000 additional video views.

- Referral traffic from social media sites to Makino's web properties increased by an average of 48 per cent, resulting in a 107 per cent increase in website conversions.

Lessons

- Work closely with internal sales to determine the specifications and behaviours of a qualified lead. Share social media results and activities with the sales force and inspire them to monitor, share and participate in social discussions.

- Nurture soft leads with the support of a robust, integrated-content marketing programme that maintains brand engagement from the early stages of interest to the final moment of purchase.

- Do not evaluate the success of a social media programme based on one-dimensional KPIs. Diversify measurements to gain a holistic view of performance and identify performance relationships that can be used to improve efficiency.

Links to campaign

- www.makino.com
- www.competitiveproduction.com
- www.moldmakermag.com
- www.radical-departures.net
- www.timachining.com
- www.facebook.com/MakinoMachine
- www.twitter.com/MakinoMachine
- www.linkedin.com/company/Makino
- plus.google.com/+makino
- www.youtube.com/user/MakinoMachineTools

About the creator

About Makino: a world leader in advanced CNC machining centres, Makino is committed to providing high-performance, leading-edge machining technologies and innovative-engineered process solutions that enable automotive, aerospace and medical manufacturers to focus on making what matters. For more information visit **www.makino.com**.

Credits

- Mark Rentschler has served within the manufacturing industry for more than 30 years. His career at Makino began in 1995 as the company's service parts manager, while later taking on the role of marketing manager in 2001. In this position, he has transitioned Makino's marketing efforts from traditional print-based media into award-winning digital marketing campaigns (Mark Rentschler, marketing manager, Makino Inc.).
- *B2B Marketing* magazine's 2013 Content Marketing Awards – Integrated Campaign Runner-Up.
- *B2B Marketing* magazine's 2013 Top 25 Digital Marketer.

Convincing your boss to invest in digital marketing

12

Note from Damian to reader:

> Since work began on *Understanding Digital Marketing* in 2007 there have been a number of references to the challenge of 'convincing the boss to invest in DM' – over the last year there have been more requests from readers for more help with this challenge than any other single knowledge area of the book. The challenge faced by me was how to integrate this into (quite deservedly) every chapter in the book – it didn't work, it became repetitive. Then by chance I met Simon Kingsnorth, a global digital marketing expert who suggested the 'challenge' merited its very own chapter. Moreover, Simon, together with Nick Massey and I, collaborated together and produced what you are about to read now...

OUR CHAPTER PLEDGE TO YOU

When you reach the end of this chapter you will have answers to the following questions:

- How do I put together a proposal?

- What are my key objectives?

- What will my decision makers be looking for?

- What are the key benefits I can use to support my argument?

- How do I build a compelling presentation?

Whether you are taking your first steps into digital marketing or are fast becoming a digital guru, the painful truth is that all your knowledge and expertise is worthless unless the decision maker buys into your plans. There are only two ways to accomplish this: first, you become the decision maker; or, second, (and far more often the case) you need to learn how to convince that decision maker that you are right.

So is it very difficult? Well, let's consider what you're trying to achieve here. You are about to try to convince an audience that your plan will be highly valuable for them. Your audience in this situation is the decision maker. That may be your president, CEO, chief financial officer, finance director, marketing director or any number of other positions, but they all have one thing in common – they are your customer. And what is your plan? Well, put simply, it is the product you are trying to sell to your customers. So what you are really trying to achieve here is to find a way to convince your customers that your product is highly valuable to them. Sound familiar? Convincing your board to invest in digital marketing is, in itself, marketing. And you know how to do that, right?

So to break this down we will look at some of the key areas you would expect when building a marketing campaign, including understanding your objectives and your target audience, getting to grips with the budgets and the key benefits of each channel. We look at the website itself and other considerations including cross-business benefit, global challenges and opportunities, competitor research and resource. Finally, we consider the key elements of building the presentation itself. So let's get started.

Understanding your objectives

As with any strategy, the first question is 'what are we trying to achieve?' You will of course have your own unique goals but you will most likely find that they will fit into one of a few distinct areas, each bringing with it a unique set of challenges; growth (eg sales volumes, international expansion), financial gain (eg revenue or profit) or brand (eg awareness or service).

For example, businesses such as Facebook and Spotify focused solely on growth in their early period and didn't overly concern themselves with monetization or profit until the business model had been proven and the user volumes were so large as to make the monetization potential and business value extremely high. More established businesses, however, or those that have a significant number of shareholders (such as financial institutions), will often be more focused on ensuring a return for their shareholders and long-term stability. Let's look at these three distinct areas and discuss how digital marketing relates to each.

If your board is looking for a digital story that supports their growth targets, how would you go about that? As with all of these goals we will

FIGURE 12.1   Digital ad spend

Digital Ad Spending Worldwide, 2010–2016
billions, % change and % of total media ad spending

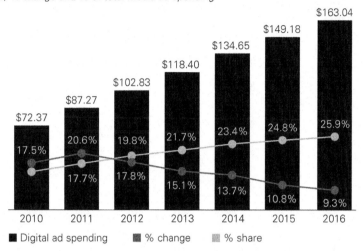

NOTE: includes advertising that appears on desktop and laptop computers as well as mobile phones and tablets, and includes all the various formats of advertising on those platforms; excludes SMS, MMS and P2P messaging based advertising

SOURCE: eMarketer, Dec 2012

start by getting to the root of the question. What does digital marketing offer from a growth perspective that other channels would not? Well, the simple answer is that digital marketing is the fastest-growing channel and will soon be the leading channel in many regions of the world (see Figure 12.1). In the United States and Western Europe online advertising is relatively mature and yet the latter continues to grow at over 20 per cent. In less developed regions, the current media profile is still heavily offline but the growth of digital marketing is enormous. Taking Latin America as an example, growth from 2011 to 2012 was a staggering 90 per cent and APAC online ad spend is expected to surpass North America and Europe combined by 2016. This naturally means that even if your business growth remains static, the growth of the digital channel itself will pass its benefits on to you.

Clearly, then, companies are spending a lot online, but you could argue that this isn't necessarily a reflection of people using the internet. Perhaps some companies are flooding the web with their advertising when the audience isn't there. Well, again, the stats speak for themselves. Throughout this book we have seen how the online population has advanced – but let's throw more petrol on the bonfire: in the developed world it is estimated that 77 per cent of people are internet users. In the developing world this number drops to

FIGURE 12.2 Global internet usage graph

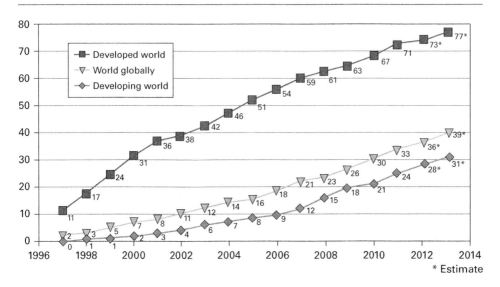

* Estimate

31 per cent but when we consider that the figure was just 21 per cent three years ago we can see the scale of the growth (see Figure 12.2). Of the 7.1 billion people on this planet there are a phenomenal 2.8 billion people using a technology that was only used by around 1 billion people just eight years ago (please note this represents an even higher estimate than cited earlier in the book, but underlines the growth and the scale of your opportunity).

The converse argument, of course, is that, by avoiding embracing digital not only does your business miss out on this growth opportunity but it also suffers from the declining offline trends. It only takes a short walk down your local high-street or to read the news from time to time (which can of course be reported in real-time online) to see the more traditional businesses that we knew and loved, struggling and disappearing altogether. Those businesses that have not embraced the digital age, or have simply been too slow to do so, have faced their inevitable end. I don't like to encourage fear tactics but this should certainly be evidence enough that the digital world is going nowhere but up.

The final challenge would be 'this is all well and good but our audience is not online'. Well, as we have already heard, this is very rarely the case. Ten years ago, when considering breaking your audience into segments you could have been forgiven for assuming that the older generations are not internet savvy and there are segments of society that are slow in taking it up. Assumptions around technology in schools and other institutions being outdated were also common. As with everything else digital, this landscape has changed enormously and young or old, rich or poor, the vast majority of audiences are online. There are some good demographic tools available (for free) online now to justify this. Google Analytics, for example, introduced demographic targeting in 2013, which is a great free way of getting a good audience snapshot.

So the argument for growth is fairly simple. But what about financial gain? This is a goal of the vast majority of businesses, of course, but why would digital marketing offer any advantage in this area? Well, again, let's look at the facts and the answer becomes quite clear.

Whether your business concentrates on cashflow, looks for rapid revenue growth or is focused on a return to shareholders, there is one thing that will be core to your finances – ensuring that every dollar spent returns two, three or more – and that is almost certainly what your decision maker will be looking for.

If we look at offline advertising channels such as TV, radio or press, we find that they are great volume drivers in terms of brand awareness and enquiries, but often at a substantial cost. This can be hard to justify and you have to start to consider the dreaded 'halo effect': ie are we getting sales from other channels due to customers first seeing our above-the-line advertising? Whether you use unique telephone numbers or unique URLs on your advertising, there is always a significant percentage of viewers who will not use them and this has always made it very difficult to measure.

Enter digital marketing. One of the most beautiful things about digital marketing (and I say that as a fan of numbers) is that not only are the channels themselves very cost-effective but they are also very measurable. Tracking users across your various touch points, through your website, along the purchase funnel to the point of sale – in detail so you know exactly who is responding to every minute detail – means you can have as close to a 100 per cent perfect view of your performance as you will get. I've never met a chief financial officer who would say no to that.

Justifying the brand argument for digital used to be a little harder. It is fairly clear that putting your spend into TV, outdoor advertising and radio can lift your brand awareness significantly. Paid search, SEO, display and e-mail are all much harder to gain real brand momentum from. I would agree with that in principle, but that was the old internet.

The rise of YouTube and Facebook alone have opened up phenomenal opportunities. We have all read the stories of YouTube users being swept off into great careers after their video 'went viral'. I'm sure most of the people reading this have reacted passionately in recent weeks to a Facebook post on a subject you care about, whether that be positively or negatively.

How much money has Psy made off 'Gangnam Style'?

Random celebrity article, by Brian Warner, 6 December 2012

Like
Tweet
+1
Pin

In case you haven't heard yet, Psy's song 'Gangnam Style' is the most liked and most viewed video in the history of YouTube. 'Gangnam Style' is about to cross 900 million views on YouTube and has been downloaded (legally) by 3 million people on iTunes alone. Suffice it to say, the song is a massive global phenomenon. But exactly how much money is Psy making off his incredible success? Millions. But even more amazingly, Psy has only sold around 100,000 physical CDs. His fortune is a modern marvel that couldn't have existed just a few years ago. If you are scratching your head wondering what I'm talking about, let me first congratulate you on waking up from that coma and, second, please watch this video (with headphones on if you're in a public place).

One of the most incredible aspects of Psy's millions is that only a tiny fraction of the money is coming from sales of physical CDs. 'Gangnam Style' was not released as a CD in the United States and has only sold around 100,000 copies in his native South Korea. Instead, Psy earns money from several different sources that did not exist just a few years ago. The first source is YouTube revenue sharing. Psy's video has been viewed 900 million times on YouTube and his account has been viewed 1.3 billion times. Every time someone watches his video or just visits his account, he or she is shown advertisements and Psy gets a cut of that revenue. By the end of the year, it is estimated that Psy will have earned US $1 million from his YouTube revenue share. The next major source is iTunes, where 'Gangnam Style' has been purchased by 3 million people, which generated roughly $2.6 million for Psy after Apple takes their 30 per cent cut. The third source of revenue is from streaming plays on platforms such as Pandora and Spotify. Unfortunately these sites pay tiny fractions of pennies for each play, so Psy's total take from worldwide streaming amounts to less than $200,000. Finally, Psy is making money through one fairly traditional source: endorsements. It is estimated that in the last six months Psy has made $5 million signing deals to endorse a range of products for brands such as Samsung and LG.

In total, Psy has made $8.8 million off the crazy success of 'Gangnam Style'. Of course, that amount does not include taxes, management fees, lawyers, agents etc... But it is still an impressive figure. Interestingly, Psy is not the only person making a fortune off his global superstardom. Psy's father and brother run a publicly traded South Korean semi-conductor company called DI Corp. A funny thing has happened to the stock price of DI Corp since June 2012 when it was sitting at an all time low of $1.20 per share. Between June and December, which happens to coincide perfectly with Psy's rise to fame, shares of DI Corp skyrocketed 188 per cent to an all time high of $5.8.

DI stock performance

According to stock analysts, it is not unusual for the price of a South Korean stock to be affected by something intangible such as public sentiment. Psy's father and brother own 10 per cent and 15 per cent of DI Corp's shares, which means they have both benefited enormously in the last six months. More specifically, his father and brother's paper net worths have increased by $12 million and $18 million, respectively, since June. On a similar note, the share price of Psy's management company, YG Entertainment, has increased more than 30 per cent since June. This increase has added $200 million to the paper net worth of YG's CEO Yang Hyun-suk. In summary, that's $8 million for Psy, $30 million for his family, and $200 million for his manager's manager. Seems like Psy is getting the short end of the stick, but keep in mind that this entire windfall comes from a silly dance and a catchy YouTube video!

The brand opportunity is literally massive online. It needs to be noted, however, that this can easily swing both ways. Brand damage is now easier than ever to achieve and customers are able to initiate direct conversations with you via the likes of Twitter. A very carefully produced and smart content plan is needed, with some skilled and experienced social people to ensure this is as effective and well managed as possible. The days of getting a few interns in to manage social media have gone. It is vital that this is taken very seriously.

One other important consideration for your objectives is to ensure that they are SMART. This technique is a very useful way of ensuring you set the best possible objectives and that they are not open to a great deal of challenge. SMART is an acronym and it breaks down as follows:

S	Specific	Don't let your objective be too broad.
M	Measurable	Ensure there is a method of measuring success and progress.
A	Attainable	Set realistic objectives, not dreams.
R	Relevant	Make sure you are not getting distracted from the core goal.
T	Time-bound	Put a deadline in place with key milestones.

Some people interpret this acronym slightly differently (eg meaningful instead of measurable) but the principles are the same.

Your market and website function

So we have looked at some of the overall goals but now we need to look at some of the specific challenges you may have. One of the first influencing factors to consider is your market. For example, are you operating in the business-to-business (B2B) or business-to-consumer (B2C) space. The B2B consumer has a different frame of mind to the B2C consumer and it's important to appreciate this: it will have an effect on your overall digital strategy, from your PR programme and distribution to your on-site funnel. To illustrate this let's look at a couple of examples of customer journeys.

A B2B company that offers contract manufacturing services may look to attract big electronics brands to its site in order to sell its services. The visitor needs to find the site when searching for specific products such as printed circuit boards or a contract manufacturer – these need to be optimized for SEO with compelling, relevant and valuable content on your site. They won't be looking for a price from your site but they will want a detailed view of your unique selling points (USPs), especially capabilities and portfolio of clients, They will want to contact you easily via a simple form and perhaps get in touch via the phone. It's vital therefore that your board invest in SEO and a strong brochureware website. You will also need a solid online PR campaign to support your position as an authority, and a good acquisition e-mail campaign will add value.

For B2C we could consider a music-streaming service. Here you need to create an exciting brand with compelling and competitive propositions as the consumer is looking to make a decision when they arrive on your site. The subscriber funnel must be simple, such as integrating it with Facebook, and it should be supported with compelling content on your site and across your social network channels. You need to be easy to find on the search engines under a wide selection of generic terms and your propositions will lend themselves well to display and performance marketing. An e-mail strategy to the right targeted segments will also pull in users. Your website needs to clearly and quickly illustrate the key benefits of the service, as the consumer will not spend long making the decision, and it must also be a slick site to build trust in the quality of your service. Finally, a free option is needed in this market – and so considering a model to migrate free users to paid is vital (e-mail upsell, for example). This is far more complex than the B2B strategy above and would need a great deal more investment and resource.

With regards to the website itself you need to understand its function. The above two examples illustrate a brochureware and transactional site and these are two key functional types, but there are many others, each with their own challenges. For example, membership sites such as clubs and magazines have to have secure areas with a great deal of easily accessible and highly valuable content, so investment in this area is key. It is vital that you take a step back and examine the core purpose of your site in order to be able to demonstrate to your decision makers that you have built your marketing strategy around the consumer and their mindset when they are shopping and arriving at your site. This needs to form a key building block of your proposal.

One good model to consider when trying to understand your market position is a matrix, as best illustrated by the Boston Consulting Group matrix. This was designed to position businesses in terms of relative market share and industry growth rates, but matrices can be used for a much wider purpose than this, such as competitive positioning and strategic direction planning. Framing your business in this way can help not only to understand your USPs and opportunities but also to frame the consumer's mindset. You can customize it as you like but below is a version of a matrix that analyses digital marketing channels in one specific market (see Figure 12.3). This example will differ depending on your market but it is a useful guide to using the matrix approach.

FIGURE 12.3   Boston Consulting Group Matrix that analyses digital marketing channels in one specific market

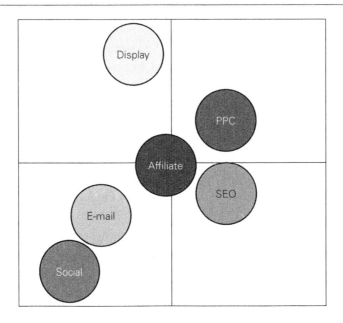

Understanding decision making and knowing your decision makers

'A camel is a horse designed by committee'

Now that we've started to assess the situation and develop some overall justification we need to ensure we understand the process that our decision makers will be going through. As I mentioned at the beginning of this chapter, what we're doing here is simply marketing, and with any marketing you need to understand your customer and their mindset.

There are several different personality types and decision-making processes that you may recognize in your organization and here we start to encroach on psychology. We do not have space here to discuss this psychology in great detail – and indeed there are many books on the subject that are worth every marketer absorbing – but we will look at some of the key areas so that you can ensure you position your proposal correctly.

The specific decision-making process your organization goes through will differ depending on the people and characters involved. You may have one decision maker who will decide the fate of your proposal alone, or you may have a group to present to who will vote on your plans. You may have one key decision maker who will consult with various other stakeholders across the organization, or that individual may simply run through a pros and cons analysis.

You will need to understand this power matrix and Table 12.1 illustrates how some of these models fit on the scale, from individual decision to group consensus. One factor that can affect the process is, of course, the bias of the individuals involved. Like it or not, we are all susceptible to bias whether it be in favour of a friend or because of our own past experience. Your decision maker will be no different. If possible, it is very valuable to find out whether your decision makers have had any previous experiences or influencers in their life that may affect the process. That will help you make the presentation relevant and also overcome any potential objections.

TABLE 12.1   Matrix of decision making

Individual	Personal preference	This is simply the preference of the individual with no analysis or consultancy
	Pros and cons or SWOT	These simple methods help to frame the decision but ultimately result in one person's decision
	Flipism	A flip of a coin. The individual cannot decide but does not look for input, leaving it to 'fate'
	Participative decision making	Where one decision maker seeks input from a group to gain additional input
	Voting-based decision making	Where a group score the various options and proceed based on the combined results
Consensus	Consensus decision making	A majority must approve the given course of action but the minority must also accept the decision

Some of the areas of bias you should consider as having an influence are listed below, but this is not by any means an exhaustive list:

- **Selective search for evidence** – gathering facts that support the decision they are looking to make. How to counter this: ensure your proposal is well-balanced.

- **Peer pressure** – certain individuals may be led by stronger personalities. How to counter this: ensure that every decision maker has an individual opportunity to ask questions and comment and gather a strong network of advocates.

- **Anchoring and adjustment** – decisions are heavily influenced by the initial information, which then shapes the way individuals perceive the remainder of the information. How to counter this: ensure your presentation/proposal tells a clear story (we will discuss this later in the chapter).

- **Recency** – people often naturally place more weight on recent information than more historic data. How to counter this: ensure your proposal is balanced and the data within covers all the key factors.

- **Credibility** – this can be a tendency to reject a proposal based on a poor opinion of the presenter, or to base their feedback or rejection on the opinion of someone they favour. How to counter this: ensure your proposal is syndicated and supported by others. Ensure the decision maker has a good opinion of you. Understand who they respect and get them on your side or consider having an advocate of yours present for you.

One final exercise on the psychology of decision making is to look at the cognitive behavioural work of Isabel Briggs Myers. Briggs Myers developed a set of four dichotomies called the Myers-Briggs Type Indicator (MBTI) and this is used by many businesses to assess the attributes of their employees. The four dichotomies are effectively scales of various personality traits and are as follows: thinking and feeling, extroversion and introversion, sensing and intuition, and judgement and perception. These can dictate whether an individual will make their decisions based on logical and analytical or more emotional factors. There is, as with most theories, much debate over the accuracy of the result and so it shouldn't be taken as an absolute indicator, but it is a worthwhile perspective.

I recommend further reading on this as it may help to frame your thinking on the mindset of your decision maker(s) (**http://www.myersbriggs.org/my-mbti-personality-type/mbti-basics/**).

It is also worth considering the key criteria often used by boards as their standard decision-making process. This will be slightly different for every business but below is a guide of the five areas you should ensure you address in your proposal:

- Logic: how does this investment fit with our strategy?
- Reward: what are the benefits? How much can we get early?
- Risk: if this fails, what will happen? Can we recover quickly?
- Execution: do we have the people, time, expertise?
- Competition: will we fall behind by not doing this?

Budget considerations

So far we have considered your organization's objectives and we have begun to understand the decision-makers themselves. It is at this point that we can begin to look at other factors that will dictate the shape of our proposal. The first of these is the budget. A bigger pot of cash certainly allows broader spend across the digital mix but it doesn't necessarily result in greater response. There will be a ceiling to the amount you can spend effectively so let's quickly try to understand how to demonstrate to your decision maker that you are using their pot of money to its best advantage.

Digital budgets vary considerably from zero to multi-million. To understand how best to allocate your budget you need to appreciate your business KPIs. Here we come back to our objectives. If your business is looking for growth you may have a budget that must be spent in order to maximize growth or, quite the opposite, no budget and therefore maximum growth possible at no cost. You may be promoting a product with a tight margin and so have a very specific cost per acquisition that must be achieved, but no overall budget, so the challenge is to maximize volume within that CPA limit. Whichever challenge your business has, there are some core principles to assigning this budget.

The first is channel optimization – to find your best-performing channel and maximize that before you move on to others. If, for example, you have a PPC campaign running and this achieves a good volume of enquiries at a highly effective CPA, then ensuring you are gaining maximum volume from your account – by optimizing keywords, ad copy, customer journey, etc – before opening up another channel is a sensible approach.

Second, you should always ensure that your website itself is optimized. This may involve some budget, depending on your technical and management set-up. This is vital as all of your digital channels will be driving traffic to your site. Optimizing this end touchpoint will effectively improve the performance of all other channels.

Third, maximizing the use of your free channels is important. Few organizations can argue against having effective social and SEO strategies in today's digital world, and these can be a fantastic source of low-cost business.

Finally, it is important to understand your business's budget cycle. This is not relevant to all businesses, but you may find that any budget you suggest in your proposal may be entirely justified but simply not available. Ensure you are fully aware of any limitations to this before you build a budget that could render the rest of your proposal worthless.

Using these principles you can begin to shape your budget allocation. Many organizations will find PPC an effective channel and SEO a key part of their strategy. The display and affiliate channels can open up further opportunities and also have brand benefits. Social can also drive volume as well as opening up a useful, low-cost customer touchpoint. E-mail can also be a cost-effective driver of digital enquiries. This book covers each channel in detail and, later in this chapter, also looks at the specific benefits of each.

Figure 12.4 shows a pie chart that illustrates a common breakdown of channel split in many organizations. It is important to note that this is simply an example and your channel split will need to take all of the above factors into consideration alongside your specific objectives and business model. For example, if your business is in the mobile industry or your consumers are primarily found on the mobile channel, then you would want to up-weight the spend there.

One other consideration is your resource. The work streams involved in managing digital marketing will include a number of skills that can be

FIGURE 12.4 A typical organizational breakdown of channel split

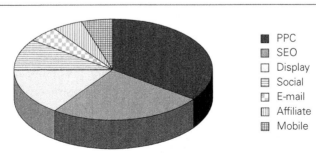

- PPC
- SEO
- Display
- Social
- E-mail
- Affiliate
- Mobile

managed in-house or at an agency. These include creative, technical build, copywriting, media buying, negotiation, technical and others. Keeping these in-house can often result in cost savings and greater control. However, agencies can offer greater depth of expertise and often have stronger media buying power. It is worth modelling a number of options, as some of these skills, such as copywriting and creative especially, are often beneficial to keep in-house. We will discuss resource allocation and agency management later in the chapter.

Key channel benefits

As mentioned above, this book covers each channel in detail and so I won't duplicate that by going into detail here. The purpose of this section is to pull out which of those channel benefits can be used to best effect when justifying digital marketing investment to your decision maker.

Whatever mix you choose when developing your digital strategy there will doubtless be multiple channels. Even if you are working with a limited budget you are still likely to at least be developing both SEO and social strategies. How these channels interact is tackled towards the end of this section, but before that we will look at the specific benefits you can use when selling-in.

SEO

Search engine optimization has been an art form since the early days of search engines and is a constantly developing channel. The core to success is, of course, developing a website and digital marketing strategy that is compelling in terms of high-quality content alongside a great user experience. What you spend on SEO can vary greatly along a scale from simple website development to a multichannel content strategy. What is constant, however, is the ability to bring in a significant volume of consumers on a wide range of search terms at a highly effective cost per visit. There is less direct control on this channel than others such as PPC, and the initial period from investment to seeing results is longer, but beginning an SEO strategy is like pushing a boulder down a hill; it's slow at first and hard to push but when it starts to roll, it will pick up pace quickly.

Your key messages here are that you can generate significant volume at an effective cost per visit/cost per acquisition. A secondary message is that the more prominent your website is, the less prominent your competitors' websites will be, as there are a limited number of spaces on that first page; therefore your share of voice is increased.

PPC

Paid search provides a fantastic source of visitors with the ultimate level of control. The ability to choose your exact keywords, provide a wide range of adverts at whichever position you are willing to bid for, at any time you choose, to whomever you choose, and to be able to switch that on or off in real time is a tool that has no comparison offline.

There are a number of ways to use this channel and therefore a number of ways to customize your selling message to meet the goals of your decision makers. It can be used to test marketing messages and audience demographics that can be used across the rest of the marketing mix. You have the ability to test the times that your audience are online or engaging in your advertising.

Paid search can also fill the gaps in your SEO performance. However successful your natural search results, you will always have gaps that need filling and that means access to 100 per cent of your potential search visitors.

And finally, paid search is able to deliver a significant volume of traffic at a highly effective cost, which is of course attractive enough on its own.

Social

The benefits of social are numerous. There are over 1 billion users on Facebook and a similar number on various social media sites in China that many people know nothing about (yet). It's clear to see that whoever your customers are, they are using social media.

So what are the key benefits? Well, the volume of users is one benefit, of course. More importantly, the ability to access advertising by their age, location and even interests is incredibly powerful. The insight available on your audience is also a hugely valuable tool. Facebook insights, for example, give you a detailed view of when your visitors are online, who they are and how they compare to the average Facebook user. You can experiment with posts at specific times with a high degree of flexibility and results in real time. All of this can again be fed back into the wider marketing plan to add significant value.

Social has also opened up the art form of viral marketing to a much greater degree than before. YouTube is filled with viral videos and Facebook has a huge number of messages and photography that have reached hundreds of thousands of users. Whilst there is no definitive guide to creating a viral marketing campaign, it is definitely true that social media is an essential part of the distribution mix for this activity. Viral marketing has the opportunity to create brand awareness that would literally cost millions of dollars to achieve on other channels. Whilst I would encourage you not to overpromise with viral campaigns, due to their unpredictability, they have an infinitely greater chance of success when employed on social channels.

Display

Display is a channel that often gets a mixed reception in marketing camps. It is a fantastic opportunity to spread a brand and its specific campaigns to a wide audience, but it generally achieves a very low click-through rate and so as a direct channel is often considered ineffective. Justifying this channel can therefore be trickier, and understanding your objectives becomes a key part of this.

If brand awareness is one of your key objectives then display has its place with little need for further explanation. The key with justifying display advertising to generate visits and sales is to look at attribution modelling and post-impression tracking. Display may not be the channel that people actually click through to your website from but that doesn't mean that it hasn't played a part in that person's journey to your site.

The internet has increasingly become a shop window. Comparison sites have become an increasing presence online and now exist for travel, financial services, utilities, homes, cars and many more services. People use the internet to consider their purchase before buying, which they then may or may not do online. This shopper mentality means that having your brand present throughout your customer's online experience increases your chance of being 'front of mind' when it comes to the purchase itself. You also have a fantastic re-marketing opportunity, which enables you to follow that customer with your unique message (including a specific price, if relevant) wherever they may go – another tool that is simply not possible offline. So when considering display marketing it is vital to look at the bigger picture, not just this single channel's conversion metrics (see Figure 12.5).

Affiliate – or performance marketing

Affiliate marketing (at times referred to as performance marketing in this book) is a channel that can involve some close monitoring. Validation, de-duplication and quality checking requires resources unless managed through an agency. Negotiation of key terms with the affiliate network or directly

FIGURE 12.5   Aggregator's graph

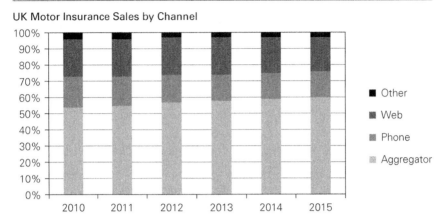

SOURCE: eBenchmarkers

with the affiliates themselves can also be time consuming and require some knowledge of the process. These considerations need to be built into your proposal as they may require resources or skills that may not exist in your current team.

The opportunity with affiliate marketing is to deliver a volume of leads from highly relevant sources such as websites or e-mail marketers operating in your market, at a CPA that you choose. Supporting this with compelling propositions and a website that converts well is essential to optimize this channel, but there are few channels where you can entirely dictate the CPA. Considering whether your business can offer an attractive bounty to affiliates, whether your propositions are competitive and whether your conversion is strong are all key before recommending this channel.

As a sales message it really is a no-brainer. Even if the volume is low for your chosen CPA this is still volume that you will not capture elsewhere. If you avoid the affiliate channel then those sources will simply be sending their volume elsewhere.

E-mail

E-mail marketing is very low-cost and there are a number of options here. Looking at your own internal database you may have lapsed or cancelled customers, previous shoppers or those who have started the purchase funnel but not completed, who may be willing to come back and buy. These win-back campaigns can be effective if you have a strong supporting proposition. This is a fairly easy sell to your decision makers.

Member-get-member (MGM) programmes can be an effective way of building your customer base by rewarding your customers for recommending a friend. An example of this is companies that pay £100 to their staff for bringing a friend in to work for the business. The incentive is key and needs to be built into your CPA. The benefit here is that the conversion on this channel is fantastic due to the borrowed trust your company achieves from the individual who is recommending you.

Cross-selling and up-selling messages are excellent through the e-mail channel and can increase customer lifetime value (CLTV) but you need to be aware of the risk of irritating or even potentially losing a customer through contacting them.

Note on CLTV

Customer lifetime value is simply a calculation of the net profit of an individual customer. This can help to shape your CPA targets and can be calculated via a number of methods that range in complexity. The simplest way to view this is:

$$\frac{\text{Average monthly revenue per customer} \times \text{gross margin per customer}}{\text{monthly churn rate}}$$

For example:

$$\frac{\$100 \text{ monthly spend} \times 20 \text{ per cent gross margin}}{10 \text{ per cent monthly churn}} = \$200.$$

Each customer in this example is therefore worth $200 to your business.

Retention marketing is also effective through the e-mail channel and can improve your chance of keeping or renewing a customer, therefore further increasing CLTV.

For acquisition e-mail marketing you will be tapping into external sources of data. This is where understanding your customer in terms of who they are and which customers convert is vital. Purchasing lists can be a minefield and so working with reputable suppliers is important, but if you get this data selection right then the CPA can be highly effective.

Finally, the actual delivery cost of the channel in terms of creative and send is also very low-cost. You therefore have the opportunity here to improve acquisition volumes and customer lifetime value at minimal cost. Again, this is a no-brainer.

FIGURE 12.6   The growth of mobile devices

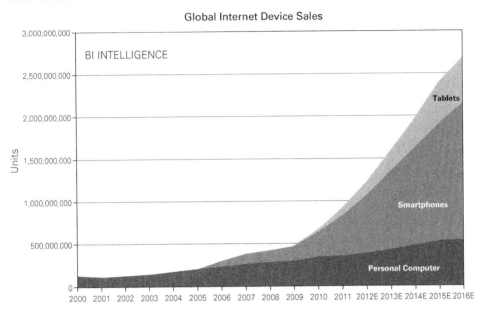

Global Internet Device Sales

SOURCE: Gartner, ID, Strategy Analytics, company filings, BI Intelligence estimates

Mobile

Mobile is a growing channel. You will have read about the multiscreen world and will most likely have a mobile phone with you – if not a tablet – as you are reading this. In recent years the number of smartphones sold has exceeded the number of PCs sold – that is an enormous statement on the growth of mobile (see Figure 12.6). There is a great deal to say on this subject, and that is a book in itself, but I recommend further reading on the growth of mobile and the opportunities it presents.

For mobile marketing specifically you need to, at the very least, ensure that your customers can access your products on their mobile devices. This may mean responsive design websites or apps. If you were to look at your websites analytics now and you have the benefit of historic performance I strongly suspect you will see that the percentage of visitors arriving on your site from mobile has increased in the last 12 months. Whether these users are converting into sales will be a telling sign of your mobile user experience. Consider the cost and benefit impact of this in your proposal.

Beyond the obvious opportunity of very real growth there are a number of other factors to consider when selling-in mobile marketing. You consumer, when engaging in your mobile site or app, will have your product in their hand. They will be able to pop you in their pocket and take you wherever they go. There is no need to remember a phone number or find a PC in order to buy your products or services. They will have access to you anywhere, anytime. That is incredibly powerful. Mobile marketing opens up SMS as a channel. Whilst this can be very invasive it can also open up the opportunity for dialogue with your customers, so should be carefully considered in the mix.

As with social media, you have fantastic viral opportunities here. It is very easy for a consumer to receive and forward a message instantly, which greatly increases the chance of that message spreading to a large consumer base.

Social media is also becoming a mobile domain, with most Twitter users tweeting from their smartphones now. Facebook also has a significant mobile user base. The opportunities here are already significant but also growing at an exceptional speed.

Channel interaction

Following our quick review of the channels and key benefits to pull out we need to look at how they interact with each other. One buzz word of marketing these days is *attribution*. This refers to exactly how the result of your marketing activity should be attributed to each channel. We touched on this when discussing display advertising earlier. Here is an example of how a customer could potentially interact with your marketing channels:

1 Ryan is watching TV and sees your commercial for some sunglasses after the end of *American Idol*. He pulls out his cell phone and searches for your offer on Google but can't remember your brand name and so clicks through to a competitor advert instead.

2 He then realizes he's late for dinner and runs out the door.

3 The next day he is having a cup of coffee and flicking through his e-mails when he notices an e-mail from you. He doesn't click on this e-mail but he remembers it.

4 Later that evening he pulls his cell phone back out and searches again on Google. This time he clicks on your paid search advert and goes on to purchase the shades. So which channel made him buy the sunglasses? It's a tricky question to answer.

The TV channel made him aware of your offer and he took action but he didn't actually come through to you and buy as a result. The e-mail prompted him to go back and specifically search for you with an intention to buy. It was the final paid search advert that brought him to your website but this had failed once before to attract him.

There are many different models for attributing value to each channel and no single model can be called the correct one. The various models to consider are listed below with their relative advantage:

- **Single source – last interaction:** this model gives the entire value of the conversion to the last interaction that a consumer had with your marketing before purchasing. In the example above this would be paid search.

- **Single source – first interaction:** this model states that the first interaction is what created the others and therefore gives all of the credit to the first channel. In the example above this is the TV advert.

- **Equal weight/ linear:** this model simply gives equal weighting to all interactions as none can be guaranteed to have been the single decision-making factor.

- **First and last priority or u-curve:** this assumes that the channel that initiated the interest and the one that finally delivered the user to the conversion funnel are the important ones and all others are less relevant. In the example above, this would mean that TV and paid search each get 50 per cent of the credit.

- **Time phased:** this model assumes that the touchpoints closer to the point of purchase are the key ones, as anything before then was simply shopping around and was not necessarily relevant in the conversion process. In the example above, this would generate the most credit for paid search, then e-mail, then TV.

There are other models but these are some of the most common. A marketing expert should have a firm grip on attribution modelling in order to build and optimize an effective multichannel strategy, and your decision makers should be made to understand it if it is relevant to your proposal.

The other factors to consider for channel interaction are your conversion levels, which will differ by channel, and the brand impact of each channel. It is essential to understand how a visitor from paid search behaves on your website compared to a visitor from natural search, for example. One may have a lower bounce rate, spend longer on your site, visit more pages, interact with you but have very low conversion rates. The other may simply arrive, buy and leave. Understanding how these specific behaviours differ per channel is essential as it will greatly affect the effectiveness of each channel.

Brand value is a more difficult value to measure without research. In digital marketing we have become spoiled with the amount of data available to us, but brand value is one metric that is not entirely scientific. We can look at performance versus competitors on search terms – and other hints of the story but never the true picture. One thing we must understand, however, is that some channels give us more opportunity than others to create brand value. This will, of course, depend heavily on targeting and creative as well as wider marketing integration.

We have mentioned above that display advertising is not always an optimum channel for driving cost-effective leads on the surface, but it gives you a significant opportunity to spread your creative and branding across a broad range of relevant sites. E-mail is also a great opportunity to disseminate your brand widely.

Figure 12.7 is a channel interaction diagram that illustrates how marketing channels influence each other and can be useful when thinking about channel interaction.

FIGURE 12.7   How marketing channels interact

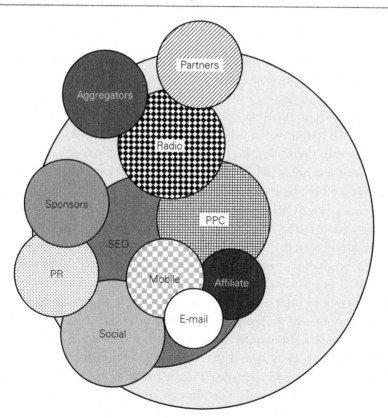

The above factors should go some way to helping you build a compelling case for your digital channels – but ultimately these customers will land on your website, so let's discuss how to justify investment there.

The perfect website

Here we look at some of the key messages to your decision makers. It is essential to ensure that your site is fast, easy to navigate, contains compelling content, has a strong conversion funnel, is tagged for optimum analysis and is built for the consumer and SEO (two factors that quite rightly go hand-in-hand these days). But how do we pull out the specific business benefit of all of these factors?

The four key building blocks for the website piece of your story break down as follows:

1 Why have a website?

2 What should we invest in functionality, look and feel?

3 How will people find our website?

4 How and why will visitors take the actions we want them to?

The first of these is highly unlikely to need an explanation in today's digital world but, very briefly, you would need to consider your consumer's use of the internet, the increasing use of digital technology, including mobile, and the cost benefits of the digital channel versus offline.

Points two to four will involve investment and so it is vital to be able to explain to your decision makers the benefit of any actions you are planning in each of these areas. What should you invest in functionality, look and feel? This is a broad question so let's break it down further. How your website operates directly affects the way a visitor reacts. If your website provides an online quote facility, for example, being able to return a quote from your pricing system is vital. Perhaps, however, your business does provide quotes but your product is complex and so conversion in a call centre delivers a better ROI. In this case, perhaps a simple data-capture form is enough or you may want to offer a live online chat facility. If your website is a shop then an e-commerce shopping basket would be required. Two out of three of these examples also require online payment processing and security. The key point to take away here is that assessing the benefits of online versus offline conversion – and a simple purchase funnel versus a full e-commerce experience – are essential when deciding to invest in website developments.

Looking at examples of your competitors and beyond is a good guide here. If there are others that have been in your market for some time, have they changed their model? Do you see patterns that you can learn from without having to go through the time-consuming and expensive process of learning them yourself? These can be used to justify your proposal. Also building financial business cases based on real or best estimations of each metric provides an incredibly useful steer. If you can support your recommended approach with financial figures that demonstrate the different scenarios then you are more likely to gain approval. Using your business's KPIs, analytics, market knowledge and any other supporting data you have available is the best approach. External data will be trusted far less.

From a look and feel perspective you will, of course, need to build in your brand values, and so the look and feel you choose cannot and should not be defined here to a great degree. You must, however, consider how your creative will impact performance. If building a new site, recommending a refresh or implementing a rebranding project, there are key points to deliver to your decision maker.

Below is a useful checklist to look through when making website changes. Each can be built into your recommendations:

- Will it make your website faster or slower? Faster pages will keep people on the site and move more of them to the goal you are steering them towards.

- Will it make it easier to find and buy your product? Help text, error messaging, signposting, removal of distracting links from purchase funnels, reducing forms – all can create an improvement in sales.

- Will it affect your digital marketing? Will it improve the conversion from your key channels or improve your organic search performance, thus driving greater volume to your site?

- Will it add extra value to your site? Extra content on your site that customers find of value is not just an SEO tool but also allows visitors to answer any questions they have, which can increase conversion and also reduce customer service requests.

- Will it raise the income from a customer? Adding up-sell and cross-sell products to your site can raise your CLTV by encouraging customers to buy add-ons or related products. If not handled correctly, however, it can interrupt your purchase funnel and reduce your conversion.

- Will it give you extra insight? Tagging your site in detail can drive a greater level of understanding of customer behaviour, which can be invaluable. However, tagging needs to be implemented correctly to avoid any technical issues such as impacting SEO performance.

- Does it integrate with your wider marketing? An integrated creative approach across all of your channels will improve conversion, as consumers who have seen your TV advertising or outdoor posters will recognize your company even if they have forgotten your name and logo. This is not, of course, a new approach to marketing but it applies equally to digital.

Further considerations

There are many other areas to consider in your proposal and there is not enough room in this chapter to discuss them all but we can look at some of the key ones that you may wish to factor in.

Trends and seasonality

Every industry has its own unique trends. Gifts are popular during the months prior to seasonal holidays. Travel products will be popular prior to your territory's key holiday seasons. Automotive-related products may be more popular prior to the launch of new cars or licence-plate updates. Understanding and appreciating the impact this has on your digital marketing is a key factor to build into your proposal. Will the strategy that you are implementing be affected immediately or in the long term by these changes?

For example, building an SEO strategy that will grow your website visits over a period of time may show a negative result for the first few months after being implemented if you launch it at the end of your seasonal peak. If this is not communicated in your proposal then you may be setting unrealistic expectations and ultimately setting yourself up for a fall. Figure 12.8 is a graph from Google Trends that demonstrates the searches for 'hotels' and 'toys' in the United States in 2012, which gives an indication of the effect of seasonal demand within different industries.

Competitor research

There are a great number of ways you can gain competitor intelligence. Some of these are through paid research organizations and others through

FIGURE 12.8   Google Trends – the effects of seasonal demand

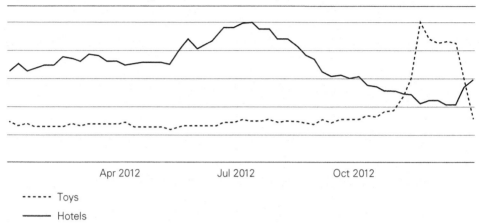

- - - - - - Toys
———— Hotels

free online tools. Whichever route you choose, understanding your competitor's performance will help shape the expectation around the results you can achieve.

A key message to your decision makers is how you will gain competitive advantage. If you can appreciate your competitor's digital strategies through reviewing their digital activity you can start to paint this picture. Even without detailed research you can gain an understanding of their paid search, social and natural search campaigns. You can also review their websites and even make enquiries or purchases through their sites in order to understand their business model. This can have the additional benefit of being added to your competitor's CRM programmes, which will give you further insight into any outbound calling, SMS or e-mail strategies they may have in place. Gathering all of this data and using it to position your strategy can be a powerful factor.

Test and learn

One principle of marketing in general is to ensure that every campaign you launch has a test element built in. This way, even if your campaign is not entirely successful, you will at least learn how to improve you future campaigns. These test and learn programmes can include creative, timing, channel, landing page variations, ad copy, demographic targeting and many other factors.

Your decision makers should be made to understand the benefits that this process can reap. Not only can this learning be fed into your future digital campaigns but they can be implemented across your business, leading to significant gains. It is worthwhile giving some examples of exactly how these programmes will be implemented and what gains can be expected.

You may also need to consider beginning your proposal as a small-scale test in order to prove the concept. This is a risk mitigation exercise and will give you a stronger chance of a more risky strategy being accepted. It will, however, also slow the impact of the overall project – and that consideration must be built in. Starting as a small test may reduce the risk but it may also open up new risks by enabling your competitors to move faster.

Future developments

One thing that I'm certain will be very clear to anyone reading this book is that time does not stand still. Just over 15 years ago (as I write this) there was no Google, no Amazon, no eBay and no YouTube. The web was used by fewer than 16 million people* and accessed by a slow dial-up connection. There was no social media and very few of us had mobile phones. There were no smartphones or tablets. Home PC processing power was comparatively miniscule, having doubled every 18 months since (in line with Moore's Law). There are many other examples of the dramatic changes in the digital world over the last 20 years and if you think we're at the peak you should think again. *Source: **http://www.internetworldstats.com/emarketing.htm**

Major players in the internet arrive regularly and can become very powerful very quickly – I give you Facebook and Twitter as just two good examples from the last 10 years. New technology is arriving all the time, such as Google Glass. The world is fast approaching, if not overtaking, the sci-fi movies of years past. For example, a technology is being developed that is eerily similar to the tri-corder made famous by *Star Trek*.

TVs have become 3D, flat screen and smart but they still take up significant space in our house – is this likely to remain the case? We have a multi-device world where people e-mail on their phone followed by playing games on their tablets, whilst watching TV. Will all of these devices be necessary in the future? The future will hold many developments, some of which are happening now and some are unforeseeable but the key here is to future-proof your digital strategy. You don't know what you don't know, but you should maximize what you do know. Keep your finger on the pulse of the digital world and this can keep you ahead of your competitors and reduce the need for future investment. Both excellent messages to give to your decision maker.

Local/global

If your business operates in multiple regions or territories then you will need to build this into your considerations. This is quite a complex area and so rather than going into a great level of detail we will just pull out a list of the key considerations when managing a global digital strategy and how these can be best used in your proposal:

Language

Deciding how best to structure your site to fit multiple languages through location detection or multiple sites will impact costs and customer engagement. Presenting a consumer with a site that is not in their language without a clear method of changing languages will dramatically increase your bounce rate. However, assuming a user in a territory speaks the national language of that territory is a risky assumption too. For example, if you are appealing to American expats worldwide then they are unlikely to want to read websites in the local language of the country they are living in, but that is not necessarily the case. Understanding the intricacies of this and demonstrating the benefits of your chosen approach to your decision makers is important. These can include bounce rates, conversion rates, engagement and build cost.

Culture

Culture is a broad area. This can include annual holidays, religion, sense of humour, digital uptake, family life, living arrangements, economy and many more factors. It is key to explain to your decision makers that these factors have been taken into account when developing your strategy. Some example questions that may apply to territories in which your business operates include:

- Is it 'Christmas' or 'holiday season' – or is it not relevant at all?
- Do certain words or names have negative connotations?
- Does the time difference affect your messaging?
- Are the personalities or phrases you refer to famous in the territory?

Seasons

If your business operates far from a central marketing office you will need to look far beyond what is outside your window when putting your strategy together – and again your decision makers will need to understand how this is built into your strategy. Questions to ask yourself here include:

- When is summer – August or February?
- Does it ever snow?
- What are the temperature and rainfall levels?
- Does the territory suffer from any earthquakes, tornadoes or other natural disasters?

Shopping behaviour

Do consumers shop online and then buy on the phone? Do they shop and buy online across a range of known brands? Do they visit a very wide range of brands by searching online? Do they use price comparison sites?

These questions all alter the KPIs of your business and how you set up your operation in every territory. You will need to demonstrate an understanding of that to your decision makers.

Part of that shopping behaviour is their chosen method of payment. Assuming consumers are comfortable buying products from your website then how do they pay? Consumers in some territories do not use credit cards online and so other methods such as PayPal are essential. Launching in territories without understanding the impact of this decision is a significant risk and one that you should ensure your decision makers are comfortable that you have assessed.

Legal and compliance

Put simply, every territory is different. Your industry may be regulated differently overseas, as may the advertising rules. Some countries, such as the United States and Australia, for example, have different laws in different states and understanding how these impact your strategy is also vital before making your proposal.

Technology

Throughout this book we have looked at the growth of digital and ensuring your website supports the fast moving trends. It is vital to understand, on the other hand, that some territories have moved faster than others. Smartphone and tablet uptake or broadband penetration are both factors that shouldn't be considered to be universal. If you optimize your strategy around mobile without considering what percentage of your global consumers can be negatively affected then this will impact your results. Building these intricacies into your presentation is key to demonstrate your understanding and to be able to accurately reflect the performance you can expect.

In-house or agency?

As mentioned above, budget considerations and cost-benefit analysis of digital marketing have to consider the resource needed to manage the activity itself. The key balance here is between expertise and control. Use of agencies can offer up-to-the-minute expertise (something vital in such a fast-paced industry) but with the activity itself you are also outsourcing your trust and your ability to fully control the individuals involved. Agencies will have a management fee and a contract termination period, all of which are additional costs. You will not, however, have salaries to pay and you will have no people concerns should you choose to restructure your strategy.

As a quick guide to this, Table 12.2 shows some of the benefits that you may wish to communicate in your proposal.

TABLE 12.2 A guide to resource investment

	Agency	In-House
Resource	Dependent on fee	Required to support all activity
Cost of work	Retainer/fees paid plus costs for ad-hoc work	Salaries cover all work
Media buying	Beneficial terms due to multiple clients	Not enough scale to gain significant advantage
Industry knowledge	Possibly good, possibly none. Unlikely to be fully up-to-date	Up-to-date expertise
Marketing expertise	Up-to-date expertise	Good but training required to stay up-to-date
Creativity	Employ specific creative people	Less creativity and harder to attract highly creative people
Control	Reliant on agency priorities	Full control with accountability
Flexibility	Highly flexible	Internal structure and processes restrict this
Technology	Technology in place at agency	Technology may need to be purchased and staff trained
Relationships	Existing relationships with Google etc	Probably no/few direct relationships

So in summary, your proposal must consider where any resource investment is best placed and what this cost will be.

Structuring your proposal

So now we come to the nitty-gritty. We've reviewed your objectives, decision makers, budget, channels and a number of other key considerations. Now, how do we tie this together into something compelling that your decision maker will applaud, or at least approve, and how do we prepare for and counter the challenges?

There are two key questions that you must answer when looking at everything you do from this point forward. The points you write, the graphs you include, the order of the slides, the conclusions you make – you must ask yourself these two questions when working through the proposal and you must answer them honestly – as you are your own judge. They are: 1) Am I telling a story?; 2) So what?

Telling a story is vital. Your proposal must flow logically (we'll look more at that shortly). 'So what?' relates to why your decision makers should care about what you're saying. What does it mean? What is the conclusion? Facts are important but interpreting them into real insights and recommendations is vital.

So let's start with the story. From what we have already discussed in this chapter you can hopefully see a story developing. How you create your own story needs to relate to your business, as we've discussed above, but there is a standard framework that you can use to shape this to best effect. The 6S framework (shown in Figure 12.9) is a useful way of remembering the key areas to cover.

It is worth noting that you will need to adapt your approach depending on whether you are producing a PowerPoint to talk through, a PDF for someone else to talk through, or a document for your decision makers to read without you there at all. If you are not there you need to be certain that your proposal is even clearer – and has all the supporting data included and all potential challenges covered.

You also need to consider that the goalposts can move. If you prepare a 60-minute presentation and then as you walk into the room you hear, 'Something's come up. You've got 10 minutes. Go!' – what do you do? Having a backup plan means you won't be flustered and miss any urgent points. This situation can make panic set in and make your proposal seem quite weak through no fault of your own, so be prepared.

FIGURE 12.9 The 6S framework

- **Synopsis** – what's the answer?
  - Executive summary
- **Scene setting** – why are we doing this?
  - Reminder of the goals and targets
  - Background
  - Company history
  - Competitors
  - Market
  - Consumer/customer
  - Approach
  - Assumptions
  - Expectations
  - Contents and what is coming next
- **Story** – what are we doing and why? Should I agree?
  - Channels
  - Website
  - Brand impact
  - Resource
  - Suppliers and partners
- **Sums** – how much does it cost?
  - Financial plans
- **Steps** – how and when does this happen?
  - Clear action plan
  - Timescales
  - Responsibilities
- **Surprise!** – What about... ?
  - Be prepared for questions

Now let's return to the *6S* framework and how each of these points relate to the proposal itself.

Synopsis

As with any report, the executive summary is simply a short, sharp presentation of the key take-outs. Try to keep this to the highlights of each section with the recommendations clearly communicated. Include bullet points and any of the supporting data that is vital to support your recommendation. Remember to ask yourself 'So what?' when putting this together. If you only read this section and nothing else, would you understand what the proposal is trying to achieve, what the recommendation is, why and what is going to be done about it?

Try to keep this to one slide or one page. A good technique is to write it then cut out anything that is unnecessary. Then, when you are happy, cut it some more. It should include facts, figures, actions, deadlines, deliverables. Do not be tempted to go into any unnecessary detail here.

Key question: if I had 30 seconds, would this this explain all the key points?

Scene setting

In this section we are trying to answer the following questions: 1) Where are we now? 2) Why are we here? This is where we bring in the objectives, market, company history and budget considerations that we mentioned earlier in this chapter. Use these to frame why you are putting this proposal together.

Ensure you include the challenges you face and how you will overcome them. Review your performance versus your competitors and how your proposal will change that. Illustrate that you understand your market positioning and what impact this proposal may have. If relevant, make the decision makers aware that you understand the budget and, if it necessary, position any restrictions that may apply. You then need to ensure that the audience understands how you went about building the proposal and why, alongside any assumptions you made.

Finally, what specifically are you going to ask the decision makers for at the end? This helps them to put your story in perspective and pick up on all the key points as they listen or read. Tackle this by breaking down into a simple format each of the key points above that apply to your proposal. This could involve showing a question and answer on the slide or page. One approach is to talk briefly about the background on one slide and then list the objectives on the next, followed by tackling each of those on its own individual slide. Then follow this with your assumptions and expectations. This frames the beginning of the story.

Key question: if I didn't know the business or history, do I now understand it?

Story

In this section we are trying to answer the following questions:

- Where do we want to go?
- How do we get there?
- Why do we want to go there?

So this is where you bring everything together. Everything we've discussed in this chapter alongside all of your plans and expertise must be poured in here. This section is the meat of your proposal and will differ enormously depending on your objectives, but the same principles apply as with the rest of the document. Keep it simple and tell the story. Every slide should follow on from the last and each should add more weight to your proposal. If, for example, you are talking about paid search, affiliate and display channels, then how will they interact? Will creative be shared or unique? How will you ensure the affiliates do not disrupt the other channels? These questions need answering here and in an order that flows as naturally as possible.

If your proposal doesn't involve any website changes, the chances are it will still impact your website in some way. Whether that be an increase in visitors, changes to conversion rates or visitor behaviour, there will be some impact – so ensure you cover that here.

As well as talking about your strategy and how it breaks down you also need to demonstrate an understanding of the business impact of the strategy. That includes the financial impact of each decision, any resource changes and associated fees, eg appointing new agencies. Do processes need to change? How will your brand be impacted and are there any legal concerns? Some of these may not be relevant but it is vital that you consider the full impact of your strategy.

As mentioned above, ensure this flows as a story. A useful format is to cover the detail with graphs, illustrations and key bullet points and then to use a summary box on each page. This box should contain all the KPIs, eg financial gain, sales, costs and risks, applied to the topic of that individual page. It should be the key summary so that a reader doesn't need to look at anything else if they choose – and it should be consistent throughout every slide in this section of your proposal to enable the audience to quickly understand everything.

Key question: do I now understand exactly what the plan is and the costs, benefits and risks?

Sums

In this section we are trying to answer the following questions: 1) What does this cost us? 2) How will we financially benefit from this? This is an area where many proposals fall down. It is vital that your maths stack up. Interrogate your numbers and try to find the gaps. What will the challenges from your audience be? There are very few decision makers that don't put significant weight on the cost of an exercise and expected returns, so you cannot walk into a presentation without knowing the numbers, having 100 per cent faith in them and understanding why and how they became what they are.

As well as the high-level summary of each element of your proposal you should also have the detail so that the audience can challenge and absorb as they see fit. This may be in the appendix of a document, or if you are presenting you may simply want to take those detailed numbers with you to ensure you can answer any challenges.

Make the numbers clear – again, simplicity is the key here. The more complex the numbers, the more explaining you have to do and so the harder it is for a decision maker to see the clear benefit of your message. You must not let your message become diluted by spending a great length of time debating unclear figures.

When a business case is produced your board will be looking for a range of figures. This may be a simple profit exercise but it may be far more complex. The key numbers expected in a full business case can include all or some of the items mentioned below, so gaining and communicating an understanding of these is important:

- capital required;
- investment horizon;
- revenue growth;
- gross profit;
- free cash flow;
- net present value (NPV);
- internal rate of return (IRR);
- break-even point;
- economic profit;
- impact on profit and loss – accretive or dilution;
- depreciation and amortization impact;

- source of funding – balance sheet, equity investment, debt;
- return – ROCE, RONA, ROTA.

Key question: do I understand the exact financial benefit and cost of this?

Steps

In this section we are trying to answer the following questions:

- When will this begin?
- When will it be complete?
- What are the key steps to get from A to B?
- Who will deliver it?

Put simply, this is a project plan. This section should demonstrate in a clear format what the timeline is to deliver your proposal. There are several programs you can use to build this. For example, looking at Microsoft alone, you could use Project, Excel or you can simply build it in PowerPoint or Word. Whatever technology you use, the most important point here is the clear formatting.

The best approach is to include a timeline at the top – this could be days, weeks, months or years, depending on your proposal. Underneath this timescale you should list all of the different workstreams that make up your project. This may include items such as:

- appoint an agency;
- launch paid search;
- launch online shopping facility.

Each of these then needs key milestones displayed on that plan. So if we look at the example of appointing an agency, it may break down into some or all of the following:

- build agency objectives and KPIs;
- produce tender document;
- select agencies for tender;
- engage agencies and send tender document;
- initial proposals from agencies;
- select shortlist;
- produce detailed second-stage tender document;

- send second-stage document to shortlisted agencies;
- final presentations from shortlisted agencies;
- select preferred agency;
- contract negotiations;
- appointment and start date.

These milestones need to be displayed clearly and simply on your project plan. When putting these in place you must ensure your timescales are realistic. Overpromising is as dangerous as underpromising so keep this in mind and challenge yourself as you build them. Each of the work streams needs an owner. There will probably be an individual who each work stream naturally fits with but you must look at the bigger picture here. The key is that the milestones are delivered within the timescale to ensure your proposal meets its objectives. If, however, one individual has received the majority of the actions, is it realistic that they can deliver all of those within the timescales whilst managing their day-to-day work and any other projects they are involved in?

Finally, it is worth considering what risks are associated with this timescale. Are there any business priorities, resource issues or market conditions that may cause these timescales to be compromised? If so you need to make the audience aware of these so as not to leave yourself in the position of giving excuses at a later date.

Key question: do I know when this will be delivered and what the steps are?

Surprise

The questions you get asked at this stage will largely depend on what hasn't been covered elsewhere in your proposal. Earlier in this chapter we discussed decision makers and decision-making techniques. Those should be referred to now.

The key to a good presentation is confidence. Confidence comes from knowing that everything you are proposing is correct and difficult to challenge. If you cover all of the points mentioned in this section then you will have countered any negatives before you get to this stage – and that is vital. The perfect proposal will answer all the questions in the previous sections and leave nothing to debate, but those are rare.

Ensure you know the background behind everything you are proposing, including the financials, why the channels are being suggested, how each channel works, what the risks are, whether the resource is available, what external factors could impact your proposal and all of the other questions we have looked at.

If you know all of this then you will be able to answer with confidence all of the challenges thrown at you. The primary reason that challenges aren't answered and proposals therefore fail is lack of preparation – and for that you only have yourself to blame, so don't fall into that trap.

Advocacy

Finally, one of the most important skills you can have in any business role is relationship management. Building excellent relationships across your business ensures that your messages can be disseminated broadly without you having to run around the entire business yourself. It also means there will be greater trust behind your proposal as it will come from various sources which, when combined, will have a larger network of trusted colleagues.

Where advocacy becomes essential, however, is when you are preparing the proposal but are not actually presenting it yourself. If a colleague is talking through the presentation or writing your plan into a document you will need to ensure that they know everything you know. The other factor is that they need to demonstrate your passion. When you build a proposal you are likely to feel passionate about driving it forward, whereas if you look at someone else's proposal you are very likely to find points you don't agree with. You therefore must ensure that they are fully on your side, or elements of your proposal might be misunderstood or compromised, which would weaken the result and reflect poorly on you.

Convincing your board – a quick take away summary

- Understand your objectives: ensure you know what your decision makers want. Are you looking for growth, financial gain, brand value, investor story or another core objective? Ensure that your proposal meets that clearly.

- Know your decision makers: understand them as individuals and what their unique perspectives are. Are they highly analytical? Do they have digital marketing knowledge? This will give you an edge in convincing them that your proposal is correct. Don't look at your proposal from your perspective, look at it from theirs.

- **Know the benefits:** whatever area of digital investment you are looking at, make sure you know it inside out. Digital marketing channels, website developments, payment portals – you must know the detail of how it works, what the challenges are and how it can be implemented.

- **Challenge yourself:** when you are building the proposal and once you have finished it, stop and challenge yourself. Interrogate what you have written. Where are the gaps? Is it clear if I don't know the detail? What are my decision makers likely to disagree with?

- **Build a compelling presentation:** create a story. Make it flow naturally and summarize the key points. Make sure you pre-empt any challenges and make it punchy. Show that you understand the detail and the broader impact on the business.

- **Prepare for the challenges:** know your stuff. All of it. Build answers to the expected challenges into your presentation – don't wait for them to come at the end. Be positive and avoid getting into any arguments with your decision makers. Use data and facts to back up your response to any challenges.

- **Advocacy:** build a strong network, ensure they are in full agreement with you, know what you know and are passionate about your message. Only trust someone else to present on your behalf if they are excellent at presenting and are in complete alignment with you.

What's next?

13

Each time I finish off a book I arrive at a blank page entitled: 'future bit'. It's where I'm supposed to polish up the old crystal ball again and make some predictions for the years ahead.

Some elements of this chapter are easier to write because I don't have to rely on fact – I just have to listen to digital marketers (and usually to investors too as their actions can dictate so much) and cogitate for several months or until my publisher starts screaming at me for copy.

It can be fun too. Like my prediction a few years back that Facebook would launch their own television channel. I cringed over that for a while until the movie *The Social Network* arrived on our screens and I felt at least semi-vindicated.

In previous editions I have taken a generic, softer look at the future. My feeling at the time was not to alienate readers by talking about flying cars and teleportation (which was lucky because I haven't got a clue how to do all that)! Rather my objective was to hypothesize a few years ahead and stay within rather safe boundaries of reason and logic. In this edition, however, I want to push a bit deeper and take some flying leaps at a range of issues that are far more open to interpretation, and while not in the far distant future are better read with an open mind – and perhaps to be taken with a small pinch of salt too. After all, in the words of my great influencer Marshall McLuhan, 'I am here to explore not to explain'!

Prediction 1 – a new internet

Recently I've been mindful of the great social issues that surround and permeate the internet and have dramatic effects on the online population. In particular I'm worried about the 'threats to a free internet', but considering the level of absolute abuse the platform attracts I now wonder if we are facing the inevitability of a full circle and a return to the famous 'walled garden' approach of the mid 1990s, where publishers sought to attract and retain audience, not wanting nor expecting them to need to look elsewhere. The questions to ask are:

- What are the implications for marketers?
- Do we think it is a good thing for marketers and the business sector to support a medium that has become deeply infected by piracy?
- What do we think about 'botnets'?

Beware the botnets!

http://www.adotas.com/2014/01/mdotlabs-warns-of-threat-to-marketers-from-athena-botnet/

The very notion of advertisers being tricked by the increasing sophistication of technology to fudge ad impressions or to condone 'ad-jacking' campaigns – where ads can appear overlaid on top of other ads – all in order to charge for eyeballs reflects an increasingly suspect and 'Wild West' type environment.

Other macro issues facing marketers include content verification and ad verification – ensuring your message appears in a 'verified' place and not discovering, as Nissan did, that their pre-roll video ad appeared beside a graphic upsetting clip of a brutal murder of a Mexican woman last October.

As a father of two blossoming daughters I am only too mindful of the ongoing horror stories of children and teenagers having too-easy access to potentially destructive content too.

The sad story of 15-year-old Tallulah Wilson:

Tallulah had 18,000 friends who loved her for who she was – online. A recent inquest heard how the teenage ballerina was killed by a train just 24 hours after the deletion of her Tumblr account. Here she had created an alter ego fuelled by cocaine, drink and had engaged with self-harm discussions, images and methodology.

Would parents pay more for access if they were guaranteed the safety of content? Should ISPs and content providers be regulated or policed in some way, knowing that if they fall foul of their own promises they stand to be blocked?

Are we in fact looking at the beginnings of an alternative internet, which sets out new standards in business behaviour, content codes of ethics and is inspired to be better with technology than the pirates and black hatters who seem to be ruining the playing field for all of us, including themselves?

I predict we will see the emergence of a '*good* internet' or perhaps good is not the description. Maybe 'marketing friendly' might be better? Either way, it will be an online environment that will ultimately cost more to conduct business but presents certain standards conducive to the world of professional commerce.

Prediction 2 – democratization of marketing knowledge

I have first-hand experience of a new shift towards the democratization of digital marketing knowledge. This is happening because the pace of change and the rising appetite for this knowledge (the demand) far outweighs the traditional channels of supply. The traditional methods of 'one to many', or if you like a 'broadcast' model for the supply of knowledge, will certainly continue for many years but I predict a dramatic rise in the collaborative pursuit of knowledge and the sharing of knowledge, especially in a sometimes-elusive space like digital marketing.

This is not going to work for everyone. The traditionalists will seek to deploy traditional methodology to impart knowledge – books (like this!) sites and events will continue for years. However, others will take the plunge and deploy a more collaborative model, sharing knowledge – and set themselves apart accordingly. Our new site, **www.gogadm.com**, will certainly feature in the collaborative camp, and in fact the future of this book will ultimately be determined by the engagement and the evolution of that site.

If we assume for a second that there are over 2 million digital marketers in the world who are spending billions finding out what works and what does not work – wouldn't you rather take part in a discussion with them as opposed to listening to just what the hundreds of suppliers have to say?

I can tell you that being an 'expert' in digital marketing these days is a complete misnomer. There are certainly experts in various aspects of digital, many of them featured in this edition, but these days a writing job like mine is much more of a co-ordinator or a curator rather than an author and expert.

So prediction two – democratization leading to greater sharing of knowledge for digital marketers. Greater openness among digital marketers – but it's not for everyone.

Prediction 3 – natural selection of content

We have all heard of Darwin and his theories of natural selection. I believe the same applies to the internet and is now leading to massive investment in the content arena. This can be supported by the development of some amazing businesses around the world who are making content generation and content distribution a force with which to be reckoned. Please refer to Chapter 11 (Content marketing) in this edition.

However, what will this mean?

I think it will lead to a marketplace where two things are going to happen: first, we will see the demise of search traffic from those already connected. I don't think this will apply to the emerging markets in the same way. While people will always want to find things on Google or Bing, I believe their desire for great content – and the publishers' goal to retain audiences – will set in place a more direct relationship where search has a different role to play.

Second, I believe it will lead to greater standards of content creation and production, and major investment in the distribution and analysis of content through all platforms. The current battle for 'native marketing' is well worth an observant eye.

I think it is going to become a more expensive market for marketers because of this content investment, but the return and the engagement will be of far greater quality: consumers more engaged with better standards of content on fewer sites, regardless of platform.

The implication for media is significant. They have to become brands rather than channels. They can no longer prevaricate over whether or not they should be on mobile or on tablet – they should become agnostic about broadcast, including radio, and build their investment to engage their audience all the time and everywhere. Does it mean the end of newspapers and books and radio stations and television channels and cinemas? I think that question has already been answered. It's what works best for the consumer not the media owner – and that's the mindset that will win the process of natural selection.

Prediction 4 – greater learning and being more competitive

A recent survey by the Confederation of British Industry fell on my desk this week. It stated that their businesses need to be fluent in social media by 2020 or they will be unable to compete, but four out of five managers felt under-equipped and somewhat behind the 8 Ball when it came to digital marketing.

That is untenable. Business leaders cannot simply rely on the skills of younger folk joining their organizations to beef up their digital marketing prowess. They must take a wider and more pragmatic view across their entire business infrastructure. They will appoint digital leaders. For some time now I have talked about the ongoing hybrid of Chief Marketing Officer with Chief Information Officer to create a new type of board member – the Chief Digital Officer.

This person's role will be manifold but certainly in larger companies it will be the complete and total directive to ensure all personnel are aligned through the various media channels that exist and that they understand how the business engages with its consumers. Given that customer engagement will take place through digital channels, this person will be fluent in IT and be able to enhance and develop the relationship between two (traditionally diverse) departments. Moreover, I also see this individual taking responsibility for the company's customer data programme. We must all accept that data marketing and 'big data' are bound to form a central part of the future of marketing. Well, where does it fit? Marketing Department? Perhaps Information Technology Department? Somewhat!

My fourth prediction is great investment in company-wide learning to capture the digital opportunity and the fostering of new internal leaders who work across marketing, IT and data. My friend and constant critic (!) Martin Scovell talks not about the irrelevance of marketing and marketers, but about 'the rise of the value engineer' – a moniker that seems to make more sense by the day.

Prediction 5 – lessons from the emerging markets

In the first chapter we read about the spectacular growth of internet users. At some point in the future everyone who wants to be online will be online irrespective of their device. Perhaps a device we are yet to see? Check out the infographic – it is staggering what now happens in an internet minute: **http://www.intel.com/content/www/us/en/communications/internet-minute-infographic.html**.

We have heard from individuals such as Eric Schmidt who referenced that every two days we now create as much content as we did from the dawn of time up to 2003. That's incredibly interesting and almost makes me seasick to think about how this will change in the future. It's not just the sheer speed of the current uptake, but what really interests me is how the lessons and the experiences gleaned by the first 2 billion people online will influence how the other 5 billion people engage, or not, as the case may be! Bear in mind that the 5 billion yet to be online are coming at this from a very different angle – their markets are consistent with conflict, instability and where the governing model can often be one of autocracy.

How much more can they teach us? How will this impact the future of digital media and the future of digital marketing as a whole? My prediction is that the emerging markets will teach more to the 2 billion than we teach to them. After all, some of us will be practically digital dinosaurs by the time this occurs. We will have been online for over 20 years and most likely will have become more set in our ways and behaviours. Along comes this whole new generation who see the opportunities to compete and will contribute vibrant business models, new levels of competition and hopefully embrace a new collaborative and openness when it comes to the online world. Of course not all countries have the freedom online that is consistent with the Western world, but there again they don't have to concern themselves too much right now with privacy and whether their online behaviour is in fact the basis of surveillance by greater powers!

My prediction is that the emerging markets and their sheer strength in numbers will teach the 2 billion of us a thing or two ! Not the other way round.

Prediction 6 – the case for a circular marketing economy...

According to Wikipedia: the generic circular economy label can be applied to, and claimed by, several different schools of thought that all gravitate around the same basic principles, which they have refined in different ways. The idea itself, which is centred on taking insights from living systems, is hardly a new one and hence cannot be traced back to one precise date or author, yet its practical applications to modern economic systems and industrial processes have gained momentum since the late 1970s, giving birth to four prominent movements, detailed below. The idea of circular material flows as a model for the economy was presented in 1966 by Kenneth E Boulding in his paper 'The Economics of the Coming Spaceship Earth'. Promoting a circular economy was identified as national policy in China's 11th five-year plan starting in 2006. The Ellen MacArthur Foundation, an independent charity established in 2010, has more recently outlined the economic opportunity of a circular economy. As part of its educational mission, the foundation has worked to bring together complementary schools of thought and create a coherent framework, thus giving the concept a wide exposure and appeal. The four movements of the circular economy are:

- **Waste is food:** waste does not exist... the biological and technical components (nutrients) of a product are designed by intention to fit within a materials cycle, designed for disassembly and repurposing. The biological nutrients are non-toxic and can be simply composted. Technical nutrients – polymers, alloys and other man-made materials – are designed to be used again with minimal energy.

- **Diversity is strength:** modularity, versatility and adaptiveness are to be prioritized in an uncertain and fast-evolving world. Diverse systems, with many connections and scales, are more resilient in the face of external shocks, than systems built simply for efficiency.

- **Energy must come from renewable sources:** as in life, any system should ultimately aim to run on 'current sunshine' and generate energy through renewable sources.

- **Systems thinking:** the ability to understand how things influence one another within a whole. Elements are considered as 'fitting in' their infrastructure, environment and social context. Whilst a machine is also a system, systems thinking usually refers to non-linear systems: systems where through feedback and imprecise starting conditions the outcome is not necessarily proportional to the input and where evolution of the system is possible – the system can display emergent properties. Examples of these systems are all living systems and any open system, such as meteorological systems or ocean currents, even the orbits of the planets, have non-linear characteristics.

So how does this apply to digital marketers?

I predict that the implications of a circular economy around product or service provision will evolve from being a 'nice to have' to become an absolute necessity. I see a short future ahead for the wasteful marketer. I see a growing intolerance for stupid packaging and an expectation of the recycling of old products. The consumption of energy and power in order for marketers to compete will become more transparent and open to feedback and engagement with consumers. Marketers will offer consumers more options regarding waste factors, perhaps even opening up more revenue streams as a result, where brand and consumer can truly collaborate on the wider implications of this whole question. Ultimately, I believe the reputation of future marketers will be scored on several factors – with 'circular' being high on the agenda.

Prediction 7 – agencies go arbitrage

If you've seen the recent movie offering by Martin Scorsese, *The Wolf of Wall Street* (which I bet will be referenced for years to come), you'll get an idea of what it looked like for brokers to be confronted with an arbitrage model, and where commission didn't seem to make much of a difference or get in the way of a good transaction. Ultimately their role was to make as much margin as possible, regardless of the stock and with absolutely nothing but disdain for the investor. Some people will say things haven't changed much in the world of finance!

From a marketing point of view I think this model is going to become far more prevalent than ever. For some marketers it is okay to accept all the risk. It's their business, their consumer and their data. If they're happy to spend 10 per cent of revenue on marketing in order to generate more orders then so be it. However, for others the ongoing development of technology, access to newer and wider markets and the availability of qualified, knowledgeable digital marketers will lead directly to a new wave of arbitrage-based agencies where risk is shared or negated in favour of practical and profitable division of revenue. Much in the same way that the Wall Street lot would absorb the risk of selling stock and divide the spoils, the same will apply to agencies but in an even greater way. This is not a new idea but it's one that is constantly evolving and I predict will play a major role in the development of new markets. Think of this: you're a marketer. You are used to getting approaches from all kinds of areas offering you everything from advertising space to access to a new database of potential customers. The balance of risk is absorbed by you. Or you take part in a performance marketing campaign (see Chapter 9) and the risk is mitigated by the sharing of revenue – that makes sense, right?

But take it up another gear: You are approached by a team of expert digital marketers who can offer you US $2.50 each for a consignment of 5,000 widgets. Their only stipulation is that they own the customer data and you agree to no conflicting marketing activity in their chosen region. It's informal, it's a quick win and it's tempting... Would you do it? The same team approach you to modify the product and stay out of their region for another 10 years, guaranteeing you the same price point and minimum orders throughout that term.

A lot of this stuff is already going on across hundreds of industry sectors and it's called a whole host of names (joint ventures, trading deals, franchises, licences etc) – but where is the value going to be? What represents the crown jewels in this equation? Either way I predict we will see a massive increase in the number of agnostic agencies deploying their unique set of digital marketing skills on an arbitrage basis. Not for leads or prospects but for actual revenue share or ownership. I see the emergence of this trend from emerging markets because I believe the opportunity to share risk will be too great for some digital marketers to resist.

Prediction 8 – fast and super fast

Great news for all those speed freaks out there. The world record for the fastest-ever broadband speed of 1.4 terabits per second has been recorded. This took place in early 2014 in a test between London and Ipswich conducted by BT and Alcatel-Lucent. Apparently that's enough oomph to download 44 high-definition movies per second – or you could snaffle the entire catalogue of the British Library four times in one minute! To put this in perspective (if that's possible) this is about 800,000 times faster than typical broadband today. Just imagine the implications of these types of speeds for digital marketers! So what's the prediction?

As the market for digital display media becomes more commoditized and brands have to compete harder for attention, I think these types of speed will lend themselves to a new renaissance in digital creativity, with agencies and advertisers seeking out more immersive forms of engagement using new devices and technologies that are probably still on the drawing board. I have always been a big fan of augmented reality and how that can be used to sell products or services, but we need to push ourselves further to realize the full power of what these types of speeds represent.

Another movie for you to watch here is *Surrogates* (2009) – a bit dated now but a fun look at the future and what technology could achieve. Set in the future it depicts a landscape where people choose to live their lives through an avatar, being the people they want to be in a completely safe environment where they cannot die or be hurt.

However, let's stay in the world of digital marketing. The implications for super-fast speeds will bring about increased investment in the creative experience. It will revolutionize the consumption of entertainment and shopping, perhaps moving beyond the screen and into a whole room-sized experience – and I think represent huge considerations for the travel and leisure industry. Why go to the gym when it can come to you? Bring on the holodecks!

Prediction 9 – radio

Wasn't video supposed to kill the radio star?

Ladies and gentlemen, I think we are about to see a complete rebirth of the radio. And from a marketing standpoint I think this could be one of the most exciting areas in the years ahead. No longer will we be bothered by the need to distinguish one wavelength over another – FM, AM, do we really care? I don't think most of us do – however, many will argue that the quality of sound via DAB sets suggests an important trend here. There has, of course, been a complete blurring of the lines in recent years already. Spotify, Pandora, Last FM and the continued rise of online radio and the integration of visual signals and effects into the delivery of sound (Soundcloud) have made for a gradual and ongoing evolution of the medium. It's a medium that also has been around for a long time now and I don't think is showing any signs of abatement. So what will change?

Personalization – where Apple helped ordinary folk to become publishers back in the early 1990s, YouTube and others have empowered us to become our own movie directors – I see the same explosion just waiting to happen with radio. Playlists are one thing and I absolutely adore sites such as GrooveShark etc, but it can go further. I refer of course to the monetization of this movement by advertisers and marketers.

Simply put, if your audience is online and listening to radio then you should be there too. If that radio stream is coming from Australia and your consumer target is in Dublin then... well, the rest is obvious right?

My ninth prediction is a boom in the online audio sector. Marketers will find new and interesting ways to engage with radio audiences, regardless of the origin of the content and the location of the consumer. Personalization plays a significant role here for all the stakeholders. Will marketers seek to empower consumers to share their music and build fan bases? *Yes*.

Prediction 10 – your online persona

This is the final prediction for this edition. It's usually where I throw in something completely out of leftfield! I had wanted to talk about the replacement of window-cleaning companies with robots but couldn't really think of a plausible angle for digital marketers! Instead a quick word about one's online persona.

Some people have a completely different online profile depending on the platform on which this is delivered, and that puzzles me – I do it myself and am starting to wonder why!

On LinkedIn people are seeking to maintain a certain gravitas in support of their careers and jobs. No problem with that, but then on Facebook they present a completely different profile featuring an interesting, fun-seeking life and lots of friends.

Twitter changes it again, as people are infinitely more opinionated on this medium. No bad thing there. In fact, depending on the online environment or platform, people seem automatically required to adjust their persona to fit the medium. I know McLuhan would have had a field day with this! The medium has most certainly become the message (or the massage). And I think that's got the potential to go horribly wrong. If the medium is in fact the message, then do we all get painted with the same brush through supporting this medium and being a small part of its overall content?

But having multipersonalities online – is this sustainable? The more I think about it the more I feel it lacks consistency. Or perhaps people don't want consistency and want to have six or seven different personalities online? It just sounds so exhausting and so untenable that I wonder if this is in fact just how people are reacting now in 2014?

So my final prediction is that in the future people will seek to have one online persona that reflects who they really are. I think it would be rather unnatural if this persona did not include their social life, their family life, their opinions, their messages, their work and all the various areas of their life – and be presented in one cohesive, consistent manner. Now they may go off, grab a surrogate and be someone completely different (!) when it suits them, but building their reputation, creating a real profile for themselves and importantly being their *own* social network is, I believe, just around the corner.

The end bit

Thanks again for reading this book. I cannot say enough about how much help and inspiration I have received from the many people who contributed along the way. My thanks to them is included in the acknowledgements section in the front of the book – please check them out because they really deserve as much kudos and ROI as possible!

Out of the five books I have authored to date this has easily been the most difficult. It has represented a significant departure from the last edition and I believe totals about 50 per cent more words too. That increase is purely consistent with the advances in digital marketing and the changing world around us.

My hope is that you have received at least *one* good idea from reading this book, which will help you become more successful in your careers. Good luck and thanks again!

CASE STUDY   UEFA Europa League

Market

Europe.

The challenge

Despite UEFA's reputation, football fans were relatively uninformed about and unengaged with the Europa League, which was established in its current format in 2009. Feedback showed that many football fans found the competition to be too large and, with 32 teams taking part, the tournament did not reflect the elite of European football.

Dog Digital worked with UEFA and decided to present a 'more' strategy that celebrated the expansive reach of the Europa League. Together they would show that the tournament offered more cities, more venues, more teams, more fans and more adventure. This turned the perceived negative of the tournament into a unique selling proposition of the event to:

- Build awareness of the UEFA Europa League competition and the clubs involved.

- Acquire new Facebook Fans over the four-month campaign period.

- Increase awareness of the dates and timelines of upcoming games.

- Build UEFA's e-mail database by 15,000 names.

- Engage fans and encourage them to interact with the UEFA brand.

- Drive traffic to the UEFA.com website.

Target audience

Football fans across Europe.

Action

- To build awareness of the UEFA Europa League and the clubs involved, the clear strategy was to grow the Facebook fan base with relevant fans. This was to be achieved by targeting with advertising the fans of the 32 teams involved in the Europa League games.

- Distributing bespoke Facebook landing pages that gave specific information regarding the UEFA Europa League to the 32 clubs as well as the broadcasters and other partners would help drive fan acquisition.

facebook

Search

UEFA Europa League 👍 Like

UEFA·com

UEFA
EUROPA
LEAGUE

presented by

SEAT

Wall
Info
Be part of our mosaic
Videos
Events
Games
Respect
Photos

About

The UEFA Europa League is European club football's second club competition....
More

115,190
like this

1,770
talking about this

Likes   See all

UEFA Champions League

UEFA.com

UEFA Under-21 Championship 2011

UEFA Training Ground

UEFA EURO 2012

Create a Page
Add to my page's favourites
Get updates via RSS
Report Page
Share

UEFA·com

UEFA
EUROPA
LEAGUE

Adventure #1 Round of 32

More fans
More adventures

WIN 1,000 UEFA.com iPhone app video centre passes to be won

Add your profile photo to our Facebook fan mosaic and show you are a supporter of European adventures. Do it now and you could **WIN** one of 1,000 vouchers for premium access to the UEFA.com iPhone app video centre, including UEFA Europa League highlights.

Add me +   **Find** me

Patent pending

More adventures **More** fans **More** cities
More memories **More** skills....**One** trophy

- Advertising the Facebook page via display banners on the clubs, broadcasters and partners, would drive traffic to and 'likes' of the Facebook page.

- The Europa League was scheduled to take place weekly at the same time and on the same day, so making fans aware of these times and when games were played was important. All match schedule information was to be posted regularly in the Facebook page.

- Encouraging interaction from all fans of a truly pan-European competition was to be achieved by the translation of all posts into eight languages.

- Producing a full content plan that used a variety of posts with fresh content would ensure engagement with the competition and the UEFA brand. As posting to the Facebook page was to be managed simultaneously by UEFA and Dog Digital staff, the content plan would be essential to ensure best practice in terms of content and timing.

- Further engagement was to be achieved with five customized apps throughout the competition's campaign. Tied in with each of the competition's knockout phases each app was to encourage users to participate by offering incentives and prizes, enticing participants to remain engaged even if their team was knocked out of the competition.

- Using premium ads and sponsored stories would highlight content and drive fans to the UEFA apps.

- The invitation to use the five Facebook apps would also serve as an e-mail collection tool to grow the size of the UEFA e-mail database.

- All informational posts and news items that fed through from the UEFA.com website would also include a link back to the UEFA website. Hyperlinks would lead them to specific content with related content links being displayed. This would ensure that visitors were more likely to stay engaged and find information that they are most interested in.

Pages

- The branding colours and logos of UEFA was applied to the visuals of the Facebook page.

- A fan gate was implemented so that targeted messages could be sent to those who had already liked the page and those who hadn't.

- Fans saw a whole world of UEFA football, including competitions, apps, and club and fixture information.

- Non-fans saw an overview of the content of the site and there was a focus on prizes that could be won through promotions and competitions. This was intended to incentivize 'liking' the page.

Content

- Dog Digital helped to create a detailed content schedule that ensured that a variety of posts were regularly sent to UEFA's vast fan base, featuring information, links, match photos and UEFA videos. As content was added by both UEFA and Dog Digital, a full schedule ensured these were sent in a timely manner. Posts peaked around match days when fans were most engaged and likely to interact with the Facebook page.

- Posting was controlled according to content, that is, UEFA.com handled football-specific posts and Dog Digital handled apps, competitions and general engagement.

- Club and fixture information was pulled in from UEFA.com XML feed, providing fresh content for Facebook fans without need for UEFA internal resource.

- Aware that images included with posts delivered best engagement, Dog Digital sourced and resized images from UEFA.com library to accompany many of its posts – this provided optimal results in terms of Facebook engagement.

- All posts were translated into eight different languages.

- UEFA employed Facebook's language- and location-targeting tool to guarantee that people only received relevant content in their own language.

- To ensure that posts from fans were suitable for family viewing, they were moderated with both automatic conditions (including the exclusion of swear words and racism, for example) as well as manual moderation. This ensured best practice and adherence to the UEFA style guide, and its moral and social principles.

Apps

Interactive apps were released with each of the five knockout stages of the competition. As per the strategy, the apps were designed to engage all fans throughout the competition, even if their team had been knocked out. They were designed to use almost every aspect of the social experience with geolocating, photo uploading, fan voting and messaging all part of the content.

- Round of 32 – More Fans: Social Mosaic app
  - This was a giant UEFA Europa League photograph mosaic, generated from the profile pictures of 10,000 fans.
  - Fans connected to an app that allowed them to add a message of support for their team and pulled their profile photo into the mosaic.
  - This app was made in collaboration with Hashtag Art.
  - Incentive: 1,000 UEFA.com video-centre vouchers.

- Round of 16 – More Cities: Light up Europe app
  - This app requested permission to view the location of the user and a pin was dropped on a map of Europe of their location. This was visualized by

a light igniting in the correct place and fans could see their light ignite and also which parts of Europe were most lit up with Europa League fans.

- Incentive: the chance to win an official UEFA Europa League ball.

- Quarterfinals – More Memories: Photo Upload app
    - Fans were encouraged to upload their own photographs from the Europa League to a fan album and were also given the opportunity to vote for their favourite photographs.
    - Incentive: top four photographs won official UEFA Europa League merchandise bundles.

- Semi-finals – One Trophy: Trophy Hunt app
    - In this app, the fan mosaic from the first round was revisited. Hidden in the 10,000 tile mosaic was a single tile with a photo of the UEFA Europa League Trophy. Finding this tile and clicking on it revealed a code that was needed to enter a prize draw.
    - Incentive: the opportunity to win a trip for two to the UEFA Europa League final.

- Final – More Skills: Facebook Fan's Favourite app
    - This app invited fans to vote for the player they wanted to crown as the Facebook Fan's Favourite.
    - Incentive: the chance to win an official match ball used in the final.

Each of the apps utilized the Facebook Connect Service and went through a strict sign-off process to ensure that they complied with UEFA's terms and conditions and legal compliances. For example, the apps used viral aspects such as posting on user's walls, but never without gaining permission beforehand, ensuring fans' privacy. All apps also had both automatic and manual moderation to uphold the UEFA brand and style guide.

As mentioned above, incentives to take part in the apps included 1,000 UEFA. com video-centre vouchers, the chance to win an official UEFA Europa League ball, Europa League merchandise bundles, the opportunity to win a trip for two to the UEFA Europa League final and the chance to win an official match ball used in the final.

Ads

To drive traffic to the Facebook page and its apps, UEFA capitalized on Facebook's full suite of advertising options, including premium ads and sponsored stories. Over 1,000 advert variations were created and ran over the course of the campaign. To maximize the impact of its extensive ad campaigns, UEFA:

- Used Facebook's enhanced targeting option to create ads tailored to the fans of each of the 32 clubs in the competition, and ensured that the customized ads were only sent to those fans.

- Posted sponsored stories featuring the names of fans who had interacted with an app to the fan's friends – this proved to be the most effective tactic in gaining additional fans, vastly extending the campaign's reach.

- Generated a large selection of ad creative and copy, ensuring that fans constantly received fresh, engaging content.

In addition to Facebook advertising, hundreds of flash banners were also designed and distributed for participating clubs, broadcasters and partners. These were displayed on their websites and linked back to the Europa League Facebook page.

Results

The Facebook campaign was hugely successful. It not only met all of the campaign objectives but surpassed all targets in terms of fan acquisition, awareness of the Europa League and engagement with the UEFA brand. Using the social media metric dashboards of Facebook Insights, the following statistics were gathered:

- The UEFA Europa League Facebook fan base grew from 160,000 to 750,000 in less than 90 days.

- Over 300,000 fans were generated from Facebook adverts alone with an overall CPA of just £0.22.

- Almost 75,000 users interacted with the apps, providing further data capture of over 40,000 e-mail addresses.

- There were over 1 billion ad impressions during the course of the three-month campaign.

- Engagement with the Facebook page was also successful, with the 'Talking About This' statistics reaching over 100,000.

- Some applications experienced a dwell time of over 15 minutes.

- Hundreds of thousands of users clicked through to UEFA.com, including to the premium Live Match Streaming service.

- The UEFA Europa League Facebook campaign was an unprecedented success. Marrying up the social nature of an international sporting tournament and the social platform of Facebook seemed a natural marketing decision, but a real challenge remained because of the sheer scale of the competition and the diversity of the fan base.

- Not only did the competition's fan base grow massively over the campaign, and 40,000 valuable e-mail addresses collected, UEFA and Dog Digital successfully overcame the challenges of the vast audience engagement by employing all of Facebook's tools in an intelligent way.

- Targeting clubs with bespoke advertising and utilizing geolocation and translation tools ensured that different national groups and fan groups received communications – in their home languages and about topics that were most important to them.

- The branding and content plan used by both UEFA and Dog Digital ensured a variety of fresh content. Similarly, the apps used nearly all of the different social functions that Facebook APIs offer. This meant that fans always had the opportunity to take part in something to their preference – for example, if a fan didn't like the idea of uploading a photograph, there was still an opportunity to take part in other rounds.

- Arguably, the biggest success of the campaign was the tangible benefits that fans received for 'liking' the Europa League page. The Facebook page was not solely a sales or informational tool. Passion was rewarded with valuable prizes – and fan engagement statistics from Facebook reflected this.

Lessons

- **Competition:** the essence of sport is competition, and that clearly translates to social media. The apps that Dog Digital built that had a competitive element to them were the best-performing in terms of numbers and engagement levels. Fans do not want to directly support UEFA or even football in general, they are passionate about their team and will interact around that more than anything else. For example, the 'Fans' Favourite' app allowed supporters to pick their player of the tournament. This was by far the most popular app, as users were able to get behind their team and star player, something they did in their tens of thousands. There was also a significant viral effect as the particularly passionate supporters shared the app in order to drum-up support for their favourite players across social media, forums, message boards and blogs.

- **Partners:** Dog Digital provided a partner toolkit to UEFA Europa League clubs, sponsors and partners to expand the reach at the outset of the campaign. This included custom Facebook pages, multilingual banners and e-mail newsletter designs. There was a low expectation for usage of this toolkit, as clubs and partners tend to have their own marketing materials. However, the uptake was positive, bringing vast levels of exposure to the campaign. In hindsight, we should have capitalized on this by providing more content and creative to the stakeholders throughout the campaign rather than only initially.

- **Quick 'touchpoints':** rather than doing this differently, the campaign really underlined our thinking that fans will only engage in quick social 'touchpoints', rather than long drawn-out activities spanning several weeks or months. We deliberately made the apps independent of each other, allowing fans to interact only with the ones that interested them. We were fully aware that fans like and use hundreds of other pages and apps, and so ours were designed to produce rewards quickly, not requiring much in the way of time or effort from the user.

Links to campaign

- https://www.facebook.com/uefaeuropaleague

- http://www.dogdigital.com/case-studies/uefa

Comment

Jon Walsh, co-founder and commercial director @OneCentralPoint, has been on the digital media scene since 1999 and worked on behalf of media owners large and small to drive advertising revenue. Since 2004, Jon has been building third-party digital media sales houses – the most successful and well known being Monetise, which was later sold to Glam Media. Jon's current focus is One Central Point – the world's only truly global, premium digital-media sales house, representing the best websites around the world and helping advertisers to run multinational campaigns with ease:

> *Bravo to UEFA and Dog Digital! In the 14 years that I have been involved in digital media, I find it hard to recollect such a well-planned and carefully nurtured campaign as this. From the simple understanding that when running international campaigns, localization and translation is crucial for an advertiser to connect with their desired audience, to the freshness of the content updates, and the simple 'stages' element of the campaign to carry it through from start to finish of the competition. Virtually (no pun intended) no stones have been left unturned. However, if I was being really hard on them, I would have liked to see a level of presence on more independent football websites too – this would have the effect of taking the Europa League conversation to a wider audience, but would have seen a slightly higher CPA overall. I would also be interested to see the Facebook statistics for 'UEFA' or 'Europa League' being mentioned in user status updates.*

I would implore more agencies and clients to take a deep look at not 'what', but 'how' this campaign was created, and how all stakeholders took responsibility for the overall success of what was achieved.

About the creator

Dog Digital: a creative agency with offices in London, Glasgow and Singapore. Established in 1996, they now have over 70 specialists. They create 21st-century communications for businesses and organizations by using the very latest technologies to spread good old-fashioned ideas.

Creative biography

Mark Elder, head of design at Dog Digital: Mark has been working in design for over 16 years. He started as a graphic designer working mainly on print material in the late 1990s, before being introduced to the world of digital. He loves working in the ever-changing online world, and is very proud of the hugely successful UEFA Europa League campaign that Dog Digital produced.

Credits

Finalist in the CIM Marketing Excellence Awards 2013 and the MiAwards 2012.

Quote

Dejah Meldem, digital marketing manager, UEFA, said:

Communicating to and engaging the multinational audience of the Europa League was a significant challenge for UEFA. We are absolutely delighted with the UEFA Europa League 2011–12 Facebook campaign that Dog Digital managed on our behalf. We were impressed with Dog's vision, analysis of our needs and technical knowledge using social media. After the success of this campaign, Facebook will continue to play a key part in our future marketing and PR strategy.

GLOSSARY

Throughout the book we've avoided technical jargon wherever possible and have tried to present information in plain, clear English. Where specific digital marketing terminology was unavoidable we provided a brief definition in the text itself. To supplement the definitions in the text and to give you a handy reference for digital marketing terms, we've included the following glossary, reproduced here with permission from the UK's Internet Advertising Bureau (**www.iabuk.net**).

abandon   When a user does not complete a transaction.

ad impression   An advertisement impression transpires each time a consumer is exposed to an advertisement (either appended to an SMS or MMS message, on mobile web (WAP) page, within a video clip, or related media).

ad serving   Delivery of online adverts to an end user's computer by an ad management system. The system allows different online adverts to be served in order to target different audience groups and can serve adverts across multiple sites. Ad technology providers each have their own proprietary models for this.

ad unit   Any defined advertising vehicle that can appear in an ad space inside of an application. For example for the purposes of promoting a commercial brand, product or service.

advertiser   Also called merchant, retailer, e-retailer, or online retailer. Any website that sells a product or service, accepts payments, and fulfils orders. An advertiser places ads and links to their products and services on other websites (publishers) and pays those publishers a commission for leads or sales that result from their site.

affiliate marketing   An affiliate (a website owner or publisher) displays an advertisement (such as a banner or link) on its site for a merchant (the brand or advertiser). If a consumer visiting the affiliate's site clicks on this advertisement and goes on to perform a specified action (usually a purchase) on an advertiser's site then the affiliate receives a commission.

algorithm   The set of 'rules' a search engine may use to determine the relevance of a web page (and therefore ranking) in its organic search results. See also *organic search results* and *search engine optimization.*

application service provider (ASP)   An online network that is accessible through the internet instead of through the installation of software. It is quickly integrated with other websites and the services are easily implemented and scalable.

avatar   A picture or cartoon used to represent an individual in chat forums, games or on a website as a help function.

bandwidth   The transmission rate of a communication line – usually measured in kilobytes per second (kbps). This relates to the amount of data that can be carried per second by your internet connection. See also *broadband.*

banner   A long, horizontal, online advert usually found running across the top of a page in a fixed placement. See also *universal advertising package, embedded format.*

BARB Broadcasters' Audience Research Board is responsible for the measurement of TV viewing.

behavioural targeting A form of online marketing that uses advertising technology to target web users based on their previous behaviour. Advertising creative and content can be tailored to be of more relevance to a particular user by capturing their previous decision making behaviour (eg: filling out preferences or visiting certain areas of a site frequently) and looking for patterns.

blog An online space regularly updated presenting the opinions or activities of one or a group of individuals and displaying in chronological order.

broadband An internet connection that is always on and that delivers a higher bit rate (128 kbps or above) than a standard dial-up connection. It allows for a better online experience as pages load quickly and you can download items faster.

buffering When a streaming media player saves portions of file until there is enough information for the file to begin playing.

button A square online advert usually found embedded within a website page. See also *universal advertising package, embedded format*.

cache memory Used to store web pages you have seen already. When you go back to those pages they'll load more quickly because they come from the cache and don't need to be downloaded over the internet again.

call to action (CTA) A statement or instruction, typically promoted in print, web, TV, radio, on-portal, or other forms of media (often embedded in advertising), that explains to a mobile subscriber how to respond to an opt-in for a particular promotion or mobile initiative, which is typically followed by a notice (see *notice*).

click-through When a user interacts with an advertisement and clicks through to the advertiser's website.

click-through rate (CTR) Frequency of click-throughs as a percentage of impressions served. Used as a measure of advertising effectiveness.

click to call A service that enables a mobile subscriber to initiate a voice call to a specified phone number by clicking on a link on a mobile internet site. Typically used to enhance and provide a direct response mechanism in an advertisement.

commission An amount of income received by a publisher for some quantifiable action such as selling an advertiser's product and/or service on the publisher's website.

content sponsorship Advertiser sponsorships of content areas (eg entire website, home page or a specific channel) to include the total value of the package including any embedded or interruptive formats. This category also includes revenue related to e-mail advertising or prioritized listing of results in search engines that are included as part of the sponsorship deal.

contextual advertising Advertising that is targeted to the content on the web page being viewed by a user at that specific time.

conversion rate Measure of success of an online ad when compared to the click-through rate. What defines a 'conversion' depends on the marketing objective, eg: it can be defined as a sale or request to receive more information, etc.

cookie A small text file on the user's PC that identifies the user's browser and hence the user so they are 'recognized' when they re-visit a site, eg: it allows usernames to be stored and websites to personalize their offering.

cost per acquisition (CPA) Cost to acquire a new customer.

cost per action (CPA) A pricing model that only charges advertising on an action being conducted, eg a sale or a form being filled in.

cost per click (CPC)   The amount paid by an advertiser for a click on their sponsored search listing. See also *PPC*.

cost per mille (CPM)/cost per thousand (CPT)   Online advertising can be purchased on the basis of what it costs to show the ad to 1,000 viewers (CPM). It is used in marketing as a benchmark to calculate the relative cost of an advertising campaign or an ad message in a given medium. Rather than an absolute cost, CPM estimates the cost per 1,000 views of the ad. (Wikipedia definition)

CRM   Customer relationship management.

deep-linking advert   Linking beyond a home page to a page inside the site with content pertinent to the advert.

display advertising on e-mail   Advertising that appears around the unrelated editorial content of e-mail newsletters. This can take the form of embedded formats like banners, or as sponsorship, and includes both opt-in (sent to customers specifically requesting it) and opt-out (sent to customers with the option to be removed at their request) e-mails.

domain name   The unique name of an internet site, eg **www.iabuk.net**.

downloading   the technology that allows users to store video content on their computer for viewing at a later date. Downloading an entire piece of media makes it more susceptible to illegal duplication.

D2C   Direct to consumer.

DRM   Digital rights management is a set of technologies used by publishers and media owners to control access to their digital content. Access can be limited to the number of times a piece of content is accessed from a single machine or user account; the number of times access permissions can be passed on; or the lifespan of a piece of content.

dynamic ad delivery   Based upon predetermined criteria, dynamic ad delivery is the process by which a mobile advertisement is delivered, via a campaign management platform, to a publisher's mobile content.

e-commerce (electronic commerce)   Business that takes place over electronic platforms, such as the internet.

e-mail bounced   Those e-mails sent as part of a mailing distribution which did not have a valid recipient e-mail address and so generated a formal failure message. (ABC Electronic jargon buster definition)

electronic programme guide (EPG)   The electronic version of a television schedule showing programme times and content on the television screen or monitor. In the case of VOD, an EPG displays the content of all of the services available to a subscriber.

embedded format   Advertising formats that are displayed in set spaces on a publisher's page. See also *banner, skyscraper, button*.

emoticons   Emoticon symbols are used to indicate mood in an electronic mode of communication, eg e-mail or instant messenger. :-)

encoding   The conversion of an analogue signal to a digital format.

EPC (average earnings per one hundred clicks)   A relative rating that illustrates the ability to convert clicks into commissions. It is calculated by taking commissions earned (or commissions paid) divided by the total number of clicks times 100.

expandable banner/skyscraper   Fixed online advertising placements that expand over the page in the response to user action, eg mouseover. See also *rich media*.

firewall software   Provides security for a computer or local network by preventing unauthorized access. It sits as a barrier between the web and your computer in order to prevent hacking, viruses or unapproved data transfer.

flash   Web design software that creates animation and interactive elements which are quick to download.

flash impression   The total number of requests made for pages holding flash-based content by users of that site in the period being measured. (ABC Electronic jargon buster definition)

geotargeting   The process of only showing adverts to people on a website and in search engines based on their physical location. This could be done using advanced technology that knows where a computer is located or by using the content of the website to determine what a person is looking for, eg someone searching for a restaurant in Aylesbury, Buckinghamshire.

GPRS   General Packet Radio Service or '2.5G' is an underlying mechanism for the networks to deliver internet browsing, WAP, e-mail and other such content. The user is 'always connected' and relatively high data rates can be achieved with most modern phones compared to a dial-up modem. Most phones default to using GPRS (if capable), and Incentivated is able to develop services that utilize this delivery mechanism.

graphic banners   A graphic mobile ad represented by a banner featuring an image. Similar to a web banner but with lower size constraints. (See *banner*.)

GSM   Global Standard for Mobiles. The set of standards covering one particular type of mobile phone system.

hit   A single request from a web browser for a single item from a web server.

hot spotting   The ability to add hyperlinks to objects in a video that enable viewers to tag a product or service. Hot spotting can be used as a direct response mechanic in internet video.

HTML   Stands for HyperText Markup Language, which is the set of commands used by web browsers to interpret and display page content to users. (ABC Electronic jargon buster definition)

image ad   An image on a mobile internet site with an active link that can be clicked on by the subscriber. Once clicked the user is redirected to a new page, another mobile internet site or other destination where an offer resides.

impressions   The metric used to measure views of a web page and its elements – including the advertising embedded within it. Ad impressions are how most online advertising is sold and the cost is quoted in terms of the cost per thousand impressions (CPM).

instant messaging   Sending messages and chatting with friends or colleagues in real time when you are both online via a special application.

Integrated Services Digital Network (ISDN)   High-speed dial-up connections to the internet over normal phone lines.

Internet Protocol TV (IPTV)   The use of a broadband connection to stream digital television over the internet to subscribed users.

internet service provider (ISP)   A company which provides users with the means to connect to the internet. Eg: AOL, Tiscali, Yahoo!

interruptive formats   Online advertising formats that appear on users' screens on top of web content (and sometimes before the web page appears) and range from static, one-page splash screens to full-motion animated advertisements. See also *overlay, pop-up*.

interstitial ads   Which appear between two content pages. Also known as splash pages and transition ads. See also *rich media*.

IPA   Institute of Practitioners in Advertising is the trade body representing advertising agencies in the UK.

IP address   The numerical internet address assigned to each computer on a network so that it can be distinguished from other computers. Expressed as four groups of numbers separated by dots.

keyword marketing   The purchase of keywords (or 'search terms') by advertisers in search listings. See also *PPC*.

LAN (local area network)   A group of computers connected together, which are at one physical location.

landing page (jump page)   The page or view to which a user is directed when they click on an active link embedded in a banner, web page, e-mail or other view. A click-through lands the user on a jump page. Sometimes the landing page is one stage upstream from what would ordinarily be considered the home page.

lead   When a visitor registers, signs up for, or downloads something on an advertiser's site. A lead might also comprise a visitor filling out a form on an advertiser's site.

link   A link is a form of advertising on a website, in an e-mail or online newsletter, which, when clicked on, refers the visitor to an advertiser's website or a specific area within their website.

location-based services (LBS)   A range of services that are provided to mobile subscribers based on the geographical location of their handsets within their cellular network. Handsets do not have to be equipped with a position-location technology such as GPS to enable the geographical trigger of service(s) being provided since the location of the cell-site can be used as a proxy. Assisted GPS combines cell-site information with satellite positioning for a more accurate read. LBS include driving directions, information about certain resources or destinations within the current vicinity, such as restaurants, ATMs, shopping, movie theatres, etc. LBS may also be used to track the movements and locations of people, as is being done via parent/child monitoring services and mobile devices that target the family market.

locator   An advertisement or service through which an advertiser's bricks-and-mortar location can be identified based on proximity of the consumer or their preferred location (can be LBS or user-defined postal code).

log files   A record of all the hits a web server has received over a given period of time.

meta-tags/-descriptions   HTML tags that identify the content of a web page for the search engines.

micro-site   A sub-site reached via clicking on an ad. The user stays on the publisher's website but has access to more information from the advertiser.

MMA   The Mobile Marketing Association (MMA) is the premier global non-profit association that strives to stimulate the growth of mobile marketing and its associated technologies. The MMA is an action-oriented association designed to clear obstacles to market development, to establish standards and best practices for sustainable growth, and to evangelize the mobile channel for use by brands and third-party content providers. The MMA has over 500 members representing 40-plus countries.

mobile data services   Includes SMS, MMS, WAP, LBS and video.

mobile internet advertising   A form of advertising via mobile phones or other wireless devices (excluding laptops). This type of mobile advertising includes mobile web banner ads, mobile internet sponsorship and interstitials (which appear while a requested mobile web page is loading) as well as mobile paid-for search listings. Mobile internet advertising does not include other forms of mobile marketing such as SMS, MMS and shortcode.

MP3   A computer file format that compresses audio files up to a factor of 12 from a .wav file.

MPEG   File format used to compress and transmit video clips online.

MSISDN   Mobile Subscriber Integrated Services Digital Network. The mobile phone number of the participating customer.

multiple purpose units (MPU)   A square online advert usually found embedded in a web page in a fixed placement. Called 'multiple purpose' as it is a flexible-shaped blank 'canvas' in which you can serve flat or more interactive content as desired. See also *rich media, universal advertising package*.

natural search results   The 'natural' search results that appear in a separate section (usually the main body of the page) to the paid listings. The results listed here have not been paid for and are ranked by the search engine (using spiders or algorithms according to relevancy to the term searched upon). See also *spider, algorithm, SEO*.

notice   An easy-to-understand written description of the information and data collection, storage, maintenance, access, security, disclosure and use policies and practices, as necessary and required of the entity collecting and using the information and data from the mobile subscriber.

NVOD   Near video on demand service is the delivery of film and television programming from a server via a cable network or the internet. Like VOD these services are nonlinear and navigated via an EPG. Programming must be downloaded and the majority of existing services require the same amount of time to download as the duration of the selected programme.

OB   Outside broadcast unit known as a 'production truck'. In the United States an OB unit is a truck containing a mobile TV production studio.

off-portal   Point of sale/access on the mobile network, but outside of the operator's 'walled garden'/portal/deck, where consumers can access/purchase information and mobile products/content/utilities.

online HD   Is the delivery of high-definition streamed video media. This typically conforms to 720p standards where 720 represents 720 lines of vertical resolution and p stands for progressive scan.

online video advertising   Video advertising accompanying video content distributed via the internet to be streamed or downloaded onto compatible devices such as computers and mobile phones. In its basic form, this can be TV ads run online, but adverts are increasingly adapted or created specifically to suit online.

on-portal   Point of sale/access within the operator's 'walled garden'/portal/deck, where consumers can access/purchase information and mobile products/content/utilities.

opt-in   An individual has given a company permission to use his/her data for marketing purposes.

opt-out An individual has stated that they do not want a company to use his/her data for marketing purposes.

organic search results The 'natural' search results that appear in a separate section (usually the main body of the page) to the paid listings. The results listed here have not been paid for and are ranked by the search engine (using spiders or algorithms) according to relevancy to the term searched upon. See also *spider*, *algorithm*, *SEO*.

overlay Online advertising content that appears over the top of the web page. See also *rich media*.

paid-for listings The search results list in which advertisers pay to be featured according to the PPC model. This list usually appears in a separate section to the organic search results – usually at the top of the page or down the right-hand side. See also *organic search results, pay per click (PPC)*.

paid inclusion In exchange for a payment, a search engine will guarantee to list/ review pages from a website. It is not guaranteed that the pages will rank well for particular queries – this still depends on the search engine's underlying relevancy process.

paid search See *PPC*.

pay for performance program Also called affiliate marketing, performance-based, partner marketing, CPA, or associate programme. Any type of revenue-sharing programme where a publisher receives a commission for generating online activity (eg leads or sales) for an advertiser.

pay per click (PPC) Allows advertisers to bid for placement in the paid listings search results on terms that are relevant to their business. Advertisers pay the amount of their bid only when a consumer clicks on their listing. Also called sponsored search/paid search.

pay per lead The commission structure where the advertiser pays the publisher a flat fee for each qualified lead (customer) that is referred to the advertiser's website.

pay per sale The commission structure where the advertiser pays a percentage or flat fee to the publisher based on the revenue generated by the sale of a product or service to a visitor who came from a publisher site.

pay per view (PPV) Is an e-commerce model that allows media owners to grant consumers access to their programming in return for payment. Micro-payments may be used for shorter programming whilst feature films may attract larger sums.

personal video recorder (PVR) Is a hard-disc-based digital video recorder (most use MPEG technology) and enables viewers to pause and rewind live TV. PVRs also interact with EPGs to automatically record favourite programmes and have led to an increase in the number of consumers watching 'time sifted' TV and skipping advertising breaks.

pharming An illegal method of redirecting traffic from another company's website (such as a bank) to a fake one designed to look similar in order to steal user details when they try to log in. See also *phishing*.

phishing An illegal method whereby legitimate looking e-mails (appearing to come from a well-known bank, for example) are used in an attempt to get personal information that can be used to steal a user's identity.

placement The area where an advertisement is displayed/placed within a publisher's mobile content.

podcasting Podcasting involves making an audio file (usually in MP3 format) of content – usually in the form of a radio programme – that is available to download to an MP3 player.

polite loading Fixed online advertising placements that load and display additional flash content after the host page on which the advert appears has finished loading. See also *flash*.

pop-under An ad that appears in a separate window beneath an open window. Pop-under ads are concealed until the top window is closed, moved, resized or minimized.

pop-up An online advert that 'pops up' in a window over the top of a web page. See also *interruptive formats*.

portal A browsable portal of links to content, pre-configured usually by the network operator, and set as the default home page to the phone's browser.

post-roll The streaming of a mobile advertising clip after a mobile TV/video clip. The mobile advert is usually 10–15 seconds.

pre-roll The name given to the adverts shown before, or whilst an online video is loading. There can be more than one and, although they all vary in length, they average 21 seconds in duration.

PSMS Premium SMS. A text message that is charged at a premium over the standard rate.

publisher Also referred to as an affiliate, associate, partner, reseller or content site. An independent party, or website, that promotes the products or services of an advertiser in exchange for a commission.

query string formation In a search engine, a query string is the set of words entered into a search engine by an individual. For example, a search for 'search engine marketing information'. Query string formation is simply the process of thinking of the correct query string to get the results required.

reach The number of unique web users potentially seeing a website one or more times in a given time period expressed as a percentage of the total active web population for that period.

real time No delay in the processing of requests for information, other than the time necessary for the data to travel over the internet.

really simple syndication (RSS) Software that allows you to flag website content (often from blogs or new sites) and aggregate new entries to this content into an easy-to-read format that is delivered directly to a user's PC. See also *blog*.

rich media The collective name for online advertising formats that use advanced technology to harness broadband to build brands. It uses interactive and audiovisual elements to give richer content and a richer experience for the user when interacting with the advert. See also *interstitial ads*, *superstitials*, *overlay* and *Rich Media Guidelines*.

Rich Media Guidelines Design guidelines produced by the IAB for effective use of rich media technologies in all forms of internet advertising. They aim to protect user experience by keeping them in control of the experience, eg: encouraging clearly labelled close, sound and video buttons.

sale When a user makes a purchase from an online advertiser.

sales house An organization which sells advertising on behalf of other media owners. These sales houses typically retain a percentage of the revenue they sell in exchange for their services. These organizations may combine a number of websites together and sell them as different packages to advertisers.

search engine marketing (SEM) The process which aims to get websites listed prominently in search engine results through search engine optimization, sponsored search and paid inclusion. See also *PPC*, *SEO* and *paid inclusion*.

search engine optimization (SEO) The process which aims to get websites listed prominently within search engines' organic (algorithmic, spidered) search results. Involves making a site 'search engine friendly'. See also *organic search results*.

serial digital interface (SDI) Is a dedicated digital video interface used to carry broadcast quality video content.

server A host computer which maintains websites, newsgroups and e-mail services.

session The time spent between a user starting an application, computer, website, etc and logging off or quitting.

SIM Subscriber identity module. A removable part of the mobile phone hardware that identifies the subscriber.

simulcast Watching an existing TV service over the internet at the same time as normal transmission.

site analytics The reporting and analysis of website activity – in particular user behaviour on the site. All websites have a weblog which can be used for this purpose, but other third-party software is available for a more sophisticated service.

skyscraper A long, vertical, online advert usually found running down the side of a page in a fixed placement. See also *universal advertising package*.

SMPP Short Message Peer-to-peer Protocol – used for exchanging SMS messages.

SMS Short Message Service.

SMSC Short Message Service Centre. A network switch for routeing SMS traffic.

sniffer software Identifies the capabilities of the user's browser and therefore can determine compatibility with ad formats and serve them an advert they will be able to see/fully interact with (eg: GIF, flash, etc).

Solus e-mail advertising Where the body of the e-mail is determined by the advertiser, including both text and graphical elements, and is sent on their behalf by an e-mail list manager/owner. Solus e-mail advertising is conducted on an opt-in basis where the recipient has given their consent to receive communications.

spam Unsolicited junk mail.

spider A programme which crawls the web and fetches web pages in order for them to be indexed against keywords. Used by search engines to formulate search result pages. See also *organic search results*.

sponsored search See *pay per click (PPC)*.

sponsorship Advertiser sponsorships of targeted content areas (eg entire website, site area or an event) often for promotional purposes.

SS7 Signalling System 7. A worldwide standard for telecommunications hardware to talk to each other.

stickiness Measure used to gauge the effectiveness of a site in retaining its users. Usually measured by the duration of the visit.

streaming media Compressed audio/video which plays and downloads at the same time. The user does not have to wait for the whole file to download before it starts playing.

superstitials A form of rich media advertising which allows a TV-like experience on the web. It is fully pre-cached before playing. See also *rich media, cache memory*.

tenancy   The 'renting' out of a section of a website by another brand who pays commission to this media owner for any revenue generated from this space. Eg: dating services inside portals or bookstores inside online newspapers.

text ad   A static appended text attached to an advertisement.

text link   Creative use for mobile advertisements – represented by highlighted and clickable text(s) with a link embedded within the highlighted text. Usually limited to 16–24 characters.

traffic   Number of visitors who come to a website.

UMTS   Universal Mobile Telephony Service or '3G' offers comprehensive voice and multimedia services to mobile customers by providing very high data rates and new functionality such as data streaming. 3G phones are backward compatible and can access all the services that 2 and 2.5G phones can, except that in this case data can be transferred a lot quicker. This means that any service that Incentivated can currently provide will work on the newer phones whose experience can be enhanced specifically based on handset type.

uniform resource locator (URL)   Technical term that is used to refer to the web address of a particular website. For example **www.iabuk.net**.

unique users   Number of different individuals who visit a site within a specific time period.

universal advertising package   A set of online advertising formats that are standardized placements as defined by the IAB. See also *banner, skyscraper, button, MPU* and *embedded format*.

universal player   A platform-agnostic media player that will allow video and audio to be played on any hardware/software configuration from a single source file.

user-generated content (UGC)   Online content created by website users rather than media owners or publishers – either through reviews, blogging, podcasting or posting comments, pictures or video clips. Sites that encourage user-generated content include MySpace, YouTube, Wikipedia and Flickr. See also *blog, podcasting*.

video on demand (VOD)   Allows users to watch what they want, when they want. This can be either 'pay per view' or a free service usually funded by advertising.

viral marketing   The term 'viral advertising' refers to the idea that people will pass on and share striking and entertaining content; this is often sponsored by a brand which is looking to build awareness of a product or service. These viral commercials often take the form of funny video clips, or interactive flash games, images, and even text.

VMNO (Virtual Mobile Network Operator)   A company that uses the infra-structure of an existing (licence-owning) telecoms network operator. Tesco and Virgin are two of the largest VMNOs in the UK.

Voice Over Internet Protocol (VOIP)   Technology that allows the use of a broadband internet connection to make telephone calls.

WAP (Wireless Application Protocol)   Standard for providing mobile data services on hand-held devices. Brings internet content such as news, weather, travel, etc to mobile phones and can also be used to deliver formatted content such as wallpapers, ringtones, video, games, portals and other useful links.

Web 2.0   The term Web 2.0 – with its knowing nod to upgraded computer applications – describes the next generation of online use. Web 2.0 identifies the consumer as a major contributor in the evolution of the internet into a two-way medium. See also *user-generated content*.

web based Requiring no software to access an online service or function, other than a web browser and access to the internet.

web portal A website or service that offers a broad array of resources and services, such as e-mail, forums, search engines, and online shopping malls.

whitelist An e-mail whitelist is a list of contacts that the user deems are acceptable to receive e-mail from and should not be sent to the trash folder. (Wikipedia definition)

Wi-Fi (Wireless Fidelity) The ability to connect to the internet wirelessly. Internet 'hotspots' in coffee shops and airports, etc use this technology.

wiki A wiki is a type of website that allows the visitors themselves to easily add, remove, and otherwise edit and change some available content, sometimes without the need for registration.

wilfing (What Was I Looking For?) Seven in 10 of Britain's 34 million users forget what they are looking for online at work and at home. Wilfing is an expression referring to browsing the internet with no real purpose.

Wireless Markup Language (WML) aka WAP 1.0 Where the mobile internet started many years ago. Hardly supported any more.

XHTML (Extensible Hypertag Markup Language) aka WAP 2.0 The language used to create most mobile internet sites.

XML (Extensible Markup Language) Language used by many internet applications for exchanging information.

INDEX

NB: page numbers in *italics* indicate figures, illustrations or tables

CPSIA information can be obtained at www.ICGtesting.com
Printed in the USA
LVOW04s1655140915

454100LV00026B/178/P